THE POSITIVIST DISPUTE IN GERMAN SOCIOLOGY

The Positivist Dispute in German Sociology

THEODOR W. ADORNO

HANS ALBERT

RALF DAHRENDORF

JÜRGEN HABERMAS

HARALD PILOT

KARL R. POPPER

Translated by Glyn Adey
and David Frisby

HEINEMANN
LONDON

Heinemann Educational Books Ltd
LONDON EDINBURGH MELBOURNE AUCKLAND TORONTO
HONG KONG SINGAPORE KUALA LUMPUR
IBADAN NAIROBI JOHANNESBURG
LUSAKA NEW DELHI

Published by Heinemann Educational Books Ltd
48 Charles Street, London W1X 8AH
Printed and bound in Great Britain by
Morrison and Gibb Ltd, London and Edinburgh

CONTENTS

INDEX OF SOURCES

DAVID FRISBY

INTRODUCTION
TO THE ENGLISH TRANSLATION

The present volume contains some of the key contributions to a controversy which has raged in social scientific and philosophical circles in Germany since 1961. The immediate origin of the controversy lay in the conference held by the German Sociological Association in Tübingen in 1961 on the logic of the social sciences in which Popper presented his twenty-seven theses on that topic. This was replied to by Adorno and the discussion which followed at that conference is summarised by Dahrendorf. In a different form, the controversy was continued by Habermas and Albert from 1963 onwards and many other writers took up various issues and aspects of the controversy. Of these other contributions, only Pilot's was added to the original German edition. In 1969 the present volume appeared in Germany with considerable additional material by Adorno. This provoked the short afterword from Albert who was dismayed at the form which the volume had taken. This translation of the 1969 volume contains an additional essay not in the original, namely, Popper's review of the German volume.

The introduction to the translation sets out to locate this controversy within a wider context. Some remarks are made on the most ambiguous notions in this dispute, namely those of positivism and scientism. The fact that no one in the controversy claims to be a positivist has led Dahrendorf to speak of 'the third man' in the debate[1] and Giddens to suggest that 'the debate is like Hamlet without the prince'.[2] On the other hand, all the contributors to the debate have claimed allegiance either to critical rationalism or to critical theory. This adherence to the central role of theoretical criticism is one reason which led Dahrendorf to suggest, with reference to the original Popper-

[1] R. Dahrendorf, *The Positivist Dispute in German Sociology*, p. 125.
[2] A. Giddens, ed., *Positivism and Sociology* (London, 1974), p. 18.

Adorno debate that a superficial glance at the controversy might incline one to the view that 'it could indeed have appeared, astonishingly enough, as if Popper and Adorno were in agreement.'[3] This is clearly far from being the case since, as the controversy proceeded, even the notion of a debate between competing standpoints became problematical.

There is some difficulty, too, in asserting that this controversy is merely a methodological dispute and can thus be seen as an extension of earlier controversies in the social sciences in Germany, notably the *Methodenstreit*, and the *Werturteilsstreit*. However, in order to examine this claim, some attempt will be made to sketch the earlier disputes in the social sciences in Germany in order to highlight the distinctive features of the present controversy. Nor should one assume that this dispute is confined to sociology as the title of the volume might suggest. Indeed, since the dispute contained in the present volume did not cease with its publication in 1969 but rather was continued, either through its extension to other areas, or to an expansion of the issues presented here, it would seem fruitful to sketch out the later stages of the controversy and some of the other commentaries upon the dispute. Finally, the issues presented in this dispute do not merely have relevance to the development of the social sciences in Germany. It can be argued that not only does the positivist dispute raise important issues for a dominant tradition in the social sciences outside Germany but that it has direct relevance for some of the recent controversies which have taken place in the philosophy of science and in the social sciences in the Anglo-American tradition in recent years.

I

Whilst positivism may be the 'ghost in the machine' in this dispute, it is certainly easy to discover a wide range of possible definitions of the constituent elements of positivism. It is difficult to find a generally acceptable nominalist definition of the term. Positivism is not a static entity but is itself dynamic and had taken different forms in various historical contexts. To take one example, Popper's assertion that he is not a positivist may be seen in the light of his criticism of the Vienna Circle, of which he was never a member. Popper had been very critical of the logical positivists

---

[3] R. Dahrendorf, loc. cit., p. 123–4.

and it is certainly not possible to classify him, in any simple manner, in that school.[4] However, as Habermas and others have argued, logical positivism is only one variant—albeit a most important one in the development of the philosophy of science in this century—of positivism.[5] Although many writers have pointed to the long history of many features of positivism, especially if one takes into account the distinctive manner in which it has incorporated features of both empiricism and rationalism, modern positivism developed with certain types of reflection upon the growth of the natural and moral sciences.

In a section of *Knowledge and Human Interests* in which Habermas attempts to reconstruct the pre-history of modern positivism, the author examines the work of the most widely-known and perhaps least read of the positivists, Auguste Comte. As well as arguing that Comte sets out to justify 'the cognitive monopoly of science' through a philosophy of history whose ultimate goal is scientific technical progress, Habermas shows that Comte's varied usages of the term 'positive' can be translated into a set of methodological rules which may be summarised as follows:

1. 'all knowledge has to prove itself through the *sense certainty* of systematic observation that secures intersubjectivity.' (*le réel*)
2. '*Methodical certainty* is just as important as sense certainty . . . the reliability of scientific knowledge is guaranteed by unity of method.' (*la certitude*)
3. 'The exactitude of our knowledge is guaranteed only by the formally cogent construction of theories that allow the deduction of lawlike hypotheses.' (*le précis*)
4. 'Scientific cognition must be technically utilizable . . . Science makes possible technical control over processes of both nature and society . . . the power of control over nature and society can be multiplied only by following rationalist principles—not through the blind expansion of empirical research, but through the development and the unification of theories.' (*l'utile*)
5. 'our knowledge is in principle *unfinished and relative*, in accord-

---

[4] It is clear that Popper has a very precise notion of positivism which his opponents in this dispute do not share. For a recent account by Popper himself of his relations with the Vienna Circle, see 'Autobiography of Karl Popper' in P. A. Schilpp, ed., *The Philosophy of Karl Popper* (La Salle, Ill., 1974), esp. pp. 62ff.

[5] For the diversity of logical positivism itself *see* the useful collection in A. J. Ayer, ed., *Logical Positivism* (New York, 1959).

ance with the "relative nature of the positive spirit".' (*le relative*)[6]

As well as illustrating the way in which this version of positivism assimilates both empiricism and rationalism, these methodological rules already point to the contradictory heritage of positivism. The sceptical or critical motive in positivism seeks to exclude whole areas of knowledge through a series of demarcations whilst its affirmative impulse seeks to secure knowledge through methodological rules. This contrast between critical enlightenment and the defence of a restrictive theory of science has been a permanent feature of positivism's history. It might be argued that in this uneasy combination of the sceptical and affirmative motives lies the instability of positivism.[7] Thus, at various points of its development, positivism has attempted to become more radical, to seek new ways of re-establishing its critical or restrictive claims.

The methodological rules which can be derived from Comte's writings also point to some modern features of positivism, which have retained Comte's positive impetus even though they may now take a different form. Von Wright suggests three basic tenets of positivism:

1. '*methodological monism*, or the idea of the unity of scientific method amidst the diversity of subject matter of scientific investigation.'

2. 'the exact natural sciences, in particular mathematical physics, set a methodological ideal for all other sciences.'

3. Causal scientific explanation which consists in 'the subsumption of individual cases under hypothetically assumed general laws of nature'.[8]

The first tenet is a more general version of the construction of Comte's second rule as well as being symptomatic of the whole process of laying down restrictive methodological rules. The second tenet is contingent upon the developments of mathematical physics in this century. Some positivist traditions might substitute formal logic for mathematical physics. The third tenet in

---

[6] J. Habermas, *Knowledge and Human Interests*, trans. J. Shapiro (Boston, 1971/London, 1972), pp. 74–77. It should be clear from this that the subsequent history of positivism emphasized different aspects of these rules at various stages of its development.

[7] This is argued in H. Schnädelbach, *Erfahrung, Begründung und Reflexion. Versuch über den Positivismus* (Frankfurt, 1971).

[8] G. H. von Wright, *Explanation and Understanding* (London, 1971), p. 4.

the social sciences might today be exemplified by Hempel's covering law model.[9] This seems to suggest the unsatisfactory nature of any historical definition of positivism. However, von Wright also suggests that positivism is often characterized as being closely bound up with 'a "scientistic" and "technological" view of knowledge and its uses'. Yet this seems to shift the problems associated with positivism onto another equally problematical term, that of scientism.

As with positivism, no one in the present controversy claims to be committed to scientism. For example, Popper has argued that those of his opponents who accept the difference between science and the humanities as being one which rests upon the method of understanding are themselves committed to scientism. Thus, Popper states, when the supporters of such a standpoint 'denounce a view like mine as "positivistic" or "scientistic", then I may perhaps answer that they themselves seem to accept, *implicitly and uncritically*, that positivism or scientism is *the only philosophy appropriate to the natural sciences*'.[10] By scientism Popper means 'a name for the aping of what is widely *mistaken* for the method of science' rather than Hayek's original notion of 'the slavish imitation of the method and language of science'.[11] For Popper, then, scientism refers to the acceptance of a false methodological position.

Habermas' notion of scientism is related to what he takes to be the replacement of theories of knowledge by the philosophy of science positivistically interpreted. ' "Scientism" means science's belief in itself: that is the conviction that we can no longer understand science as *one* form of possible knowledge, but rather must identify knowledge with science'.[12] As such of course, it is closely bound up with the development of positivism. Indeed Habermas goes further and argues that 'Positivism stands and falls with the principle of scientism, that is that the meaning of knowledge is defined by what the sciences do and can thus be adequately explicated through the methodological analysis of scientific procedures. Any epistemology that transcends the framework of methodology as such now succumbs to the same

---

[9] *See* C. G. Hempel, *Aspects of Scientific Explanation* (New York/London, 1965), esp. pp. 333ff.

[10] K. R. Popper, *Objective Knowledge* (Oxford, 1972), p. 185.

[11] Ibid.

[12] J. Habermas, loc. cit., p. 4.

sentence of extravagance and meaninglessness that it once passed on metaphysics.'[13] In the present controversy, Habermas takes as a crucial feature of scientism that it equates scientific rationality with rationality in general. This is central to the exchanges between Habermas and Albert.

Other contributors to the controversy have taken scientism to imply other basic tenets. Lorenzen, for example, in his contribution to the later debate, 'Szientismus versus Dialektik', takes scientism to be a characterization of theories which hold that a rational legitimation of practical principles is impossible.[14] Such a polemical notion extends far beyond the confines of a preoccupation with methodology and has been related to subsequent attempts to reconstitute practical philosophy.[15] Apel, in his contributions to the later controversy, also starts out from a broader notion of scientism as implying that reflection on the subject of the scientific process is minimal since this subject is itself understood as a scientific object.[16] In the extension of scientism to the practical sphere, Apel argues that scientism as the absolutism of value-free scientific rationality rests upon three premises. Firstly, that intersubjective validity is equivalent to the objectivity of the subjects of science; secondly, that science is the value-free description and explanation of facts (secured, in part, through formal logic); and thirdly, that no value judgments can be derived from facts. All these premises lie at the heart of the Habermas–Albert dispute where the nature of science as a specific form of activity and the particular type of practice derived from such a notion of science are placed in question.

It might be argued that much of the positivist dispute is the

---

[13] Ibid, p. 67. Elsewhere Habermas writes, 'By scientism I mean a basic orientation prevailing in analytical philosophy, until recently the most differentiated and influential philosophy of our time. This orientation says that a scientific philosophy, just like science itself, must proceed *intentione recta*, i.e. it must have its object before itself (and is not allowed to approach it reflexively)', in 'A Postscript to *Knowledge and Human Interests*', trans. C. Lenhardt, *Philosophy of the Social Sciences*, vol. 3, 1973, p. 158.

[14] P. Lorenzen, 'Szientismus versus Dialektik' in R. Bubner, K. Cramer, R. Wiehl, eds., *Hermeneutik und Dialektik*, vol. 1 (Tübingen, 1970).

[15] *See* the collection, M. Riedel, ed., *Rehabilitierung der praktischen Philosophie* (Freiburg, vol. 1, 1972; vol. 2, 1974). Also F. Kambartel, ed., *Praktische Philosophie und konstruktive Wissenschaftstheorie* (Frankfurt, 1974).

[16] K.-O. Apel, *Transformation der Philosophie*, 2 vols. (Frankfurt, 1973), esp. 'Einleitung', 'Szientismus, Hermeneutik, Ideologiekritik' and 'Szientismus oder transzendentale Hermeneutik?'. *See* further his 'The A Priori of Communication and the Foundation of the Humanities', *Man and World*, vol. 5, 1972.

result of terminological confusion since it is certainly the case that the participants claim their views are misunderstood, not examined or not held up to genuine criticism. Yet this apparent process of talking past one another might in turn have its origin not in conceptual confusion as such but in the situation which Feyerabend refers to as the incommensurability of theories.[17] The main groupings in this dispute lay claim to the development of a critical stance, either as critical rationalism or as a critical theory of society. However, once again the dispute centres around the nature of the criticism and the foundations of such criticism and rationalism. It does begin to look as if one difficulty in this debate is that there is more than one ghost in the machine.[18]

II

This is certainly not the first time that many of the issues raised in this dispute have been the subject of heated controversy. It is a feature of the development of the social sciences in Germany that they have historically produced a number of important controversies, ostensibly concerned with methodology but actually more wide-ranging. At times they have provided a degree of reflection upon the activity of doing social science which has no comparable development in other social scientific traditions. The earlier controversies will be briefly presented in order to locate the present dispute within some historical perspective. One cannot, of course, appeal to these past controversies in order to offer easy solutions to the present dispute, but it is necessary to show how the positivist dispute both continues earlier themes or develops new points of departure.

Long before the original Schmoller–Menger *Methodenstreit* in economics in the 1870s and 1880s in Germany, one can discern aspects of contrary positions which are relevant to the present dispute. Within the empiricist tradition of philosophy, Hume's discussion of values is relevant for the later *Werturteilsstreit*. Habermas has pointed to the contrary motives of the Scottish

---

[17] The incommensurability argument is made most forcefully in P. Feyerabend, 'Against Method', in M. Radnor and S. Winokur, eds., *Minnesota Studies in the Philosophy of Science*, vol. 4 (Minneapolis, 1970). For an expanded version *see* P. Feyerabend, *Against Method* (London, 1975). This argument is rejected by Popper especially in his remarks on 'the myth of the framework'. *See* K. Popper, 'Normal Science and its Dangers' in I. Lakatos and A. Musgrave, eds., *Criticism and the Growth of Knowledge* (Cambridge, 1970), pp. 56ff.

[18] *See* K. Popper, 'Wider die grossen Worte', *Die Zeit*, 24.9.1971.

Economists in the second half of the eighteenth century who, though they directed their research against existing institutions and authorities, did not basically question the postulate of continuous progress in society.[19] Their early version of sociology can be seen as the precursor of what Brinkmann was later to refer to as sociology as an 'oppositional science'. That critical tradition of sociology was continued in the immediate post French Revolution period by Saint Simon, the conservative tradition by de Bonald.[20] Negt has high-lighted the opposition of a Hegelian and Comtean social theory, an opposition which still has relevance for the contenders in the present positivist dispute.[21] The whole of Marx's critique of political economy stands as a critical chapter in the development of methodological reflection upon critical social science, though its relevance for the methodological controversies later in the century is hardly ever drawn.[22] This is all the more surprising since Marx and Engels were engaged in the development of a methodology which they saw as both logical and historical. As Engels remarks cryptically 'the logical method of approach was therefore the only suitable one. This however is indeed nothing but the historical method, only stripped of the historical form and divested of chance occurrences.'[23] In a very different form, the controversy sur-

---

[19] J. Habermas, 'Kritische und konservative Aufgaben der Soziologie' in *Theorie und Praxis* (Neuwied/Berlin, 1963).

[20] H. Marcuse, *Reason and Revolution* (New York, 1941).

[21] O. Negt, *Strukturbeziehungen zwischen den Gesellschaftslehren Comtes und Hegel* (Frankfurt, 1964).

[22] An exception is O. Morf, *Geschichte und Dialektik in der politischen Ökonomie* (Frankfurt, 1970).

[23] F. Engels, 'Review' (of Marx's *A Contribution to the Critique of Political Economy*) appended to K. Marx, *A Contribution to the Critique of Political Economy* (London/New York, 1971), p. 225. For Marx the logical method did not imply applying Hegel's logic abstractly to the subject matter of political economy. As Marx himself remarked of a writer's attempt 'to present political economy in the Hegelian manner . . . He will learn to his cost that to bring a science by criticism to the point where it can be dialectically presented is an altogether different thing from applying an abstract ready-made system of logic to mere inklings of such a system', K. Marx and F. Engels, *Selected Correspondence* (Moscow, 2nd ed., 1965), p. 102. Marx also avoided the polarization of history and nature which was so characteristic of later controversies in Germany. On this *see* A. Schmidt, *The Concept of Nature in Marx*, trans. B. Fowkes (London, 1971). In *The German Ideology* Marx writes, 'We know only a single science, the science of history. History can be contemplated from two sides, it can be divided into the history of nature and the history of mankind. However, the two sides are not to be divided off; as long as men exist, the history of nature and the history of men are mutually conditioned.' Quoted in A. Schmidt, loc. cit., p. 49.

rounding a historical or logical approach lay at the centre of the Schmoller–Menger *Methodenstreit*.

In the early pages of his most important contribution to the *Methodenstreit* published in 1883 Menger, with reference to economics, writes 'the progress of our science at present is hindered by the sway of erroneous methodological principles'.[24] In the course of that decade Menger and Schmoller debated whether economics should proceed according to the 'exact' or 'historical', the 'deductive' or the 'inductive', the 'abstract' or the 'empirical' method.[25] Menger argued that the world of phenomena supply two types of knowledge for science—concrete phenomena which are individual and empirical forms which are general. Those empirical forms which are repeated, Menger terms types, whilst relations which regularly recur are typical relations. Knowledge of these latter are as important as concrete phenomena. Thus for Menger, without cognition of typical relations we would be deprived of a deeper understanding of the world and of the prediction and control of phenomena. Menger goes on to suggest that there are three groups of economic science: historical economics, concerned with individual concrete phenomena, individual relations, individual knowledge; theoretical economics concerned with types, typical relations and general knowledge; and practical economics concerned with techniques, with economic policy and finance. Menger argues that the historical and theoretical are exclusive approaches. However, Menger does refer to the role of understanding in his commitment to the theoretical orientation. He argues that understanding is gained in two ways; as historical understanding where we investigate a phenomenon's individual process of development, and as theoretical understanding where we recognize a phenomena to be a special case of certain regularity in the succession or co-existence of phenomena. These two types of understanding should be strictly separated. The theoretical

---

[24] C. Menger, *Problems of Economics and Sociology*, trans. F. Nock, ed. and introd. L. Schneider (Urbana, 1963), p. 31. This is a translation of C. Menger, *Untersuchungen über die Methode der Sozialwissenschaften und der politischen Ökonomie insbesondere* (Leipzig, 1883).

[25] The battle lines of that debate were in fact more complex. *See* G. Ritzel, *Schmoller versus Menger. Eine Analyse des Methodenstreits im Hinblick auf den Historismus in der Nationalökonomie* (Frankfurt, 1950); R. Hansen, 'Der Methodenstreit in den Sozialwissenschaften zwischen Gustav Schmoller und Karl Menger', in A. Diemer, ed., *Beiträge zur Entwicklung der Wissenschaftstheorie in 19. Jahrhundert* (Meisenheim, 1968); D. Lindenlaub, 'Richtungskämpfe im Verein für Sozialpolitik', *Vierteljahrsschrift für Sozial-und Wirtschaftsgeschichte*, (Beiheft 52, 1967), pp. 96f.

approach in economics proceeds through a realistic empirical method to give us real types and empirical laws, and through what Menger terms the exact scientific method to enable us to move from the simplest to the most complex elements.

Schmoller, the leading figure in the historical school, questioned the role of general theories in the social sciences.[26] Menger's version of economics, he argued, could only lead to the empirically empty formation of models, including Robinsonades, based on abstract principles. Menger had argued that historical economics could fulfil only a subordinate role in economics. Schmoller saw historical science as itself generating rules which should explain reality and which must be tested. Further, Schmoller sought to distance metaphysics, abstract thought and ideals from economic theory and concentrate upon the actual life process of society. Habermas argues that the historical school countered Menger's approach with two related theses: firstly that 'economics is not concerned with the functions of quantities of goods but rather with the interdependence of economic actions' and secondly that 'since intentional action can only be interpreted through understanding, a strict mathematically formulated scientific economic theory is not possible'.[27] Yet Schmoller did attempt to thrust aside the separation of history and economic theory and to make history a necessary part of theory. However, he hoped to do this whilst rejecting both Menger's characterization of historical method and that implicit in Rickert's and Windelband's distinction between the natural and cultural sciences. The degree of concretion demanded by the historical school was often lacking. Weber, for example, later rightly criticized Roscher's reduction of the complex interaction of nature, society and the individual to the abstract reified notion of 'the people'.[28]

It is difficult to characterize the issues at stake in the original *Methodenstreit*, since they cannot be taken to rest upon a simple

[26] *See* G. Schmoller, 'Zur Methodologie der Staats-und Sozialwissenschaften', *Schmollers Jahrbuch*, 1883. The debate was continued with the publication of K. Menger, *Die Irrtümer des Historismus in der deutschen Nationalökonomie* (Vienna, 1884).

[27] J. Habermas, 'Zur Logik der Sozialwissenschaften', *Philosophische Rundschau*, Beiheft 5 (Tübingen, 1967). Reprinted with additional material (Frankfurt 1971), p. 128.

[28] M. Weber, 'Roscher und Knies und die logischen Probleme der historischen Nationalökonomie', *Gesammelte Aufsätze zur Wissenschaftslehre*, 3rd ed. (Tübingen, 1968). For a brief account of Weber's relation to the *Methodenstreit see* W. Cahnman, 'Weber and the Methodological Controversy', in W. Cahnman and A. Boskoff, eds., *Sociology and History* (New York, 1964).

debate between inductionism and deductionism. Schmoller, for example, was aware that induction and deduction must go together but did not realize the real meaning of their combination. In this controversy it was perhaps not the relation of theory to reality which was at issue but rather what constitutes theory, in a context in which both Schmoller and Menger rejected classical political economy.[29]

The later stages of the *Methodenstreit* roughly coincide historically with the development of the neo-Kantian attempt to ground the separation of the natural from the historical or cultural sciences, a separation which many see to be a central error in the positivist dispute. As Popper argues, 'Labouring the difference between science and the humanities has long been a fashion, and has become a bore. The method of problem solving, the method of conjecture and refutation, is practised by both. It is practised in reconstructing a damaged text as well as in constructing a theory of radioactivity.'[30] Against this view the predominance of the unified science ideal and of methodological monism has been seen by Habermas as the reason why 'the lively discussion of the methodological distinction between natural and cultural scientific research which was first opened by neo-Kantianism is today forgotten; the problematic which it sparked off does not appear real any more'.[31] Habermas goes on to argue that whilst the dominant positivist interpretation of research has adopted the unified science thesis and accounted for any dualism in science in terms of distinctions between levels of development, it still remains true that research continues to take separate paths which take little notice of one another, either as a general methodology of empirical science or as a general hermeneutics of social and

---

[29] In many ways the lines between the historical and theoretical traditions in political economy were more clearly drawn in the later Böhm-Bawerk–Hilferding controversy concerning Marx's methodology. *See* E. von Böhm-Bawerk, *Zum Abschluss des Marxschen Systems* (Berlin, 1896); R. Hilferding, 'Böhm-Bawerk's Marx-Kritik' in M. Adler and R. Hilferding, eds., *Marx Studien*, vol. 1 (Vienna, 1904). These are translated in P. Sweezy, ed., *Karl Marx and the Close of his System and Böhm-Bawerk's Criticism of Marx* (New York, 1949). *See* also Böhm-Bawerk's own contribution to the *Methodenstreit* in Böhm-Bawerk, 'The Historical versus the Deductive Method in Political Economy', *Annals of the American Academy of Political and Social Science*, vol. 1, 1890. For a commentary on the Böhm-Bawerk–Hilferding controversy *see* B. Rüther, *Die Auseinandersetzung zwischen Böhm-Bawerk and Hilferding über Marx. Darstellung und Kritik* (Cologne, 1926); E. Kauder, 'Austro-Marxism versus Austro-Marginalism', *Journal of the History of Political Economy*, 1971.

[30] K. Popper, *Objective Knowledge*, loc. cit., p. 185.

[31] J. Habermas, 'Zur Logik der Sozialwissenschaften', 2nd ed., p. 71.

historical science. For this reason, and since the neo-Kantian distinctions play an important role in the *Werturteilstreit* and Weber's attempted resolution, it is useful to return to these writers.

Windelband and Rickert were the leading figures in the South-West School of neo-Kantianism.[32] Windelband's distinction between history—already a well developed study in Germany—and natural science in his rectoral address of 1894 was not, as many later interpreters suggest, based on a metaphysical dualism of nature and spirit (*Geist*), which Windelband explicitly rejected. Rather, this distinction was based on the formal character of their cognitive goals. Unlike Dilthey's earlier division, Windelband's is not based on psychological or hermeneutic grounds but is instead logically based. Windelband's concern is with the methods of research and not with the object of research, which could, he argued, be investigated by either method. It is in this way that we should understand Windelband's distiction between a science generating laws and a science of individual events, between nomothetic and idiographic sciences. It is thus not an ontological demarcation of scientific realms but a typology of scientific modes of procedure. As Schnädelbach comments 'The application of nomothetic or idiographic procedures is thereby directed not according to the object but according to the cognitive interest or the cognitive goal.'[33] In terms of utility, Windelband ascribes to the natural sciences a technical goal or interest and to the historical-idiographic sciences a practical goal or cognitive interest. He argues strongly against the view that our knowledge can only be nomothetic and for the view that the dualism of 'these two moments of human knowledge' are not reducible to one another and cannot be transcended.

---

[32] There were two schools of neo-Kantian philosophy, only one of which concerns us here. The Marburg School, whose central figures were Cohen and Natorp, was interested primarily in natural scientific knowledge and took scientific cognition to be the prototype of all cognition worthy of the name. Epistemology for them was therefore the analysis of the logical foundations of the exact sciences. In some respects modern positivism has its roots in this tradition. The South-West School, whose leading figures were Windelband and Rickert, focused their attention on the historical and cultural sciences. The original statement of their position was W. Windelband, 'Geschichte und Naturwissenschaft', *Präludien*, vol. 2, new ed. (Tübingen, 1924). Amongst Rickert's most relevant works are H. Rickert, *Kulturwissenschaft und Naturwissenschaft* (Tübingen, 1899), and H. Rickert, *Die Grenzen der naturwissenschaftlichen Begriffsbildung* (Tübingen/Leipzig, 1902).

[33] H. Schnädelbach, *Geschichtsphilosophie nach Hegel* (Freiburg/Munich, 1974), pp. 141–2. Schnädelbach provides a very concise account of the neo-Kantian tradition in this volume.

Rickert followed Windelband in his commitment to an epistemological and logical starting point for his analysis and to the thesis that 'the value relevance (*Wertbeziehung*) of the objects of knowledge possess central importance for the special position of disciplines to which history belongs'.[34] However, Rickert extended his analysis and distanced himself from Windelband in important respects. As well as relativizing the nomothetic-idiographic distinction to a relative typological opposition between generalizing and individualizing methods, Rickert changed the distinction itself to one between natural and cultural sciences in order to remove any association of the Geisteswissenschaften with psychology.[35] Whereas Windelband based his opposition of nomothetic and idiographic upon the logical dualism of general and particular judgments, Rickert shifted the basis for the distinction to the level of scientific concept formation. This was necessary for Rickert since, as Schnädelbach explains 'if, with Kant, one starts out not from facts as finished objects, but from facts of consciousness in the sense of a variety of sensory perceptions then a *constitution of facts as scientific objects* is required *before* one can apply judgement to the facts'.[36] This insistence on the epistemological priority of concept formation over the activity of judgment—and in this he was following Kant—led Rickert to transfer Windelband's problem of classification to the level of scientific concept formation.

The specific realm of the cultural sciences are for Rickert constituted from the prior value relevance of empirical material whereas the dominant perspective in the choice and synthesis of data is generation of laws. Thus value and law generation are the two organizational principles in cultural and natural scientific concept formation. However, not only is our constitution of cultural objects a process of individualizing concept formation

---

[34] Ibid, p. 144.

[35] It is worth pointing out here that the term '*Geisteswissenschaften*' was originally introduced into German through the 1863 translation of J. S. Mill's *A System of Logic*, when Schiel, the translator, interpreted the title of Book VI of that work, 'On the Logic of the Moral Sciences' as 'Von der Logic der Geisteswissenschaften oder moralischen Wissenschaften'. Dilthey had brought the term into more familiar usage and, in the period in which Rickert was writing, had tended to make the association between psychology and Geisteswissenschaften, though this was hardly his intention. On Dilthey's examination of the cultural sciences *see* J. Habermas, *Knowledge and Human Interests*, loc. cit., chs. 7 and 8.

[36] H. Schnädelbach, loc. cit., p. 146.

but the importance of values takes on new meaning. For Rickert
'the unity and objectivity of the cultural sciences is determined
by the unity and objectivity of our concept of the cultural and
this in turn, by the unity of and objectivity of values which we
value'.[37] At this point, however, Rickert must move on to a
cultural philosophy and a philosophy of value. Yet such a
philosophy would be relegated to the level of metaphysics within
the neo-Kantian tradition. Their strict interpretation of epistemology as a logic of science would necessarily lead them to a
strict separation of the critique of knowledge and hermeneutics,
such that the latter would be removed from consideration.
Rickert construed the concept of culture on the basis of transcendental idealism: 'culture as the essence of appearances under a
system of valid values has a transcendental meaning—it says
nothing about the objects, but rather determines the conditions
for the possible interpretation of objects'.[38] For Rickert science
can only ask of values whether they are valid, not whether they
exist. This can only lead to a restriction of the notion of understanding. As Habermas argues, Rickert remains trapped in the
dichotomies of facts and values, empirical existence and transcendental validity and nature and culture.[39]

If the South West German neo-Kantian tradition did pose basic
problems for the cultural sciences in terms of their relation to
values then they did so at a largely theoretical and formal level.
This is in contrast with the heated controversy known as the
Werturteilsstreit, a controversy which has not only continued to
exist in the social sciences but one which, in the context of the
positivist dispute, Dahrendorf argues 'Even if the fronts have
perhaps been reversed, the controversy over value judgments has
forfeited little of its explosiveness in German Sociology after fifty
years'.[40]

The original *Werturteilsstreit* commenced in earnest in 1909 at
the Vienna general meeting of the *Verein für Sozialpolitik* and

[37] H. Rickert, *Kulturwissenschaften und Naturwissenschaften*, loc. cit., p. 137.
[38] J. Habermas, *Zur Logik der Sozialwissenschaften*, loc. cit., p. 76.
[39] In terms of one of the debates which has succeeded the positivist dispute, namely the Habermas-Luhmann controversy, Bubner has suggested that it is possible to trace Luhmann's position, especially on the notion of meaning, back to Rickert. *See* R. Bubner, 'Wissenschaftstheorie und Systembegriff. Zur Position von N. Luhmann und deren Herkunft', in R. Bubner, *Dialektik und Wissenschaft* (Frankfurt, 1973).
[40] R. Dahrendorf, 'Remarks on the Discussion', *The Positivist Dispute*, p. 127.

continued in the years up to 1914.[41] The *Verein* had been founded
in 1872 as a social reform movement which opposed both the
isolation of economic life from the rest of society, which was seen
to be exemplified in the work of the Manchester School of
economics, and revolutionary socialism. However, though a
reform movement it never took up a concrete social political
programme as such but published studies of specific concrete
problems in the socio-economic sphere.

The original 1909 discussion placed in question the conditions
for the possibility of a normative social and economic science,
with Sombart arguing that what was decisive was whether
economics could be considered a science, whilst his opponent
Knapp argued that the *Verein*, by its very nature, must be engaged
in political activity. Max Weber, though he argued for the principle of a value free (*Wertfreiheit*) science whilst recognizing the
value relevance (*Wertbeziehung*) of all scientific research, maintained that the *Verein* must remain a forum for the discussion of
political evaluations and goals. If the *Verein* was to remain
concerned with the political sphere then some other organization
should perhaps concern itself with value free scientific research.
In fact, one important consequence of the 1909 meeting was the
foundation of a separate sociological association which had its
first meeting in 1910. This move heralded the professionalization
of sociology in Germany and its increasing separation from
politics and from the study of economics which was itself caught
up in attempts to separate positive economics (*Volkswirtschaftslehre*) from normative economics (*Volkswirtschaftspolitik*). Symptomatic of the latter split and of the attempt to develop a scientific
study of values and norms is Weber's definition of sociology as
'the scientific investigation of the general cultural meaning of the
socio-economic structure of human communal life'. This split did
not mean that the discussion of the role of value judgments in
social science ceased in either of the two institutions. The discussion papers circulated by Max Weber, Schmoller and others
in 1912 as a preliminary basis for a meeting of the *Verein* in 1913
showed that the debate was hardly over. Schmoller asserted the
possibility of 'objective value judgments' and the hope that

---

[41] For a detailed account of the *Verein*, see D. Lindenlaub, loc. cit. *See* also W.
Hofmann, *Gesellschaftslehre als Ordnungsmacht. Die Werturteilsfrage-heute* (Berlin, 1961);
C. von Ferber, 'Der Werturteilsstreit. 1909/59', *Kölner Zeitschrift für Soziologie*,
vol. 11, 1959; H. Albert and E. Topitsch, eds., *Werturteilsstreit* (Darmstadt, 1971).

ethics might increasingly become an empirical science. Weber, however, asserted the permanent struggle of a plurality of values, even 'the ethical irrationality of the world', and the need for science in its study of values to examine their existence but not their validity. Behind this demand for value free science lies an epistemological conception derived from the neo-Kantians, namely, that value judgments are not the result of cognitive acts. In fact Weber later saw the justification of practical judgments as meaningless: 'It is [therefore] in principle meaningless, since the diverse value orders of the world stand in an insoluble struggle with one another'.[42]

At the first meeting of the newly founded German Sociological Association, Weber was not alone in asserting the non-partisan nature of sociology. Töinnes, too, argued that the new association was a learned society and not a school and that consequently 'We wish therefore as sociologists to concern ourselves only with what is, not with what, from whatever viewpoint, on whatever grounds, should be'.[43] Such views were not accepted by some members of the association and the issues continued to be debated up to the outbreak of the First World War.

Whilst it is hardly possible to develop the methodological standpoint of Max Weber in this context, it is important to point out at this juncture that Weber's work in this period was not solely preoccupied with methodological issues in the abstract.[44] As well as being concerned with the abstract theories of economics and specifically the development of the notion of the ideal type from Menger, Weber was deeply preoccupied with developments in historical research too.[45] Nor was he concerned merely with philosophical issues surrounding methodology, but rather with

---

[42] M. Weber, *Wissenschaftslehre*, loc. cit., p. 603.

[43] F. Töinnes, 'Wege und Ziele der Soziologie', *Verhandlungen des Ersten Deutschen Soziologentages, 1910* (Tübingen, 1911), p. 23.

[44] On Weber's methodology *see* F. Tenbruck, 'Die Genesis der Methodologie Max Webers', *Kölner Zeitschrift für Soziologie*, vol. 11, 1959; H. Baier, *Von der Erkenntnistheorie zur Wirklichkeitswissenschaft. Eine Studie über die Begrundung der Soziologie bei Max Weber*, unpublished habilitation thesis (Münster, 1969). For a classic earlier analysis *see* A. von Schelting, *Max Webers Wissenschaftslehre* (Tübingen, 1934).

[45] See the collection by W. Mommsen, *Gesellschaft, Politik und Geschichte* (Frankfurt, 1974), esp. the essays, 'Soziologische Geschichte und historische Soziologie' and ' "Verstehen" und "Idealtypus". Zur Methodologie einer historischen Soziologie'. In the latter essay, Mommsen points to Weber's interest in the methodological dispute in history surrounding Karl Lamprecht's attempt to ground an exact cultural history. Cf. Mommsen, loc. cit., pp. 211f.

the development of an empirical science, a science of reality (*Wirklichkeitswissenschaft*). Thus, as Rickert argued, 'Logical investigations for Weber certainly never remained an end in itself' but were always directed towards 'actual questions of social life'.[46] Yet much of Weber's methodological writing has suffered from later interpretation which have extracted problems which he raised, e.g. the role of value judgments and understanding, and so distanced them from empirical study by placing them firmly in the sphere of an autonomous meta-science of methodology that their real relevance for the practice of scientific research is often lost. For example, it is a distortion of Weber's viewpoint to relegate his category of understanding to a heuristic device as is often the case in neo-positivist interpretations of his work. Even though Weber did not use understanding as a way of distinguishing the natural from the human sciences, and although he was critical of the notion of *Verstehen*, he did not give it a subordinate place to nomological explanation; rather understanding and explanation were seen as complementary, whilst at the same time understanding served as a connecting link between causal knowledge of social phenomena and a value relevant interpretation of social phenomena.[47]

In the field of sociology in the post First World War period the value problem received a more radical statement in the development of the sociology of knowledge in Germany, particularly as exemplified by Mannheim's *Ideology and Utopia*.[48] This enterprise is sharply criticized in the present positivist dispute by both Popper and Adorno. Of more relevance for the present dispute were the rise of critical theory and the development of logical positivism. Horkheimer, in a number of essays written in the nineteen thirties, particularly 'Traditional and Critical Theory' and 'The Latest attack on Metaphysics', sought both to distinguish critical theory from contemporary notions of theory and to attack

---

[46] Quoted in H. Baier, loc. cit., p. 62.

[47] *See* W. Mommsen, loc. cit., pp. 208ff.

[48] K. Mannheim, *Ideologie und Utopie* (Bonn, 1929). It is possible to see Mannheim's position in this work as a radical version of Weber's notion of value pluralism. Weber's later discussion of the value problem in relation to science has been seen as part of a further controversy generated in the early 1920s, which Kracauer terms 'the so-called *Wissenschaftsstreit*'. *See* S. Kracauer, 'Die Wissenschaftskrisis' in S. Kracauer, *Das Ornament der Masse* (Frankfurt, 1963). *See* also K. Singer, 'Die Krisis der Soziologie', *Weltwirtschaftliches Archiv*, vol. 16, 1920–21; E. Wittenberg, 'Die Wissenschaftskrisis in Deutschland im Jahre 1919', *Theoria*, vol. 3, 1937.

the logical positivism of the Vienna Circle.[49] Horkheimer summarizes the difference between traditional and critical theory thus: 'Theory in the traditional sense established by Descartes and everywhere practised in the pursuit of the specialized sciences organizes experience in the light of questions which arise out of life in present-day society. The resultant network of disciplines contains information in a form which makes it useful in any particular circumstances for the greatest number of possible purposes. The social genesis of problems, the real situations in which science is put to use, and the purposes which it is made to serve are all regarded by science as external to itself'[50] Horkheimer contrasts this with a critical theory of society which 'has for its object men as producers of their historical way of life in its totality. The real situations which are the starting point of science are not regarded simply as data to be verified and to be predicted according to the laws of probability. Every datum depends not on nature alone but also on the power man has over it. Objects, the kind of perception, the questions asked, and the meaning of the answers all bear witness to human activity and the degree of man's power.'[51] In the period in which these remarks were written, Horkheimer still assumed as his model of critical theory Marx's critique of political economy, despite critical theory's precarious relation to it. However, these articles do not form part of a genuine controversy since they were written while Horkheimer and other members of the Frankfurt School were in exile. They are important, as Wellmer has argued more recently, in that they foreshadow some aspects of the critique of positivism offered by Habermas.[52]

The logical positivism which Horkheimer attacked also came under attack from a different quarter. When Horkheimer wrote these essays, logical positivism had already gone beyond its radical phase. The analytical theory of science had moved in two diverse directions which sometimes overlapped, 'one concerned with the

---

[49] *See* M. Horkheimer, *Critical Theory* (trans. M. O'Connell *et al.*), (New York, 1972/London, 1973). For a concise account of the development of the Frankfurt School's methodological position *see* A. Wellmer, 'Empirico-Analytical and Critical Social Science', in his *Critical Theory of Society* (trans. J. Cumming) (New York, 1971). More generally on the early history of the Frankfurt School *see* M. Jay, *The Dialectical Imagination* (Boston and Toronto/London, 1973).

[50] M. Horkheimer, 'Postscript', in *Critical Theory*, loc. cit., p. 244.

[51] Ibid.

[52] A. Wellmer, loc. cit.

logical reconstruction of scientific languages and the other with the logico-methodological reconstruction of the research process itself'.[53] Whilst both traditions at times placed great emphasis on formal logic, it is worth pointing out that it would be difficult to argue that formal logic is intrinsic to positivism or the analytical theory of science. The former tradition of reconstruction of scientific languages, exemplified in Carnap's work, was later to influence the development of a much broader linguistic philosophy which has been known as ordinary language philosophy.[54] The second tradition is perhaps best represented by Popper who, from 1919 onwards, developed his concept of falsificationism and rejected logical positivism's verificationism. Popper later broadened his theory of scientific method to incorporate the social and political world.[55]

III

The preceding brief outline of earlier methodological controversies in the social sciences in Germany now opens the way to an estimation of what is distinctive about the present positivist dispute. It is clear that the present controversy appears to bear little direct relation to the original *Methodenstreit* in the sense that competing approaches to a recognized discipline and subject matter are at issue. A *purely* methodological dispute would presuppose that the scientific division of labour is so advanced that certain groups are concerned only with methodology as an independent discipline. Whilst such a conception would, pushed to its limits, be an impossibility since it would be difficult to conceive of a discussion of methodology without reference to the actual objects concerned, many writers have argued that precisely this tendency exists in the neo-positivist philosophy of science even to the extent that it is cut off from what scientists are

---

[53] A. Wellmer, loc. cit., p. 18.

[54] For an attempt to classify these various traditions *see* G. Radnitsky, *Contemporary Schools of Metascience* (Göteborg, 1968).

[55] Most notably in K. Popper, *The Open Society and its Enemies*, 5th ed. (London, 1966). Popper suggests that his social theory differs from his theory of method in an important respect, namely 'that my own social theory, which favours gradual and piecemeal reform, strongly contrasts with my theory of method, which happens to be a theory of scientific and intellectual revolution'. Cf. 'Reason or Revolution?', *European Journal of Sociology*, 11, 1970, p. 255.

actually doing.[56] Yet if the works of the major figures in the development of sociology are examined, for example those of Marx, Weber and Durheim, then it is apparent that for them, despite their diverse orientations, methodology was not an exclusive interest but rather existed only in relation to, and formed an integral part, of their orientation towards specific areas of social life. The distinction between 'theory' and 'methods' appeared later with the institutionalization of the discipline.

In the present instance, the cause of the lamented lack of genuine discussion may lie elsewhere. A discussion of methodology usually presupposes that we know and agree on the object to which the methodology is related or at least that there exists some measure of agreement as to where this object lies. In the present dispute this is not the case. Some protagonists do not recognize as a genuine object what others argue is the real object of social research. That the methodological standpoints and their interpretation are divergent, suggests that methodology may not be taken in isolation from its object nor from the critical reflection upon its own activity. For example, in the present dispute, Habermas argues that the neo-positivist position restricts the cognitive interest in the acquisition of knowledge to a purely technical interest, and ignores both the practical interest by which we come to make our expressions intelligible and the emancipatory interest which is usually reduced to the technical.

Thus what is at issue here is the attempt to reduce science to methodology in such a way that what characterizes science is its methodology in the abstract. This was apparent in the neo-Kantian conception of science, and not merely the South West School but also the Marburg School, with reference to which Tenbruck argues 'the methodological inclinations of that epoch result from the naturalistic image of reality's lack of structure. Science itself *is* here nothing other than methodology, namely a procedure. In this hypertrophy, methodologizing looses its original function as a way towards knowledge of reality. The conflict of methodologies is then only a methodological conflict.'[57]

---

[56] This argument has perhaps most often been advanced by Feyerabend. *See* his most recent work, P. Feyeraband, *Against Method*, loc. cit.

[57] F. Tenbruck, loc. cit., p. 600. It was perhaps this reduction of science to methodology which prompted Nietzsche to comment, 'It is not the triumph of *science* which distinguishes our nineteenth century but the triumph of scientific *method* over science', F. Nietzsche, *Werke*, vol. 3, ed. K. Schlechta (Munich, 1965), p. 814.

Such considerations are pertinent to the positivist controversy.

A different line of argument is advanced by Schnädelbach in a postscript to the controversy.[58] He argues that it is a mistake to see the positivist dispute as the third methodological controversy since methodology is not at issue. 'The central controversies do not at all relate to methodological questions in the restricted sense. In the critique of a positivist scientific practice, that is, of a collection of facts without theory and of reference to the "given" in problems of foundation, both parties were in agreement; positivism provided no reason for dispute.'[59] Particularly in Adorno's introduction, it is noticeable that he holds up for criticism a naïve positivism which is hardly at issue amongst any of the disputants even though it may remain in operation in much social scientific practice. Nor could one look for the source of the controversy in scientific practice as such 'since a consensus concerning the standards and directions for action for scientific practice cannot be a basis of agreement for a debate on it since this practice, which follows from those standards and directions for action itself must be interpreted'.[60] Schnädelbach suggests that rather than methodological conceptions as such being at issue, one may look for one source of controversy in the concepts of interpretation of methods. Similarly, in the case of interpretation of social scientific methodology what would be required would be some prior consensus of the conditions for understanding of 'how scientific methods themselves were to be interpreted: and this, no longer a methodological but a hermeneutic minimal consensus, was not provided'.[61] If Schnädelbach's argument is conceded then the issues in the controversy must be sought elsewhere. If the positivist dispute is not in the strict sense a *Methodenstreit*, then perhaps one may see some of the issues raised in it as deriving from the controversy which succeeded it and which retained some of the same participants, namely the *Werturteilsstreit*. Lorenzen, who sees the dispute as one of 'scientism versus dialectics' does indeed argue that the *Werturteilsstreit* is 'the immediate predecessor of the present controversy' whilst at the same time suggesting that the central problem of that controversy has taken

---

[58] H. Schnädelbach, 'Über den Realismus', *Zeitschrift für allgemeine Wissenschaftstheorie*, vol. 3, 1972.

[59] Ibid, p. 88.

[60] Ibid, p. 89.

[61] Ibid, p. 89.

on a somewhat different importance.[62] In general, he sees the
problem as that of 'scientific value judgments, the problem whether
reason is practical, whether norms can be grounded in reason'.[63]
The possibility of the rehabilitation of practical reason is certainly
one issue in the positivist dispute which has generated considerable further discussion.

The original *Werturteilsstreit* emerged in a context in which,
not only had the methodology of the social sciences been the
source of controversy, but the aims of the social sciences had also
been made problematic. It is the aims of the social sciences which
have again been placed in question in the positivist controversy.
Baier, for example, has argued that this aspect of the controversy
is manifested at three levels.[64] Firstly, whether the role of
sociology is the replication or reproduction of existing social
reality or rather whether it is to be concerned with the transformation of that reality; secondly, whether sociology engages
in its empirical world unhistorically or historically; finally,
whether theories generated possess a globalizing or individualizing
tendency. In other words, the Habermas–Albert debate is concerned with the connection of social scientific theory and practice.
Both positions, Baier argues, 'see an essential criterion of social
scientific theory *in its practical relevance.* . . . Both are certainly in
agreement that social scientific theory by means of social
criticism, by means of social technology and by means of rational
politics, can and should be practical.'[65] Any reading of the debate
will, however, reveal that agreement is only an appearance.

The diversity of issues which are contained in the positivist
dispute, however much of a misnomer the title of the dispute may
be, suggests that there is not merely one but several debates
taking place. The connection between the various debates and
the diverse levels of analysis has hardly been made. One way of
highlighting the various issues is by examining the later development of the controversy since it in no way came to an end with
the volume translated here.

[62] P. Lorenzen, 'Szientismus versus Dialektik', loc. cit., p. 58.
[63] Ibid, p. 58.
[64] H. Baier, 'Soziale Technologie oder soziale Emanzipation? Zum Streit zwischen
Positivisten und Dialektikern über die Aufgabe der Soziologie', in B. Schäfers, ed.,
Thesen zur Kritik der Soziologie (Frankfurt, 1969).
[65] H. Baier, 'Soziologie und Geschichte', *Archiv für Rechts-und Sozialphilosophie*,
vol. 52, 1966, p. 362.

IV

Any overview of the succeeding controversy remains inadequate
in so far as it is not possible to develop in any detail the various
issues raised. Only the focal points of the debates can be sum-
marized since their presentation would necessitate several more
volumes of collected contributions. The volume translated here
was published in the same year as the transactions of the German
Sociological Association Conference of 1968.[66] This Conference,
whose theme was 'Late Capitalism or Industrial Society?', and
more especially the heated debate within it, led to the temporary
demise of the sociological association. Whilst the major themes
of the conference did not bear directly upon the positivist dispute
—with two exceptions, one of which was a paper by Scheuch on
methodological problems of total societal analysis which was
intended as a dialogue with Habermas[67]—the discussion many
times took up the issue of the role of value-judgments in a context
which many viewed as an extreme polarization of viewpoints.[68]
At the same congress, Luhmann presented a paper on 'Modern
systems theory as a form of total societal analysis'[69] which subsequently sparked off a further debate, first with Habermas and
then with many other contributors.[70] This debate was still to the
fore in 1974 at the first sociology congress since 1968.[71] Some
writers have characterized it as 'the second major post-war
controversy in West German sociology',[72] the first being the
positivist dispute. Unlike the latter, however, this new debate

---

[66] T. W. Adorno, ed., *Spätkapitalismus oder Industriegesellschaft? Verhandlungen
des 16. Deutschen Soziologentages* (Tübingen, 1969).

[67] E. Scheuch, 'Methodische Probleme gesamtgesellschaftlicher Analysen', in
Spätkapitalismus, loc. cit., pp. 153ff.

[68] It should be pointed out here that the conference took place at the height of the
student movement in Germany.

[69] N. Luhmann, 'Moderne Systemtheorien als Form gesamtgesellschaftlicher
Analyse', in *Spätkapitalismus*, loc. cit., pp. 253f.

[70] The original debate is collected in J. Habermas/N. Luhmann, *Theorie der
Gesellschaft oder Sozialtechnologie- was leistet die Systemforschung?* (Frankfurt, 1971).
Further contributions are collected in F. Maciejewski, ed., *Beiträge zur Habermas-
Luhmann-Diskussion. Theorie-Diskussion Supplement 1* (Frankfurt, 1973); F. Macie-
jewski, ed., *Neue Beiträge zur Habermas-Luhmann-Diskussion. Supplement 2* (Frankfurt,
1974).

[71] See *Verhandlungen des 17. Deutschen Soziologentages, Kassel, 1974* (Tübingen, 1975)
(forthcoming).

[72] K. O. Hondrich, 'Systemtheorie als Instrument der Gesellschaftsanalyse', in
F. Maciejewski, ed., loc. cit. (1973), p. 88.

developed at a more concrete level of analysis and has centred
around the implications of systems theory in the social sciences.
Nor has it generated the same intransigence on the part of the
opponents as is manifested in the positivist dispute. The notion
of positivism has not been at issue in this later controversy since
both Habermas and Luhmann have been critical of its consequences for social research.

This is not to suggest that this later controversy between
systems theory and critical theory is totally unconnected with the
earlier positivist dispute. Habermas' essay in the present volume,
'The Analytical Theory of Science and Dialectics', starts out from
some points of difference between the analysis of society from
the standpoint of a dialectical theory of society and an analysis
which utilizes functional notions of social system. In some ways,
the Habermas–Luhmann debate may be seen as an amplification
of these differences. Similarly, Max Weber's theoretical and
methodological standpoint has been at issue in the present debate
since Popper's original paper, 'The Logic of the Social Sciences'
and been contested, in a more muted manner, in the Habermas–
Luhmann controversy.[73] It is worth adding here that three years
after Popper presented his paper, Weber's work was the theme of
the Fifteenth German Sociological Congress in 1964.[74]

More specifically, however, the Habermas–Luhmann controversy develops issues which are not merely evident in the
positivist dispute but which are central to it. For example,
Habermas argues that Luhmann's systems theory possesses many
features of a theory generated from a restricted technical interest
which adopts a decisionistic stance with regard to practical questions: 'this theory represents the advanced form of a technocratic
consciousness, which today permits practical questions to be
defined from the outset as technical ones, and thereby withholds
them from public and unconstrained discussion'.[75] This controversy once more raises the issue of the possibility of grounding
the normative basis of science as well as raising more concrete
issues, such as how to conceptualize the complexity of societies

---

[73] B. Heidtmann, 'Traditionelle und ideologische Determinanten einer Theorie
sozialer Systeme und ihre Kritik', in F. Maciejewski, ed., loc. cit. (1974), pp. 154f.

[74] O. Stammer, ed., *Max Weber and Sociology Today* (trans. K. Morris) (Oxford,
1971).

[75] J. Habermas, 'Theorie der Gesellschaft oder Sozialtechnologie?' in J. Haber-
mas/N. Luhmann, loc. cit., p. 145.

which Luhmann takes to be a central issue. In short, and in terms of the history of sociology, it renews the attempt, which had been placed in question in the positivist dispute, to analyse society as a whole. In so doing, it has relevance for the methodological individualism debate which has persisted in Anglo-American discussions.[76]

This is not the only direction in which the subsequent controversy has moved. Albert, for example, from the standpoint of critical rationalism, has extended his criticism of a hermeneutical-dialectical sociology to recent attempts, notably that of Holzkamp, to develop a critical psychology.[77] It remains to examine two further developments which have emerged out of the problematics of the positivist dispute. These are the attempt to extend the critique of the analytical philosophy of science by Apel and the rejoinders by Albert, and various attempts to develop a practical philosophy.

In Habermas' contributions to the present volume reference is often made to the hermeneutic dimension in the interpretation of theories and life experience. At the same time as the positivist dispute was in progress Habermas and Apel were developing a critical version of hermeneutics which incorporates the critique of ideology. This has led some observers to characterize this project as a hermeneutic-dialectical theory of society.[78] In order to introduce this dimension of the debate, reference will be made to the work of Apel since this is the subject of a critical volume by Albert.[79]

If, as Apel suggests, we compare the dominant neo-positivist

---

[76] Much of this debate is usefully presented in J. O'Neill, ed., *Modes of Individualism and Collectivism* (London, 1973).

[77] H. Albert and H. Keuth, eds., *Kritik der kritischen Psychologie* (Hamburg, 1973). The work criticized is K. Holzkamp, *Kritische Psychologie* (Frankfurt, 1972).

[78] As does, for example, G. Radnitsky, *Contemporary Schools of Metascience*, 2nd ed. (Göteborg, 1970). As well as providing a useful summary of this tradition and of what he terms 'logical empiricism', Radnitsky attempts to reconcile critical rationalism with the hermeneutic-dialectical tradition.

[79] Much of Apel's recent work is collected in K.-O. Apel, *Transformation der Philosophie*, 2 vols. (Frankfurt, 1973). See also K.-O. Apel, 'Communication and the Foundation of the Humanities', *Man and World*, vol. 5, 1972; K.-O. Apel, *Analytic Philosophy of Language and the Geisteswissenschaften* (Dordrecht, 1967); K.-O. Apel, 'Das Problem der philosophischen Letzbegründung im Lichte einer transzendentalen Sprachpragmatik (Versuch einer Metakritik des "kritischen Rationalismus")' in B. Kanitscheider, ed., *Festschrift für Gerhard Frey*, 1974. On the relation between hermeneutics and dialectics *see* K.-O. Apel *et al.*, *Hermeneutik und Ideologiekritik* (Frankfurt, 1971).

theory of science with Kant's theory of knowledge, which critical rationalism claims as its heritage, then it becomes apparent that the question of the conditions for the possibility of knowledge have not been enlarged but have been substantially reduced. Kant's notion of transcendental philosophy recognized that recourse to the critique of pure reason was not possible without placing the question of the possibility of science and the conditions for its validity. Apel argues that neo-positivism reduces Kant's transcendental logic to formal logic or to a logic of science. In its extreme form, the problem of the synthetic constitution of the data of experience plays no role. This is contrasted with an enlarged conception of the conditions for the possibility of knowledge, which Apel favours, in which the constitution of experiential data is dependent not only upon the synthetic capacity of human understanding but on an engaged world understanding, that is, a meaning constitutive cognitive interest. However, Apel argues that neo-positivism seeks to eliminate the question of cognitive interests from the basic problematic of the logic of science. The latter's restricted level of reflection becomes apparent when it seeks to extend its methodological ideals beyond the realms of natural science.

In the process of extrapolation from scientific methodology to a critical social philosophy, Apel argues that Popper is guilty of two 'abstractive fallacies'. The first, a scientistic-technicistic fallacy, derives from the fact that 'Popper makes the methodological ideal of *unified science* together with *social technology* ("social engineering") the *foundation* of critical rationality in the social politics of an "open society".'[80] The fallacy in such an extrapolation, Apel argues, lies in the fact that 'social technology does not possess its ideal precondition in the model of the "open society", but in a society which—on the basis of stable, quasi-archaic structures of domination—is split up into the informed and non-informed, manipulating and manipulated, and subject and object of science and technology'.[81] Social technology does not function at its best when all mature citizens make its goals and norms the basis of informed criticism and discussion, but rather when the object of technology 'can be reduced to the status of dumb natural objects which can be investigated in replicable

[80] K.-O. Apel, *Transformation der Philosophie*, loc. cit., vol. i, p. 14.
[81] Ibid.

experiments and instrumentally manipulated under binding objectives'.[82] Even if one wishes to secure the organization of intersubjective understanding of technical scientific objectivations of human behaviour, this cannot be achieved through improvement of the social technology or of increasing its 'feed-back'. 'The organization of *understanding concerning* necessary standards of social technology is, however, not itself a standard of social technology, and it cannot be supported merely on the basis of the results of a science which has itself already made the subjects of understanding into the objects of empirical-analytical behavioural explanation.'[83] The meaning and boundaries of such standards can only be generally secured through argumentation.

The second 'abstractive fallacy' derives from the transfer of the ideal of the community of scientists to a wider framework. Thus Apel suggests that one might interpret the starting point for the extrapolation of scientific methodological ideals in critical rationalism as lying not in the methods of the natural sciences but in 'the *method of critical argumentation* which elevates the *community of scientists* to the paradigm for an "open society".'[84] The implication of this extrapolation is that ' "criticism" in the community of argumentation of (natural) scientists refers exclusively to cognitive and thought operations, which already presuppose the self-evident cognitive interest of (natural) science; it refers in no way to the concrete needs and interests of socialized men which—consciously or unconsciously—also lie at the basis of the cognitive interest of (natural) science'.[85] With regard to the question as to whether the ideal of critical argumentation can be so extrapolated and institutionalized in society at large as a communication community, Apel argues that society is neither merely the object of science and technology nor is it yet the real subject of science.

Apel suggests that it is the deep-seated prejudice of the Popperian School against a non-scientistically orientated enlargement of the idea of methodical rationality which characterizes the inner limit to the fruitful conception of critical rationalism. He sees this prejudice as being conditioned by commitment to the axiom of unified science or unified methodology, and

[82] Ibid.
[83] Ibid. p. 15.
[84] Ibid, p. 16.
[85] Ibid, p. 17.

by failing to attend to the conditions for the possibility and validity of philosophy as criticism. Critical rationalism, however, does not believe in 'an, in principle, *transcendental reflection* upon the conditions for the possibility and validity of knowledge in the broadest sense'.[86] Further, Apel argues, critical rationalism rules out other cogitive paradigms within philosophy as methodologically irrelevant or obscurantist. In this manner it disposes of both hermeneutics in the human sciences and a social critical dialectics which have at least been concerned with the central problem of the modern human sciences and social philosophy, namely, 'the identity and non-identity of the subject and object of communicative knowledge and action as interaction in an "open society".'[87] Apel sees this failure to take account of hermeneutic dialectical philosophy, but perhaps an implicit recognition of the need for it, as being manifested within the critical rationalist tradition itself. Evidence for this view is the controversy over Kuhn's work and 'a practical *continuum between the theory of science and the history of science*', the controversy over a normatively relevant 'reconstruction' of an 'internal history' of science in Lakatos's work, and over the sceptical relativism in Feyerabend's challenge to a 'normatively binding idea of rational progress'.[88]

Apel's notion of a critical hermeneutics and his attempt to develop Kant's transcendental philosophy in a transcendental pragmatic direction has come under attack from Albert in a number of articles and most recently in a volume devoted to the criticism of Apel's philosophy.[89] Albert has elsewhere defended critical rationalism and developed its relevance for the social

---

[86] Ibid, pp. 18–19.

[87] Ibid, p. 20.

[88] Ibid, p. 22. It is not possible to develop here Apel's other contributions to the present controversy except to note that he has discussed further the three cognitive interests introduced by himself and Habermas, namely the technical, the practical (hermeneutics) and the emancipatory (critique of ideology) and argued that the study of science should include all three dimensions. He has specifically countered neo-positivism's reduction of understanding and hermeneutics to a heuristic device and argued for a critical hermeneutics which sees hermeneutics and the critique of ideology as complementary.

[89] Cf. H. Albert, 'Hermeneutik und Realwissenschaft' in H. Albert, *Plädoyer für kritischen Rationalismus* (Munich, 1971); H. Albert, *Konstruktion und Kritik* (Hamburg, 1972), esp. Part III, 'Geschichte, Recht und Verstehen: Zur Kritik des hermeneutischen Denkens', pp. 195f. The volume devoted to criticism of Apel's position is H. Albert, *Transzendentale Träumereien. Karl-Otto Apels Sprachspiele und sein hermeneutischer Gott* (Hamburg, 1975).

sciences.[90] In so doing, Albert has often combined Popper's philosophy with an interpretation of Max Weber's philosophy which suggests affinities between the latter and critical rationalism. For example, he sees Weber as combining 'an idea of rational cognitive practice' with the 'idea of a rational politics', whilst his immediate scientific concern was to establish 'a nomologically orientated value-free science'.[91]

Albert argues that recent attempts to re-establish a demarcation between nature and history are orientated towards 'a new transcendental idealism with a hermeneutic character'[92] which is basically anti-naturalist in intent. Albert takes the origins of hermeneutics to lie in Christian theology and the extension of Heidegger's philosophy, especially in the work of Gadamer. In short, this tradition is characterized as fundamentally conservative —though now incorporated into presumed radical stances—and fundamentally opposed to the Enlightenment tradition from which critical rationalism sees itself emanating. The hermeneutic tradition rejects nomological explanation as inappropriate for the historical-social world and favours the method of understanding directed at uncovering meaning. In this, Albert argues, the current hermeneutic tradition has much in common with that linguistic philosophy which was influenced by Wittgenstein's later works, and possesses similar distinctive characteristics, notably, '(1) the *linguistic* orientation and with it emphasis on the problem of linguistic meaning; (2) the *transcendental philosophical* tendency, that is, the falling back upon ontological arguments in the direction of an apriorism in which language is elevated to an unmistakable transcendental factor; and (3) the *methodological claim to autonomy* for the *Geisteswissenschaften* on hermeneutic grounds, which already characterized the earlier historicism'.[93] It therefore suffers from the weaknesses of that tradition.[94]

---

[90] As well as the volumes mentioned above, *see* H. Albert, *Traktat über kritische Vernunft* (Tübingen, 1968).

[91] H. Albert, 'Wissenschaft und Verantwortung' in *Plädoyer*, loc. cit., pp. 90–91.

[92] H. Albert, 'Hermeneutik und Realwissenschaft', in *Plädoyer*, loc. cit., p. 107. On anti-naturalist arguments *see* K. Popper, *The Poverty of Historicism*, 2nd ed. (London, 1960).

[93] H. Albert, *Plädoyer*, loc. cit., p. 110.

[94] The most notable presentation of this position in the social sciences has been P. Winch, *The Idea of a Social Science* (London, 1958). For a critique *see* E. Gellner, 'The New Idealism', in I. Lakatos and A. Musgrave, eds., *Problems in the Philosophy of Science* (Amsterdam, 1968).

The hermeneutic tradition tends to devalue natural scientific theory as instrumentalist and reduces it to knowledge generated from one cognitive interest amongst others. Albert sees the quasi-transcendental cognitive interests introduced by Habermas and Apel—the technical, practical and emancipatory—as 'the product of a secularization of Scheler's conception'[95] of a hierarchy of types of knowledge—knowledge for domination, education or formation and salvation. Again, the implication is that this tradition has its origins in a conservative philosophy. Albert argues that Apel's attempt to develop a cognitive anthropology diverts attention away from the actual empirical problems faced by the different sciences and instead seeks 'to undermine trans-cendentally the actual cognitive practice in the diverse groups of disciplines and thereby, at the same time, to justify the different modes of cognition which clearly predominate in them'.[96]

On the crucial role of understanding in the human sciences, Albert argues that the analysis of the problem of understanding in the hermeneutic tradition places emphasis upon the notion of meaning in terms of the meaning of signs rather than the meaning of actions. This distinction was already implicit in Weber's notion of understanding and orientates analysis towards a teleological conception of meaning directed at intentional behaviour. At this level, however, 'the *explanation of understanding* . . . thus *implies* the *explicability of meaningful behaviour* as such, an implication which is largely rejected by the advocates in the humanities of the alternatives of understanding and explanation'.[97] Such a notion of understanding cannot form the basis for the human science's claim to autonomy. Albert elsewhere suggests that the social sciences might do well to take as their model not the historicist understanding of historical research but instead the development of neo-classical economic theory which, despite its failings, has generated a considerable number of general explanatory theories.[98]

The central disagreement between Apel and Albert would appear to lie in the 'distinction between "transcendental," and

---

[95] H. Albert, *Plädoyer*, loc. cit., p. 111; *see* also Apel's comments on this criticism in K.-O. Apel, *Transformation der Philosophie*, loc. cit., p. 31.

[96] H. Albert, *Plädoyer*, p. 114.

[97] Ibid, p. 137.

[98] *See* H. Albert, 'Theorie, Verstehen und Geschichte' in *Konstruktion und Kritik*, oc. cit., pp. 206f. For Albert's critical analysis of economic theory *see* H. Albert, *Marktsoziologie und Entscheidungslogik* (Neuwied/Berlin, 1967).

"empirical" preconditions for the possibility of knowledge, understanding, criticism and action'.[99] Thus Albert finds it difficult to see 'what "transcendental" preconditions might possibly be other than preconditions whose *realization* is necessary —or even sufficient—for the actualization of the phenomena in question'.[100] The resort to transcendental philosophy is unnecessary. From the standpoint of critical rationalism 'it is clearly possible to utilize the results of the empirical sciences for the clarification of philosophical problems . . . The problem of knowledge itself belongs therefore to those problems which apply to the structural features of reality.'[101] The solution to the problem of knowledge does not require us 'to constitute a "transcendental subject" from which a guarantee of truth can be expected for specific insights but to make clear the basic features of the factual cognitive efforts of real subjects'.[102]

If the Apel–Albert controversy has centred round the foundation of the sciences and can be related back to the positivist dispute, then so too can the attempts to resurrect practical philosophy and to reopen the possibilities for a rational discourse concerning normative orientations. Even here, however, as far as the social sciences are concerned, it is possible to trace a concerted attempt to develop a practical philosophy in Aristotle's work, if not earlier. In the more recent history of sociology, opposition to such an enterprise within the social sciences came most forcefully from Max Weber who rigidly separated the 'completely *heterogeneous* problems' of securing facts and making normative judgments.[103]

More recently, however, attempts have been made not merely to resurrect practical philosophy but also to examine the normative basis of both social action and science. On the one hand, Habermas in the present dispute and elsewhere points to a rational normative foundation of science and of interaction.[104] Habermas argues that we employ counterfactual presuppositions (idealizations through

[99] H. Albert, *Transzendental Trämereien*, loc. cit., p. 146.

[100] Ibid, p. 146.

[101] Ibid.

[102] Ibid, pp. 148–9.

[103] *See* Max Weber, 'Science as a Vocation' in H. Gerth and C. W. Mills, eds., *From Max Weber* (New York/London, 1948).

[104] *See* J. Habermas, 'Vorbereitende Bemerkungen zu einer Theorie der kommunikative Kempetenz' in Habermas/Luhmann, loc. cit.; J. Habermas, *Legitimation Crisis*, trans. T. McCarthy (Boston/London, 1975), section 3.

which we seek to implement ideal postulates) in everyday speech and interaction. These relate to the assumption of rationality on the part of participants and to a domination-free discourse as well as the assumption that we could, if we wished, ground our norms discursively. Habermas' theory requires a consensus theory of truth which can be applied to theoretical as well as practical orientations.[105] From a different direction, the Erlangen School, notably Lorenzen and others, have developed a 'constructive theory of science' which is directed against the purely formalistic interpretation of scientific theories.[106] This has led in the direction of a dialogical foundation of logic and an attempt to construct the normative foundations of science. Though there are substantial differences between the two positions,[107] they are both agreed that 'it is possible to judge, in a *rational* manner, evaluative orientations in social and particularly scientific practice'.[108]

V

Readers of the contributions to the positivist dispute may discern the convergence of some of the issues raised with debates which have already been under way for some time in Anglo-American philosophy and social science. This is, in part, due to the critical assimilation of Anglo-American traditions in some German circles.[109] More significantly, however, some debates in Anglo-

[105] J. Habermas, 'Wahrheitstheorien', *Festschrift für Walter Schulz* (Pfullingen, 1973).

[106] *See* P. Lorenzen, *Methodisches Denken* (Frankfurt, 1968); P. Lorenzen and O. Schwemmer, *Konstruktive Logik, Ethik und Wissenschaftstheorie* (Mannheim, 1973); O. Schwemmer, *Philosophie der Praxis* (Frankfurt, 1971). For the Konstanz group *see* J. Mittelstrass, *Die Möglichkeit von Wissenschaft* (Frankfurt, 1974); F. Kambartel and J. Mittelstrass, eds., *Zum normativen Fundament der Wissenschaft* (Frankfurt, 1973); F. Kambartel, *Theorie und Begründung* (Frankfurt, 1974); P. Janich/F. Kambartel/J. Mittelstrass, *Wissenschaftstheorie als Wissenschaftskritik* (Frankfurt, 1974).

[107] The debate is contained in F. Kambartel, ed., *Praktische Philosophie und konstruktive Wissenschaftstheorie* (Frankfurt, 1974).

[108] Ibid, p. 9.

[109] This would include the German critical rationalists' assimilation and development of the Anglo-American philosophy of science tradition. For a recent example *see* H. Spinner, *Pluralismus als Erkenntnismodell* (Frankfurt, 1974). Also Apel's reception to the pragmatist tradition, especially that of Peirce, and to linguistic philosophy, as well as Habermas' recent attempt to develop a consensus theory of truth which relies on, amongst others, Searle and Austin, cf. J. Habermas, 'Wahrheitstheorien', in H. Fahrenbach, ed., *Wirklichkeit und Reflexion. Festschrift für Walter Schulz* (Pfullingen, 1973).

American philosophy have raised, in a different manner, some of the issues debated here.

The debate surrounding Kuhn's work on the relation between the philosophy and history of science, Lakatos's attempts to redevelop the internal history of science and Feyerabend's radical pluralism have all, Apel suggests, pointed to issues concerning the normative status of science, the notion of scientific rationality and the interpretation of theories, all of which have animated contributions to the positivist controversy. The implications of the Kuhn debate on the growth of science certainly extend to the social sciences or what Kuhn terms the 'protosciences'.[110] As Lakatos remarked, the dispute 'has implications not only for theoretical physics but also for the underdeveloped social sciences and even for moral and political philosophy'.[111] However, this did not imply, for some contestants, that one should turn to sociology, psychology or history for assistance in clarifying the aims of science. As Popper pointed out, this would be a dangerous enterprise since 'compared with physics, sociology and psychology are riddled with fashions and with uncontrolled dogmas. The suggestion that we can find anything here like "objective, pure description" is clearly mistaken. Besides, how can the regress to these often spurious sciences help us in this particular difficulty?'[112] Such a view is consistent with Popper's attempt to preserve the autonomy of science and secure 'third world' status for its theories.

It is clear from the contributions to the positivist dispute that another central issue concerns the notion of rationality. This is most apparent in the criticism of the reduction of scientific rationality to the canons of formal logic and methodology, and the possible extension of scientific rationality as the dominant paradigm of rationality to other areas of social life. Such views have been challenged within the Anglo-American tradition. Toulmin, for example, in a recent work attempts to develop the

---

[110] The debate is contained in I. Lakatos and A. Musgrave, eds., *Criticism and the Growth of Knowledge* (Cambridge, 1970) and was sparked off by T. Kuhn, *The Structure of Scientific Revolutions* (Chicago, 1962). *See* also R. Harre, ed., *Problems of Scientific Revolution* (Oxford, 1975).

[111] I. Lakatos, 'Falsification and the Methodology of Scientific Research Programmes', in *Criticism and the Growth of Knowledge*, loc. cit., p. 93. *See* also I. Lakatos, 'History of Science and its Rational Reconstructions', in R. Buck and R. Cohen, eds., *Boston Studies in the Philosophy of Science*, vol. 8 (Dordrecht, 1971).

[112] K. Popper, 'Normal Science and its Dangers', in Lakatos and Musgrave, eds., loc. cit., pp. 57–8.

concept of rationality within a historical dimension and suggests
that 'what has to be demonstrated is not that the rational procedures of scientific inquiry have, after all, a kind of "logic" of
their own: rather it is, how the formal structures and relations of
propositional logic are put to work in the service of rational
enterprises at all'.[113] From a different standpoint, Feyerabend,
who characterizes critical rationalism as 'the most liberal positivistic methodology in existence today',[114] also challenges the
notion of critical rationalism, both at the level of scientific
activity and in its extension to other realms.[115] However,
Feyerabend's own alternative to what he takes to be a restricted
concept of rationality, namely, a radical theoretical pluralism and
an anti-methodology of 'anything goes' has been seen by many to
entail an irrationalist response to this problem.

In other areas too the positivist dispute has taken up earlier
controversies. O'Neill argues that the positivist dispute extends
the earlier debate surrounding methodological individualism,
though not merely at the level of 'the nature of concept formation
and the logic of explanation in the social sciences'. Rather, 'what
is at stake besides methodological issues, is the question of the
conservative and radical roots of social science knowledge'.[116]
This is perhaps made most apparent in Adorno's introduction
and in Habermas' 'Analytical Theory of Science and Dialectics'.
Their opponents continue a tradition in the social sciences which,
in the recent past and within the history of the present dispute,
goes back to Max Weber who wrote, 'If I am now a sociologist
... I am so essentially in order to put an end to the use of collective
concepts, a use which still haunts us. In other words: even
sociology can only start from the action of one or a few, or many
individuals, i.e. pursue a strictly "individualistic" method.'[117]

In recent years in the social sciences, and especially in sociology,
the positivist framework has come under attack from the

[113] S. Toulmin, *Human Understanding*, vol. 1 (Oxford/Princeton, 1972), p. 479.
[114] P. Feyerabend, *Against Method* (London, 1975), p. 171.
[115] He argues that 'critical rationalism arose from the attempt to solve Hume's problem and to understand the Einsteinian revolution, and it was then extended to politics and even to the conduct of one's private life. (Habermas and others therefore seem to be justified in calling Popper a positivist)' ibid, p. 175.
[116] J. O'Neill, loc. cit., p. 5.
[117] M. Weber in a letter to R. Liefmann (1920). Quoted in W. J. Mommsen, 'Discussion on Max Weber and Power-politics', in O. Stammer, ed., *Max Weber and Sociology Today*, loc. cit., p. 115.

phenomenological and ethnomethodological traditions.[118] Whilst
the former has, following Schutz and others, examined an
alternative theoretical grounding for the social sciences, the
ethnomethodological tradition has challenged the type of research
activity and strategies generated from a positivist paradigm. It
has also provided a much wider basis for rationality and for the
consideration of theories of the everyday world.[119] It is one of
the ironies of the German positivist dispute that whilst the
analytical theory of science and its research strategies were
criticized, this did not immediately lead to the presentation and
development of alternative methodologies. In fact, as has been
previously remarked, the debate did not take up actual research
methodology, though some of the contributors have discussed
concrete social research elsewhere.

Any summary of the issues raised by the positivist dispute must
make apparent the complex range of controversies held together
under the umbrella of a 'positivist dispute'. As one commentator
somewhat acidly remarks, 'on the one hand, this dispute is still
relatively unfruitful, and on the other, it already covers so much
ground'.[120] But this may only point to the fact that controversy
is certainly not foreign to the social sciences. Indeed the history
of almost continuous dispute suggests that controversy must
characterize 'normal science' in the social sciences. Their problematic role and the problematic nature of their inquiry has a
history as long as that of the sciences themselves. It was perhaps
this state of affairs which J. S. Mill was commenting upon over a
century ago in his *A System of Logic*. There Mill, in his opening
remarks on the logic of the moral sciences, asserts that whilst
'concerning the physical nature of man as an organized being'
there exists 'a considerable body of truths which all who have
attended to the subject consider to be fully established' this is
certainly not true for 'the laws of Mind' and especially those of
society which 'are so far from having attained a similar state of

---

[118] A. Schutz, *The Phenomenology of the Social World*, trans. G. Walsh and F. Lehnert
(Evanston, 1967); A. Schutz, *Collected Papers*, 3 vols. (Hague, 1964, 1966, 1967);
A. V. Cicourel, *Method and Measurement in Sociology* (New York/London, 1964);
A. V. Cicourel, *Cognitive Sociology* (London, 1973); H. Garfinkel, *Studies in Ethno-
methodology* (New York, 1967).

[119] See H. Garfinkel, 'The Rational Properties of Scientific and Commonsense
Activities', *Behavioral Science*, 1960. Reprinted in *Studies in Ethnomethodology* loc. cit.

[120] B. Willms, 'System und Subjekt oder die politische Antinomie der Gesell-
schaftstheorie' in F. Maciejewski, ed., loc. cit. (1973), p. 45.

even partial recognition, that it is still a controversy whether they are capable of becoming subjects of science in the strict sense of the term; and amongst those who are agreed on this point there reigns the most irreconcilable diversity on almost every other'.[121]

---

[121] J. S. Mill, *A System of Logic* (London, 1961), p. 572. For a valuable recent collection of confrontations on the social sciences *see* R. Borger and F. Cioffi, eds., *Explanation in the Behavioural Sciences* (Cambridge, 1970).

THEODOR W. ADORNO

*INTRODUCTION**

For Fred Pollock on his seventy-fifth birthday in cordial friendship

'Open Sesame! I want to get out.'
Stanislav Jerzy Lec

In his incisive remarks on the Tübingen discussion of the two papers which marked the beginning in Germany of the public controversy on dialectics and positivistic sociology in the broadest sense,[1] Ralf Dahrendorf regrets that the discussion 'generally lacked the intensity that would have been appropriate to the actual differences in views'.[2] According to him, some of the participants in the discussion censured 'the lack of tension between the symposiasts' papers'.[3] Dahrendorf, for his part, senses 'the irony of such points of agreement' and suggests that profound differences in the matters discussed are hidden behind similarities in formulation. But the conciliatory attitude of the two symposiasts was not the only reason why no discussion actually came about in which reasons and counter-reasons might have interacted upon one another. The symposiasts were primarily concerned to make their positions in general theoretically commensurable. Nor was it merely a question of the attitude of

---

* Special gratitude is due to Albrecht Wellmer for a paper read at a private seminar (held by Ludwig v. Friedeburg and the author) on the philosophy of science in the summer semester of 1967.

[1] Cf. the introduction to E. Durkheim, *Soziologie und Philosophie*, Frankfurt 1967, pp. 8f., footnote. It must be restated in advance here that Popper and Albert distance themselves from the specific position of logical positivism. The reason why they are nevertheless regarded as positivists should be evident from what follows.

[2] Ralf Dahrendorf, 'Remarks on the Discussion of the Papers of Karl R. Popper and Theodor W. Adorno', *see* below, p. 123.

[3] loc. cit.

I

several participants in the discussion who asserted their estrangement from philosophy—an estrangement which, in some cases, has only recently been acquired. The dialecticians have explicit recourse to philosophy, but the methodological interests of the positivists are hardly less alien to naïvely practised research activity. Both speakers, however, ought to plead guilty to one genuine lack which obstructed the discussion. Both failed to achieve the complete mediation of their theoretical interests with sociology as such. Much of what they said referred to science in general. A degree of bad abstraction is posited in all epistemology, and even in the criticism of it.[4] Anyone who does not remain satisfied with the immediacy of scientific procedure and renounces its requirements secures, together with a less restricted view, illegitimate advantages. However, the claim that was occasionally voiced, namely that the Tübingen discussion confined itself to preliminaries and consequently was of no use to sociology as a distinctive discipline, misses the point. Arguments which commit themselves to the analytical theory of science without inquiring into its axioms—and 'preliminaries' can only imply this—become caught up in the infernal machine of logic. No matter how faithfully one may observe the principle of immanent critique, it cannot be applied in an unreflected manner when logical immanence itself, regardless of any particular content, is elevated to the sole standard. The critique of its constraining character is included in an immanent critique of an unleashed logic. Thought assumes this constraining character through unthinking identification with formal logical processes. Immanent critique has its limitation in the fetishized principle of immanent logic: this principle must be called by its proper name. Moreover, the material relevance of the supposedly preliminary discussions is by no means excluded in sociology. For instance, whether one can talk of ideology depends directly upon whether one can distinguish between illusion and essence, and is thus a central piece of sociological doctrine extending into all ramifications of the subject. This material relevance of what sounds like epistemological or logical preliminaries is explained by the fact that the relevant controversies are, for their part, of a latently material nature. Either, knowledge of society is interwoven with the latter, and society enters the science of society in a concrete form, or society is

---

[4] Cf. Hans Albert, 'The Myth of Total Reason', pp. 167f.

simply a product of subjective reason, beyond all further inquiry about its own objective mediations.

But behind the censured abstractness of the discussion lie far more serious difficulties. For the discussion to be possible it must proceed according to formal logic. But the thesis concerning the priority of the latter is, in turn, the core of the positivistic or— to replace the perhaps all too loaded term with one which might be acceptable to Popper—scientistic view of any science, sociology and the theory of science included. Amongst the topics in the controversy which must be considered is the question whether the inescapable logicality of the procedure actually gives absolute primacy to logic. But thoughts which demand the critical self-reflection of the primacy of logic in concrete disciplines inevitably end in a tactical disadvantage. They must reflect upon logic with the aid of means which, in turn, are largely logical—a contradiction of the type that Wittgenstein, as the most reflective positivist, realized all too clearly. If the present inevitable debate became one of 'Weltanschauungen' and were conducted from externally opposed standpoints, then it would a priori be unfruitful. But if it enters into argumentation then there is the danger that if the rules governing one position were to be tacitly recognized then this would inevitably supply the object of the discussion.

Dahrendorf answered my remark that it was not a matter of difference in standpoint but rather of determinable differences, with the question 'whether the first statement was correct but the latter false'.[5] Whilst in his view the two positions did not exclude discussion and argument, the differences in the type of argumentation were so profound 'that one must doubt whether Popper and Adorno could even agree upon a procedure with the aid of which their differences could be decided'.[6] The question is a genuine one. It can only be answered after the attempt has been made to produce such a decision and not before. This attempt should be made since the amiable tolerance towards two different coexisting types of sociology would amount to nothing more than the neutralization of the emphatic claim to truth. The task itself is paradoxical. The controversial questions must be discussed without logicistic prejudice, but also without dogmatism. Habermas implies this effort, and not crafty eristic arts, with the formulations 'flanking strategy' or 'behind positivism's back'. A

---

[5] Dahrendorf, p. 128 below.
[6] loc. cit., p. 128.

theoretical position ought to be found from which one can respond to the other person without, however, accepting a set of rules which are themselves a theme of the controversy—an intellectual no man's land. But this position cannot be conceived, in terms of a model derived from extensional logic, as something even more general than the two opposing positions. It is made concrete since even science, including formal logic, is not only a social force of production but also a social relation of production. One may doubt whether this is acceptable to the positivists. It critically affects the basic thesis of the absolute independence of science and its constitutive character for all knowledge. One ought to ask whether a valid disjunction exists between knowledge and the real life-process, or whether it is not rather the case that knowledge is mediated through the latter; or whether its own autonomy, through which it has made itself productively independent of its genesis and objectivated itself, can be derived, in turn, from its social function; or whether it forms an immanent context and yet, in terms of its constitution, is situated in a field which surrounds it and even acts upon its immanent structure. But such a dual nature, no matter how plausible, would clash with the principle of non-contradiction. Science would then be both independent and dependent. A dialectics which advocated this could, in so doing, no more act as if it were 'privileged thought' than it could elsewhere. It cannot set itself up as a specific subjective capacity, with which one person is gifted but which is denied to others. Nor can it present itself as intuitionism. Conversely, the positivists must make sacrifices. They must relinquish the attitude which Habermas calls the 'systematic pretence of failure to understand', and not unhesitatingly disqualify out of hand as unintelligible anything that fails to coincide with their 'criteria of meaning'. In view of their increasing animosity towards philosophy, one suspects that certain sociologists are taking great pains to shake off their own past. But the past usually takes its revenge.

At first sight the controversy seems to be that the positivists' position represents a strict concept of objective scientific validity which is weakened by philosophy, whilst the dialecticians proceed speculatively, as the philosophical tradition would suggest. However, everyday linguistic usage converts the concept of the speculative into its opposite. It is no longer interpreted, as it was by Hegel, in the sense of the critical self-reflection of the intellect, of self-reflection's boundedness and self-correction. But rather it is imperceptibly interpreted in a popular manner. Here, he who speculates is viewed as an unrestricted wild thinker who in his vanity dispenses with logical self-criticism and any confrontation with the facts. Since the collapse of the Hegelian system, and perhaps as a consequence of it, the idea of speculation has become so inverted that it resembles the Faustian cliché of the beast on the barren heath. What was once intended to signify the thought that renounces its own narrowness and in so doing gains objectivity, is now equated with subjective caprice. It is caprice since speculation lacks generally valid restraints; it is subjectivism since the concept of the fact of speculation is dissolved through emphasis upon mediation, through the 'concept' which appears as a relapse into scholastic realism and according to positivistic ritual, as that product of the thinker which boldly confuses itself with an entity in itself. On the other hand, stronger than the *tu quoque* argument which Albert regards with suspicion, is the thesis that the positivist position, where pathos and influence are inherent in its claim to objectivity, is in turn, subjectivist. This was anticipated by Hegel's critique of what he termed the philosophy of reflection. Carnap's jubilation was based on the claim that nothing remained of philosophy but its method. His method of logical analysis is the prototype of the quasi-ontological predisposition towards subjective reason.[7] Positivism, to which contradictions are anathema, possesses its innermost contradiction, unbeknown to itself, in the following: namely, that it adheres to an objectivity which is most external to its sentiments and purged of all subjective projections, but thereby simply becomes all the more entangled in the particularity of mere subjective, instrumental reason. Those who regard themselves as victors over idealism are far closer to it than critical theory. They hypostatize the knowing subject, not as an absolute subject or a source, but as the *topos noetikos* of all validity—of scientific control. Whilst they wish to liquidate philosophy, they advocate a philosophy which, resting on the authority of science, seeks to immunize itself against itself. In Carnap's work, the final link in the Hume-Mach-Schlick chain, the connection with the older subjective positivism is still revealed through his sensualist interpretation of protocol statements. Since these scientific statements are

---

[7] The concept of subjective reason is developed in Max Horkheimer, *The Eclipse of Reason* (New York 1947) repr. 1974.

simply given in language and are not immediately given as sense certainty, this sensualist interpretation gave rise to Wittgenstein's problematic. But the latent subjectivism is in no way penetrated by the language theory of the *Tractatus*. There, one reads: 'Philosophy does not result in "philosophical propositions", but rather in the clarification of propositions. Without philosophy thoughts are, as it were, cloudy and indistinct: its task is to make them clear and to give them sharp boundaries.'[8] But clarity is only accorded to subjective consciousness. In a scientific spirit, Wittgenstein exaggerates the claim of objectivity to such an extent that it dissolves and yields to the total paradox of philosophy, which forms Wittgenstein's nimbus. Latent subjectivism has formed a counterpoint to the objectivism of the entire nominalist Enlightenment, the permanent *reductio ad hominem*. Thought need not adapt to it. It has the power to reveal critically the latent subjectivism. It is amazing that the supporters of scientism, including Wittgenstein, were no more disturbed by this antagonism than by the permanent antagonism between the formal logical and empiricist currents, which, distorted within positivism, brings to light an extremely real antagonism. Even for Hume the doctrine of the absolute validity of mathematics was heterogenously contrasted with sceptical sensualism. Here the relative failure of scientism to achieve a mediation between facticity and concept becomes evident. If the two are not united then they become logically incompatible. One can neither advocate the absolute priority of the individual entity over 'ideas', nor can one maintain the absolute independence of the purely ideal, namely the mathematical, realm. No matter how one interprets it, as long as Berkeley's *esse est percipi* is retained, it is difficult to see where the claim to validity of the formal disciplines is derived from, for this claim is not founded in anything sensuous. Conversely, all the connecting mental operations of empiricism, for which the connectedness of statements is a criterion of truth, postulate formal logic. This simple consideration ought to be sufficient to induce scientism to take up dialectics. The unsatisfactory abstract polarity of the formal and the empirical is extended, in a highly tangible manner, to the social sciences. Formal sociology is the external complement to what Habermas has termed restricted experience. The theses of sociological formalism,

---

[8] Ludwig Wittgenstein, *Tractatus Logico-Philosophicus*, 4.112 (London 1961), p. 49.

for instance those of Simmel, are not in themselves false. Yet the mental acts are false which detach these from the empirical, hypostatize them and then subsequently fill them out through illustration. The favourite discoveries of formal sociology, such as the bureaucratization of proletarian parties, have their *fundamentum in re*, but they do not invariably arise from the higher concept 'organization in general' but rather from societal conditions, such as the constraint of asserting oneself within an overwhelming system whose power is realized through the diffusion of its own organizational forms over the whole. This constraint infects the opponents of the system and not merely through social contamination but also in a quasi-rational manner—so that the organization is able, at any time, to represent effectively the interests of its members. Within a reified society, nothing has a chance to survive which is not in turn reified. The concrete historical generality of monopolistic capitalism extends into the monopoly of labour, with all its implications. A relevant task for empirical sociology would be to analyse the intermediate members and to show in detail how the adaptation to the changed capitalist relations of production includes those whose objective interests conflict, in the long run, with this adaptation.

The predominant positivistic sociology can rightly be termed subjective in the same sense as subjective economics. In the work of one of economics' major representatives, Vilfredo Pareto, contemporary sociological positivism has one of its roots. 'Subjective' has a double meaning here. Firstly, as Habermas expresses it, such a sociology operates with catalogues of hypotheses or schemata imposed upon the material. Whilst undoubtedly, in this operation, it is the material which prevails, depending upon the section into which it must be incorporated, what is more decisive is whether the material—the phenomena—is interpreted in accordance with its own predetermined structure, and not simply established by science in a classificatory manner. Just how decisive is the choice of the supposed system of co-ordinates, is exemplified by the alternative of subsuming certain social phenomena under concepts such as prestige and status, or deriving them from objective relations of domination. According to the latter interpretation, status and prestige are subject to the dynamics of class relations and, in principle, they can be conceptualized as capable of abolition. But their classificatory subsumption, on the other hand, tends to accept such categories as simply given, and probably untransformable. A distinction which apparently concerns only methodology therefore has vital concrete consequences. The subjectivism of positivistic sociology accords with this in its second meaning. In quite a considerable area of its activity at least, it takes as its starting point opinions, modes of behaviour and the self-understanding of individual subjects and of society. In such a conception, society is largely what must be investigated statistically: the average consciousness or unconsciousness of societalized and socially acting subjects, and not the medium in which they move. The objectivity of the structure which, for the positivists, is a mythological relic is, according to dialectical theory, the *a priori* of cognitive subjective reason. If subjective reason became aware of this then it would have to determine the structure of its own law-like nature and not present it independently according to the procedural rules of conceptual order. The condition and the content of the social facts to be derived from individual subjects are provided by this structure. Regardless of the extent to which the dialectical conception of society has realized its claim to objectivity, and whether this is still possible for it, the dialectical conception takes this claim more seriously than do its opponents, who purchase the apparent security of their objectively valid findings by foregoing, from the outset, the emphatic idea of objectivity, which was once intended with the concept of the in-itself. The positivists prejudice the outcome of the debate in so far as they insinuate that they represent a new advanced type of thought whose views, as Albert puts it, have as yet not prevailed everywhere, but compared with which dialectics has become archaic. This view of progress disregards the price paid which sabotages it. The mind is to advance by fettering itself as mind for the benefit of the facts—truly a logical contradiction. Albert asks, 'Why should not new ideas similarly receive a chance to prove themselves?'[9] By 'new ideas' he means a mentality which is not generally favourably disposed towards ideas. Its claim to modernity can only be that of advanced Enlightenment. But this claim requires the critical self-reflection of subjective reason. The advance of the latter, which is permeated to its innermost core with the dialectics of Enlightenment, cannot, without difficulty, be assumed to be a higher objectivity. This is the focal point of the controversy.

---

[9] Hans Albert, 'The Myth of Total Reason', p. 175 below.

Since dialectics is not a method independent of its object, it cannot, unlike a deductive system, be represented as a for-itself [*Für sich*]. It does not accede to the criterion of the definition but instead it criticizes it. What is more serious is that, after the irrevocable collapse of the Hegelian system, dialectics has forfeited the former, profoundly questionable, consciousness of philosophical certainty. The accusation of the positivists, namely that dialectics lacks a foundation upon which everything else might be constructed, is held against it even by currently predominant philosophy with the claim that it lacks ἀρχή*. In its idealist version, dialectics ventured, through numerous mediations and, in fact, by virtue of Being's own non-identity with Spirit, to present Being as perfectly identical with the latter. This was unsuccessful and consequently, in its present form, dialectics adopts a position towards the 'myth of total reason' no less polemical than Albert's scientism. Dialectics is unable to take its claim to truth as guaranteed, as it did in its idealist phase. For Hegel the dialectical movement was able, with difficulty, to consider itself to be a comprehensive explanatory principle—to be 'science'. For, in its first steps and positings, the thesis of identity was always present, a thesis which in the development of the analyses was neither corroborated nor explicated. Hegel described it with the metaphor of the circle. Such closedness, which necessarily implied that nothing remained essentially unrecognized or fortuitous outside dialectics, has been exploded, along with its constraint and unambiguity. Dialectics does not possess a canon of thought which might regulate it. Nevertheless, it still has its raison d'être. In terms of society, the idea of an objective system-in-itself is not as illusory as it seemed to be after the collapse of idealism, and as positivism asserts. The notion of the great tradition of philosophy, which positivism considers to be outdated,[10] is not indebted to the allegedly aesthetic qualities of intellectual achievements but rather to a content of experience which, because of its transcendence into individual consciousness, would tempt me to hypostatize it as being absolute. Dialectics is able to legitimize itself by translating this content back into the experience from which it arose. But this is the experience of the mediation of all that is individual through the objective societal

[10] Cf. Helmut F. Spinner, 'Wo warst du, Platon. Ein kleiner Protest gegen eine "grosse Philosophie",' *Soziale Welt*, vol. 18, 1967, No. 2/3, p. 174 footnote.
* A source of origin.

totality. In traditional dialectics, it was turned on its head with the thesis that antecedent objectivity—the object itself, understood as totality—was the subject. Albert objects that in my Tübingen paper there are merely hints at totality.[11] Yet it is almost tautological to say that one cannot point to the concept of totality in the same manner as one can point to the facts, from which totality distances itself as a concept. 'And to this first, still quite abstract approximation, let us add a further qualification, namely the dependency of all individuals on the totality which they form. In such a totality, everyone is also dependent on everyone else. The whole survives only through the unity of the functions which its members fulfil. Each individual without exception must take some function on himself in order to prolong his existence; indeed, while his function lasts, he is taught to express his gratitude for it.'[12]

Albert accuses Habermas of adhering an idea of total reason, together with all the sins of the philosophy of identity. In objective terms, Albert claims that dialectics carries on, in an obsolete Hegelian manner, with a notion of the societal whole that cannot be realized by research and which thus belongs on the rubbish dump. The fascination exerted by Merton's 'theory of the middle range' can certainly be explained by the scepticism towards a category of totality, whilst the objects of such theorems are violently torn from the encircling contexts. According to the simplest common sense, the empirical strives towards totality. If one studies social conflict in a case such as the hostile reactions in Berlin towards students in 1967, then the occasion of the individual situation is not sufficient for an explanation. A thesis such as the following: that the population simply reacted in a spontaneous manner towards a group which it considered to be endangering the interests of a city maintained under precarious conditions—would be inadequate, and not only because of the doubtfulness of the political and ideological connections assumed. Such a thesis in no way makes plausible the rage against a specific visible minority, easily identifiable according to popular prejudice, which immediately exploded into physical violence. The most widespread and effective stereotypes in vogue against the students

---

[11] Cf. Albert, loc. cit., p. 164, footnote 1.
[12] Theodor W. Adorno, 'Gesellschaft', in *Evangelische Staatslexikon* (Stuttgart, 1967) column 637. English trans. F. Jameson, 'Society' in *Salmagundi*, no. 10–11, 1969–70, p. 145.

—that they demonstrate instead of working (a flagrant untruth), that they squander the taxpayers' money which pays for their studies, and similar statements—apparently have nothing to do with the acute situation. The similarity between such slogans and those of the jingoistic press is obvious. But this press would scarcely be influential if it did not act upon dispositions of opinion and instinctive reactions of numerous individuals and both confirm and strengthen them. Anti-intellectualism and the readiness to project discontent with questionable conditions onto those who express the questionableness, make up the reactions to immediate causes which serve as a pretence or as a rationalization. If it were the case that even the situation in Berlin was a factor which helped to release the mass psychological potential, then it could not be understood other than within the wider context of international politics. It is a narrow line of thought which deduces from the so-called Berlin situation what arises from power struggles actualized in the Berlin conflict. When lengthened, the lines lead to the social network. Owing to the infinite plurality of its moments, it can, of course, scarcely be encapsulated by scientific prescriptions. But if it is eliminated from science then the phenomena are attributed to false causes, and the dominant ideology regularly profits from this. That society does not allow itself to be nailed down as a fact actually only testifies to the existence of mediation. This implies that the facts are neither final nor impenetrable, even though the prevailing sociology regards them as such in accordance with the model of sense data found in earlier epistemology. In them there appears that which they are not.[13] Not the least significant of the differences between the positivist and dialectical conceptions is that positivism, following Schlick's maxim, will only allow appearance to be valid, whilst dialectics will not allow itself to be robbed of the distinction between essence and appearance. For its part, it is a societal law that decisive structures of the social process, such as that of the inequality of the alleged equivalency of exchange, cannot become apparent without the intervention of theory. Dialectical thought counters the suspicion of what Nietzsche termed nether-worldly [*hinterweltlerisch*] with the assertion that concealed essence is non-essence. Dialectical thought, irreconcilable with the philosophical tradition, affirms this non-essence, not

---

[13] Cf. Max Horkheimer, loc. cit.

because of its power but instead it criticizes its contradiction of 'what is appearing' [*Erscheinendes*] and, ultimately, its contradiction of the real life of human beings. One must adhere to Hegel's statement that essence must appear. Totality is not an affirmative but rather a critical category. Dialectical critique seeks to salvage or help to establish what does not obey totality, what opposes it or what first forms itself as the potential of a not yet existent individuation. The interpretation of facts is directed towards totality, without the interpretation itself being a fact. There is nothing socially factual which would not have its place in that totality. It is pre-established for all individual subjects since they obey its 'contrainte' even in themselves and even in their monado-logical constitution and here in particular, conceptualize totality. To this extent, totality is what is most real. Since it is the sum of individuals' social relations which screen themselves off from individuals, it is also illusion—ideology. A liberated mankind would by no means be a totality. Their being-in-themselves is just as much their subjugation as it deceives them about itself as the true societal substratum. This certainly does not fulfil the desideratum of a logical analysis of the concept of totality,[14] as the analysis of something free from contradiction, which Albert uses against Habermas, for the analysis terminates in the objective contradiction of totality. But the analysis should protect recourse to totality from the accusation of decisionistic arbitrariness.[15] Habermas, no more than any other dialectician, disputes the possibility of an explication of totality; he simply disputes its verifiability according to the criterion of facts which is trans-cended through the movement towards the category of totality. Nevertheless, it is not separate from the facts but is immanent to them as their mediation. Formulated provocatively, totality is society as a thing-in-itself, with all the guilt of reification. But it is precisely because this thing-in-itself is not yet the total societal subject—nor is it yet freedom, but rather extends nature in a heteronomous manner—that an indissoluble moment is objective to it such as Durkheim, though somewhat onesidedly, declared to be the essence of the social as such. To this extent it is also 'factual'. The concept of facticity, which the positivistic view guards as its final substratum, is a function of the same society about which scientistic sociology, insistent upon this opaque

---

[14] Cf. Hans Albert, 'The Myth of Total Reason', pp. 167f.
[15] Cf. loc. cit., p. 168.

substratum, promises to remain silent. The absolute separation
of fact and society is an artificial product of reflection which must
be derived from, and refuted through, a second reflection.

In a footnote, Albert writes the following:

'Habermas quotes in this context Adorno's reference to the
untestability of the dependence of each social phenomenon
"upon the totality". The quotation stems from a context in
which Adorno, with reference to Hegel, asserts that refutation
is only fruitful as immanent critique; see Adorno, "On the
Logic of the Social Sciences", pp. 113f. Here the meaning of
Popper's comments on the problem of the critical test is
roughly reversed through "further reflection". It seems to me
that the untestability of Adorno's assertion is basically linked
with the fact that neither the concept of totality used, nor the
nature of the dependence asserted, is clarified to any degree.
Presumably, there is nothing more behind it than the idea that
somehow everything is linked with everything else. To what
extent any view could gain a methodical advantage from such
an idea would really have to be demonstrated. In this matter,
verbal exhortations of totality ought not to suffice.'[16]

However, the 'untestability' does not reside in the fact that no
plausible reason can be given for recourse to totality, but rather
that totality, unlike the individual social phenomena to which
Albert's criterion of testability is limited, is not factual. To the
objection that behind the concept of totality there lies nothing
more than the triviality that everything is linked with everything
else, one should reply that the bad abstraction of that statement
'is not so much the sign of feeble thinking as it is that of a shabby
permanency in the constitution of society itself: that of exchange.
The first, objective abstraction takes place; not so much in the
scientific account of it, as in the universal development of the
exchange system itself, which happens independently of the
qualitative attitudes of producer and consumer, of the mode of
production, even of need, which the social mechanism tends to
satisfy as a kind of secondary by-product. A humanity classified
as a network of consumers, the human beings who actually have
the needs, has been socially preformed beyond anything which
one might naïvely imagine, and this not only by the technical

---

[16] loc. cit., p. 175, footnote 26.

level of productive forces but just as much by the economic relationships themselves in which they function. The abstraction of exchange value is a priori allied with the domination of the general over the particular, of society over its captive membership. It is not at all a socially neutral phenomenon as the logistics of reduction, of uniformity of work time pretend. The domination of men over men is realized through the reduction of men to agents and bearers of commodity exchange. The concrete form of the total system requires everyone to respect the law of exchange if he does not wish to be destroyed, irrespective of whether profit is his subjective motivation or not.'[17] The crucial difference between the dialectical and the positivistic view of totality is that the dialectical concept of totality is intended 'objectively', namely, for the understanding of every social individual observation, whilst positivistic systems theories wish, in an uncontradictory manner, to incorporate observations in a logical continuum, simply through the selection of categories as general as possible. In so doing, they do not recognize the highest structural concepts as the precondition for the states of affairs subsumed under them. If positivism denigrates this concept of totality as mythological, pre-scientific residue then it mythologizes science in its assiduous struggle against mythology. Its instrumental character, or rather its orientation towards the primacy of available methods instead of towards reality and its interest, inhibits insights which affect both scientific procedure and its object. The core of the critique of positivism is that it shuts itself off from both the experience of the blindly dominating totality and the driving desire that it should ultimately become something else. It contents itself with the senseless ruins which remain after the liquidation of idealism, without interpreting, for their part, both liquidation and what is liquidated, and rendering them true. Instead, positivism is concerned with the disparate, with the subjectivistically interpreted datum and the associated pure thought forms of the human subject. Contemporary scientism unites these now fragmented moments of knowledge in a manner as external as that of the earlier philosophy of reflection which, for this reason, deserved to be criticized by speculative dialectics. Dialectics also contains the opposite of idealistic hubris. It abolishes the illusion of a somehow natural-transcendental dignity

---

[17] Adorno, 'Gesellschaft', loc. cit., column 639. English trans. F. Jameson, *Salmagundi*, loc. cit., pp. 148–9. Original slightly revised.

of the individual subject and becomes conscious of it in its forms
of thought as something societal in itself. To this extent, dialectics
is 'more realistic' than scientism with all its 'criteria of meaning'.

But since society is made up of human subjects and is constituted through their functional connection, its recognition
through living, unreduced subjects is far more commensurable
with 'reality itself' than in the natural sciences which are compelled, by the alien nature of a non-human object, to situate
objectivity entirely within the categorial mechanism, in abstract
subjectivity. Freyer has drawn attention to this. The distinction
between the nomothetic and idiographic, made by the south-west
German neo-Kantian school, can be left out of consideration all
the more readily since an unabbreviated theory of society cannot
forego the laws of its structural movement. The commensur-
ability of the object—society—with the knowing subject exists
just as much as it does not exist. This too is difficult to combine
with discursive logic. Society is both intelligible and unintelligible.
It is intelligible in so far as the condition of exchange, which is
objectively decisive, itself implies an abstraction and, in terms of
its own objectivity, a subjective act. In it the human subject
truly recognizes himself. In terms of the philosophy of science,
this explains why Weberian sociology concentrates upon the
concept of rationality. In rationality, regardless of whether
consciously or unconsciously, Weber sought what was identical
in subject and object, namely that which would permit something
akin to knowledge of the object [*Sache*], instead of its splintering
into data and its processing. Yet the objective rationality of
society, namely that of exchange, continues to distance itself
through its dynamics, from the model of logical reason. Consequently, society—what has been made independent—is, in turn,
no longer intelligible; only the law of becoming independent is
intelligible. Unintelligibility does not simply signify something
essential in its structure but also the ideology by means of which
it arms itself against the critique of its irrationality. Since rationality or spirit has separated itself as a partial moment from the
living human subjects and has contended itself with rationalization, it moves forward towards something opposed to the
subjects. The aspect of objectivity as unchangeability, which it
thus assumes, is then mirrored in the reification of the knowing
consciousness. The contradiction in the concept of society as
intelligible and unintelligible is the driving force of rational

critique, which extends to society and its type of rationality, namely the particular. If Popper seeks the essence of criticism in the fact that progressive knowledge abolishes its own logical contradictions, then his own ideal becomes criticism of the object if the contradiction has its own recognizable location in it, and not merely in the knowledge of it. Consciousness which does not blind itself to the antagonistic nature of society, nor to society's immanent contradiction of rationality and irrationality, must proceed to the critique of society without μετάβασις εἰς ἄλλο γένος, without means other than rational ones.

In his essay on the analytical theory of science, Habermas has justified the necessity of the transition to dialectics with particular reference to social scientific knowledge.[18] According to Habermas' argument, not only is the object of knowledge mediated through the subject, as positivism would admit, but the reverse is just as true: namely, that the subject, for its part, forms a moment of the objectivity which he must recognize; that is, it forms a moment of the societal process. In the latter, with increasing scientization, knowledge becomes to an increasing extent a force of production. Dialectics would like to confront scientism in the latter's own sphere in so far as it strives for a more correct recognition of contemporary societal reality. It seeks to help to penetrate the curtain hanging before reality—a curtain which science helps to weave. The harmonistic tendency of science, which makes the antagonisms of reality disappear through its methodical processing, lies in the classificatory method which is devoid of the intention of those who utilize it. It reduces to the same concept what is not fundamentally homonymous, what is mutually opposed, through the selection of the conceptual apparatus, and in the service of its unanimity. In recent years, an example of this tendency has been provided by Talcott Parsons' well-known attempt to create a unified science of man. His system of categories subsumes individual and society, psychology and sociology alike, or at least places them in a continuum.[19] The ideal of continuity, current since Descartes and Leibniz especially, has become dubious, though not merely as a result of recent natural scientific

---

[18] Cf. Jürgen Habermas, 'The Analytical Theory of Science and Dialectics. A postscript to the Controversy between Popper and Adorno', p. 162 below.

[19] Cf. Theodor W. Adorno, 'Zum Verhältnis von Soziologie und Psychologie', in *Sociologica*, Frankfurter Beiträge zur Sociologie, 1955, vol. 1, pp. 12ff. English trans. as 'Sociology and Psychology' in *New Left Review*, No. 46, 1967, No. 47, 1968.

development. In society this ideal conceals the rift between the general and the particular, in which the continuing antagonism expresses itself. The unity of science represses the contradictory nature of its object. A price has to be paid for the apparently contagious satisfaction that nonetheless can be derived from the unified science: such a science cannot grasp the societally posited moment of the divergence of individual and society and of their respective disciplines. The pedantically organized total scheme, which stretches from the individual and his invariant regularities to complex social structures, has room for everything except for the fact that the individual and society, although not radically different, have historically grown apart. Their relationship is contradictory since society largely denies individuals what it—always a society of individuals—promises them and why society coalesces at all; whilst on the other hand, the blind, unrestrained interests of individuals inhibit the formation of a possible total societal interest. The ideal of a unified science merits an epithet, but one which it would by no means please it, namely, that of the aesthetic—just as one speaks of 'elegance' in mathematics. The organizatory rationalization in which the programme of unified science results, as opposed to the disparate individual sciences, greatly prejudices questions in the philosophy of science which are thrown up by society. If, in Wellmer's words, 'meaningful becomes a synonym for scientific', then science, socially mediated, guided and controlled, paying existing society and its tradition a calculable tribute, usurps the role of the *arbiter veri et falsi*. For Kant, the epistemological constitutive question was that of the possibility of science. Now, in simple tautology, the question is referred back to science. Insights and modes of procedure which, instead of remaining within valid science affect it critically, are banished *a limine*. Thus it is that the apparently neutral concept of 'conventionalist bond' has fatal implications. Through the back door of conventionalism social conformism is smuggled in as a criterion of meaning for the social sciences. The effort of analysing in detail the entanglement of conformism and the self-enthronement of science proved worthwhile. More than thirty years ago, Horkheimer drew attention to the whole complex in 'The Latest Attack upon Metaphysics'.[20] The concept of

---

[20] Now in: Max Horkheimer, *Kritische Theorie* (Frankfurt, 1968), vol. 2, pp. 82ff. English trans. by M. J. O'Connell *et al.*, *Critical Theory* (New York, 1973/London 1974), pp. 132ff.

science is also assumed by Popper as if it were self-evident. But such a concept contains its own historical dialectic. When Fichte's *Theory of Science* and Hegel's *Science of Logic* were written at the turn of the eighteenth century, the present concept of science with its claim to exclusiveness would have been critically placed on the level of the pre-scientific, whilst nowadays what was then termed science, no matter how chimerically it was called absolute knowledge, would be rejected as extra-scientific by what Popper refers to as scientism. The course of history, and not merely of intellectual history, which led to this is by no means unqualified progress, as the positivists would have it. All the mathematical refinement of the highly developed scientific methodology does not allay the suspicion that the elaboration of science into a technique alongside others has undermined its own concept. The strongest argument for this would be that what appears as a goal to scientific interpretation, namely fact-finding, is only a means towards theory for emphatic science. Without theory the question remains open as to why the whole enterprise was undertaken. However, the reformulation of the idea of science begins even with the idealists, in particular with Hegel, whose absolute knowledge coincides with the manifest concept of what exists thus—and not otherwise [*so und nicht anders Seiendes*]. The point of attack for the critique of this development is not the crystallization of particular scientific methods the fruitfulness of which is beyond question but rather the now dominant suggestion, crudely urged on the authority of Max Weber, that extra-scientific interests are external to science and that the two should be strictly separated. Whilst, on the one hand, the allegedly purely scientific interests are rigid channels and are frequently neutralizations of extra-scientific interests which, in their weakened form, extend into science, the scientific body of instruments, on the other hand, which provides the canon of what is scientific, is also instrumental in a manner in which instrumental reason has never dreamt. This body of instruments is the means for answering questions which both originate beyond science and strive beyond it. In so far as the ends–means rationality of science ignores the *Telos* which lies in the concept of instrumentalism and becomes its own sole purpose, it contradicts its own instrumentality. But this is what society demands of science. In a determinably false society that contradicts the interests both of its members and of the whole, all knowledge

Sense of 'positivism' being used in the book. Contrast
with Bryant's two notions of 'positivism'. Tendency to
confuse the two, or to impose one as exclusive on
sociological theorizing, esp. from a philosophical base.
Examination of actual sociologists (not philosophers
talking abstractly about sociology) indicates that there
are few true 'positivists' in sociology, though there
are a fair number of empiricists and inductivists.
Most sociologists are not positivists in the sense used
by philosophers. [Detail with examples]. Still, the
charge of 'positivism' does reverberate within sociology
more often as a ritual incantation, than as a reasoned
attack. [Various uses, e.g.s] Reent attacks on
'positivism': anti-theory, anti-generality, etc.
    Modelled on mistaken notion of science,

which readily subordinates itself to the rules of this society that
are congealed in science, participates in its falsehood.

The current academically attractive distinction between the
scientific and the pre-scientific, to which even Albert adheres,
cannot be upheld. The revision of this dichotomy is legitimated
by a fact which can constantly be observed and is even confirmed
by positivists, namely, that there is a split in their thinking in that,
regardless of whether they speak as scientists or non-scientists,
they nevertheless utilize reason. What is classified as pre-scientific
is not simply what has not yet passed through, or avoided, the
self-critical work of science advocated by Popper. But rather it
subsumes all the rationality and experience which are excluded
from the instrumental determinations of reason. Both moments
are necessarily dependent upon one another. Science, which
incorporates the pre-scientific impulses without transforming
them, condemns itself to indifference no less than do amateur
arbitrary procedures. In the disreputable realm of the pre-
scientific, those interests meet which are severed by the process of
scientization. But these interests are by no means inessential. Just
as there certainly would be no advance of consciousness without
the scientific discipline, it is equally certain that the discipline
also paralyses the organs of knowledge. The more science is
rigified in the shell which Max Weber prophesied for the world,
the more what is ostracized as pre-scientific becomes the refuge of
knowledge. The contradiction in the relationship of the spirit to
science responds to the latter's own contradiction. Science
postulates a coherent immanent connection and is a moment of
the society which denies it coherence. If it escapes this antinomy,
be it by cancelling its truth content through a sociology of knowledge relativization, or by failing to recognize its entanglement in
the faits sociaux, and sets itself up as something absolute and self-
sufficient, then it contents itself with illusions which impair
science in what it might achieve. Both moments are certainly
disparate but not indifferent to one another. Only insight into
science's inherent societal mediations contributes to the objectivity
of science, since it is no mere vehicle of social relations and
interests. Its absolutization and its instrumentalization, both
products of subjective reason, are complementary. Scientism
becomes false with regard to central states of affairs by engaging
itself one-sidedly in favour of the unified moment of individual
and society for the sake of logical systematics, and by devaluing

as an epiphenomenon the antagonistic moment which cannot be
incorporated into such logical systematics. According to pre-
dialectical logic, the constitutum cannot be the constituens and
the conditioned cannot be the condition for its own condition.
Reflection upon the value of societal knowledge within the
framework of what it knows forces reflection beyond this simple
lack of contradiction. The inescapability of paradox, which
Wittgenstein frankly expressed, testifies to the fact that generally
the lack of contradiction cannot, for consistent thought, have
the last word, not even when consistent thought sanctions its
norm. Wittgenstein's superiority over the positivists of the Vienna
Circle is revealed in a striking manner here: the logician perceives
the limit of logic. Within its framework, the relationship between
language and world, as Wittgenstein presented it, could not be
treated unambiguously. For him language forms a closed immanent context through which the non-verbal moments of knowledge, for instance sense data, are mediated. But it is not the
intention of language to refer to what is non-verbal. Language is
both language and autarchy. In accord with the scientistic assumption of rules only being valid within it, it is as a moment within
reality, a fait social.[21] Wittgenstein had to account for the fact
that it removed itself from all that factually exists since the latter
is only 'given' through it, and yet is conceivable only as a moment
of the world which, in his view, can only be known through
language. At this point, he had reached the threshold of a dialectical awareness of the so-called problems of constitution and
had reduced *ad absurdum* scientism's right to cut off dialectical
thought. This affects both the current scientistic notion of the
subject, even of the transcendental subject of knowledge, which

---

[21] The dual nature of language is revealed in that it—and to this extent it is allied
with the positivists—gains objectivity solely through subjective intention. The
objectivity of language is recognized and strengthened only by the person who
expresses what he intends subjectively as precisely as possible, whilst every attempt
to rely upon language's being-in-itself, or upon its ontological essence, ends in the
bad subjectivism of the hypostasis of verbal figures. This was perceived by Benjamin.
In positivism itself, with the exception of Wittgenstein, this positivistic motif is
not accorded its proper due. The stylistic negligence of many adherents to scientism,
which may become rationalized with the taboo on the moment of expression in
language, betrays reified consciousness. Since science is dogmatically made into an
objectivity which cannot be mediated through the subject, linguistic expression is
trivialized. Anyone who posits states of affairs as existent in themselves without
subjective mediation will be indifferent towards the formalization at the cost of
idolizing reality.

is seen as dependent upon its object as a precondition for its own possibility, and it also affects the current scientistic notion of the object. It is no longer an X whose substratum must be composed from the context of subjective determinations but rather, being itself determined, it helps to determine the subjective function.

The validity of knowledge, and not only of natural laws, is certainly largely independent of its origin. In Tübingen the two symposiasts were united in their critique of the sociology of knowledge and of Pareto's sociologism. Marx's theory opposes it. The study of ideology, of false consciousness, of socially necessary illusion would be nonsense without the concept of true consciousness and objective truth. Nevertheless, genesis and validity cannot be separated without contradiction. Objective validity preserves the moment of its emergence and this moment permanently affects it. No matter how unassailable logic is, the process of abstraction which removes it from attack is that of the controlling will. It excludes and disqualifies what it controls. In this dimension logic is 'untrue'; its unassailability is itself the intellectualized societal taboo. Its illusory nature is manifested in the contradictions encountered by reason in its objects. In the distancing of the subject from the object, which realizes the history of the mind, the subject gave way to the real superiority of objectivity. Its domination was that of the weaker over the stronger. Perhaps in no other way would the self-assertion of the human species have been possible. The process of scientific objectivation would certainly not have been possible. But the more the subject seized for itself the aims of the object, the more it, in turn, unconsciously rendered itself an object. This is the prehistory of the reification of consciousness. What scientism simply assumes to be progress was always, at the same time, a sacrifice. What in the object does not correspond to the ideal of a 'pure' subject foritself, alienated from its own living experience, slips through the net. To this extent, advancing consciousness was accompanied by the shadow of false consciousness. Subjectivity has in itself eradicated what does not yield to the unambiguousness and identity of its claim to domination. Subjectivity, which is really always object, has reduced itself no less than its object. One should also recall the moments which are lost in scientific methodology's curtailment of objectivity, and similarly the loss of the spontaneity of knowledge inflicted by the subject upon himself in order to master his own restricted achievements. Carnap, one of the most radical positivists, once characterized as a stroke of good luck the fact that the laws of logic and of pure mathematics apply to reality. A mode of thought, whose entire pathos lies in its enlightened state, refers at this central point to an irrational—mythical—concept, such as that of the stroke of luck, simply in order to avoid an insight which, in fact, shakes the positivistic position; namely, that the supposed lucky circumstance is not really one at all but rather the product of the ideal of objectivity based on the domination of nature or, as Habermas puts it, the 'pragmatistic' ideal of objectivity. The rationality of reality, registered with relief by Carnap, is simply the mirroring of subjective *ratio*. The epistemological metacritique denies the validity of the Kantian claim to the subjective a priori but affirms Kant's view to the extent that his epistemology, intent on establishing validity, describes the genesis of scientistic reason in a highly adequate manner. What to him, as a remarkable consequence of scientistic reification, seems to be the strength of subjective form which constitutes reality is, in truth, the *summa* of the historical process in which subjectivity—liberating itself from nature and thus objectivating itself—emerged as the total master of nature, forgot the relationship of domination and, thus blinded, re-interpreted this relationship as the creation of that ruled by the ruler. Genesis and validity must certainly be critically distinguished in the individual cognitive acts and disciplines. But in the realm of so-called constitutional problems they are inseparably united, no matter how much this may be repugnant to discursive logic. Since scientistic truth desires to be the whole truth it is not the whole truth. It is governed by the same *ratio* which would never have been formed other than through science. It is capable of criticism of its own concept and in sociology can characterize in concrete terms what escapes science—society.

Both Tübingen symposiasts were in agreement in their emphasis upon the concept of criticism.[22] Following a remark by Peter Ludz, Dahrendorf pointed out that the concept had been used equivocally. For Popper it signifies, without any concrete determinacy, a 'pure mechanism of the temporary corroboration of the general statements of science', for Adorno 'the development of

---

[22] In abstract generality, Popper's twenty-first thesis contains something like a common denominator. Cf. Popper, 'The Logic of the Social Sciences', loc. cit., p. 101.

the contradictions of reality through knowledge of them';
nevertheless, I had already laid bare this equivocation.[23] But it is
not a mere contamination of various meanings in the same word,
rather it is concretely grounded. If one accepts Popper's purely
cognitive or, possibly, 'subjective' concept of criticism, which is
to apply only to the unanimity of knowledge and not to the
legitimation of the reality recognized, then thought cannot leave
it at that. For here and there critical reason is similar. It is not the
case that two 'capacities' are in operation. The identity of the
word is no accident. Cognitive criticism, of knowledge and
especially of theorems, necessarily also examines whether the
objects of knowledge are what they claim to be according to their
own concept. Otherwise it would be formalistic. Immanent
criticism is never solely purely logical but always concrete as
well—the confrontation of concept and reality. It is for criticism
to seek out the truth which the concepts, judgments and theorems
themselves desire to name and it does not exhaust itself in the
hermetic consistency of formation of thought. It is in a largely
irrational society that the scientifically stipulated primacy of
logic is at issue. Material concretion, which no knowledge—not
even purely logical procedure—can entirely dismiss, demands
that immanent critique, in so far as it is directed towards what is
intended by scientific statements and not towards 'statements in
themselves', does not generally proceed in an argumentative
manner but rather demands that it investigate whether this is the
case. Otherwise, disputation falls prey to the narrowness which
can often be observed in ingenuity. The notion of argument is
not as self-evident as Popper believes but requires critical analysis.
This was once expressed in the phenomenological slogan, 'back
to the things themselves'. Argumentation becomes questionable
as soon as it assumes discursive logic to be opposed to content.
In his *Science of Logic*, Hegel did not argue in a traditional manner
and in the introduction to the *Phenomenology of Mind* he demanded
'pure reflection'. On the other hand, Popper, who sees the objectivity of science in the objectivity of the critical method,
elucidates it with the statement 'that the main instrument of

---

[23] Initially I declared myself to be in agreement with Popper's criticism of 'misguided and erroneous methodological . . . naturalism or scientism' (cf. Popper, loc.
cit., p. 90, and Adorno 'On the Logic of the Social Sciences', p. 108), but did not
then conceal that, in my presentation of criticism, I had to go further than Popper
would approve (cf. Adorno, loc. cit., pp. 108ff.).

logical criticism—the logical contradiction—is objective'.[24] This certainly does not raise an exclusive claim for formal logic such as that criticism only possesses its *organon* in the latter, but such a claim is at least suggested. Albert, following Popper, can hardly interpret criticism differently.[25] He certainly permits the type of 'investigations of such factual connections as Habermas himself mentions'[26] but he wishes to keep them and the logical connections. The unity of both types of criticism, which indicates their concepts, is conjured away through a conceptual order. But if logical contradictions appear in social scientific statements, such as the relevant contradiction that the same social system unleashes and leashes the forces of production, then theoretical analysis is able to reduce such logical inconsistencies to structural moments of society. It must not eliminate them as mere maladjustments of scientific thought since, in any case, they can only be removed through a change in reality itself. Even if it were possible to translate such contradictions into merely semantic contradictions, that is, to demonstrate that each contradictory statement refers to something different, their form still expresses the structure of the object more sharply than a procedure which attains scientific satisfaction by turning its back upon what is unsatisfactory in the non-scientific object of knowledge. Moreover, the possibility of devolving objective contradictions onto semantics may be connected with the fact that Marx, the dialectician, did not possess a completely developed notion of dialectics. He imagined that he was simply 'flirting' with it. Thinking, which teaches itself that part of its own meaning is what, in turn, is not a thought, explodes the logic of non-contradiction. Its prison has windows. The narrowness of positivism is that it does not take this into account and entrenches itself in ontology as if in a last refuge, even if this ontology were simply the wholly formalized, contentless ontology of the deductive connection of statements in themselves.

The critique of the relationships of scientific statements to that to which they refer is, however, inevitably compelled towards a critique of reality. It must rationally decide whether the insufficiencies which it encounters are merely scientific, or whether reality insufficiently accords with what science, through its concept, expresses about it. The separation between the structures

[24] Popper, 'The Logic of the Social Sciences', p. 90.
[25] Cf. Hans Albert, 'Behind Positivism's Back?', pp. 242ff.
[26] loc. cit., p. 244.

of science and reality is not absolute. Nor may the concept of truth be attributed solely to the structures of science. It is no less meaningful to speak of the truth of a societal institution than of the truth of theorems concerned with it. Legitimately, criticism does not normally imply merely self-criticism—which is what it actually amounts to for Popper—but also criticism of reality. In this respect, Habermas' reply to Albert has its pathos.[27] The concept of society, which is specifically bourgeois and anti-feudal, implies the notion of an association of free and independent human subjects for the sake of the possibility of a better life and, consequently, the critique of natural societal relations. The hardening of bourgeois society into something impenetrably and inevitably natural is its immanent regression. Something of the opposing intention was expressed in the social contract theories. No matter how little these theories were historically correct, they penetratingly remind society of the concept of the unity of individuals, whose conscious ultimately postulates their reason, freedom and equality. In a grand manner, the unity of the critique of scientific and meta-scientific sense is revealed in the work of Marx. It is called the critique of political economy since it attempts to derive the whole that is to be criticized in terms of its right to existence from exchange, commodity form and its immanent 'logical' contradictory nature. The assertion of the equivalence of what is exchanged, the basis of all exchange, is repudiated by its consequences. As the principle of exchange, by virtue of its immanent dynamics, extends to the living labours of human beings it changes compulsively into objective inequality, namely that of social classes. Forcibly stated, the contradiction is that exchange takes place justly and unjustly. Logical critique and the emphatically practical critique that society must be changed simply to prevent a relapse into barbarism are moments of the same movement of the concept. Marx's procedure testifies to the fact that even such an analysis cannot simply ignore the separation of what has been compounded, namely of society and politics. He both criticized and respected the separation. The same person who, in his youth wrote the 'Theses on Feuerbach', remained throughout his life a theoretical political economist. The Popperian concept of criticism inhibits logic by restricting it to scientific statements

---

[27] Cf. Jürgen Habermas, 'A Positivistically Bisected Rationalism', p. 210.

without regard for the logicity of its substratum which it requires in order to be true to its own meaning. Popper's 'critical rationalism' has something pre-Kantian about it; in terms of formal logic, this is at the expense of its content. Sociological constructs, however, which contented themselves with their logical freedom from contradiction, could not withstand concrete reflection. They could not withstand the reflection of a thoroughly functional society—though one which perpetuates itself solely through the harshness of relentless repression *ad calendas Graecas*—because that society is inconsistent; because the constraint under which it keeps itself and its members alive does not reproduce their life in a form which would be possible given the state of the rationality of means, as is specifically presupposed by integral bureaucratic domination. Endless terror can also function, but functioning as an end in itself, separated from why it functions, is no less a contradiction than any logical contradiction, and a science which fell silent before it would be irrational. Critique does not merely imply the decision as to whether suggested hypotheses can be demonstrated as true or false; it moves transparently over to the object. If theorems are full of contradictions then by modifying Lichtenberg's statement one might say that they are not always to blame. The dialectical contradiction expresses the real antagonisms which do not become visible within the logical-scientistic system of thought. For positivists, the system, according to the logical-deductive model, is something worth striving for, something 'positive'. For dialecticians, in real no less than in philosophical terms, it is the core of what has to be criticized. One of the decaying forms of dialectical thought in dialectical materialism is that it reprimands critique of the dominant system. Dialectical theory must increasingly distance itself from the system. Society constantly distances itself from the liberal model which gave it its systematic character, and its cognitive system forfeits the character of an ideal since, in the post-liberal form of society, its systematic unity as a totality is amalgamated with repression. Today, wherever dialectical thought all too inflexibly adheres to the system, even and precisely in what is criticized, it tends to ignore determinate being and to retreat into illusory notions. It is a merit of positivism that it draws attention to this, if its concept of the system, as merely internal-scientific and classificatory, is not to be enticed to hypostasis. Hypostatized dialectics becomes undialectical and requires correction by the fact finding whose interest is realized by empirical social research, which then, in turn, is unjustly hypostatized by the positivistic theory of science. The pre-given structure which does not merely stem from classification—Durkheim's impenetrable—is essentially negative and is incompatible with its own goal, namely the preservation and satisfaction of mankind. Without such a goal the concept of society, seen in concrete terms, would indeed be what the Viennese positivists used to term devoid of meaning. To this extent, sociology even as a critical theory of society is 'logical'. This compels us to extend the concept of criticism beyond its limitations in Popper's work. The idea of scientific truth cannot be split off from that of a true society. Only such a society would be free from contradiction and lack of contradiction. In a resigned manner, scientism commits such an idea to the mere forms of knowledge alone.

By stressing its societal neutrality, scientism defends itself against the critique of the object and replaces it with the critique merely of logical inconsistencies. Both Albert and Popper seem to bear in mind the problematic of such a restriction of critical reason or, as Habermas expressed it, of the fact that scientific asceticism encourages the decisionism of ends or that irrationalism inherent even in Weber's theory of science. Popper concedes that 'protocol sentences are not inviolable' and that this 'represents, in [his] opinion, a notable advance'.[28] His concession that universal law-like hypotheses could not be meaningfully regarded as verifiable, and that this even applies to protocol sentences,[29] indeed furthers the concept of criticism in a productive manner. Whether intentionally or not, it has taken into account that the referent of so-called sociological protocol statements, namely simple observations, are preformed through society which, in turn, cannot be reduced to protocol statements. But if one replaces the traditional positivist postulate of verification by the postulate of 'the capacity for confirmation' then positivism forfeits its intention. All knowledge requires confirmation; it must rationally distinguish between true and false without autologically setting up the categories of true and false in accordance with the rules of established science. Popper contrasts his

---

[28] Popper, *The Logic of Scientific Discovery* (London/New York, 6th imp., 1972), p. 97.
[29] 'The fate of being deleted can even befall a protocol sentence'. Otto Neurath, 'Protokollsätze', in *Erkenntnis*, vol. 3, 1932/33, p. 209.

'sociology of knowledge' [*Soziologie des Wissens*] with that familiar since Mannheim and Scheler [*Wissenssoziologie*]. He advocates a 'theory of scientific objectivity'. But it does not transcend scientistic subjectivism[30]; rather it can be subsumed under Durkheim's still valid statement that 'Between "I like this" and "a certain number of us like this" there is no essential difference.'[31] Popper elucidates the scientific objectivity which he advocates in the following manner: 'Objectivity can only be explained in terms of social ideas such as competition (both of individual scientists and of various schools); tradition (mainly the critical tradition); social institution (for instance, publication in various competing journals and through various competing publishers; discussion at congresses); the power of the state (its tolerance of free discussion).'[32] The questionable nature of such categories is striking. For instance, in the category of competition there lies the entire competitive mechanism, together with the fatal factor denounced by Marx, namely, that market success has primacy over the qualities of the object, even of intellectual formations. The tradition upon which Popper relies, has apparently developed within the universities into a fetter of productive forces. In Germany a critical tradition is completely lacking—'discussions at congresses' aside—which Popper might hesitate to recognize empirically as an instrument of truth, just as he will not over-estimate the actual range of the political 'tolerance of free discussion' in science. His forced innocence with regard to all this breathes the optimism of despair. The a priori negation of an objective structure of society, and its substitution by ordering schemata, eradicates thoughts which turn upon this structure, whilst Popper's enlightening impulse strives after such thoughts. In accordance with its pure form, the denial of social objectivity leaves such thoughts undisturbed. An absolutized logic is ideology. Habermas sums up Popper's position as follows: 'Popper, in opposing a positivist solution to the basis problem, adheres to the view that the observational statements which lend themselves to the falsification of law-like hypotheses cannot be justified in an empirically compelling manner; instead, it must be decided in each case whether the acceptance of a basic statement

[30] *See* above, pp. 5f.
[31] Emile Durkheim, *Sociology and Philosophy*. English trans. D. F. Pocock (London, 1965), p. 83.
[32] Popper, 'The Logic of the Social Sciences', loc. cit., p. 96 below.

is sufficiently motivated by experience. In the process of research, all the observers who are involved in attempts at falsifying certain theories must, by means of relevant observational statements, arrive at a provisional consensus which can be refuted at any time. This agreement rests, in the last instance, upon a decision; it can be neither enforced logically nor empirically.'[33] Popper's Tübingen paper corresponds to this where he claims, 'It is a mistake to assume that the objectivity of a science depends upon the objectivity of the scientist.'[34] But in fact this objectivity suffers less under the personal equation which has been made from time immemorial, than from the objective societal pre-formation of the objectivated scientific apparatus. Popper the nominalist can provide no stronger corrective than intersubjectivity within organized science: 'What may be described as scientific objectivity is based solely upon a critical tradition which, despite resistance, often makes it possible to criticise a dominant dogma. To put it another way, the objectivity of science is not a matter of the individual scientist but rather the social result of their mutual criticism, of the friendly-hostile division of labour among scientists, of their co-operation and also of their competition.'[35] The belief that very divergent positions, by virtue of the recognized rules of co-operation, will 'get together' and thereby achieve the particular attainable level of objectivity in knowledge, follows the outmoded liberal model of those who gather at a round table in order to work out a compromise. The forms of scientific co-operation contain an infinite amount of societal mediation. Popper in fact calls them a 'social concern' but does not concern himself with their implications. They stretch from the mechanism of selection which controls whether someone is academically co-opted and receives a call—a mechanism in which conformity with prevailing group opinion is apparently decisive— to the form of *communis opinio* and its irrationalities. After all sociology, whose topics deal with explosive interests, is also in its own form, not only privately but also in its institutions a complete microcosm of these interests. The classificatory principle in itself has already taken care of this. The scope of concepts which seek to be simply abbreviations of particular existent facts, does not lead beyond their compass. The deeper the approved method

[33] Habermas 'The Analytical Theory of Science and Dialectics', loc. cit., p. 151.
[34] Popper, loc. cit., p. 95.
[35] Ibid, p. 95.

descends into societal material the more apparent its partisanship becomes. If the sociology of the 'mass media'—the accepted notion purveys the prejudice that by questioning the human subjects, the consumer masses, one must establish what is planned and kept alive in the sphere of production—seeks to ascertain simply the opinions and attitudes of those socially categorized and tested and to elicit 'socially critical' consequences, then the given system, centrally guided and reproducing itself through mass reactions, tacitly becomes its own norm. The affinity of the whole sphere of what Paul F. Lazarsfeld has called administrative research with the goals of administration in general is almost tautological. What is no less evident here is that these goals, if one does not forcibly taboo the concept of the structure of objective domination, according to the needs of the latter, are formed frequently over the heads of individual administrators. Administrative research is the prototype of a social science which is based upon the scientitic theory of science and which, in turn, acts as a model for the latter. In societal and concrete terms, both political apathy and the much-praised scientific neutrality prove to be political facts. Ever since Pareto, positivistic scepticism has come to terms with the specific existing power, even that of Mussolini. Since every social theory is interwoven with real society, every social theory can certainly be misused ideologically or operationalized in a distorted manner. Positivism, however, specifically lends itself, in keeping with the entire nominalist-sceptical tradition,[36] to ideological abuse by virtue of its material indeterminacy, its classificatory method and, finally, its preference for correctness rather than truth.

The scientific measure of all things, the fact as the fixed and irreducible entity which the human subject is not allowed to undermine, is borrowed from the world—a world, however, that *more scientifico* still has to be constituted from the facts and from their connection formed according to logical rules. The entity to which scientistic analysis leads, the final subjective phenomenon postulated by a critique of knowledge and one which cannot be further reduced, is in turn the inadequate copy of the objectivity reduced here to the subject. In the spirit of an unswerving claim to objectivity, sociology cannot content itself with the fact, with what is only in appearance most objective. Anti-idealistically,

---

[36] Cf. Max Horkheimer, 'Montaigne und die Funktion der Skepsis', in *Kritische Theorie*, II (Frankfurt, 1968), p. 220 *passim*.

something of idealism's truth content is preserved in it. The equation of subject and object is valid in so far as the subject is an object, initially in the sense emphasized by Habermas that sociological research, for its part, belongs to the objective context which it intends to study.[37] Albert replies, 'Does he [Habermas] wish to declare common sense—or somewhat more sublimely expressed, "the natural hermeneutics of the social life-world"—to be sacrosanct? If not, then wherein does the specificity of his method lie? To what extent is "the object" (*Sache*) treated more "in accord with its own significance" than in the usual methods of the empirical sciences?'[38] But dialectical theory in no way inhibits in an artificial-dogmatic manner, as Hegel once did, the critique of so-called pre-scientific consciousness. At the Frankfurt sociology conference in 1968, Dahrendorf addressed the dialecticians ironically with the words: you simply know much more than I do. He doubted the knowledge of antecedent social objectivity since the social in itself is mediated through subjective categories of the intellect. The predominance of the method attacked by the dialecticians was, he claimed, simply the advancing reflection of the *intentio recta* through which the advance of science is accomplished. But it is epistemological critique— the *intentio obliqua*—in its results which the dialecticians criticize. Here, however, they annul the prohibitions in which scientism, including the recent development of 'analytical philosophy', has culminated, since these prohibitions are maintained at the expense of knowledge. The concept of the object itself does not, as Albert suspects, revive 'certain prejudices' or even the priority of intellectual 'origin' as opposed to 'achievement'; and incidentally, the achievement of scientism within the field of sociology is not so very impressive. Popper's view, referred to by Albert, according to which theorems 'can be understood as attempts to illuminate the structural characteristics of reality',[39] is not so very far removed from the concept of the object itself. Popper does not deny the philosophical tradition as Reichenbach had done. Criteria such as that of 'relevance'[40] or of 'explanatory power',[41]

---

[37] Cf. Habermas, 'A Positivistically Bisected Rationalism', loc. cit., p. 220 below.
[38] Albert, 'The Myth of Total Reason', loc. cit., p. 173 below.
[39] Albert, 'Behind Positivism's Back?', loc. cit., p. 241, also footnote 41: 'Cf. Popper, "Die Zielsetzung der Erfahrungswissenschaft" [in *Ratio*, vol. 1, 1957]'. Revised version . . . in K. R. Popper, *Objective Knowledge* (Oxford, 1972).'
[40] Popper, 'The Logic of the Social Sciences', loc. cit., p. 97.
[41] Ibid, p. 97.

which he certainly interprets later in a sense closer to the natural-scientific model, would have little meaning if, in spite of everything, there were not an implicit underlying concept of society which several positivists—for instance, König and Schelsky in Germany—would prefer to abolish. The mentality which refuses to admit an objective social structure draws back from the object which it taboos. In caricaturing their opponents as visionary metaphysicians the followers of scientism become unrealistic. Operationally ideal techniques inevitably withdraw from the situations in which what is to be investigated is located. In particular, this could be demonstrated in the social-psychological experiment but it could also be demonstrated in the alleged improvements in scale construction. Objectivity, which actually should be served by the finishing touches of methodology and the avoidance of sources of error, becomes something secondary, something graciously dragged along by the operational ideal. What is central becomes peripheral. If the methodological will to make problems unambiguously determinable and 'falsifiable' predominates in an unreflected manner, then science is reduced to alternatives, which only emerged through the elimination of 'variables', that is, by abstracting and thereby changing the object. Methodological empiricism works according to this scheme in the opposite direction to experience.

In sociology, *interpretation* acquires its force both from the fact that without reference to totality—to the real total system, untranslatable into any solid immediacy—nothing societal can be conceptualized, and from the fact that it can, however, only be recognized in the extent to which it is apprehended in the factual and the individual. It is the societal physiognomy of appearance. The primary meaning of 'interpret' is to perceive something in the features of totality's social givenness. The idea of the 'anticipation' of totality, which perhaps a very liberal positivism would be prepared to accept, is insufficient. Recalling Kant, it envisages totality as something in fact indefinitely relinquished and postponed, but something in principle to be fulfilled through the given, without regard for the qualitative gap between essence and appearance in society. Physiognomy does better justice to it since it realizes totality in its dual relationship to the facts which it deciphers—a totality which 'is', and does not represent a mere synthesis of logical operations. The facts are not identical with totality but the latter does not exist beyond the facts. Knowledge of society which does not commence with the physionomic view is poverty-stricken. In this view appearance is categorically suspect. But knowledge cannot adhere to this. By developing mediations of the apparent and of what expresses itself in these mediations, interpretation occasionally differentiates and corrects itself in a radical manner. As distinct from what in fact is a pre-scientific, dull registration, knowledge worthy of human cognizance begins by sharpening the sense for what is illuminated in every social phenomenon. This sense, if anything, ought to be defined as the *organon* of scientific experience. Established sociology banishes this sense—hence its sterility. Only if this sense is first developed can it be disciplined. Its discipline requires both increased exactness of empirical observation and the force of theory which inspires interpretation and transforms itself in it. Several followers of scientism may generously accept this, but the divergence still remains. The divergence is one of conceptions. Positivism regards sociology as one science among others and, since Comte, has considered that the proven methods of older science, in particular of natural science, can be transferred to sociology. The actual *pseudos* is concealed here. For sociology has a dual character. In it, the subject of all knowledge—society, the bearer of logical generality—is at the same time the object. Society is subjective because it refers back to the human beings who create it, and its organizational principles too refer back to subjective consciousness and its most general form of abstraction —logic, something essentially subjective. Society is objective because, on account of its underlying structure, it cannot perceive its own subjectivity, because it does not possess a total subject and through its organization it thwarts the installation of such a subject. But such a dual character modifies the relationship of social-scientific knowledge with its object; positivism does not take this into account. It simply treats society, potentially the self-determining subject, as if it were an object, and could be determined from outside. It literally objectivates what, for its part, causes objectivation and what can provide an explanation for objectivation. Such a substitution of society as object for society as subject constitutes the reified consciousness of sociology. It is not recognized that by recourse to the subject as something estranged from itself and objectively confronting the researcher, the subject implied, in other words the very object of sociology, becomes another. Certainly the change through the orientation of knowledge possesses its *fundamentum in re*. The development within society, moves, for its part, towards reification; this provides a reified consciousness of society with its *adaequatio*. But truth demands that this *quid pro quo* also be included. Society as subject and society as object are the same and yet not the same. The objectivating acts of science eliminate that in society by means of which it is not only an object, and the shadow of this falls upon all scientistic objectivity. For a doctrine whose supreme norm is the lack of contradiction it is most difficult to perceive this. Here lies the innermost difference between a critical theory of society and what is commonly known as sociology. Despite all the experience of reification, and in the very expression of this experience, critical theory is orientated towards the idea of society as subject, whilst sociology accepts reification, repeats it in its methods and thereby loses the perspective in which society and its law would first reveal themselves. This relates back to the sociological claim to domination raised by Comte; a claim which today is more or less openly reproduced in the notion that, since it is possible for sociology to control successfully particular societal situations and fields, it can extend its control to the whole. If such a transfer were somehow possible, if it did not crassly fail to recognize the power relations through whose givenness sociology is constituted, then the scientifically totally controlled society would remain an object—that of science—and as unemancipated as ever. Even in the rationality of a scientific management of the whole society which had apparently thrown off its shackles, domination would survive. Even against their will, the domination of the scientists would amalgamate with the interests of the powerful cliques. A technocracy of sociologists would retain an elitist character. On the other hand, one of the moments which must remain common to philosophy and sociology, and which must rank highly if the two are not to decline—the latter to a lack of content, the former to a lack of concepts—is that inherent to both is something not wholly transformable into science. In both nothing is meant in a completely literal manner, neither statement of fact nor pure validity. This unliteralness— according to Nietzsche a part of a game—paraphrases the concept of interpretation which interprets being as non-being. What is not quite literal testifies to the tense non-identity of essence and appearance. Emphatic knowledge does not lapse into irrationalism if it does not absolutely renounce art. The scientistic adult mockery of 'mind music' simply drowns the creaking of the cupboard drawers in which the questionnaires are deposited —the sound of the enterprise of pure literalness. It is associated, with the trusty objection to the solipsism of self-satisfying thought about society which neither respects the latter's actual condition nor fulfils a useful function in it. Nevertheless there are many indications that theoretically trained students who have a flair for reality and what holds it together, are more capable, even in reality, of reasonably fulfilling their allotted tasks than recruited specialists for whom method is paramount. The catchword 'solipsism', however, turns the state of affairs upon its head. In that the individual, to which even Max Weber believed he had to have recourse in his definition of social action, does not count as a substratum for dialectics, the latter does not content itself with a subjective concept of reason. But all solipsism rests upon the individual as a substratum. All this has been explicated in detail in the philosophical publications of the Frankfurt School. The illusion of solipsism is furthered by the fact that apparently in the present situation the subjectivistic spell is only penetrated by what remains unenthusiastic about subjective sociology's general pleasure in communication. Recently something of this has been manifested in rebellious public opinion which feels that it can believe only what, through the form of 'communication', does not leer at consumers of culture who are about to have something foisted upon them.

What jars like discordant music in the positivists' ears is that which is imperfectly present in objective circumstances and requires linguistic form. The closer the latter follows the objective circumstances, the more it surpasses mere signification and comes to resemble expression. What was hitherto unfruitful in the controversy surrounding positivism probably stems from the fact that dialectical knowledge was taken all too literally by its opponents. Literalness and precision are not the same but rather the two diverge. Without the broken, the inauthentic there can be no knowledge which might be more than an ordering repetition. That, thereby, the idea of truth is nevertheless not sacrificed, as it tends to be in the most consistent representatives of positivism, expresses an essential contradiction: knowledge is, and by no means *per accidens*, exaggeration. For just as little as something particular is 'true' but rather by virtue of its mediatedness is always its own other, so the whole is no less true. It is an expression of its own negativity that it remains unreconciled with the particular. Truth is the articulation of this relationship. In ancient times leading philosophers still knew it: Plato's philosophy, which pre-critically raises the extreme claim to truth, continually sabotages this claim in its presentational form of the 'aporetic' dialogues as a literally fulfilled claim. Speculations which related Socratic irony to this would not be out of place. The cardinal sin of German idealism which today takes its revenge upon it through positivistic critique, consisted in deceiving itself and its followers about such disjointedness by means of the subjective pathos of fully attained identity with the object in absolute knowledge. Thereby German idealism transferred itself to the show-place of the statements of fact and of validity's *terre à terre*, upon which it is then inevitably defeated by a science which can demonstrate that idealism does not meet its desiderata. The interpretative method becomes weak at the moment when, terrorized by the progress of individual sciences, it professes to be as good a science as the others. There is no more stringent objection to Hegel than that already uttered by Kierkegaard, namely, that he took his philosophy literally. But interpretation is by no means arbitrary. History mediates between the phenomenon and its content which requires interpretation. The essential which appears in the phenomenon is that whereby it became what it is, what was silenced in it and what, in painful stultification, releases that which yet becomes. The orientation of physiognomy is directed towards what is silenced, the second level of phenomena. One should not assume that Habermas' phrase 'the natural hermeneutics of the social life-world',[42] which Albert censures, applies to the first level of phenomena, but rather it is the expression which emergent social processes receive in what has emerged. Nor should interpretation be absolutized according to the usage of phenomenological invariance. It remains enmeshed in the total process of knowledge. According to Habermas, 'the dependence of these ideas and interpretations upon the interests of an objective configuration of societal reproduction makes it impossible to remain at the level of subjective meaning—comprehending hermeneutics; an objective meaning-comprehending theory must also account for that moment of reification which the objectifying

---

[42] Habermas, 'The Analytical Theory of Science and Dialectics', loc. cit., p. 134; *see* p. 31 above.

procedures exclusively have in mind'.[43] Sociology is only peri-
pherally concerned with the ends-means-relation subjectively
carried out by actors. It is more concerned with the laws realized
through and against such intentions. Interpretation is the opposite
of the subjective meaning endowment on the part of the knowing
subject or of the social actor. The concept of such meaning
endowment leads to an affirmative fallacy that the social process
and social order are reconciled with the subject and justified as
something intelligible by the subject or belonging to the subject.
A dialectical concept of meaning would not be a correlate of
Weber's meaningful understanding but rather the societal essence
which shapes appearances, appears in them and conceals itself in
them. It is not a general law, understood in the usually scientistic
sense, which determines the phenomena. Its model would be
Marx's law of crisis—even if it has become so obscured as to be
unrecognizable—which was deduced from the tendency of the
rate of profit to fall. Its modifications, for their part, should also
be derived from it. The efforts to ward off or postpone the system
immanent tendency are already prescribed within the system. It is
by no means certain that this is possible indefinitely or whether
such efforts enact the law of crisis against their own will. The
writing on the wall suggests a slow inflationary collapse.

The employment of categories such as totality and essence
strengthens the prejudice that the dialecticians concern themselves uncommittedly with the global, whilst the positivists deal
with solid details and have purged the facts of all doubtful conceptual trappings. One should oppose the scientistic habit of
stigmatizing dialectics as theology, which has crept in through the
back door, with the difference between society's systematic
nature and so-called total thought. Society is a system in the sense
of a synthesis of an atomized plurality, in the sense of a real yet
abstract assemblage of what is in no way immediately or 'organically' united. The exchange relationship largely endows the
system with a mechanical character. It is objectively forced onto
its elements, as implied by the concept of an organism—the model
which resembles a celestial teleology through which each organ
would receive its function in the whole and would derive its
meaning from the latter. The context which perpetuates life
simultaneously destroys it, and consequently already possesses in

[43] Ibid, p. 139.

itself the lethal impulse towards which its dynamic is propelled. In its critique of total and organicist ideology, dialectics lacks none of positivism's incisiveness. Similarly, the concept of societal totality is not ontologized, and cannot be made into a primary thing-in-itself. Positivists who ascribe this to dialectical theory, as Scheuch did recently, simply misunderstand it. The concept of a primary thing-in-itself is just as little generally accepted by dialectical theory as by the positivists. The *telos* of the dialectical view of society runs contrary to the global view. Despite reflection upon totality, dialectics does not proceed from above but rather it attempts to overcome theoretically the antinomic relationship between the general and the particular by means of its procedure. The followers of scientism suspect that the dialecticians are megalomaniacs for, instead of striding through the finite in all direction in a Gothean masculine manner and fulfilling the requirement of the day within the attainable, they enjoy themselves in the uncommitted infinite. Yet as a mediation of all social facts totality is not infinite. By virtue of its very systematic character it is closed and finite, despite its elusive nature. Even if the great metaphysical categories were a projection of innerworldly societal experience onto the spirit which was itself socially derived, it remains true that, once retrieved into society, they do not retain the illusion of the absolute which the projections created in them. No social knowledge can profess to be master of the unconditioned. Nevertheless, its critique of philosophy does not imply that the latter is submerged in this knowledge without a trace. Consciousness which retreats to the societal domain also liberates, through its self-reflection, that element in philosophy which does not simply dissolve in society. But if it is argued that the societal concept of system, as the concept of something objective, secularizes metaphysic's concept of system, then this argument is true but applies to everything and therefore to nothing. It would be no less justifiable to criticize positivism on the grounds that its concept of secure certainty is a secularization of celestial truth. The accusation of crypto-theology is incomplete. The metaphysical systems apologetically projected the constraining character of society onto being. Anyone who desires to extricate himself from the system through thought, must translate it from idealistic philosophy into the societal reality from which it was abstracted. Thereby, the concept of totality, preserved by the followers of scientism such as Popper in the notion of the deductive system, is confronted with enlightenment. What is untrue but also what is true in it can be determined. The accusation of megalomania is no less unjust in concrete terms. Hegel's logic knew totality as what it is in its societal form: not as anything preformed before the singular or, in Hegel's language, preformed before the moments, but rather inseparable from the latter and their motion. The individually concrete has more weight in the dialectical conception than in the scientistic conception which fetishizes it epistemologically and, in practical terms, treats it as raw material or as an example. The dialectical view of society is closer to micrology than is the positivistic view which *in abstracto* certainly ascribes to the singular entity primacy over its concept but, in its method, skims over it in that timeless haste which is realized in computers. Since the individual phenomenon conceals in itself the whole society, micrology and mediation through totality act as a counterpoint to one another. It was the intention of a contribution to the theory of social conflict today[44] to elucidate this; the same point was central to the earlier controversy with Benjamin concerning the dialectical interpretation of societal phenomena.[45] Benjamin's social physiognomy was criticized for being too immediate, for lacking reflection upon the total societal mediation. He suspected the latter of being idealistic, but without it the materialistic construction of social phenomena would lag behind theory. The firmly established nominalism, which relegates the concept to the status of an illusion or an abbreviation, and represents the facts as something concept-free or indeterminate in an emphatic sense, thereby becomes necessarily abstract. Abstraction is the indiscrete incision between the general and the particular. It is not the apprehension of the general as the determination of the particular in itself. In as far as abstraction can be attributed to the dialectical method, as opposed to the sociographic description of individual findings, it is dictated by the object, by the constancy of a society which actually does not tolerate anything qualitatively different—a society which drearily repeats itself in the details. Nevertheless, the individual phenomena expressing the general are far more substantial than they would be if they were merely its logical representatives. The dialectical formulation of social laws as historically concrete laws accords

---

[44] Cf. Theodor W. Adorno and Ursula Jaerisch, 'Anmerkungen zum sozialen Konflikt heute' in *Gesellschaft, Recht und Politik* (Neuwied/Berlin, 1968), pp. 1ff.
[45] Cf. Walter Benjamin, *Briefe* (Frankfurt, 1966), pp. 782ff.

with the emphasis on the individual, an emphasis which, for the sake of its immanent generality it does not sacrifice to comparative generality. The dialectical determinacy of the individual as something simultaneous particular and general alters the societal concept of law. It no longer possesses the form 'if—then' but rather 'since—must'. In principle, it is only valid under the precondition of lack of freedom, since, inherent in the individual moments, is already a determinate law-likeness which follows from the specific social structure, and is not merely a product of the scientific synthesis of individual moments. It is in this way that Habermas' remarks on the historical laws of movement should be interpreted—in the context of the objective—immanent determinacy of the individual himself.[46] Dialectical theory refuses to contrast sharply historical and societal knowledge as a knowledge of the individual with knowledge of laws since what is supposed to be merely individual—individuation is a societal category—embodies within itself a particular and a general. Even the necessary distinction between the two possesses the character of a false abstraction. Models of the process of the general and the particular are the development tendencies within society, such as those leading to concentration, over-accumulation and crisis. Empirical sociology realized long ago what it forfeited in specific content through a statistical generalization. Something decisive about the general is frequently apprehended in the detail, and escaped mere generalization; hence, the fundamental complementation of statistical inquiries through case studies. The goal of even quantitative social methods would be qualitative insight; quantification is not an end in itself but a means towards it. Statisticians are more inclined to recognize this than is the current logic of the social sciences. The behaviour of dialectical thought towards the singular can perhaps best be underlined in contrast with one of Wittgenstein's formulations quoted by Wellmer: 'The simplest kind of proposition, an elementary proposition, asserts the existence of a state of affairs.'[47] The apparently self-evident view that the logical analysis of statements leads to elementary statements is anything but self-evident. Even Wittgenstein still repeats the dogma of Descartes' *Discours de la Méthode*, namely, that the most simple—whatever one could imagine this

---

[46] Cf. Habermas, 'The Analytical Theory of Science and Dialectics', loc. cit., p. 139; *see also* Adorno, 'Sociology and Empirical Research', p. 76.

[47] Wittgenstein, *Tractatus*, 4.21, loc. cit., p. 51.

to be—is 'more true' than what is composed, and therefore that the reduction of the more complicated to the simple a priori deserves greater merit. In fact, for the followers of scientism, simplicity is a value criterion of social scientific knowledge. This is exemplified in the fifth thesis of Popper's Tübingen paper.[48] Through its association with honesty, simplicity becomes a scientific virtue. The overtone is unmistakable here, namely that the complicated arises from the confusion or the pomposity of the observer. But the objects decide objectively whether social theorems should be simple or complex.

Popper's statement that 'What really exists are problems and solutions, and scientific traditions'[49] depends upon his own insight which immediately precedes this one, that a so-called scientific discipline is a conglomeration of problems and attempts at solution. The selection of tacitly circumscribed problems as the scientistic 'sole reality' installs simplification as a norm. Science is to concern itself solely with determinable questions. The material seldom poses these questions in such a concise form. In the same spirit, Popper defines the method of the social sciences 'like that of the natural sciences'. It 'consists in trying out tentative solutions to certain problems: the problems from which our investigations start, and those which turn up during the investigation. Solutions are proposed and criticized. If a proposed solution is not open to pertinent criticism, then it is excluded as unscientific for this reason, although perhaps only temporarily.'[50] The concept of a problem employed here is hardly less atomistic than Wittgenstein's criterion of truth. It is postulated that everything with which sociology legitimately ought to concern itself can be dissected into individual problems. If one interprets Popper's thesis in a strict sense then, despite its common sense which recommends it at a first glance, it becomes an obstructive censure upon scientific thought. Marx did not suggest the 'solution of a problem'—in the very concept of suggestion, the fiction of consensus as a guarantor of truth creeps in. Does this mean that *Das Kapital* is therefore not a contribution to the social sciences? In the context of society, the so-called solution of each problem presupposes this context. The panacea of trial

---

[48] Cf. Popper, 'The Logic of the Social Sciences', loc. cit., p. 88.
[49] loc. cit., p. 92.
[50] loc. cit., pp. 89ff.

and error exists at the expense of moments, after whose removal the problems are licked into shape *ad usum scientiae* and possibly become pseudo-problems. Theory has to bear in mind that the connections, which disappear through the Cartesian dissection of the world into individual problems, must be mediated with the facts. Even if an attempted solution is not immediately amenable to the 'pertinent criticism' stipulated by Popper, that is, if it is not amenable to refutation, the problem can nevertheless be central with regard to the object. Whether or not capitalist society will be impelled towards its collapse, as Marx asserted, through its own dynamic is a reasonable question, as long as questioning is not manipulated; it is one of the most important questions with which the social sciences ought to concern themselves. As soon as they deal with the concept of the problem, even the most modest and therefore the most convincing theses of social-scientific scientism gloss over what are actually the most difficult problems. Concepts such as that of hypothesis and the associated concept of testability cannot be blithely transferred from the natural to the social science. This does not imply approval of the cultural-scientific ideology that the superior dignity of man will not tolerate quantification. The society based on domination has not simply robbed itself and human beings—its compulsory members—of such a dignity, but rather it has never permitted them to become the emancipated beings who, in Kant's theory, have a right to dignity. What befalls them nowadays, as earlier in the form of an extended natural history, is certainly not above the law of large numbers, which astonishingly prevails in the analysis of elections. But the context in itself has a different, or at least a more recognizable, form than it did in the older natural science from which the models of scientistic sociology are derived. As a relationship between human beings, this context is just as much founded in them as it comprehends and constitutes them. Societal laws are incommensurable with the concept of hypothesis. The Babylonian confusion between positivists and critical theorists emerges when the former, although professing tolerance, rob theory, by its transformation into hypotheses, of that moment of independence which endows hypotheses with the objective hegemony of social laws. Moreover, social facts are not as predictable as natural-scientific facts within their relatively homogeneous continua—a point to which Horkheimer first drew attention. Included in the objective law-like nature of

society is its contradictory character, and ultimately its irrationality. It is the task of social theory to reflect upon this too
and, if possible, to reveal its origins, but not to argue it away
through an overzealous adaptation to the ideal of prognoses
which must either be corroborated or refuted.

Similarly, the concept—also borrowed from the natural
sciences—of the general, quasi-democratic, empathetic reconstructability [*Nachvollziehbarkeit*] of cognitive operations and
insights is by no means as axiomatic in the social sciences as it
pretends to be. It ignores the power of the necessarily false
consciousness which society imposes upon its members—a
consciousness which in turn must be critically penetrated. It is
embodied in the aspiring type of social science research assistant
as the contemporary form of the world spirit. Anyone who has
grown up under the influence of the culture industry so entirely
that it has become his second nature is initially hardly able and
inclined to internalize insights which apply to the culture
industry's functions and role in the social structure. Like a reflex
action he will fend off such insights preferably, by referring to
the scientistic guide-line of general empathetic reconstructability.
It took thirty years for the critical theory of the culture industry
to prevail. Even today numerous instances and agencies attempt
to stifle it since it is harmful to business. The knowledge of
objective societal invariant regularities and, in particular, its
uncompromisingly pure, undiluted representation by no means
measures itself against the *consensus omnium*. Opposition to the
repressive total tendency can be reserved for small minorities
who even have to suffer being castigated for an élitist stance.
Empathetic reconstructability is a potential possessed by mankind and does not exist here and now under existing conditions.
It is certainly the case that what *one* person can understand can
potentially be understood by another, for in the interpreter
[*der Verstehende*] that whole is operative through which generality
is also posited. Yet in order to realize this possibility, it is not
sufficient to appeal to the intellect of others as they are, nor even
to education. Probably a change in the whole would be required
—that whole which today, in terms of its own law, deforms
rather than develops awareness. The postulate of simplicity
harmonizes with such a repressive disposition. Since it is incapable of any mental operations other than those which, for all
their perfection, proceed mechanically, this disposition is even

proud of its intellectual honesty. Involuntarily it denies the complicated nature of precisely those social relations which are indicated by such currently overworked terms as alienation, reification, functionality and structure. The logical method of reduction to elements, from which the social is constructed, virtually eliminates objective contradictions. A secret agreement exists between the praise for simple life and the anti-intellectual preference for the simple as what is attainable by thought. This tendency prescribes simplicity for thought. Social scientific knowledge, however, which expresses the complex nature of the process of production and distribution, is apparently more fruitful than the dissection into separate elements of production by means of surveys on factories, individual companies, individual workers and the like. It is also more fruitful than reduction to the general concept of such elements which, for their part, only attain their importance in the more complex structural context. In order to know what a worker is one must know what capitalist society is; conversely, the latter is surely no 'more elementary' than are the workers. If Wittgenstein justifies his method by the statement: 'Objects form the substance of the world. Therefore they cannot be compound',[51] then in so doing he follows, with the positivist's naïvety, the dogmatic rationalism of the seventeenth century. Scientism certainly regards the *res*—the individual objects—as the sole true existent, but thereby dispossesses them of all their determinations, as mere conceptual superstructure, to such an extent that this solely real entity becomes wholly nugatory for scientism and then, in fact, merely serves as an illustration for what, in nominalistic belief, is a similarly nugatory generality.

The positivist critics of dialectics rightly demand models at least of sociological methods which, although they are not tailored to empirical rules, prove to be meaningful. Here however the empiricist's so-called 'meaning criterion' would have to be altered. The *index verborum prohibitorum* demanded by Otto Neurath in the name of the Vienna Circle would then be abolished. One might name as a model something which certainly did not emerge as science, namely, the critique of language, which Karl Kraus, who strongly influenced Wittgenstein, practised for decades in *Die Fackel*. His critique, often directed at journalistic

---

[51] Wittgenstein, *Tractatus*, 2.021, loc. cit., p. 11.

corruptions of grammar, was immanently inscribed. From the outset, however, aesthetic criticism possessed a social dimension. For Kraus linguistic impoverishment was the herald of real impoverishment. Already in the First World War he witnessed the realization of the malformations and rhetoric whose muted cry he had heard long before. This process is the prototype of a non-verbal one. The worldly-wise Kraus knew that language, no matter how much it might be a *constituens* of experience, did not simply create reality. Through its absolutization, language analysis became for Kraus both a distorted mirror of real tendencies and a medium in which his critique of capitalism was concretized into a second immediacy. The linguistic abominations which he created, and whose disproportion to the real abominations is most readily emphasized by those who wish to gloss over the real ones, are excretions of the societal processes which appear archetypically in words before they abruptly destroy the supposedly normal life of bourgeois society in which, beyond current scientific observation, they matured almost imperceptibly. Consequently, the physiognomy of language developed by Kraus contains a greater penetrative power over society than do largely empirical sociological findings since it records seismographically the monster which science, out of a sense of pure objectivity, narrow-mindedly refuses to deal with. The figures of speech cited and pilloried by Kraus parody and surpass what research only tolerates under the sloppy heading of 'juicy quotes'. Kraus' non-science or anti-science puts science to shame. Sociology may contribute mediations which Kraus would in fact scorn as mitigations of his diagnoses that still inevitably lag behind reality. Even during his lifetime, the Viennese socialist workers' newspaper was aware of social conditions which made Viennese journalism into what Kraus recognized it to be. In *History and Class Consciousness* Lukács defined the social type of the journalist as the dialectical extreme of reification. In this extreme case, the commodity character conceals what is simply contrary to the essence of commodities and devours it; namely, the primary spontaneous capacity for reaction on the part of human subjects, which sells itself on the market. Kraus' physiognomy of language would not have had such a profound effect upon science and upon the philosophy of history without the truth content of the underlying experiences which are dismissed by the clique with a subordinate's arrogance as mere art.[52] The analyses micrologically attained by Kraus, are by no means so 'unconnected' with science as would be acceptable to the latter. More specifically, his language-analytical theses on the mentality of the commercial traveller—of the future office worker—must, as a neo-barbaric norm, concur with those aspects of Weber's theory of the dawning of bureaucratic domination which are relevant to the sociology of education. In addition, Kraus' analyses also concur with the decline of education explained by Weber's theory. The strict relation of Kraus' analyses to language and their objectivity lead them beyond the promptly and automatically recorded fortuitousness of merely subjective forms of reaction. The analyses extrapolate from the individual phenomena a whole which comparative generalization cannot master, and which is co-experienced as pre-existent in the approach adopted in Kraus' analysis. His work may not be scientific but a discipline which lay claim to scientific status would have to emulate it. Freud's theory in the phase of its diffusion, was ostracized by Kraus. Nevertheless, and despite Freud's own positivistic mentality, his theory ran as counter to established science as Kraus' own work. Since it was developed on the basis of a relatively small number of individual cases, according to the scientific system of rules, it would be judged to be a false generalization from the first to the last statement.

---

[52] The positivist usage of the concept of art would require critical analysis. For positivists it serves as a rubbish bin for everything which the restricted concept of science wishes to exclude. But since it accepts intellectual life all too readily as a fact, this concept of science must admit that intellectual experience is not exhausted merely in what it tolerates. In the positivist concept of art emphasis is laid upon the supposedly free invention of fictitious reality. This has always been secondary in works of art, but recedes entirely in modern painting and literature. Consequently art's participation in knowledge, namely, that it can express the essential which eludes science and must bear the cost of this, is not recognized or is disputed in advance according to hypostatized scientistic criteria. If one committed oneself so strictly to given states of affairs—as positivism implies—then one would be bound to them even as far as art is concerned. One could not regard art as the abstract negation of science. The positivists, although they treat art *en canaille* and reveal little knowledge of it, do not nevertheless go so far in their rigorism as to prohibit art in earnest, as might be consistent with this view. Their uncritical neutral attitude is responsible for this which mainly benefits the culture industry. Unsuspectingly, like Schiller, they regard art as a realm of freedom. But this is not entirely the case. They frequently behave in an alien or hostile manner towards radical modernism which turns its back upon pictorial realism. They secretly measure even what is not science by scientific standards such as that of the actual or even a picture theory of reality which appears so strangely in Wittgenstein's theory of science. Everywhere throughout positivist writings the gesture of 'I don't understand that' becomes an automatic response. At heart, hostility to art and hostility to theory are identical.

But without its productivity for the understanding of social modes of behaviour and, in particular, the understanding of the 'cement' of society, one could not imagine what might possibly be registered as actual progress of sociology over recent decades. Freud's theory which, for reasons of a complex nature, prompted established science to shrug its shoulders—and psychiatry has still not grown out of this habit—provided intra-scientifically practicable hypotheses for the explanation of what otherwise cannot be explained; namely, that the overwhelming majority of human beings tolerate relations of domination, identify themselves with them and are motivated towards irrational attitudes by them—attitudes whose contradiction with the simplest interests of their self-preservation is obvious. But one must doubt whether the transformation of psycho-analysis into hypotheses does justice to its specific type of knowledge. Its utilization in survey procedures takes place at the expense of the immersion in detail to which it owes its wealth of new societal knowledge, even if it placed its hopes in general law-like regularities in accordance with the model of traditional theory.

Albert seems to be well disposed towards such models.[53] But what is actually at issue in the controversy is unfortunately disguised in his concept of testability in principle. If a sociological theorist repeatedly observes on the posters of New York subway stations that one of the dazzling white teeth of an advertising beauty is blacked out then he will infer, for example, that the glamour of the culture industry, as a mere substitute satisfaction through which the spectator pre-consciously feels himself to be deceived, simultaneously arouses aggression in the latter. In terms of the epistemological principle Freud constructed his theorems in a similar manner. It is very difficult to test such extrapolations empirically, unless one were to light upon particularly ingenious experiments. Such observations can, however, crystallize into social-psychological thought structures which, in a different context and condensed into 'items', lend themselves to questionnaire and clinical methods. But if, on the other hand, the positivists insist that the dialecticians, unlike themselves, are unable to cite any binding rules of behaviour for sociological knowledge and that they therefore defend the *aperçu*, then this postulate presupposes the strict separation of

---

[53] Cf. Hans Albert, 'The Myth of Total Reason', loc. cit., p. 175.

reality and method which is attacked by dialectics. Anyone who wishes to follow the structure of his object and conceptualizes it as possessing motion in itself does not have at his disposal a method independent of the object.

As a counterpart to the general positivist thesis of the verifiability of meaning a valuable model will be cited here from the author's own work in the sociology of music. This is not because the author overestimates the status of the work, but rather since a sociologist naturally becomes aware of the interdependence of material and methodological motives most readily in his own studies. In the 1936 article 'Über Jazz', published in the *Zeitschrift für Sozialforschung* and reprinted in *Moments musicaux*, the concept of a 'jazz subject' was employed, an *ego-imago* which occurs quite generally in this type of music. Jazz was regarded as a totally symbolic process in which this jazz subject, confronted by the collective demands represented by the basic rhythm, falters, stumbles and 'drops out' but, while 'dropping out', reveals himself in a kind of ritual to be similar to all the other helpless subjects and is integrated into the collective at the price of his self-cancellation. One can neither put one's finger on the jazz subject in protocol statements, nor reduce the symbolism of the process to sense data in a completely stringent manner. Nevertheless, the construction which interprets the smooth idiom of jazz, stereotypes of which await such deciphering like a secret code, is hardly devoid of meaning. This construction should promote the investigation of the interiority of the jazz phenomenon, namely of what it generally signifies in societal terms, more than do surveys of the views of various population—or age-groups on jazz, even if the latter were based upon solid protocol statements such as the original comments of those randomly sampled and interviewed. Presumably one could only decide whether the juxtaposition of positions and criteria was quite irreconcilable after a concentrated attempt had been made to realize theorems of this type in empirical research projects. Up till now, this has hardly interested social research, although the possible gain in cogent insight can scarcely be denied. Without indulging in a shoddy compromise one can readily detect possible meaning criteria for such interpretations. This is exemplified in extrapolations from the technological analysis of a phenomenon of mass culture—this is the point of the theory of the jazz subject—or the capacity to combine theorems with other phenomena closer to the usual criteria: phenomena such as the eccentric clown and certain older types of film. In any case, what is implied by such a thesis as that of the jazz subject, in his capacity as the latent embodiment of this type of popular music, is intelligible even if it is neither verified nor falsified by the reactions of the jazz listeners questioned. Subjective reactions by no means need to coincide with the determinable content of cultural phenomena which provoke a reaction. The moments which motivate the ideal construction of a jazz subject must be adduced. No matter how inadequately, this was attempted in the above-mentioned article on jazz. As an evident meaning criterium there emerges the question whether, and to what extent, a theorem illuminates questions which would otherwise remain obscure and whether, through this theorem, diverse aspects of the same phenomenon are mutually elucidated. The construction can fall back upon far-reaching societal experiences, such as that of the integration of society in its monopolistic phase at the expense of the virtually powerless individuals and by means of them. Hertha Herzog, in a later study of the 'soap operas' popular at that time on American radio—radio series for housewives—applied the formula closely related to jazz theory of 'getting into trouble and getting out of it', to such programmes. This study took the form of a content analysis, empirical in terms of the usual criteria, and achieved analogous results. The positivists themselves must state whether the internal positivistic extension of the so-called verifiability criterion makes room for the above-cited models, in that it does not restrict itself to observations requiring verification, but rather includes statements for which any pre-conditions for their verification can be created at all,[54] or whether the all too indirect possibility of verification of these statements—a possibility burdened down by additional 'variables'—as usual renders them unacceptable.

It ought to be the task of sociology to analyse which problems can be dealt with adequately by means of an empirical approach and which problems cannot be analysed in this manner without forfeiting some degree of meaning. A strictly a priori judgment on this question cannot be made. One can presume that a gap exists between empirical research actually carried out and posi-

[54] Cf. Wellmer, loc. cit., p. 15.

tivist methodology. Even in the form of 'analytical philosophy', the latter, until now, has contributed little that is positive to sociological research, and the reason for this is probably that, in research, interest in the object (*Sache*) has, in fact, asserted itself—sometimes through crudely pragmatistic considerations—against methodological obsessions. Living science must be rescued from the philosophy which, having been culled from it, holds it in tutelage. One should simply ask oneself whether, for all its faults, the F-scale of *The Authoritarian Personality*—a study which operated with empirical methods—could ever have been introduced and improved if it had been developed, from the outset, with the aid of the positivist criteria of the Gutman scale. The dictum of the academic teacher that 'You are here to do research, not to think', mediates between the subordinate status of numerous social scientific surveys and their social standpoint. The inquiring mind which neglects the question 'what' in favour of the question 'how', or neglects the goal of knowledge in favour of the means of knowledge, changes itself for the worse. As a heteronomous cog, it forfeits all its freedom in the machinery. It becomes despiritualized through rationalization.[55] Thought, harnessed to the functions of an office worker, becomes an office worker's mentality in itself. The despiritualized spirit must virtually lead *ad absurdum*, since it flounders when faced with its own pragmatic tasks. The defamation of fantasy, and the inability to conceive of what does not yet exist, become sand in the mechanism of the apparatus itself, as soon as it finds itself confronted with phenomena not provided for in its schemata. Undoubtedly, part of the blame for the Americans' helplessness in the Vietnamese guerilla war is borne by what the Americans call 'top brass'. Bureaucratic generals pursue a calculating strategy that is unable

---

[55] At the height of philosophical rationalism, Pascal emphatically distinguished between two types of spirit: the 'esprit de géométrie' and the 'esprit de finesse'. According to the great mathematician's insight, which anticipated many things, the two are seldom united in one person—yet they can be reconciled. At the inception of a development which has since proceeded unopposed, Pascal still perceived which productive intellectual forces fall prey to the process of quantification. Moreover, he conceived of 'pre-scientific' human common sense as a resource which could just as easily benefit the spirit of mathematics as vice versa. The reification of science in the following three centuries put an abrupt end to such a reciprocal relationship. The 'esprit de finesse' has been disqualified. The fact that the term was rendered as 'Geist des Feinsinns' ['spirit of refinement'] in Wasmuth's 1946 German translation, demonstrates both the disgraceful growth of this latter spirit and the decline of 'finesse' as the qualitative moment of rationality.

to anticipate Giap's tactics, which are irrational according to their norms. Scientific management, which is what the strategy of warfare has become, results in military disadvantage. Moreover, in societal terms, the prohibition of fantasy is all too compatible with societal statics, with the decline in capitalist expansion which, despite all protestations to the contrary, is becoming discernible. What, by virtue of its own nature, strives for enlargement becomes, as it were, superfluous, and this in turn damages the interests of capital which must expand in order to survive. Anyone acting in accordance with the maxim 'safety first' is in danger of losing everything. They are a microcosm of the prevailing system whose stagnation is precipitated both by the surrounding dangerous situation and by deformations immanent in progress.

It would be worthwhile to write an intellectual history of fantasy, since the latter is the actual goal of positivist prohibitions. In the eighteenth century, both in Saint-Simon's work and in d'Alembert's *Discours préliminaire*, fantasy along with art is included in productive labour and participates in the notion of the unleashing of the forces of production. Comte, whose sociology reveals an apologetic, static orientation, is the first enemy of both metaphysics and fantasy simultaneously. The defamation of fantasy or its relegation to a special domain, marked off by the division of labour, is the original phenomenon of the regression of the bourgeois spirit. However, it does not appear as an avoidable error of this spirit, but rather as a consequence of a fatality which instrumental reason—required by society—couples with this taboo. The fact that fantasy is only tolerated when it is reified and set in abstract opposition to reality, makes it no less of a burden to science than to art. Legitimate science and art desperately seek to redeem the mortgage that burdens them. Fantasy implies an intellectual operation rather than free invention —without the equivalent of hastily realized facticity. But this is precisely what is prevented by the positivist theory of the so-called meaning criterion. In quite formal terms, for instance, this is exemplified in the famous postulate of clarity: 'Everything that can be thought at all can be thought clearly. Everything that can be put into words can be put clearly'.[56] But everything which is not sensuously realized retains a halo of indeterminacy. No abstraction is ever quite clear; every abstraction is also indistinct

[56] Wittgenstein, *Tractatus*, 4.116, loc. cit., p. 51.

on account of the diversity of possible concretizations. Moreover, one is surprised by the language-philosophical apriorism as Wittgenstein's thesis. Knowledge as free from prejudice of positivism requires would have to confront states of affairs that, in themselves, are anything but clear and are, in fact, confused. There is no guarantee that they can be expressed clearly. The desire to do so, or rather the desire that expression must do strict justice to the object, is legitimate. But this can only be satisfied gradually, and not with the immediacy expected of language only by a view alien to it, unless one dogmatically regards the priority of the instrument of knowledge, even up to the subject-object relation, as prestabilized—a standpoint emanating from Descartes' theory of the *clara et distincta perceptio*. Just as it is certain that the object of sociology, contemporary society, is structured, so there is no doubt that, in its immanent claim to rationality, it possesses incompatible characteristics. These possibly give rise to the effort to conceptualize, in a clear manner, what is not clear—but this cannot be made into a criterion for the object itself. Wittgenstein would have been the last to overlook the unfathomable; namely, whether the conceptualization of something which is, for its part, unclear can ever be clear of itself. In social science, new experiences which are only just developing completely mock the criterion of clarity. If one were to measure them here and now against this criterion, then the tentatively developing experience would not be permitted to become active at all. Clarity is a moment in the process of knowledge, but it does not exhaust this process. Wittgenstein's formulation closes its own horizon against expressing mediately, in a complex manner, and in constellations, what cannot be expressed clearly and immediately. In this respect, his own behaviour was far more flexible than his pronouncements. For instance, he wrote to Ludwig von Ficker, who had presented Georg Trakl with a considerable sum of money donated by Wittgenstein, to say that, although he did not understand Trakl's poems, he—Wittgenstein—was convinced of their high quality. Since the medium of poetry is language, and since Wittgenstein deal with language as such and not merely with science, he unintentionally confirmed that one can express what cannot be expressed. Such paradoxicality was hardly alien to his mode of thought. It would be a sign of equivocation to attempt to evade this paradox by claiming a dichotomy between knowledge and poetry. Art is knowledge *sui generis*. In poetry, that upon which Wittgenstein's theory of science lays stress is emphatic: namely, language.

Wittgenstein's hypostasis of the cognitive moment, clarity, as the canon of knowledge clashes with some of his other major theorems. His formulation, 'The world is everything that is the case', which has become an article of faith for positivism, is in itself so ambiguous that it is inadequate as a 'criterion of meaning', in terms of Wittgenstein's own postulate of clarity. Its apparent incontestability and its ambiguity are surely inextricably linked. The statement is armed with a language form which prevents its content from being fixed. To be 'the case' can mean the same as to exist in factual terms, in the sense of what exists [*das Seiende*] in philosophy τὰ ὄντα; but it can also mean: to have logical validity—that two times two is four is 'the case'. The positivists' basic principle conceals the conflict between empiricism and logistics, which the positivists have never settled. In fact, this conflict prevails throughout the entire philosophical tradition and only penetrates positivism as something new since positivism would prefer to know nothing about this tradition. Wittgenstein's statement is grounded in his logical atomism, rightly criticized within positivism. Only single states of affairs—something, for their part, abstracted—can be 'the case'. Recently, Wellmer has criticized Wittgenstein by asserting that one looks in vain for examples of elementary statements in the *Tractatus*.[57] For there 'are' none with the conclusiveness upon which Wittgenstein would have to insist. In announcing examples he implicitly reveals the critique of the category of the 'First'. If one strives for it, then it evaporates. Unlike the actual positivist members of the Vienna Circle, Wittgenstein opposed the desire to replace a positivism hostile to philosophy with a philosophy which was itself questionable—and ultimately, sensualist—through the primacy of the concept of perception. On the other hand, the so-called protocol statements actually transcend language, within whose immanence Wittgenstein wishes to entrench himself. Antinomy is inevitable. The magic circle of reflexion upon language is not breached by recourse to crude, questionable notions such as that of the immediately 'given'. Philosophical categories, such as that of the idea, the sensual, as well as dialectics, all of which have been in existence since Plato's

---

Theaetetus, arise in a theory of science hostile to philosophy, thereby revoking its hostility towards philosophy. One cannot dispose of philosophical questions by first deliberately forgetting them, and then rediscovering them with the effect of *dernière nouveauté*. Carnap's modification of Wittgenstein's criterion of meaning is a retrogressive step. Through the question concerning the criteria of validity he represses the question of truth. Most of all, they would like to relegate this question to metaphysics. In Carnap's opinion, 'metaphysical statements are not "empirical statements"' [*Erfahrungssätze*][58]—a simple tautology. What motivates metaphysics is not sense experience, to which Carnap ultimately reduces all knowledge, but rather mediated experience. Kant did not tire of pointing this out.

The fact that the positivists extrapolate from science, in a gigantic circle, the rules which are to ground and justify it, has its fateful consequences, even for the science whose actual progress includes types of experience which, in turn, are not prescribed and approved by science. The subsequent development of positivism confirmed just how untenable Carnap's assertion is that 'protocol sentences . . . themselves do not require corroboration, but rather they served as a basis for all the other statements of science.'[59] Presumably, both logically and within science itself, immediacy is essential; otherwise the category of mediation, for its part, would lack any rational meaning. Even categories which distance themselves as greatly from immediacy as society does, could not be conceptualized without something immediate. Anyone who does not primarily perceive in social phenomena the societal, which expresses itself in them, cannot advance to an authentic concept of society. But in the progress of knowledge the moment of immediacy must be transcended. The objections raised by Neurath and Popper as social scientists against Carnap, namely that protocol sentences can be revised, indicates that these statements are mediated. In the first instance, they are mediated through the subject of perception, presented in accordance with the model of physics. Since Hume, positivism has regarded careful reflection upon this subject as superfluous and, as a result, the subject has constantly crept in as an unnoticed presupposition. The consequences are borne by the truth-content of protocol sentences. They are both true and not true. They would have to

---

[58] loc. cit., p. 10.
[59] loc. cit., p. 14.

be elucidated on the basis of several questionnaires such as are used in surveys in political sociology. As preliminary material, the answers are certainly 'true' and, despite their reference to subjective opinions, they are themselves a part of social objectivity to which opinions themselves belong. The people sampled have affirmed this, or put a cross against this and nothing else. On the other hand, however, in the context of the questionnaires, the answers are frequently inconsistent and contradictory; on an abstract level, they might be pro-democratic whilst, with regard to concrete 'items', they are anti-democratic. Hence sociology cannot be satisfied with the data, but rather it must attempt to reveal the derivation of the contradictions; empirical research proceeds accordingly. When viewed subjectively, the philosophy of science's *ab ovo* scorn for such considerations common in science, presents the dialectical critique with its point of attack. The positivists have never wholly shaken off the latent anti-intellectualism which was already present in Hume's dogmatic degradation of ideas to mere copies of impressions. For them thought is nothing more than reconstruction [*Nachvollzug*]; anything beyond this is an evil. Undoubtedly, such a disguised anti-intellectualism, with its unintended political overtones, increases the influence of the positivist doctrine. Amongst its followers, there is one particular type who distinguishes himself both through the lack of a reflective dimension, and through resentment towards those intellectual modes of behaviour which essentially operate within such a dimension.

Positivism internalizes the constraints exercised upon thought by a totally socialized society in order that thought shall function in society. It internalizes these constraints so that they become an intellectual outlook. Positivism is the puritanism of knowledge.[60] What puritanism achieves in the moral sphere is, under

---

[60] At the Frankfurt Congress in 1968, Erwin Scheuch, in particular, advocated a sociology 'which seeks to be nothing more than sociology'. At times, scientific modes of behaviour recall the neurotic fear of bodily contact. Purity becomes over-valued. If one were to strip sociology of everything which, for instance, does not strictly correspond to Weber's definition in the opening pages of *Economy and Society* [*Wirtschaft und Gesellschaft*], then there would be nothing left. Without all the economic, historical, psychological and anthropological moments it would shuffle aimlessly around every social phenomenon. Its raison d'être is not that of an area of study, of an academic 'subject', but rather the constitutive—and therefore neglected—context of those areas of study of an older type. It is a piece of intellectual compensation for the division of labour, and should not, in turn, be unconditionally fixed in accordance with the division of labour. But it is no more true to claim that

positivism, sublimated to the norms of knowledge. Kant's equivocally phrased warning not to digress into intelligible worlds, which Hegel countered with his ironic comment on 'evil houses', forms a prelude to this development; but only, of course, as one vocal line in the polyphonic structure of the philosophical score, whereas, for the positivists, it has become the trivially dominant melody of the soprano part. From the outset, knowledge denies what it seeks, what it ardently desires, since this is denied by the desideratum of socially useful labour. Knowledge then projects the taboo which it has imposed upon itself onto its goal, and proscribes what it cannot attain. The process which otherwise might be unbearable for the subject—namely, the integration of thought into what confronts it and what must be penetrated by it—is integrated into the subject by positivism and made into his own affair. The felicity of knowledge is not to be. If one wished to subject positivism to the *reductio ad hominem* which it so readily practises on metaphysics, then one would surmise that positivism grants a logical form to the sexual taboos which were converted into prohibitions on thought some time ago. Within positivism, it becomes a maxim of knowledge itself that one should not eat from the tree of knowledge. Curiosity is punished in the novelty of thought; utopia must be expelled from thought in every form it takes—including that of negation. Knowledge resigns itself to being a mere repetitive reconstruction. It becomes impoverished just as life is impoverished under work discipline. In the concept of the facts to which one must adhere, and from which one cannot distance oneself, not even through an interpolation of them, knowledge is reduced to the mere reproduction of what is, in any case, present. This is expressed by recourse to logic in the ideal of the continuous deductive system from which nothing is

---

sociology simply brings the contents of these areas of study into a more or less fruitful contact. What is called interdisciplinary co-operation cannot be equated with sociology. It is the task of the latter to reveal the mediations of the object categories —each one of which leads to the next. Sociology is orientated towards the immanent interplay of the elements dealt with in a relatively independent manner by economics, history, psychology and anthropology. It attempts to restore scientifically the unity which they form, in themselves, as societal elements, and which they constantly forfeit through science—though not only through science. This can be most easily apprehended in psychology. Even in the Freudian school, with its monadological approach, society lies hidden in innumerable moments. The individual, its substratum, has made himself independent of society for social reasons. Formalism, which is the result of the instrumentalization, or virtual mathematization, of sociological reason, completely liquidated the qualitative difference between sociology and other sciences and thus its autarchy, proclaimed by the advocates of scientism.

excluded. Insensible enlightenment is transformed into regression. The subordinate and trivial in positivist doctrine is not the fault of its representatives. Frequently, when they set aside their gowns, they derive no profit from it. Objective bourgeois spirit has risen up as a replacement for philosophy. One cannot fail to recognize in this the *parti pris* for the exchange principle, abstracted to the norm of being-for-another (*Füranderessein*), with which the criterion of empathetic reconstructability and the concept of communication, ultimately formed in the culture industry, comply as the measure of all that is intellectual. It is hardly disloyal to interpret what the positivists mean by 'empirical' as what something is for something else; the object itself is never to be apprehended. The positivists react to the simple shortcoming that knowledge does not attain its object but merely places it in relations external to the object, by registering this shortcoming as immediacy, purity, gain and virtue. The repression, which the positivist mind creates for itself, suppresses what is not like itself. This causes positivism—despite its avowal of neutrality, if not by virtue of this avowal—to be a political fact. Its categories are latently the practical categories of the bourgeois class, whose enlightenment contained, from the outset, the notion that one cannot have recourse to ideas which cast doubt upon the rationality of the prevailing *ratio*.

Such a physiognomy of positivism is also that of its central concept: the empirical, experience. In general, categories are only dealt with if, in Hegel's terminology, they are no longer substantial, or if they are no longer unquestionably alive. In positivism, a historical condition of the mind is documented which no longer knows experience and, consequently, both eradicates the indictments of experience and presents itself as its substitute—as the only legitimate form of experience. The immanency of the system, which virtually isolates itself, neither tolerates anything qualitatively different that might be experienced, nor does it enable the human subjects adapted to it to gain unregimented experience. The state of universal mediation and reification of all the relations between human beings sabotages the objective possibility of specific experience of the object—can this world be experienced at all as something living?—together with the anthropological capacity for this. Schelsky rightly called the concept of unregimented experience one of the central points of controversy between dialecticians and positivists. The regimented experience prescribed by positivism nullifies experience itself and, in its intention, eliminates the experiencing subject. The correlate of indifference towards the object is the abolition of the subject, without whose spontaneous receptivity, however, nothing objective emerges. As a social phenomenon, positivism is geared to the human type that is devoid of experience and continuity, and it encourages the latter—like Babbitt—to see himself as the crown of creation. The appeal of positivism must surely be sought in its a priori adaptation to this type. In addition, there is its pseudo-radicalism which makes a clean sweep without attacking anything substantially, and which deals with every substantially radical thought by denouncing it as mythology, as ideology and outdated. Reified consciousness automatically turns upon every thought which has not been covered in advance by facts and figures, with the objection: 'where is the evidence?'. The vulgar-empirical praxis of concept-free social science, which usually takes no notice of analytical philosophy, betrays something about the latter. Positivism is the spirit of the age, analogous to the mentality of jazz fans. Similar, too, is the attraction it holds for young people. This is augmented by the absolute certainty which it promises, after the collapse of traditional metaphysics. But this certainty is illusory; the pure non-contradiction, to which it contracts, is simply a tautology—the empty compulsion to repeat, which has developed into a concept. Certainty becomes something quite abstract and transcends itself. The desire to live in a world without anxiety is satisfied by the pure identity of thought with itself. Paradoxically, security, which fascinates positivism, is similar to the alleged safety which the functionaries of authenticity derive from theology, and for whose sake they advocate a theology which no one believes in. In the historical dialectics of enlightenment, ontology shrinks to a zero point. But this point, although in fact nothing, becomes the bastion—or the ineffable—for the advocates of scientism. This is in keeping with the consciousness of the masses, who sense that they are societally superfluous and ineffectual, and at the same time cling to the fact that the system, if it is to survive, cannot let them starve. Ineffectuality is savoured as destruction, whilst empty formalism is indifferent, and therefore conciliatory, towards whatever exists. Real impotence itself consciously becomes an authoritarian mental attitude. Perhaps objective emptiness holds a special attraction for the emergent anthropological type of the empty being lacking experience. The affective realization of an instrumental thought alienated from its object is mediated through its technification. The latter presents such thought as if it were avant-garde.

Popper advocates an 'open' society. The idea of such a society is contradicted, however, by the close regimented thought postulated by his logic of science as a 'deductive system'. The most recent form of positivism fits the administered world perfectly. In the early days of nominalism, and even for early bourgeois society, Bacon's empiricism implied the emancipation of experience from the *ordo* of pre-given concepts—the 'open' as liberation from the hierarchical structure of bourgeois society. Since, however, the liberated dynamics of bourgeois society are nowadays moving towards a new statics, this openness is obstructed through the restitution of closed intellectual control-systems by the scientistic syndrome of thought. If one applies to positivism its own supreme maxim, one might say that positivism —with its elective affinity to the bourgeoisie—is self-contradictory in that it declares experience to be its ultimate, and yet in the very same breath prohibits it. The exclusivity which it ascribes to the ideal of experience both systematizes it and thereby potentially transcends it.

Popper's theory is more flexible than normal positivism. He does not insist upon value-freedom in such an unreflected manner as does the most influential tradition in German sociology since Weber. Albert, for instance, writes: 'Adorno's judgement that the whole value problem is falsely posed, bears no relation to a definite formulation of this problem, and can therefore hardly be judged; it is an assertion which sounds comprehensive but carries no risk.'[61] To this one must reply that the criticized abstractness of formulation corresponds to a dichotomy which has been sacrosanct in Germany since Weber, and that its inaugurators and not its critics should be censured. The antinomies in which positivism has been entangled through the norm of value-freedom, however, can be made concrete. Just as a strictly apolitical stance becomes a political fact, as does capitulation in the face of might in the political play of forces, so value neutrality generally subordinates itself, in an unreflected manner, to what the positivists call valid value systems. Even Popper with his

---

[61] Albert, 'The Myth of Total Reason', loc. cit., p. 184 below.

demand 'that it should be one of the tasks of scientific criticism
to point out confusions of value and to separate purely scientific
value problems of truth, of relevance, simplicity, and so forth,
from extra-scientific problems',[62] takes back to some extent,
what he originally permits. The problem of this dichotomy
can actually be traced in concrete terms to the social sciences. If
one applies value freedom as vigorously as Max Weber did on
public occasions—but not always in his texts—then sociological
studies can easily violate the criterion of relevance, which Popper
after all includes. If the sociology of art seeks to brush aside the
question of the quality of works whose effects it studies, then it
fails to apprehend such relevant complexes as that of manipulation
through the consciousness industry, the truth or falsity content of
'stimuli' to which a random sample of people is exposed, and
ultimately the determinate insight into ideology as societally false
consciousness. A sociology of art, unable or unwilling to
distinguish between the quality of an honest and significant work
and that of a kitsch product, calculated in terms of its influence,
forfeits not only the critical function it seeks to exercise, but also
the knowledge of such *faits sociaux* as the autonomy or heteronomy
of intellectual works, which depends upon their social location
and determines their social influence. If this is ignored, then we
are left with the empty remains of a 'head count'—at most,
mathematically perfected—of likes and dislikes, of no consequence for the social significance of the registered likes and
dislikes. The critique of the evaluative procedure of the social
sciences should not be refuted, nor should, for instance, the
entological theory of value of Scheler's middle period be restored
as a norm for the social sciences. The dichotomy between value
and value freedom, and not the one or the other, is untenable. If
Popper concedes that the scientistic ideals of objectivity and value
freedom are, in turn, values, then this extends to the truth of
judgments. Their meaning is implied by the 'evaluative' notion
that a true judgment is better than a false one. Analysis of any
substantive social-scientific theorems would necessarily encounter
their axiological elements, even if the theorems do not give an
account of them. But this axiological moment does not stand in
abstract opposition to making a judgment, but rather is immanent to it. Value and value freedom are not separate; rather,

---

they are contained in one another. Each, by itself, would be false—both the judgment which is fixed to an external value and a judgment which paralysed itself through the extirpation of its immanent and inextinguishable evaluative moment. One has to be completely blind to separate the *thema probandum*, together with the line of argument in Weber's treatise on the Protestant Ethic, from the—by no means value-free—intention of his critique of Marx's base-superstructure theorem. This intention nourishes the individual arguments, but above all it also supports the insulation of the investigation against the socio-economic origin of the *theologumena*, which, it is claimed, constituted capitalism. Weber's anti-materialist standpoint not only provides the motivation—as he would admit—for the questions raised in his sociology of religion, but also its focus of attention, the selection of material and the mental complex. Self-consciously, his line of argument turns the economic derivation upon its head. The rigidity of the concept of value, external to thought and object alike, was, for both sides, precisely what was unsatisfactory in the debate on value-freedom. Moreover, without mentioning Weber, a positivist such as Durkheim stated frankly that cognitive and evaluative reason were the same and that, consequently, the absolute separation of value and knowledge was invalid. With respect to the latter, positivists and ontologists are in agreement. The solution of the alleged problem of value, which Albert finds lacking in the dialecticians' work, must surely be sought—to use a positivist concept on this occasion—in the fact that the alternative is apprehended as a pseudo-problem (*Scheinproblem*), as an abstraction which dissolves when confronted with the concrete view of society and reflection upon consciousness of society. This was the point of the thesis concerning the reification of the problem of value, namely, that the so-called values—whether they are regarded as something to be eliminated from the social sciences, or as their blessing—are elevated to something independent, quasi self-constitutive; whereas, neither in real historical terms, nor as categories of knowledge, are they anything of the kind. Value-relativism is the correlate to the absolutist apotheosis of values. As soon as values are removed from the arbitrariness and affliction of the knowing consciousness, and are torn away from its reflection and from the historical context in which they emerge, they fall prey to this very relativity which an invocation of these values sought to banish. The economic concept of value, which served as a model both for Lotze's philosophical concept, and that of the South West German School, and subsequently for the dispute on objectivity, is the original phenomenon of reification—namely, the exchange-value of the commodity. Starting out from the latter, Marx developed his analysis of fetishism, which interpreted the concept of value as the reflection of the relationship between human beings as if it were a characteristic of objects. The normative problems arise from historical constellations, and they themselves demand, as it were, mutely and 'objectively', that they be changed. What subsequently congeals as values for historical memory are, in fact, question-forms (*Fragegestalten*) of reality, and formally they do not differ so greatly from Popper's concept of a problem. For instance, as long as the forces of production are not sufficient to satisfy the primitive needs of all, one cannot declare, in abstract terms, as a value that all human beings must have something to eat. But if there is still starvation in a society in which hunger could be avoided here and now in view of the available and potential wealth of goods, then this demands the abolition of hunger through a change in the relations of production. This demand arises from the situation, from its analysis in all its dimensions, independently of the generality and necessity of a notion of value. The values onto which this demand, arising from the situation, is projected are the poor and largely distorted copy of this demand. The mediating category is immanent critique. It contains the moment of value freedom in the form of its undogmatic reason, succinctly expressed in the confrontation between what a society appears to be and what it is. The value moment, however, lives in the practical challenge which must be construed from the situation; to fulfil this task, however, one requires a theory of society. The false *chorismos* of value freedom and value reveals itself to be the same as that of theory and practice. Society, if it is understood as the functional context of human self-preservation, 'means' this: namely, that it aims objectively at a reproduction of its life which is consonant with the state of its powers. Otherwise, every societal arrangement— even societalization itself—in the simplist cognitive sense is absurd. As soon as it were no longer actually retarded by societal or scientistic authoritative orders, the subjective reason of the ends-means relation would be transformed into objective reason, which is contained in the axiological moment as a moment of knowledge itself. Value and value freedom are mediated dialectically through one another. No knowledge orientated towards the mediated essence of society would be true if it desired a different state of affairs. To this extent, it would be an 'evaluative' knowledge. Nothing can be demanded of society which does not emerge from the relationship between the concept and the empirical, which is not therefore essentially knowledge.

A dialectical theory of society does not simply brush aside the desideratum of value freedom, but rather seeks to transcend it, together with the opposing desideratum. It should adopt this attitude towards positivism in general. It may be that out of a feeling of aversion towards philosophy, dialectics treat Marx's distinction between the representation and origin of knowledge philosophically in a manner that is all too light. With this distinction, Marx intended to ward off the objection that he was devising a deductive system. What is true here, however, is the heavy accent upon the existent as opposed to the unleashed concept—the sharpening of critical theory against idealism. It is an innate temptation for thought which proceeds immanently to disregard the facts. But the dialectical concept is mediation, not something which exists in itself. This imposes on the dialectical concept the duty of not pretending that there is any truth set apart from the mediated, from the facts. A dialectical critique of positivism finds its most important point of attack in reification, in the reification of science and of unreflected facticity. And consequently, such critique must not reify its concepts either. Quite correctly, Albert recognizes that such central concepts as society or collectivity, which are not however sensorily verifiable concepts, should not be hypostatized nor posited and fixed in a naïvely realistic manner as things that exist in themselves. Nevertheless, a theory endangered by such reification is persuaded to become a theory of the object while the object itself is so hardened that it recurs in the theory— provided that the theory merely 'reflects'—as its dogma. If society, a functional and not a substantial concept, remains hierarchically above all individual phenomena in an apparently objective manner, then even dialectical sociology cannot ignore the aspect of their reified nature. Otherwise it distorts that which is decisive, namely, the relationships of domination. Even Durkheim's concept of the collective consciousness, which so obviously reifies mental phenomena, derives its truth content from the constraint exerted by societal mores. But this constraint ought, in turn, to be derived from the relationships of domination in the real life process, and not accepted as an ultimate pregiven or as a thing [*Sache*]. Perhaps, in primitive societies, the lack of food necessitates organizational modes of constraint which recur in situations of scarcity in supposedly mature societies where such situations are caused by the relations of production and are consequently unnecessary. The question which comes first, the socially necessary separation of physical and mental labour or the usurpatory privilege of the medicine man resembles the debate over the chicken and the egg. In any case, the shaman requires ideology and without him it would not be possible. For the sake of sacrosanct theory one cannot exorcise the possibility that social constraint might be an animal or biological inheritance. The inescapable spell of the animal world is reproduced in the brutal domination of a society, still caught up in natural history. But one should not apologetically conclude from this that constraint is immutable. Ultimately it is positivism's most profound moment of truth—even if it is one against which positivism rebels as it does against the word which holds it in its spell—that the facts, that which exists in this manner and not in any other, have only attained that impenetrable power which is then reinforced by the scientistic cult of facts in scientific thought, in a society without freedom of which its own subjects are not masters. Even the philosophical preservation of positivism would require the procedure of interpretation prohibited by positivism—the interpretation of that which, in the course of the world, prevents interpretation. Positivism is the conceptless appearance of negative society in the social sciences. In the debate, dialectics induces positivism to become conscious of such negativity, of its own negativity. The traces of such consciousness are not lacking in Wittgenstein. The further positivism is driven the more energetically it drives itself beyond its boundaries. Wittgenstein's statement, emphasized by Wellmer, 'that much must be prepared in language in order that mere naming has a meaning',[63] achieves no less than the recognition of the fact that tradition is constitutive for language and consequently, precisely in Wittgenstein's sense, for knowledge as such. Wellmer touches a nerve-point when he detects in this an objective denial of the reductionism of the Vienna Circle, a

---

[63] Wellmer, loc. cit., p. 12.

rejection of the criterion of validity for protocol statements. Reductionism has even less of a claim to an authoritative model for the social sciences. According to Wellmer, even Carnap relinquishes the principle of the reduction of all terms to observational predicates and introduces alongside observational language a theoretical one which has been only partially interpreted.[64] In this one may reasonably detect a decisive developmental tendency for the whole of positivism. It is consumed by increasing differentiation and self-reflection. By using a widespread typification its apologetics is able to profit from this; central objections to the school are rejected as outdated when compared with the school's current level of development. Recently Dahrendorf implied that the positivism criticized by the Frankfurt School no longer existed. But the more the positivists are unable to maintain their harsh but suggestive norms, the more the appearance of a legitimation for their scorn for philosophy and for the methods penetrated by the latter vanishes. Like Popper, even Albert seems to abandon prohibitive norms.[65] Towards the end of his essay, 'The Myth of Total Reason', it becomes difficult to draw a sharp dividing line between Popper's and Albert's concept of science and dialectical reflection on society. As a difference there remains the following, 'the dialectical cult of total reason is too fastidious to content itself with "specific" solutions. Since there are no solutions which meet its demands, it is forced to rest content with insinuation, allusion and metaphor'.[66] Dialectical theory, however, does not indulge in a cult of total reason; it criticizes such reason. But whilst arrogance towards specific solutions is alien to it, it does not allow itself to be silenced by them.

Nevertheless, one should not lose sight of what continues to survive untouched in positivism. Dahrendorf's ironic comment that the Frankfurt School is the last school of sociology is symptomatic. What was probably meant here was that the age of schools within sociology was past and that unified science has triumphantly ousted the schools as archaically qualitative entities. But no matter how democratic and egalitarian the prophecy is intended to be, its fulfilment would be intellectually totalitarian and would decisively undermine the very dispute which Dahrendorf himself regards as the agent of all progress. The ideal of

---

[64] Cf. loc. cit., pp. 23f.
[65] Cf. Albert, 'Behind Positivism's Back', loc. cit., p. 227 below.
[66] Albert, 'The Myth of Total Reason', loc. cit., p. 197 below.

progressive technical rationalization, even of science, disavows the pluralistic conceptions to which the opponents of dialectics otherwise pay homage. Anyone who, when faced with such a slogan as that of the last school, recalls the question of the little girl upon seeing a large dog—how long can such a dog live?—does not need to subscribe to any sociological psychologism.

Despite the avowed intention of both sides to conduct the controversy in a rational spirit, the controversy retains its thorny nature. In the press comments on the dispute over positivism, particularly after the Sixteenth German Sociology Congress, which incidentally often did not even follow the course of the debate in an adequate and informed manner, one repeatedly finds the stereotyped statement that no progress was made, that the arguments were already familiar, that no settlement of the opposing viewpoints was in sight. Consequently, doubt was thrown upon the fruitfulness of the debate. These misgivings, which are full of rancour, miss the point. They expect tangible progress in science at a point where its tangibility is just as much in question as its current conception. It has not been established whether the two positions can be reconciled through mutual criticism as they might be in Popper's model. Albert's cheap comments *ad spectatores* on the whole subject of Hegel, not to mention his most recent comments, provide little ground for hope. To protest that one has been misunderstood does not further the discussion any more than the nudging appeal for agreement by refering to the notorious unintelligibility of the opponent. If one contaminates by association dialectics and irrationalism then one blinds oneself to the fact that criticism of the logic of non-contradiction does not suspend the latter but rather reflects upon it. One can generalize the observations made even in Tübingen on the ambiguities contained in the word criticism. Even when the same concepts are used, in fact, even where consensus is achieved, the opposing parties actually mean and strive after such diverse things that the consensus remains a façade covering the antagonisms. A continuation of the controversy would surely have to make visible those underlying antagonisms, which have by no means been fully articulated as yet. It could often be observed in the history of philosophy that doctrines which consider themselves to be the true representation of another diverge because of the climate of the intellectual context right up to the last detail. The relationship of Fichte to Kant would provide the most striking example. In sociology matters are no different; no matter whether sociology as a science has to maintain society in its particular functioning form, as was the tradition from Comte to Parsons, or whether sociology strives for the change of society's basic structures as a result of societal experience, this is determined down to the last category by the theory of science and therefore can scarcely be decided in terms of the theory of science. It is not even the immediate relationship to praxis which is decisive; but rather what role one accords science in the life of the mind and ultimately in reality. Divergencies here are not those of world view. They have their rightful place in logical and epistemological questions, in the interpretation of contradiction and non-contradiction, of essence and appearance, of observation and interpretation. Dialectics remains intransigent in the dispute since it believes that it continues to reflect beyond the point at which its opponents break off, namely before the unquestioned authority of the institution of science.

THEODOR W. ADORNO

SOCIOLOGY AND
EMPIRICAL RESEARCH

1

The modes of procedure assembled under the name of sociology as an academic discipline are united in an extremely abstract sense, namely, in that all of them in some way deal with society. But neither their object nor their method is uniform. Some apply to societal totality and its laws of movement, others, in pointed opposition, apply to individual social phenomena which one relates to a concept of society at the cost of ostracization for being speculative. Accordingly, the methods vary. In the former case, insight into the societal context is supposed to follow from structural basic conditions, such as the exchange relationship. In the latter, such an endeavour, even though it may in no way desire to justify the factual from the standpoint of an autocratic mind, is dismissed as philosophical residue in the development of science, and is to give way to the mere establishment of what is the case. Historically divergent models underlie both conceptions. The theory of society originated in philosophy whilst, at the same time, it attempts to reformulate the questions posed by the latter by defining society as the substratum which traditional philosophy called eternal essences or spirit. Just as philosophy mistrusted the deceit of appearances and sought after interpretation, so the more smoothly the façade of society presents itself, the more profoundly does theory mistrust it. Theory seeks to give a name to what secretly holds the machinery together. The ardent desire for thought, to which the senselessness of what merely exists was once unbearable, has become secularized in the desire for disenchantment. It seeks to raise the stone under which the monster lies brooding. In such knowledge alone meaning has been preserved for us. Sociological research into facts opposes such a desire. Disenchantment of the kind that Max Weber accepted, is merely a special case of sorcery for such research, and reflection upon that which governs secretly and would have to be changed, is viewed as a mere waste of time on the way towards the alteration of the manifest. This is especially the case since what nowadays generally bears the name empirical social science has taken, more or less avowedly since Comte's positivism, the natural sciences as its model. The two tendencies refuse to be reduced to a common denominator. Theoretical reflections upon society as a whole cannot be completely realized by empirical findings; they seek to evade the latter just as spirits evade para-psychological experimental arrangements. Each particular view of society as a whole necessarily transcends its scattered facts. The first condition for construction of the totality is a concept of the object [*Sache*], around which the disparate data are organized. From the living experience, and not from one already established according to the societally installed control mechanisms, from the memory of what has been conceived in the past, from the unswerving consequence of one's own reflection, this construction must always bring the concept to bear on the material and reshape it in contact with the latter. But if theory is not to fall prey to the dogmatism over whose discovery scepticism—now elevated to a prohibition on thought—is always ready to rejoice, then theory may not rest here. It must transform the concepts which it brings, as it were, from outside into those which the object has of itself, into what the object, left to itself, seeks to be, and confront it with what it is. It must dissolve the rigidity of the temporally and spatially fixed object into a field of tension of the possible and the real: each one, in order to exist, is dependent upon the other. In other words, theory is indisputably critical. But, for this reason, hypotheses derived from it—forcasts of what can be regularly expected—are not completely sufficient for it. What can merely be expected is itself a piece of societal activity, and is incommensurable with the goal of criticism. The cheap satisfaction that things actually come about in the manner which the theory of society had suspected, ought not to delude the theory, that, as soon as it appears as a hypothesis, it alters its inner composition. The isolated observation through which it is verified belongs, in turn, to the context of delusion which it desires to penetrate. The concretization and certainty gained must be paid for with a loss in penetrating force; as fas as the principle is concerned it will be reduced to the phenomenon against which it is tested. But if, conversely, one wishes to proceed in accordance with general scientific custom from individual investigations to the totality of society then one gains, at best, classificatory higher concepts, but not those which express the life of society itself. The category 'a society based on the division of labour in general' is higher and more general than 'capitalistic society'—but it is not more substantial. Rather, it is less substantial and tells us less about the life of the people and what threatens them. This does not mean, however, that a logically lower category such as 'urbanism' would say more. Neither upwards nor downwards do sociological levels of abstraction correspond simply to the societal knowledge value. For this reason, one can expect so little from their systematic standardization by means of a model such as Parsons' 'functional' model. But still less can be expected from the promises repeatedly made, and postponed since sociological prehistory, of a synthesis of the theoretical and the empirical, which falsely equate theory with formal unity and refuse to admit that a theory of society, purged of the substantive contents, displaces all its emphases. It should be remembered how indifferent recourse to the 'group' is as opposed to recourse to industrial society. Societal theory formation, based on the model of classificatory systems, substitutes the thinnest conceptual residue for what gives society its law. The empirical and the theoretical cannot be registered on a continuum. Compared with the presumption of insight into the essence of modern society, empirical contributions are like drops in the ocean. But according to the empirical rules of the game, empirical proofs for central structural laws remain, in any case, contestable. It is not a matter of smoothing out such divergences and harmonizing them. Only a harmonistic view of society could induce one to such an attempt. Instead, the tensions must be brought to a head in a fruitful manner.

2

Nowadays, in the train of disappointment with both culturalscientific [*Geisteswissenschaftlich*] and formal sociology, there is a predominant tendency to give primacy to empirical sociology. Its immediate practical utilizability, and its affinity to every type of administration, undoubtedly play a role here. But the reaction against either arbitrary or empty assertions made about society from above is legitimate. Nevertheless, empirical procedures do not merit simple priority. It is not merely the case that there exist other procedures besides these. Disciplines and modes of thought are not justified by their mere existence but rather their limit is prescribed for them by the object [*Sache*]. Paradoxically, the empirical methods, whose power of attraction lies in their claim to objectivity, favour the subjective—and this is explained by their origins in market research. At most, this preference abstracts from statistical data of the census type—such as sex, age, marital status, income, education and the like, and also opinions and attitudes—the behavioural modes of human subjects. So far, at any rate, only within this compass has what is specific to them asserted itself. As inventories of so-called objective states of affairs they could only be distinguished with some difficulty from pre-scientific information for administration purposes. In general, the objectivity of empirical social research is an objectivity of the methods, not of what is investigated. From surveys of varying numbers of individuals, statements are derived by means of statistical processing which are generalizable and independent of individual fluctuations in accordance with the laws of the theory of probability. But even if their validity be objective, in most cases the mean values remain objective statements about human subjects, and, in fact, they remain statements about how human subjects see themselves and reality. The empirical methods— questionnaire, interview and whatever combination and supplementation of these is possible—have ignored societal objectivity, the embodiment of all the conditions, institutions and forces within which human beings act, or at most, they have taken them into account as accidentals. At fault here are not only those interested in commissioning research who consciously or unconsciously prevent the elucidation of such conditions and who in America are careful to make sure—even when distributing research projects on mass communications for instance—that only reactions within the dominant 'commercial system' are recorded and that the structure and implications of the system itself are not analysed. Moreover, even the empirical means are objectively fashioned to this end. This involves the largely pre-ranked questioning of many individuals and its statistical evaluation which, in advance, tend to recognize widely-held—and, as such, preformed—views as justification for judgment on the object itself. In these views, objectivities may also be reflected but certainly not entirely, and often in a distorted form. In any case, as the most cursory glance at the manner in which working people function in their jobs will demonstrate, the weight of subjective opinions, attitudes and modes of behaviour is secondary compared with such objectivities. No matter how positivistic the modes of procedure, they are implicitly based upon the notion—derived from the ground rules of democratic elections and all-too unhesitatingly generalized—that the embodiment of the contents of man's consciousness or unconsciousness which form a statistical universe possesses an immediate key role for the societal process. Despite their objectification, in fact on account of it, the methods do not penetrate the objectification of the object, or in particular, the constraint of economic objectivity. For them, all opinions possess virtually the same validity, and they capture such elementary differences as that of the weight of opinions in proportion to societal power purely through additional refinements such as the selection of key groups. The primary becomes the secondary. Such shifts within the method are not, however, indifferent to what is investigated. For all the aversion of empirical sociology to the philosophical anthropologies which became fashionable in the same period, it shares with them a standpoint; namely, the belief that already in the here and now it is man as such who is central, instead of determining socialized human beings in advance as a moment of societal totality—in fact, predominantly as the object of the latter. The reified nature [*Dinghaftigkeit*] of the method, its inherent tendency to nail down the facts of the case, is transferred to its objects, that, to the subjective facts which have been ascertained, as if they were things in themselves and not hypostatized entities. The method is likely both to fetishize its object and, in turn, to degenerate into a fetish. Not for nothing—and quite rightly as far as the logic of scientific procedures under discussion is concerned—in discussions of empirical social research do questions of method outweigh substantive questions. As a criterion, the dignity of the objects to be examined is frequently replaced by the objectivity of the findings which are to be ascertained by means of a method. In the empirical scientific process, the selection of the research objects and the starting point of the investigation are guided, if not by practical administrative considerations and not so much by the essential nature of what is investigated, but rather by the available methods which, at most, must be developed further. This explains the undoubted irrelevance of so many empirical studies. The procedure of operational or instrumental definition generally current in empirical techniques—which will define a category such as 'conservatism' by means of certain numerical values of the answers to questions within the investigation itself—sanctions the primacy of the method over the object, and ultimately sanctions the arbitrariness of the scientific enterprise itself. The pretence is made to examine an object by means of an instrument of research, which through its own formulation, decides what the object is; in other words, we are faced with a simple circle. The gesture of scientific honesty, which refuses to work with concepts that are not clear and unambiguous, becomes the excuse for superimposing the self-satisfied research enterprise over what is investigated. With the arrogance of the uninstructed, the objections of the great philosophical tradition to the practice of definition are forgotten.[1] What this tradition rejected as scholastic residue is dragged along in an unreflected manner by individual disciplines in the name of scientific exactitude. But as soon as there is any extrapolation from the instrumentally defined concepts even to the conventionally common concepts—and this is almost inevitable—research is guilty of the impurity which it intended to eradicate with its definitions.

3

It is in the nature of society itself that the natural scientific model cannot be happily and unreservedly transferred to it. But although the ideology suggests otherwise, and this is rationalized by the reactionary opposition to new techniques in Germany, this is not because the dignity of man, for the gradual abolition of which mankind is avidly working, would be excluded from methods which regard him as a part of nature. Instead, it is more true to say that mankind commits a flagrant sin in so far as man's claim to domination represses the remembrance of his natural being and thus perpetuates blind natural spontaneity (*Naturwüchsigkeit*) than when human beings are reminded of their natural instincts

---

[1] Cf. Kant, *Critique of Pure Reason*, trans. N. Kemp Smith (London/New York, 1933), pp. 586f.; *Hegel's Science of Logic*, trans. A. V. Miller (London/New York, 1969), pp. 795ff.; and numerous passages in Nietzsche.

(*Naturhaftigkeit*). 'Sociology is not a cultural science (*Geisteswissenschaft*).'[2] Insofar as the obduracy of society continually reduces human beings to objects and transforms their condition into 'second nature', methods which find it guilty of doing just this are not sacrilegious. The lack of freedom in the methods serves freedom by attesting wordlessly to the predominant lack of freedom. The enraged, indignant protests and the subtler defensive gestures provoked by Kinsey's investigations are the most powerful argument for Kinsey. Wherever human beings are, in fact, reduced under the pressure of conditions to the 'amphibious' mode of reaction,[3] as they are in their capacity as compulsive consumers of the mass media and other regimented joys, opinion research, which infuriates lixiviated humanism, is better suited to them than, for instance, an 'interpretative' sociology. For, the substratum of understanding, namely human behaviour, which is in itself unified and meaningful, has already been replaced in the human subjects themselves by mere reaction. A social science which is both atomistic, and ascends through classification from the atoms to generalities, is the Medusan mirror to a society which is both atomized and organized according to abstract classificatory concepts, namely those of administration. But in order to become true, this *adaequatio rei atque cogitationis* requires self-reflection. Its legitimation is solely critical. In that moment in which one hypostatizes that state which research methods both grasp and express as the immanent reason of science, instead of making it the object of one's thought, one contributes intentionally or otherwise to its perpetuation. Then, empirical social research wrongly takes the epiphenomenon— what the world has made of us—for the object itself. In its application, there exists a presupposition which should not be deduced from the demands of the method but rather the state of society, that is, historically. The hypostatized method postulates the reified consciousness of the people tested. If a questionnaire inquires into musical taste and, in so doing, offers a choice between the categories 'classical' and 'popular', then it rightly believes that it has ascertained that the audience in question listens in accordance with these categories. Similarly, one auto-

[2] 'Sociology and Empirical Social Research' in *Aspects of Sociology* (London/Boston 1973), p. 124 (amended translation).
[3] M. Horkheimer and T. W. Adorno, *Dialectic of Enlightenment* (New York, 1972/ London, 1973), p. 36.

matically recognizes, without reflection, when one turns on the radio, whether one has found a popular music programme, or what is considered serious music, or the background music to a religious act. But as long as the societal conditions for such forms of reaction are not met, the correct finding is also misleading. It suggests that the division of musical experience into 'classical' and 'popular' is final and even natural. But the societally relevant question only arises with this division, with its perpetuation as something self-evident, and necessarily implies the question whether the perception of music under the a priori sectors most acutely affects the spontaneous experience of the perceived. Only the insight into the genesis of the existing forms of reaction and their relationship to the meaning of that experienced would permit one to decipher the phenomenon registered. The predominant empiricist habit, however, would reject any discussion of the objective meaning of the particular work of art, and would discuss such meaning as a mere subjective projection by the listeners and relegate the structure to the mere 'stimulus' of a psychological experimental arrangement. In this manner, it would, from the outset, exclude the possibility of discussing the relationship between the masses and the products forced upon them by the culture industry. Ultimately, the products themselves would be defined through the reactions of the masses whose relation to the products was under discussion. But it is all the more urgent today to proceed beyond the isolated study since, with the hold of the media on the population growing stronger, the pre-formation of their consciousness also increases so that there is scarcely a gap left which might permit an awareness of this very pre-formation. Even such a positivistic sociologist as Durkheim, who in his rejection of *Verstehen* was in agreement with social research, had good reason for associating the statistical laws, to which he also adhered, with the 'contrainte sociale'[4] and even for recognizing in the latter the criterion of society's general law-like nature. Contemporary social research denies this connection and thereby also sacrifices the connection between its generalizations and concrete, societal determinations of structure. But if such perspectives are pushed aside and considered to be the task of special investigations which must be carried out at some point, then scientific mirroring indeed remains a mere

---

[4] Cf. Emile Durkheim, *Les Règles de la méthode sociologique* (Paris, 1950), pp. 6ff.

duplication, the reified apperception of the hypostatized, thereby distorting the object through duplication itself. It enchants that which is mediated into something immediate. As a corrective, it is not then sufficient simply to distinguish descriptively between the 'collective realm' and the 'individual realm', as Durkheim intended, but rather the relationship between the two realms must be mediated and must itself be grounded theoretically. The opposition between quantitative and qualitative analysis is not absolute. It is not the last word in the matter. It is well known that whoever quantifies must always first abstract from qualitative differences in the elements, and everything that is societally individual contains the general determinations for which the quantitative generalizations are valid. The proper categories of the latter are always qualitative. A method which does not do justice to this fact and rejects qualitative analysis as incompatible with the essence of the collective realm distorts what it should investigate. Society is one. Even where the major societal forces have not yet made their influence felt, the 'undeveloped' spheres are functionally inter-related with those spheres which have advanced towards rationality and uniform socialization (*Vergesellschaftung*). Sociology, which disregards this and remains content with such weak and inadequate concepts as induction and deduction,[5] supports what exists in the over-zealous attempt to say what exists. Such sociology becomes ideology in the strict sense—a necessary illusion. It is illusion since the diversity of methods does not encompass the unity of the object and conceals it behind so-called factors into which the object is broken up for the sake of convenience; it is necessary since the object, society, fears nothing more than to be called by name, and therefore it automatically encourages and tolerates only such knowledge of itself that slides off its back without any impact. The conceptual dichotomy of induction and deduction is the scientistic substitute for dialectics. But just as a binding theory of society must have fully immersed itself in its material, so the fact to be processed must itself throw light on the societal totality by virtue of the process which apprehends it. If, however, the method has already rendered it a *factum brutum*, then no light can subsequently penetrate it. In the rigid opposition and complementation of

---

[5] Cf. Erich Reigrotzki, *Soziale Verflechtungen in der Bundesrepublik* (Tübingen, 1956), p. 4.

formal sociology and the blind establishment of facts, the relationship between the general and the particular disappears. But society draws its life from this relationship, which therefore provides sociology with its only humanly worthy object. If one subsequently adds together what has been separated, then the material relationship is stood upon its head by the gradation of the method. The eagerness to quantify immediately even the qualitative findings is not fortuitous. Science wishes to rid the world of the tension between the general and the particular by means of its consistent system, but the world gains its unity from inconsistency.

4

This inconsistency is the reason why the object of sociology—society and its phenomena—does not posses the type of homogeneity which so-called classical natural science was able to count upon. In sociology one cannot progress to the same degree from partial assertions about societal states of affairs to their general, even if restricted, validity, as one was accustomed to infer the characteristics of lead in general from the observation of the characteristics of one piece of lead. The generality of social-scientific laws is not at all that of a conceptual sphere into which the individual parts can be wholly incorporated, but rather always and essentially relates to the relationship of the general to the particular in its historical concretion. In negative terms, this attests to the lack of homogeneity of the state of society—the 'anarchy' of all history up till now—whilst, in positive terms, it attests to the moment of spontaneity which cannot be apprehended by the law of large numbers. Anyone who contrasts the human world with the relative regularity and constancy of the objects in the mathematical natural sciences, or at least in the 'macro-realm', does not transfigure this world. The antagonistic character of society is central and this is conjured away by mere generalization. Homogeneity, rather than its absence, requires clarification insofar as it subjects human behaviour to the law of large numbers. The applicability of this law contradicts the *principium individuationis* namely that, despite everything, it cannot be overlooked that human beings are not merely members of a species. Their modes of behaviour are mediated through their intellect. The latter certainly contains a moment of the general which can very easily recur in the statistical generality. Yet it is also specified by means of the interests of particular individuals which diverge in bourgeois society and, even given uniformity, tend to be opposed to one another, not to mention the irrationality in individuals, reproduced under the societal constraints. It is only the unity of the principle of an individualistic society which unites the dispersed interests of the individuals in the formula of their 'opinion'. The currently widespread talk about the social atom certainly does justice to the powerlessness of the individual confronted with the totality, yet it remains merely metaphorical when compared with the natural scientific concept of the atom. Even in front of the television screen, the similarity of the smallest social units, that is the similarity of individuals, cannot be seriously asserted with the strictness possible in the case of physical-chemical matter. Yet empirical social research proceeds as if it took the idea of the social atom at its face value. That it is to some extent successful, is a critical reflection upon society. The general law-like nature of society, which disqualifies statistical elements, testifies that the general and the particular are not reconciled, that precisely in individualistic society the individual is blindly subjected to the general and is himself disqualified. Talk about society's 'character mask' once recorded this state of affairs, but contemporary empiricism has forgotten it. The communal social reaction is essentially that of social pressure. It is only on this account that empirical research, with its conception of the collective realm, is able to brush individuation aside in such a high-handed manner, since the latter has remained ideological up to the present, and since human beings are not yet human beings. In a liberated society, statistics would become, in a positive manner, what today it can only be in negative terms: an administrative science, but really a science for the administration of objects—namely, consumer-goods—and not of people. Yet despite its awkward basis in the social structure, empirical social research should retain its capacity for self-criticism to the extent that the generalizations which it achieves should not immediately be attributed to reality, to the standardized world, but instead they should always be attributed to the method as well. For even through the generality of the question put to individuals or their restricted selection—the cafeteria—the method prepares in advance what is to be ascertained—the opinions to be investigated—in such a manner that it becomes an atom.

5

Insight into the heterogeneity of sociology as a scientific construct, that is, insight into the heterogeneity of the categorial, and not merely graded and easily bridgeable, divergence between disciplines such as social theory, the analysis of objective social conditions and institutions, and subjectively orientated social research in the narrower sense, does not imply that one should simply accept the sterile division between the disciplines. The formal demand for the unity of a science is certainly not to be respected when the science itself bears the marks of an arbitrary division of labour and cannot set itself up as if it could discern without difficulty the much-favoured totalities, whose social existence is, in any case, questionable. But the critical amalgamation of divergent sociological methods is required for concrete reasons, for the cognitive goal. In view of the specific nexus of social theory formation and specific social interests, a corrective of the type offered by the research methods is salutary no matter how entangled with particular interests the latter may be by virtue of their 'administrative' structure. Numerous stalwart assertions of social theories—and here we shall only mention for the purpose of illustration, Max Scheler's assertion about the typical lower-class forms of consciousness[6]—can be tested and refuted with the aid of strict investigations. On the other hand, social research is dependent upon confrontation with theory and with knowledge of objective social structures, otherwise it would degenerate into irrelevancy or willingly comply with apologetic slogans such as those of the family, which occasionally gain popularity. Isolated social research becomes untrue as soon as it wishes to extirpate totality as a mere crypto-metaphysical prejudice, since totality cannot, in principle, be apprehended by its methods. Science then pledges itself to the mere phenomena. If one taboos the question of being as an illusion, as something which cannot be realized with the aid of the method, then the essential connections—what actually matters in society—are protected a priori from knowledge. It is futile to ask whether these essential connections are 'real', or merely conceptual structures. The person who attributes the conceptual to social reality need

---

[6] Cf. 'Ideologie und Handeln' in Max Horkheimer and Theodor W. Adorno, *Sociologica II, Reden und Vorträge, Frankfurter Beiträge zur Soziologie*, vol. 10, 2nd ed. (Frankfurt, 1967), pp. 41f.

not fear the accusation of being idealistic. What is implied here is
not merely the constitutive conceptuality of the knowing subject
but also a conceptuality which holds sway in reality (*Sache*) itself.
Even in the theory of the conceptual mediation of all being, Hegel
envisaged something decisive in real terms. The law which
determines how the fatality of mankind unfolds itself is the law of
exchange. Yet, in turn, this does not represent a simple immediacy
but is conceptual. The act of exchange implies the reduction of the
products to be exchanged to their equivalents, to something
abstract, but by no means—as traditional discussion would
maintain—to something material. This mediating conceptuality is,
however, not a general formulation of average expectations, nor
is it an abbreviating addition on the part of a science which
creates order. Instead, society obeys this conceptuality *tel quel*, and
it provides the objectivity valid model for all essential social
events. This conceptuality is independent both of the consciousness of the human beings subjected to it and of the consciousness
of the scientists. Confronted with physical reality and all the hard
data, one might call this conceptual entity illusion, since the
exchange of equivalents proceeds both justly and unjustly. It is
not an illusion to which organizing science sublimates reality but
rather it is immanent to reality. Moreover, talk about the un-
reality of social laws is only justified critically, namely with regard
to the commodity's fetish character. Exchange value, merely a
mental configuration when compared with use value, dominates
human needs and replaces them; illusion dominates reality. To
this extent, society is myth and its elucidation is still as necessary
as ever. At the same time, however, this illusion is what is most
real, it is the formula used to bewitch the world. The critique of
this illusion has nothing to do with the positivistic scientific
critique according to which one cannot regard the objective nature
of exchange as valid. This validity is unremittingly corroborated
by reality itself. But if sociological empiricism claims that the law
is not something that exists in real terms, then it involuntarily
denotes something of the social illusion in the object—an illusion
which sociological empiricism wrongly attributes to the method.
It is then precisely the alleged anti-idealism of the scientific
mentality which benefits the continued existence of ideology. The
latter is supposed to be inaccessible to science since it is not, of
course, a fact. Yet nothing is more powerful than the conceptual
mediation which conjures up before human beings the being-for-

another (*das Füranderesseiende*) as an in-itself, and prevents them
from becoming conscious of the conditions under which they live.
As soon as sociology opposes recognition of what is known as its
'fact' and remains content simply to register and order it—in so
doing, mistaking the rules distilled for the law which governs the
facts and in accordance with which they develop—then it has
already succumbed to justification, even if it does not suspect
that it has done so. In the social sciences, one cannot therefore
proceed from the part to the whole as one can in the natural
sciences, since it is something conceptual, totally different in its
logical extension and in the unity of features of any individual
elements, which constitutes the whole. Nevertheless, because of
its mediated conceptual nature, this whole has nothing in common with 'totalities' and forms, which necessarily must always be
conceptualized as being immediate. Society has more in common
with the system than with the organism. An empirical research
devoid of theory which gets by with mere hypotheses is blind to
society as a system, its authentic object, since its object does not
coincide with the sum of all the parts. It does not subsume the
parts nor is it made up, like a geographical map, of their juxtaposition of 'country and people'. No social atlas in the literal and
figurative sense represents society. Insofar as society is more than
the immediate life of its members and the related subjective and
objective facts, research which exhausts itself in the investigation
of such immediacy misses its mark. For all the hypostatization of
the method, even by virtue of such hypostatization as the idoliza-
tion of what can be simply observed, it produces an illusion of
being alive, an illusion of neighbourliness, as it were, from
countenance to countenance. A dissolution of such an illusion
would not be the last of the tasks for social knowledge if it had not
already been dissolved. Today, however, it is repressed. In this
respect, the transfiguring metaphysics of existence and the rigid
description of what is the case are equally guilty. Moreover, to a
considerable extent, the practice of empirical sociology does not
even comply with its own admission that hypotheses are necessary.
Whilst the necessity of the latter is reluctantly conceded, each
hypothesis is met with suspicion since it might become a 'bias' and
lead to an infringement of impartial research.[7] This view is based
upon a 'residual theory of truth', upon the notion that truth is

[7] Cf. René König, 'Beobachtung und Experiment in der Sozialforschung', in
Praktische Sozialforschung (Cologne, 1956), II, p. 27.

what remains after the allegedly mere subjective addition, a sort of cost price, has been deducted. Since Georg Simmel and Freud, psychology has realized that the conclusiveness of the experience of objects, if the latter in turn are essentially subjectively mediated like society, is increased and not decreased by the degree of subjective participation of the knowing subject. But this insight has not yet been incorporated into the social sciences. As soon as individual common sense is suspended in favour of the responsible behaviour of the scientist, people seek salvation in procedures which are as free from hypotheses as possible. Empirical social research ought to dismiss completely the superstition that research must begin like a *tabula rasa*, where the data that are assembled in an unconditioned manner are prepared. In so doing, it ought to recall epistemological controversies which are indeed fought out long ago, but are forgotten all too willingly by short-winded consciousness in its reference to the urgent requirements of the research process. Scepticism with regard to its own ascetic ideals befits a sceptical science. The readily-quoted statement that a scientist needs 10% inspiration and 90% perspiration is secondary and leads to a prohibition on thought. For a long time, the abstinent work of the scholar has mainly consisted in renouncing for poor pay those thoughts which he did not have in any case. Nowadays, since the better paid executive has succeeded the scholar, lack of intellect is not only celebrated as a virtue on the part of the modest well-adapted person who is incorporated into the team, but, in addition, it is institutionalized through the establishment of levels of research which hardly recognize the spontaneity of individuals as anything other than as indices of friction. But the antithesis of grandiose inspiration and solid research work is, as such, of secondary importance. Thoughts do not come flying along but rather they crystallize in protracted subterranean processes, even if they emerge suddenly. The abruptness of what research technicians condescendingly call intuition marks the penetration of living experience through the hardened crust of the *communis opinio*. It is the long drawn-out breath of opposition to the latter, and by no means the privilege of highly gifted moments, which permits unregimented thought that contact with being which is often inexorably sabotaged by the distended apparatus that intervenes. Conversely, scientific assiduity is always both the operation and exertion of the concept, the opposite of the mechanical, doggedly unconscious procedure with which it is equated. Science should be the recognition of the truth and untruth of what the phenomenon under study seeks to be. There is no knowledge which is not, at the same time, critical by virtue of its inherent distinction between true and false. Only a sociology which set the petrified antitheses of its organization in motion would come to its senses.

6

The categorial difference between the discipline is confirmed by the fact that what should be fundamental, namely the combination of empirical investigations with theoretically central questions, has—despite isolated attempts—not yet been achieved. The most modest demand and yet, in terms of immanent critique, the most plausible demand for empirical social research in accordance with its own rules of 'objectivity', would be to confront all its statements directed at the subjective consciousness and unconsciousness of human beings and groups of human beings with the objective factors of their existence. What seems merely accidental or mere 'background study' to the domain of social research provides the precondition for the possibility of social research ever reaching the essential. Inevitably, in these given factors, it will first emphasize what is connected with the subjective opinions, feelings and behaviour of those studied, although these connections, in particular, are so wide-ranging that such a confrontation ought not really to content itself with the knowledge of individual institutions but instead should have recourse to the structure of society. The categorial difficulty is not removed by means of a comparison between certain opinions and certain conditions. But even with this weighty reservation, the results of opinion research acquire a different value as soon as they can be measured against the real nature of what opinions are concerned with. The differences which thereby emerge between social objectivity and the consciousness of the subjectivity, no matter in what form this consciousness may be generally distributed, mark a place at which empirical social research reaches knowledge of society—the knowledge of ideologies, of their genesis and of their function. Such knowledge would be the actual goal, although not of course the only goal, of empirical social research. Taken in isolation, however, the latter does not have the weight of social knowledge.

The laws of the market, in whose system it remains in an un-reflected manner, remain a façade. Even if a survey provided the statistically overwhelming evidence that workers no longer con-sider themselves to be workers and deny that there still exists such a thing as the proletariat, the non-existence of the proletariat would in no way have been proved. But rather, such subjective findings would have to be compared with objective findings, such as the position of those questioned in the production process, their control or lack of control over the means of pro-duction, their societal power or powerlessness. The empirical findings concerning the human subjects would certainly still retain their significance. One would not simply have to ask within the content of the theory of ideology how such modes of conscious-ness come about, but also whether something essential has changed in social objectivity through their very existence. In the latter, the nature and self-consciousness of human beings, no matter how this is produced and reproduced, can only be neglected by erroneous dogma. Even the existence of such consciousness, whether as an element of the affirmation of what exists or as a potential for something different, is a moment in societal totality. Not only theory but also its absence becomes a material force when it seizes the masses. Empirical social research is not only a corrective in that it prevents blindly superimposed constructions, but also in the relationship between appearance and essence. If the task of a theory of society is to relativize critically the cognitive value of appearance, then conversely it is the task of empirical research to protect the concept of essential laws from mythologization. Appearance is always also an appearance of essence and not mere illusion. Its changes are not indifferent to essence. If no one in fact knows any more that he is a worker then this affects the inner composition of the concept of the worker even if its objective definition—through separation from the means of production—is still fulfilled.

7

Empirical social research cannot evade the fact that all the given factors investigated, the subjective no less than the objective relations, are mediated through society. The given, the facts which, in accordance with its methods, it encounters as something final, are not themselves final but rather are conditioned. Consequently, empirical social research cannot confuse the roots of its knowledge—the givenness of facts which is the concern of its method—with the real basis, a being in-itself of facts, their immediacy as such, their fundamental character. It can protect itself against such a confusion in that it is able to dissolve the immediacy of the data through refinement of the method. This accounts for the significance of motivational analyses although they remain under the spell of subjective reaction. They can indeed seldom rest upon direct questions; and correlations indicate functional connections but do not elucidate causal dependencies. Consequently, the development of indirect methods is, in principle, the opportunity for empirical social research to reach beyond the mere observation and preparation of superficial facts. The cognitive problem of its self-critical development remains, namely that the facts ascertained do not faithfully reflect the underlying societal conditions but rather they simultaneously constitute the veil by means of which these conditions, of necessity, disguise themselves. For the findings of what is called— not without good reason—'opinion research' Hegel's formulation in his *Philosophy of Right* concerning public opinion is generally valid: it deserves to be respected and despised in equal measure.[8] It must be respected since even ideologies, necessary false consciousness, are a part of social reality with which anyone who wishes to recognize the latter must be acquainted. But it must be despised since its claim to truth must be criticized. Empirical social research itself becomes ideology as soon as it posits public opinion as being absolute. This is the fault of an unreflectedly nominalistic concept of truth which wrongly equates the 'volonté de tous' with truth in general, since a different truth cannot be ascertained. This tendency is particularly marked in American empirical social research. But it should not be dogmatically confronted with the mere assertion of a 'volonté générale' as a truth in-itself, for instance in the form of postulated 'values'. Such a procedure would be loaded with the same arbitrariness as the installation of popular opinion as objectively valid. Historically, since Robespierre, the establishment of the 'volonté générale' by decree has possibly caused even more harm than the concept-free assumption of a 'volonté de tous'. The only way out of the fateful

---

[8] Cf. *Hegel's Philosophy of Right*, trans. T. M. Knox (Oxford/New York, 1952), §318, p. 205.

alternative was provided by immanent analysis; the analysis of the consistency or inconsistency of opinion in itself and of its relationship to reality (*Sache*), not however the abstract antithesis of the objectively valid and of opinion. Opinion should not be rejected with Platonic arrogance, but rather its untruth is to be derived from the truth: from the supporting societal relationship and ultimately from the latter's own untruth. On the other hand, however, average opinion does not represent an approximate value of truth, but instead the socially average illusion. In the latter, there participate what unreflective social research imagines to be its *ens realissimum*: those questioned, the human subjects. Their own nature, their being as subjects, depends upon the objectivity, upon the mechanisms which they obey, and which constitute their concept. This can only be determined, however, if one perceives in the facts themselves the tendency which reaches out beyond them. That is the function of philosophy in empirical social research. If it is not realized or suppressed, if merely the facts are reproduced then such a reproduction is at the same time a corruption of facts into ideology.

KARL R. POPPER

THE LOGIC OF THE SOCIAL SCIENCES

First Contribution to the Symposium*

I propose to begin my paper on the logic of the social sciences with two theses which formulate the opposition between our knowledge and our ignorance.

First thesis: We know a great deal. And we know not only many details of doubtful intellectual interest but also things which are of considerable practical significance and, what is even more important, which provide us with deep theoretical insight, and with a surprising understanding of the world.

Second thesis: Our ignorance is sobering and boundless. Indeed, it is precisely the staggering progress of the natural sciences (to which my first thesis alludes) which constantly opens our eyes anew to our ignorance, even in the field of the natural sciences themselves. This gives a new twist to the Socratic idea of ignorance. With each step forward, with each problem which we solve, we not only discover new and unsolved problems, but we also discover that where we believed that we were standing on firm and safe ground, all things are, in truth, insecure and in a state of flux.

My two theses concerning knowledge and ignorance only appear to contradict one another. The apparent contradiction is primarily due to the fact that the words 'knowledge' and 'ignorance' are not used in the two theses as exact opposites. Yet both ideas are important, and so are both theses: so much so that I propose to make this explicit in the following third thesis.

Third thesis: It is a fundamentally important task for every theory of knowledge, and perhaps even a crucial requirement, to

---

* This was the opening contribution to the Tübingen symposium, followed by Professor Adorno's reply. The translation was revised by the author for the present publication. A few small additions have been made. See also the last contribution to the present volume.

do justice to our first two theses by clarifying the relations between our remarkable and constantly increasing knowledge and our constantly increasing insight that we really know nothing.

If one reflects a little about it, it becomes almost obvious that the logic of knowledge has to discuss this tension between knowledge and ignorance. An important consequence of this insight is formulated in my fourth thesis. But before I present this fourth thesis, I should like to apologize for the many numbered theses which are still to come. My excuse is that it was suggested to me by the organizers of this conference that I assemble this paper in the form of numbered theses [in order to make it easier for the second symposiast to present his critical counter-theses more sharply]. I found this suggestion very useful despite the fact that this style may create the impression of dogmatism. My fourth thesis, then, is the following.

Fourth thesis: So far as one can say at all that science, or knowledge, 'starts from' something, one might say the following: Knowledge does not start from perceptions or observations or the collection of data or facts, but it starts, rather, from *problems*. One might say: No knowledge without problems; but also, no problems without knowledge. But this means that knowledge starts from the tension between knowledge and ignorance. Thus we might say not only, no problems without knowledge; but also, no problems without ignorance. For each problem arises from the discovery that something is not in order with our supposed knowledge; or, viewed logically, from the discovery of an inner contradiction between our supposed knowledge and the facts; or, stated perhaps more correctly, from the discovery of an apparent contradiction between our supposed knowledge and the supposed facts.

While my first three theses may perhaps, because of their abstract character, create the impression that they are somewhat removed from our topic—that is, the logic of the social sciences —I should like to say that with my fourth thesis we have arrived at the heart of our topic. This can be formulated in my fifth thesis, as follows.

Fifth thesis: As in all other sciences, we are, in the social sciences, either successful or unsuccessful, interesting or dull, fruitful or unfruitful, in exact proportion to the significance or interest of the problems we are concerned with; and also, of course, in exact proportion to the honesty, directness and simplicity with which we tackle these problems. In all this we are in no way confined to theoretical problems. Serious practical problems, such as the problems of poverty, of illiteracy, of political suppression or of uncertainty concerning legal rights were important starting-points for research in the social sciences. Yet these practical problems led to speculation, to theorizing and thus to theoretical problems. In all cases, without exception, it is the character and the quality of the problem—and also of course the boldness and originality of the suggested solution—which determine the value, or the lack of value, of a scientific achievement.

The starting-point, then, is always a problem; and observation becomes something like a starting-point only if it reveals a problem; or in other words, if it surprises us, if it shows us that something is not quite in order with our knowledge, with our expectations, with our theories. An observation creates a problem only if it clashes with certain of our conscious or unconscious expectations. But what in this case constitutes the starting-point of our scientific work is not so much an observation pure and simple, but rather an observation that plays a particular role; that is, an observation which creates a problem.

I have now reached the point where I can formulate my *main thesis*, as thesis number six. It consists of the following.

Sixth thesis:

(a) The method of the social sciences, like that of the natural sciences, consists in trying out tentative solutions to certain problems: the problems from which our investigations start, and those which turn up during the investigation.

Solutions are proposed and criticized. If a proposed solution is not open to pertinent criticism, then it is excluded as unscientific, although perhaps only temporarily.

(b) If the attempted solution is open to pertinent criticism, then we attempt to refute it; for all criticism consists of attempts at refutation.

(c) If an attempted solution is refuted through our criticism we make another attempt.

(d) If it withstands criticism, we accept it temporarily; and we accept it, above all, as worthy of being further discussed and criticized.

(e) Thus the method of science is one of tentative attempts to solve our problems; by conjectures which are controlled by

severe criticism. It is a consciously critical development of the
method of 'trial and error'.

(f)   The so-called objectivity of science lies in the objectivity
of the critical method. This means, above all, that no theory is
beyond attack by criticism; and further, that the main instrument of logical criticism—the logical contradiction—is objective.

The basic idea which lies behind my central thesis might also
be put in the following way.

Seventh thesis: the tension between knowledge and ignorance
leads to problems and to tentative solutions. Yet the tension is
never overcome. For it turns out that our knowledge always
consists merely of suggestions for tentative solutions. Thus the
very idea of knowledge involves, in principle, the possibility that
it will turn out to have been a mistake, and therefore a case of
ignorance. And the only way of 'justifying' our knowledge is
itself merely provisional, for it consists in criticism or, more
precisely, in an appeal to the fact that *so far* our attempted solutions appear to withstand even our most severe attempts at
criticism.

There is no positive justification: no justification which goes
beyond this. In particular, our tentative solutions cannot be shown
to be probable (in any sense that satisfies the laws of the calculus
of probability).

Perhaps one could describe this position as *the critical approach*
('critical' alludes to the fact that there is here a relation to Kant's
philosophy).

In order to give a better idea of my main thesis and its significance for sociology it may be useful to confront it with certain
other theses which belong to a widely accepted methodology
which has often been quite unconsciously and uncritically accepted
and absorbed.

There is, for instance, the misguided and erroneous methodological approach of naturalism or scientism which urges that it is
high time that the social sciences learn from the natural sciences
what scientific method is. This misguided naturalism establishes
such demands as: begin with observations and measurements;
this means, for instance, begin by collecting statistical data;
proceed, next, by induction to generalizations and to the formation of theories. It is suggested that in this way you will approach

the ideal of scientific objectivity, so far as this is at all possible in the social sciences. In so doing, however, you ought to be conscious of the fact that objectivity in the social sciences is much more difficult to achieve (if it can be achieved at all) than in the natural sciences. For an objective science must be 'value-free'; that is, independent of any value judgment. But only in the rarest cases can the social scientist free himself from the value system of his own social class and so achieve even a limited degree of 'value freedom' and 'objectivity'.

Every single one of the theses which I have here attributed to this misguided naturalism is in my opinion totally mistaken: all these theses are based on a misunderstanding of the methods of the natural sciences, and actually on a myth—a myth, unfortunately all too widely accepted and all too influential. It is the myth of the inductive character of the methods of the natural sciences, and of the character of the objectivity of the natural sciences. I propose in what follows to devote a small part of the precious time at my disposal to a critique of this misguided naturalism.*

Admittedly, many social scientists will reject one or other of the theses which I have attributed to this misguided naturalism. Nevertheless this naturalism seems at present to have gained the upper hand in the social sciences, except perhaps in economics; at least in English-speaking countries. I wish to formulate the symptoms of this victory in my eighth thesis.

Eighth thesis: Before the Second World War, sociology was regarded as a general theoretical social science, comparable, perhaps, with theoretical physics, and social anthropology was regarded as a very special kind of sociology—a descriptive sociology of primitive societies. Today† this relationship has been completely reversed; a fact to which attention should be drawn. Social anthropology or ethnology has become a general social science, and sociology has resigned itself more and more to playing the part of a special kind of social anthropology: the social anthropology of the highly industrialized West European or American forms of society. Restated more briefly, the relationship

---

* (Note to the English edition.) What my Frankfurt opponents call positivism seems to me the same as what I here call 'misguided naturalism'. They tend to ignore my rejection of it.

† (Note to the English edition.) Since this was written in 1961, there has been a strong reaction to the tendencies here criticized.

between sociology and anthropology has been reversed. Social anthropology has been promoted from an applied descriptive discipline to a key theoretical science and the anthropologist has been elevated from a modest and somewhat short-sighted descriptive fieldworker to a far-seeing and profound social theorist and social depth-psychologist. The former theoretical sociologist however must be happy to find employment as a fieldworker and a specialist: his function is to observe and to describe the totems and taboos of the natives of the white race in Western Europe and the United States.

But one probably should not take this change in the fate of the social scientist too seriously; particularly as there is no such thing as the essence of a scientific subject. This leads me to my ninth thesis.

Ninth thesis: A so-called scientific subject is merely a conglomerate of problems and attempted solutions, demarcated in an artificial way. What really exists are problems and solutions, and scientific traditions.

Despite this ninth thesis, the complete reversal in the relations between sociology and anthropology is extremely interesting, not on account of the subjects or their titles, but because it points to the victory of a pseudo-scientific method. Thus I come to my next thesis.

Tenth thesis: The victory of anthropology is the victory of an allegedly observational, allegedly descriptive and allegedly more objective method, and thus of what is taken to be the method of the natural sciences. It is a Pyrrhic victory: another such victory and we—that is, both anthropology and sociology—are lost.

My tenth thesis may be formulated, I readily admit, a little too pointedly. I admit of course that much of interest and importance has been discovered by social anthropology, which is one of the most successful social sciences. Moreover, I readily admit that it can be fascinating and significant for us Europeans to see ourselves, for a change, through the spectacles of the social anthropologist. But although these spectacles are perhaps more coloured than others, they hardly are, for this reason, more objective. The anthropologist is not the observer from Mars which he so often believes himself to be and whose social role he often attempts to play (and not without gusto); quite apart from the fact that there is no reason to suppose that an inhabitant of Mars would see us more 'objectively' than we, for instance, see ourselves.

In this context I should like to tell a story which is admittedly extreme but in no way unique. Although it is a true story, this is immaterial in the present context: should the story seem improbable to you then, please, take it as an invention, as a freely invented illustration, designed to make clear an important point by means of crass exaggeration.

Years ago, I was a participant in a four-day conference, organized by a theologian, in which philosophers, biologists, anthropologists and physicists participated—one or two representatives from each discipline; in all eight participants were present. The topic was, I think, 'Science and Humanism'. After several initial difficulties and the elimination of an attempt to impress us by exalted depth ['*erhabene Tiefe*' is a term of Hegel's who failed to see that an exalted depth is just a platitude] the joint efforts of roughly four or five participants succeeded in the course of two days in raising the discussion to an uncommonly high level. Our conference had reached the stage—or so it appeared to me at least—at which we all had the happy feeling that we were learning something from one another. At any rate, we were all immersed in the subject of our debate when out of the blue the social anthropologist made his contribution.

'You will, perhaps, be surprised', he said, 'that I have said nothing so far in this conference. This is due to the fact that I am an observer. As an anthropologist I came to this conference not so much in order to participate in your verbal behaviour but rather to study your verbal behaviour. This is what I have succeeded in doing. Concentrating on this task, I was not always able to follow the actual content of your discussion. But someone like myself who has studied dozens of discussion groups learns in time that the topic discussed is relatively unimportant. We anthropologists learn'—this is almost verbatim (so far as I remember)—'to regard such social phenomena from the outside and from a more objective standpoint. What interests us is not the what, the topic, but rather the how: for example, the manner in which one person or another attempts to dominate the group and how his attempts are rejected by the others, either singly or through the formation of a coalition; how after various attempts of this type a hierarchical order and thus a group equilibrium develops and also a group ritual of verbalization; these things are always very similar no matter how varied the question appears to be which serves as the topic of the discussion.'

We listened to our anthropological visitor from Mars and to all he had to say; and then I put two questions to him. First, whether he had any comment to make on the actual content and result of our discussion; and then, whether he could not see that there were such things as impersonal reasons or arguments which could be valid or invalid. He replied that he had had to concentrate too much on the observation of our group behaviour to have been able to follow our argument in detail; moreover, had he done so, he would have endangered (so he said) his objectivity; for he might have become involved in the argument; and had he allowed himself to be carried away by it, he would have become one of us—and that would have been the end of his objectivity. Moreover, he was trained not to judge the literal content of verbal behaviour (he constantly used the terms 'verbal behaviour' and 'verbalization'), or to take it as being important. What concerned him, he said, was the social and psychological function of this verbal behaviour. And he added something like the following. 'While arguments or reasons make an impression on *you*, as participants in a discussion, what interests *us* is the fact that through such means you can mutually impress and influence each other; and also of course the symptoms of this influence. We are concerned with concepts such as emphasis, hesitation, intervention, and concession. We are actually not concerned with the factual content of the discussion but only with the role which the various participants are playing: with the dramatic interplay as such. As to the so-called arguments, they are of course only one aspect of verbal behaviour and not more important than the other aspects. The idea that one can distinguish between arguments and other impressive verbalizations is a purely subjective illusion; and so is the idea of a distinction between objectively valid and objectively invalid arguments. If hard pressed, one could classify arguments according to the societies or groups within which they are, at certain times, accepted as valid or invalid. That the time element plays a role is also revealed by the fact that seemingly valid arguments, which are at one time accepted in a discussion group such as the present one, may nevertheless be attacked or rejected at a later stage by one of the participants.'

I do not wish to prolong the description of this incident. I imagine that it will not be necessary to point out, in the present gathering, that the somewhat extreme position of my anthropological friend shows in its intellectual origin the influence not only of the behaviouristic ideal of objectivity but also of certain ideas which have grown on German soil. I refer to the idea of philosophical relativism: historical relativism, which believes that there is no objective truth but instead merely truths for this or that age; and sociological relativism, which teaches that there are truths or sciences for this or that class or group or profession, such as proletarian science and bourgeois science. I also believe that the sociology of knowledge has its full share of responsibility, for it contributed to the pre-history of the dogmas echoed by my anthropological friend. Admittedly, he adopted a somewhat extreme position at that conference. But this position, especially if one modifies it a little, is neither untypical nor unimportant.

But this position is *absurd*. Since I have criticized historical and sociological relativism and also the sociology of knowledge in detail elsewhere, I will forego criticism here. I will confine myself to discussing very briefly the naïve and misguided idea of scientific objectivity which underlies this position.

Eleventh thesis: It is a mistake to assume that the objectivity of a science depends upon the objectivity of the scientist. And it is a mistake to believe that the attitude of the natural scientist is more objective than that of the social scientist. The natural scientist is just as partisan as other people, and unless he belongs to the few who are constantly producing new ideas, he is, unfortunately, often very biased, favouring his pet ideas in a one-sided and partisan manner. Several of the most outstanding contemporary physicists have also founded schools which set up a powerful resistance to new ideas.

However, my thesis also has a positive side and this is more important. It forms the content of my twelfth thesis.

Twelfth thesis: What may be described as scientific objectivity is based solely upon a critical tradition which, despite resistance, often makes it possible to criticize a dominant dogma. To put it another way, the objectivity of science is not a matter of the individual scientists but rather the social result of their mutual criticism, of the friendly-hostile division of labour among scientists, of their co-operation and also of their competition. For this reason, it depends, in part, upon a number of social and political circumstances which make this criticism possible.

Thirteenth thesis: The so-called sociology of knowledge which tries to explain the objectivity of science by the attitude of impersonal detachment of individual scientists, and a lack of objectivity in terms of the social habitat of the scientist, completely misses the following decisive point: the fact that objectivity rests solely upon pertinent mutual criticism. What the sociology of knowledge misses is nothing less than the sociology of knowledge itself—the social aspect of scientific objectivity, and its theory. Objectivity can only be explained in terms of social ideas such as competition (both of individual scientists and of various schools); tradition (mainly the critical tradition); social institution (for instance, publication in various competing journals and through various competing publishers; discussion at congresses); the power of the state (its tolerance of free discussion).

Such minor details as, for instance, the social or ideological habitat of the researcher, tend to be eliminated in the long run; although admittedly they always play a part in the short run.

In a way similar to that in which we have solved the problem of objectivity, we can also solve the related problem of the freedom of science from involvement in value judgments ('value freedom'); and we can do so in a freer, a less dogmatic way, than is usually done.

Fourteenth thesis: In a pertinent critical discussion we may distinguish such questions as: (1) The question of the truth of an assertion; the question of its relevance, of its interest and of its significance relative to the problems in which we are interested. (2) The question of its relevance and of its interest and of its significance for various *extra-scientific problems*, for example, problems of human welfare or the quite differently structured problems of national defence; or (by contrast) of an aggressive nationalist policy; or of industrial expansion; or of the acquisition of personal wealth.

It is clearly impossible to eliminate such extra-scientific interests and to prevent them from influencing the course of scientific research. And it is just as impossible to eliminate them from research in the natural sciences—for example from research in physics—as from research in the social sciences.

What is possible and what is important and what lends science its special character is not the elimination of extra-scientific interests but rather the differentiation between the interests which do not belong to the search for truth and the purely scientific interest in truth. But although truth is our regulative principle, our decisive scientific value, it is not our only one. Relevance, interest, and significance (the significance of statements relative to a purely scientific problem situation) are likewise scientific values of the first order; and this is also true of values like those of fruitfulness, explanatory power, simplicity, and precision.

In other words, there exist *purely* scientific values and disvalues and *extra*-scientific values and disvalues. And although it is impossible to separate scientific work from extra-scientific applications and evaluations, it is one of the tasks of scientific criticism and scientific discussion to fight against the confusion of value-spheres and, in particular, to separate extra-scientific evaluations from *questions of truth*.

This cannot, of course, be achieved once and for all, by means of a decree; yet it remains one of the enduring tasks of mutual scientific criticism. The purity of pure science is an ideal which is presumably unattainable; but it is an ideal for which we constantly fight—and should fight—by means of criticism.

In formulating this thesis I have said that it is practically impossible to achieve the elimination of extra-scientific values from scientific activity. The situation is similar with respect to objectivity: we cannot rob the scientist of his partisanship without also robbing him of his humanity, and we cannot suppress or destroy his value judgments without destroying him as a human being *and as a scientist*. Our motives and even our purely scientific ideals, including the ideal of a disinterested search for truth, are deeply anchored in extra-scientific and, in part, in religious evaluations. Thus the 'objective' or the 'value-free' scientist is hardly the ideal scientist. Without passion we can achieve nothing —certainly not in pure science. The phrase 'the passion for truth' is no mere metaphor.

It is, therefore, not just that objectivity and freedom from involvement with values ('value freedom') are unattainable in practice for the individual scientist, but rather that objectivity and freedom from such attachments are themselves *values*. And since value freedom itself is a value, the unconditional demand for freedom from any attachment to values is paradoxical. I do not regard this argument of mine as very important; but it should be noted that the paradox disappears quite of its own accord if we replace the demand for freedom from attachment to all values by the demand that it should be one of the tasks of scientific criticism to point out confusions of value and to separate purely scientific value problems of truth, relevance, simplicity, and so forth, from extra-scientific problems.

I have so far attempted to develop briefly the thesis that the method of science consists in the choice of interesting problems and in the criticism of our always tentative and provisional attempts to solve them. And I have attempted to show further, using as my examples two much discussed questions of method in the social sciences, that this critical approach to methods (as it might be called) leads to quite reasonable methodological results. But although I have said a few words about epistemology, about the logic of knowledge, and a few critical words about the methodology of the social sciences, I have made so far only a small positive contribution to my topic, the logic of the social sciences.

I do not wish to detain you by giving reasons why I consider it important to identify scientific method, at least in first approximation, with the critical method. Instead, I should like now to move straight to some purely logical questions and theses.

Fifteenth thesis: The most important function of pure deductive logic is that of an organon of criticism.

Sixteenth thesis: Deductive logic is the theory of the validity of logical inferences or of the relation of logical consequence. A necessary and decisive condition for the validity of a logical consequence is the following: if the premisses of a valid inference are *true* then the conclusion must also be *true*.

This can also be expressed as follows. Deductive logic is the theory of the transmission of truth from the premisses to the conclusion.

Seventeenth thesis: We can say: if all the premisses are true and the inference is valid, then the conclusion *must* also be true; and if, consequently, the conclusion is false in a valid inference, then it is not possible that all the premisses are true.

This trivial but decisively important result can also be expressed in the following manner: deductive logic is not only the theory of the *transmission of truth* from the premisses to the conclusion, but it is also, at the same time, the theory of the *retransmission of falsity* from the conclusion to at least one of the premisses.

Eighteenth thesis: In this way deductive logic becomes the theory of rational criticism. For all rational criticism takes the form of an attempt to show that unacceptable conclusions can be derived

THE LOGIC OF THE SOCIAL SCIENCES

from the assertion we are trying to criticize. If we are successful in deriving, logically, unacceptable conclusions from an assertion, then the assertion may be taken to be refuted.

Nineteenth thesis: In the sciences we work with theories, that is to say, with deductive systems. There are two reasons for this. First, a theory or a deductive system is an attempt at explanation, and consequently an attempt to solve a scientific problem—a problem of explanation. Secondly, a theory, that is, a deductive system, can be criticized rationally through its consequences. It is, then, a tentative solution which is subject to rational criticism.

So much for formal logic as the organon of criticism.

Two fundamental ideas which I have used here require a brief elucidation: the idea of truth and the idea of explanation.

Twentieth thesis: The concept of truth is indispensable for the critical approach developed here. What we criticize is, precisely, the claim that a theory is true. What we attempt to demonstrate as critics of a theory is, clearly, that this claim is unfounded: that it is false.

The important methodological idea that *we can learn from our mistakes* cannot be understood without the regulative idea of truth: any mistake simply consists in a failure to live up to the standard of objective truth, which is our regulative idea. We term a proposition 'true' if it corresponds to the facts, or if things are as described by the proposition. This is what is called the absolute or objective concept of truth which each of us constantly uses. The successful rehabilitation of this absolute concept of truth is one of the most important results of modern logic.

This remark hints at the fact that the concept of truth had been undermined. Indeed, this was the driving force which produced the dominant relativistic ideologies of our time.

This is the reason why I am inclined to describe the rehabilitation of the concept of truth by the logician and mathematician Alfred Tarski as the philosophically most important result of mathematical logic.

I cannot of course discuss this result here; I can merely say quite dogmatically that Tarski succeeded, in the simplest and most convincing manner, in explaining wherein the agreement of a statement with the facts lies. But this was precisely the task whose apparently hopeless difficulty led to sceptical relativism—with social consequences which I do not need to spell out here.

The second concept which I have used and which may require elucidation is the idea of explanation or, more precisely, the idea of a *causal explanation*.

A purely theoretical problem—a problem of pure science—always consists in the task of finding an explanation, the explanation of a fact or of a phenomenon or of a remarkable regularity or of a remarkable exception from a rule. That which we hope to explain can be called the explicandum. The tentative solution of the problem—that is, the explanation—always consists of a theory, a deductive system, which permits us to explain the explicandum by connecting it logically with other facts (the so-called initial conditions). A completely explicit explanation always consists in pointing out the logical derivation (or the derivability) of the explicandum from the theory strengthened by some initial conditions.

Thus the basic logical schema of every explanation consists of a (logical) deductive inference whose premisses consist of a theory and some initial conditions,* and whose conclusion is the explicandum.

This basic schema has a remarkable number of applications. One can point out with its aid, for example, the distinction between an *ad-hoc* hypothesis and an independently testable hypothesis. Further—and this might be of more interest to you—one can analyse logically, in a simple manner, the distinction between theoretical problems, historical problems, and problems of applied science. Another result is that the famous *distinction* between theoretical or nomothetic and historical or ideographic sciences can be logically justified—provided one understands here under the term 'science' not merely 'natural science' (as in English) but any attempt to solve a definite, logically distinguishable, set of problems.

So much for the elucidation of the logical concepts which I have employed so far.

The two concepts under discussion, that of truth, and that of explanation, make possible the logical analysis of further concepts which are perhaps even more important for the logic of knowledge or methodology. The first of these concepts is that of

---

* (Note to the English edition.) In the social sciences, the premises of the explanation usually consist of a situational model and of the so-called 'rationality principle'. These 'explanations of situational logic' are briefly discussed in my twenty-fifth and twenty-sixth theses, below.

approximation to the truth and the second that of the *explanatory power* or the *explanatory content* of a theory.

These two concepts are purely logical concepts since they may be defined with the help of the purely logical concepts of the truth of a statement and of the content of a statement—that is, the class of the logical consequences of a deductive theory.

Both are relative concepts. Although each statement is simply true or false, nevertheless *one* statement can represent a better approximation to the truth than *another* statement. This will be so, for example, if the one statement has 'more' true and 'less' false logical consequences than the other. (It is presupposed here that the true and the false sub-sets of the set of consequences of the two statements are comparable.) It can then easily be shown why we rightly assume that Newton's theory is a better approximation to the truth than Kepler's. Similarly it can be shown that the explanatory power of Newton's theory is greater than Kepler's.

Thus we analyse here logical ideas which underlie the appraisal of our theories, and which permit us to speak meaningfully of progress or regress with reference to scientific theories.

So much for the general logic of knowledge. Concerning, in particular, the logic of the social sciences, I should like to formulate some further theses.

Twenty-first thesis: There is no such thing as a purely observational science; there are only sciences in which we theorize (more or less consciously and critically). This of course also holds for the social sciences.

Twenty-second thesis: Psychology is a social science since our thoughts and actions largely depend upon social conditions. Ideas such as (a) imitation, (b) language, (c) the family, are obviously social ideas; and it is clear that the psychology of learning and thinking, and also, for instance, psychoanalysis, cannot exist without utilizing one or other of these social ideas. Thus psychology presupposes social ideas; which shows that it is impossible to explain society exclusively in psychological terms, or to reduce it to psychology. Thus we cannot look upon psychology as the basis of the social sciences.

What we cannot, in principle, explain psychologically, and what we must presuppose in every psychological explanation, is man's social environment. The task of describing this social environment (that is, with the help of explanatory theories since—as stated before—theory-free descriptions do not exist) is the fundamental task of social science. It might well be appropriate to allot this task to sociology. I therefore assume this in what follows.

Twenty-third thesis: Sociology is autonomous in the sense that, to a considerable extent, it can and must make itself independent of psychology. Apart from the dependence of psychology on social ideas (mentioned in my twenty-second thesis), this is due to the important fact that sociology is constantly faced with the task of explaining unintended and often undesired consequences of human action. An example: competition is a social phenomenon which is usually undesirable for the competitors, but which can and must be explained as a (usually inevitable) unintended consequence of (conscious and planned) actions of the competitors. Thus even though we may be able to explain psychologically some of the actions of the competitors, the social phenomenon of competition is a psychologically inexplicable consequence of these actions.

Twenty-fourth thesis: But sociology is also autonomous in a second sense; that is, we cannot reduce to psychology what has often been termed '*verstehende Soziologie*' (the sociology of [objective*] understanding).

Twenty-fifth thesis: The logical investigation of economics culminates in a result which can be applied to all social sciences. This result shows that there exists *a purely objective method* in the social sciences which may well be called the method of *objective* understanding, or situational logic. A social science orientated towards objective understanding or situational logic can be developed independently of all subjective or psychological ideas. Its method consists in analysing the social *situation* of acting men sufficiently to explain the action with the help of the situation, without any further help from psychology. Objective understanding consists in realizing that the action was objectively *appropriate to the situation*. In other words, the situation is analysed far enough for the elements which initially appeared to be psychological (such as wishes, motives, memories, and associations) to be transformed into elements of the situation. The man with certain wishes therefore becomes a man whose situation may be characterized by the fact that he pursues certain objective *aims*; and a man with certain memories or associations becomes a man

---

* (Note to the English edition.) For a fuller discussion (including some examples) of an *objective* theory of understanding, see my paper 'On the Theory of the Objective Mind', which forms chapter 4 of my book *Objective Knowledge*.

whose situation can be characterized by the fact that he is equipped objectively with certain theories or with certain information.

This enables us then to understand actions in an objective sense so that we can say: admittedly I have different aims and I hold different theories (from, say, Charlemagne): but had I been placed in his situation thus analysed—where the situation includes goals and knowledge—then I, and presumably you too, would have acted in a similar way to him. The method of situational analysis is certainly an individualistic method and yet it is certainly not a psychological one; for it excludes, in principle, all psychological elements and replaces them with objective situational elements. I usually call it the 'logic of the situation' or 'situational logic'.

Twenty-sixth thesis: The explanations of situational logic described here are rational, theoretical reconstructions. They are oversimplified and overschematized and consequently in general *false*. Nevertheless, they can possess a considerable truth content and they can, in the strictly logical sense, be good approximations to the truth, and better than certain other testable explanations. In this sense, the logical concept of approximation to the truth is indispensable for a social science using the method of situational analysis. Above all, however, situational analysis is rational, empirically criticizable, and capable of improvement. For we may, for instance, find a letter which shows that the knowledge at the disposal of Charlemagne was different from what we assumed in our analysis. By contrast, psychological or characterological hypotheses are hardly ever criticizable by rational arguments.

Twenty-seventh thesis: In general, situational logic assumes a physical world in which we act. This world contains, for example, physical resources which are at our disposal and about which we know something, and physical barriers about which we also know something (often not very much). Beyond this, situational logic must also assume a social world, populated by other people, about whose goals we know something (often not very much), and, furthermore, *social institutions*. These social institutions determine the peculiarly social character of our social environment. These social institutions consist of all the social realities of the social world, realities which to some extent correspond to the things of the physical world. A grocer's shop or a university institute or a police force or a law are, in this sense, social institutions. Church, state, and marriage are also social institutions, as are certain coercive customs like, for instance, harakiri in Japan. But in European society suicide is not a social institution in the sense in which I use the term, and in which I assert that the category is of importance.

That is my last thesis. What follows is a suggestion and a short concluding remark.

Suggestion: We may, perhaps, accept provisionally, as the fundamental problems of a purely theoretical sociology, the general situational logic of and the theory of institutions and traditions. This would include such problems as the following:

1. Institutions do not act; rather, only individuals act, in or for or through institutions. The general situational logic of these actions will be the theory of the quasi-actions of institutions.
2. We might construct a theory of intended or unintended institutional consequences of purposive action. This could also lead to a theory of the creation and development of institutions.

Finally, a further comment. I believe that epistemology is important not only for the individual sciences but also for philosophy, and that the religious and philosophical uneasiness of our time, which surely concerns us all, is, to a considerable degree, the result of uneasiness about the philosophy of human knowledge. Nietzsche called it the European nihilism and Benda the treason of the intellectuals. I should like to characterize it as a consequence of the Socratic discovery that we know nothing; that is, that we can never justify our theories rationally. But this important discovery which has produced, amongst many other malaises, the malaise of existentialism, is only half a discovery; and nihilism can be overcome. For although we cannot justify our theories rationally and cannot even prove that they are probable, we can criticize them rationally. And we can often distinguish better from worse theories.

But this was known, even before Socrates, to Xenophanes who told us*:

The gods did not reveal from the beginning,
All things to us; but in the course of time,
Through seeking we may learn, and know things better . . .

---

* (Note to the English edition.) Cf. my *Conjectures and Refutations*, p. 152. (The translation is mine.)

THEODOR W. ADORNO

ON THE LOGIC OF
THE SOCIAL SCIENCES

Second Contribution

Generally, the discussant has to choose between behaving like a
pedant or a parasite. First of all, I should like to thank Popper
for freeing me from such an embarrassing situation. I can take
up what he has said without having to begin with elementary
matters, but also without having to adhere so closely to the text
of his paper, that I would be dependent upon it. With authors of
so diverse intellectual origins, this is no less astonishing than are
the numerous substantive points of agreement. Often, I do not
need to oppose his theses with counter-theses, but instead I can
take up what he has said and attempt to reflect on it further.
However, I interpret the concept of logic more broadly than
Popper does. I understand this concept as the concrete mode of
procedure of sociology rather than general rules of thought, of
deduction. Here, I do not wish to touch upon the problems of
the latter in sociology.

Instead, I shall commence with Popper's distinction between
the abundance of knowledge and boundless ignorance. It is
plausible enough, certainly in sociology. At any rate, the latter is
continually admonished for not so far having produced a corpus
of acknowledged laws comparable to that of the natural sciences.
But this distinction contains a dubious potential, that of a current
view which Popper surely does not have in mind. According to
this view, sociology, on account of its conspicuous retardedness
in relation to the exact sciences, should initially content itself
with collecting facts and elucidating methods before it raises the
claim to reliable and, at the same time, relevant knowledge.
Theoretical reflections on society and its structure are then
frequently tabooed as an impermissible anticipation of the future.
But if one views sociology as beginning with Saint-Simon rather

than with its godfather Comte then it is more than 160 years old. It should no longer flirt bashfully with its youth. What appears as temporary ignorance is not to be simply replaced in progressive research and methodology by that characterized in such an awkward and inappropriate term as synthesis. Rather, reality [*die Sache*] opposes the clean, systematic unity of assembled statements. I do not have in mind the traditional distinctions between the natural and cultural sciences [*Geisteswissenschaften*], such as Rickert's distinction between the nomothetic and idiographic method, which Popper views more positively than I do. But the cognitive ideal of the consistent, preferably simple, mathematically elegant explanation falls down where reality itself, society, is neither consistent, nor simple, nor neutrally left to the discretion of categorial formulation. Rather, on the contrary, it is anticipated by its object as the categorial system of discursive logic. Society is full of contradictions and yet determinable; rational and irrational in one, a system and yet fragmented; blind nature and yet mediated by consciousness. The sociological mode of procedure must bow to this. Otherwise, out of puristic zeal to avoid contradiction, it will fall into the most fatal contradiction of all, namely, that existing between its own structure and that of its object. Society does not elude rational knowledge; in so far as its contradictions and their preconditions are intelligible, they cannot be conjured away by means of intellectual postulates abstracted from a material which is, as it were, indifferent with regard to knowledge—a material which offers no resistance to scientific activities that usually accommodate themselves to cognitive consciousness. Social-scientific activity is permanently threatened by the fact that, out of its love for clarity and exactness, it could fail to apprehend that which it intends to apprehend. Popper objects to the cliché that knowledge passes through a series of stages from observation to the ordering, processing and systematization of its materials. This cliché is so absurd in sociology because the latter does not have unqualified data at its disposal but only such data as are structured through the context of societal totality. To a large extent, the alleged sociological ignorance merely signifies the divergence between society as an object and traditional method. It can therefore hardly be outstripped by a knowledge which denies the structure of its object in deference to its own methodology. On the other hand, however—and undoubtedly Popper would also concede

Frisby/Adey's defence pf the CT's use of 'positivism'
will not hold up to sustained examination. F/A want
to acknowledge that, though used loosây, the CT's
use of 'positivism' is o.k. 1) Insofar as the
opposnent is Popper, cannot charge with being a
positivist, unless carefully specify terms; 2) Further
positivism has various uses. Comteian, LE,
methodological, plus the innumerable loose uses which
tie it to a) anti-metaphysics, b) empiricism (or
'vulgar empiricism'), c) fact-value distinction, and
a host of other issues.

Frisby/Adey's defence of the CT's use of 'positivism'
will not hold up to sustained examination. I/We want
to acknowledge that, though used loosely, the CT's
use of 'positivism' is o.k. (1 Insofar as the
opponent is Popper, cannot charge with being a
positivist, unless carefully specify terms; (2 Further
positivism has various uses. Comtetan. If,
methodological, plus the innumerable loose uses which
tie it to a) anti-metaphysics, b) empiricism (or
'vulgar empiricism'), c) fact-value distinction, and
a host of other issues.

this—the usual empirical asceticism with regard to theory cannot be sustained. Without the anticipation of that structural moment of the whole, which in individual observations can hardly ever be adequately realized, no individual observation would find its relative place. This is not to advocate anything similar to the tendency in cultural anthropology to superimpose upon Western civilization the centralistic and total character of some primitive societies by means of a selected co-ordinate system. One may even cherish as few illusions as I do about its gravitation towards total forms and about the decline of the individual, but the differences between a pre- and post-individual society are still decisive. In the democratically governed countries of industrial societies, totality is a category of mediation, not one of immediate domination and subjugation. This implies that in industrial market societies by no means everything pertaining to society can simply be deduced from its principle. Such societies contain within themselves countless non-capitalist enclaves. At issue here is whether, in order to perpetuate itself under the present relations of production, it necessarily needs such enclaves as that of the family. Their specific irrationality compliments, as it were, that of the structure as a whole. Societal totality does not lead a life of its own over and above that which it unites and of which it, in its turn, is composed. It produces and reproduces itself through its individual moments. Many of these moments preserve a relative independence which primitive-total societies either do not know or do not tolerate. This totality can no more be detached from life, from the co-operation and the antagonism of its elements than can an element be understood merely as it functions without insight into the whole which has its source [*Wesen*] in the motion of the individual himself. System and individual entity are reciprocal and can only be apprehended in their reciprocity. Even those enclaves, survivals from previous societies, the favourites of a sociology which desires to unburden itself of the concept of society—as it might of an all too spectacular philosopheme—become what they are only in relation to the dominant totality from which they deviate. This is presumably underestimated in the present most popular sociological conception, that of middle-range theory.

In opposition to the view held since Comte, Popper advocates the priority of problems, of the tension between knowledge and ignorance. I am in agreement with every criticism Popper makes

of the false transposition of natural scientific methods, of the 'misguided and erroneous methodological . . . naturalism or scientism'.
If he accuses his social anthropologist of extracting himself from
the problem of truth or falsehood by means of the allegedly
greater objectivity of someone who observes social phenomena
from outside, then this is surely good Hegel. In the preface to the
Phenomenology of Mind, Hegel scorns those who only stand above
things because they do not stand amidst things. I hope that König
will not chide me and will not criticize the discussion with Popper
for being philosophy and not sociology. It seems to me worth
mentioning that a scholar, for whom dialectics is anathema, finds
himself reduced to formulations which reside in dialectical
thought. Moreover, the problems of social anthropology examined by Popper are presumably closely associated with a method
rendered independent of reality. Like Veblen's theory of a barbaric
culture, a comparison of the frictionless mores of a late capitalist
society with the rights of the Trobrianders, who by now have
presumably been overstudied, certainly has its merits. Yet the
alleged freedom in the choice of a system of co-ordinates is transformed into a falsification of the object, since for every member of
the modern state the fact that he belongs to the latter's economic
system means, in real terms, far more than the finest analogies
with totem and taboo.

In my agreement with Popper's critique of scientism, and with
his thesis concerning the primacy of the problem, I must perhaps
go further than he would approve. For the object of sociology
itself, society, which keeps itself and its members alive but
simultaneously threatens them with ruin, is a problem in an
emphatic sense. This means, however, that the problems of
sociology do not constantly arise through the discovery 'that
something is not in order with our supposed knowledge; . . . from
the discovery of an apparent contradiction between our supposed
knowledge and the facts'. The contradiction must not, as Popper
at least presumes here, be a merely 'supposed' contradiction
between subject and object, which would have to be imputed to
the subject alone as a deficiency of judgment. Instead, the contradiction can, in very real terms, have its place in reality and can in
no way be removed by increased knowledge and clearer formulation. The oldest sociological model of such a contradiction which
necessarily develops in reality is the now-famous section 243 in
Hegel's *Philosophy of Right*: 'The amassing of wealth is intensified

by generalizing (a) the linkage of men by their needs, and (b) the methods of preparing and distributing the means to satisfy these needs, because it is from this double process of generalization that the largest profits are derived. That is one side of the picture. The other side is the subdivision and restriction of particular jobs. This results in the dependence and distress of the class tied to work of that sort.'[1] It would be easy to accuse me of equivocation, namely, that for Popper a problem is something merely epistemological and for me, at the same time, it is something practical—in the last instance, even a problematic condition of the world. But we are concerned here with the legitimacy of precisely this distinction. One would fetishize science if one radically separated its immanent problems from the real ones, which are weakly reflected in its formalisms. No doctrine of logical absolutism, Tarski's no more than formerly Husserl's, would be in a position to decree that the facts obey logical principles which derive their claim to validity from a purgation of all that pertains to reality. I must content myself with a reference to the critique of logical absolutism in *Metakritik der Erkenntnistheorie*[2] which is there associated with a critique of sociological relativism, in which respect I am in agreement with Popper. The conception of the contradictory nature of societal reality does not, however, sabotage knowledge of it and expose it to the merely fortuitous. Such knowledge is guaranteed by the possibility of grasping the contradiction as necessary and thus extending rationality to it.

Methods do not rest upon methodological ideals but rather upon reality. Popper implicitly acknowledges this in the thesis concerning the priority of the problem. When he establishes that the quality of social scientific achievement stands in an exact relationship to the significance or to the interest of its problems, then unquestionably one can detect here the awareness of an irrelevance to which countless sociological investigations are condemned in that they follow the primacy of the method and not that of the object. They either wish to develop methods further for their own sake or, from the outset, they so select objects that they can be treated with already available methods. When Popper talks about significance or interest one can sense the gravity of the

---

[1] Hegel, WW7, *Grundlinien der Philosophie des Rechts*, ed. Glockner (Stuttgart, 1927 onwards), p. 318. English trans. T. M. Knox, *Hegel's Philosophy of Right* (Oxford/New York, 1969), pp. 149-50.
[2] T. W. Adorno, *Zur Metakritik der Erkenntnistheorie* (Stuttgart, 1956).

matter to be dealt with. It would only have to be qualified by the fact that it is not always possible to judge a priori the relevance of objects. Where the categorical network is so closely woven that much of that which lies beneath is concealed by conventions of opinion, including scientific opinion, then eccentric phenomena which have not yet been incorporated by this network at times, take on an unexpected gravity. Insight into their composition also throws light upon what counts as the core domain but which often is not. This scientific-theoretical motive was surely involved in Freud's decision to concern himself with the 'fragments of the world of appearance' [*Abhub der Erscheinungswelt*]. Similarly, it proved to be fruitful in Simmel's sociology when, mistrustful of the systematic totality, he immersed himself in such social specifics as the stranger or the actor. Nor would one be able to dogmatize about the demand for problem relevancy; to a large extent, the selection of research objects is legitimated by what the sociologist can read from the object which he has selected. This should not, however, provide an excuse for the countless projects merely carried out for the good of one's academic career, in which the irrelevance of the object happily combines with the pedestrian mentality of the research technician.

I should like, however, to urge a certain caution concerning the attributes which Popper ascribes, together with the relevance of the problem, to the true method. Honesty—or, in other words, that one does not cheat, that one expresses what has been apprehended without tactical considerations—ought to be a matter of course. In the actual course of science, however, this norm is frequently terroristically misused. Completely abandoning oneself to reality then implies that one confronts reality with nothing of oneself but instead one merely reduces oneself to a piece of registering apparatus. The renunciation of fantasy or the lack of productivity is passed off as scientific ethos. One should not forget what Cantril and Allport have contributed to the critique of the ideal of sincerity in America. Even in the sciences, honesty is frequently attributed to the person who thinks what everyone thinks, devoid of the supposed vanity of desiring to perceive something special and, for this reason, prepared to bleat sheep-like with the others. Similarly, directness and simplicity are not unquestionable ideals when the matter [*Sache*] is complex. The replies of common sense derive their categories to such an extent from that which immediately exists that they tend to strengthen its opacity instead of penetrating it. As far as the directness is concerned, the path along which one approaches knowledge can hardly be anticipated. In view of the present state of sociology, I would place, from amongst the criteria of scientific quality mentioned by Popper, the greatest emphasis upon the boldness and originality [*Eigenart*] of the suggested solution, which naturally, in its turn, has to be constantly criticized. In the last instance, the category of the problem should not be hypostatized. Anyone who checks his own work in an unbiased manner will encounter a state of affairs which only the taboos of alleged presuppositionlessness make it difficult to admit. It is not uncommon that one has solutions; something suddenly occurs to one and one subsequently constructs the question. But this is not fortuitous. The priority of society as that of something all-encompassing and consolidated above its individual manifestations is expressed in societal knowledge by means of insights which stem from the concept of society and which are only transformed into individual sociological problems through the subsequent confrontation of what was anticipated with the particular material. Expressed in more general terms, the epistemologies, as they were developed and handed down relatively independently by the great philosophical tradition since Bacon and Descartes, are conceived from above even by the empiricists. They have frequently remained inappropriate to the living tradition of knowledge; they have trimmed the latter in accordance with a conception of science, as an inductive or deductive continuum, which is alien and external to this living tradition. By no means the last of the necessary tasks of epistemology—and Bergson sensed this—would be to reflect upon the actual process of cognition instead of describing in advance the cognitive achievement in accordance with a logical or scientific model to which, in truth, productive knowledge in no way corresponds.

In Popper's categorial framework, the concept of a problem is associated with that of a solution. Solutions are to be suggested and criticized. With the key nature of criticism, a decisive point is reached in opposition to the primitive doctrine of observation, a doctrine estranged from knowledge. Sociological knowledge is, indeed, criticism. But crucial nuances are involved here, such as how the decisive distinctions between scientific positions are often more likely to be found in the nuance than they are to be expressed in grandiose concepts expressive of a view of life [*Weltanschauung*].

According to Popper, if an attempted solution is not accessible to factual criticism, then it will be excluded as unscientific for this reason even if, perhaps, only temporarily. This is, to say the least, ambiguous. If such criticism implies reduction to so-called facts, the complete redemption of thought through what is observed, then this desideratum would reduce thought to hypothesis and would rob sociology of that moment of anticipation which essentially belongs to it. There are sociological theorems which, as insights into the mechanisms of society which operate behind the façade, in principle, even for societal reasons, contradict appearances to such an extent that they cannot be adequately criticized through the latter. Criticism of them is incumbent upon systematic theory, upon further reflection but not, for instance, upon the confrontation with protocol statements. (Popper, incidentally, does not formulate it this way either.) For this reason, facts in society are not the last thing to which knowledge might attach itself, since they themselves are mediated through society. Not all theorems are hypotheses; theory is the *telos* not the vehicle of sociology.

One could also enlarge upon the equation of criticism and the attempt at refutation. Refutation is only fruitful as immanent criticism. Hegel already knew that. The second volume of the larger *Logic* provides statements on the 'judgment of the notion' which must simultaneously outweigh most of what has been proclaimed about values since then: '. . . the predicates *good, bad, true, beautiful, correct,* etc. express that the thing is *measured* against its universal *Notion* as the simply presupposed *ought-to-be* and is, or is not, in *agreement* with it.'[3] Viewed from without, everything and nothing is refutable. Scepticism is appropriate in discussion. It testifies to a confidence in organized science as an instance of truth confronted with which the sociologist should show reserve. In the face of scientific thought control, whose preconditions sociology itself names, it is particularly important that Popper grants the category of criticism a central position. The critical impulse is at one with the resistance to the rigid conformity of each dominant opinion. This motive also occurs in Popper. In his twelfth thesis, he strictly equates scientific objectivity with the critical tradition which, 'despite resistance, often makes it possible

[3] Hegel, WW5, *Wissenschaft der Logik*, part 2, ed. Glockner, loc. cit., pp. 110f. English trans. A. V. Miller, *Hegel's Science of Logic* (London/New York, 1969), pp. 657f.

to criticize a dominant dogma'. Like Dewey and previously Hegel, he appeals for open, unfixed, unreified thought. An experimental, not to say a playful, moment is unavoidable in such thought. I would hesitate, however, both to equate it simply with the concept of 'attempted solution' [*Lösungsversuch*] and even to adopt the maxim of trial and error. In the climate from which the latter stems, the phrase 'attempted solution' is ambiguous. It is precisely this phrase which carries with it natural-scientific associations and is directed against the independence of every thought which cannot be tested. But some thoughts and, in the last instance, the essential ones recoil from tests and yet they have a truth content—Popper agrees even with this. Probably no experiment could convincingly demonstrate the dependence of each social phenomenon on the totality for the whole which preforms the tangible phenomena can never itself be reduced to particular experimental arrangements. Nevertheless, the dependence of that which can be socially observed upon the total structure is, in reality, more valid than any findings which can be irrefutably verified in the particular and this dependence is anything but a mere figment of the imagination. If, in the last analysis, one does not wish to confuse sociology with natural-scientific models, then the concept of the experiment must also extend to the thought which, satiated with the force of experience, is projected beyond the latter in order to comprehend it. In sociology, in contrast to the situation in psychology, experiments in the narrower sense are, in any case, mainly unproductive. The speculative moment is not a necessity of societal knowledge but is, rather, an indispensable moment of it even though idealist philosophy, which once glorified speculation, may be a thing of the past. To the above, one might add that criticism and the solution can in no way be separated from one another. Solutions are at times primary and direct; they instigate the criticism through which they are mediated in order to advance the process of knowledge. Above all, however, the construct [*Figur*] of criticism, if it fulfils its latent possibilities, can, conversely, already imply the solution; the latter hardly ever appears from without. It was to this that the philosophical concept of determinate negation referred, a concept which is in no way alien to Popper although he is in no way enamoured of Hegel. Insofar as he identifies the objectivity of science with the critical method, he raises the latter to the organon of truth. No dialectician today would demand more. From this, however, I would draw a consequence which is not mentioned in Popper's paper, and I am not sure whether he would accept it. He calls his standpoint, in a very un-Kantian sense, 'the critical approach' [*Kritizistisch*]. Yet, if one takes the dependency of the method upon reality [*Sache*] as seriously as is inherent in some of Popper's definitions, such as in that of relevance and interest as measures for societal knowledge, then the critical work of sociology could not be restricted to self-criticism—to reflection upon its statements, theorems, conceptual apparatus and methods. It is, at the same time, a critique of the object upon which, in fact, all these subjectively localized moments are dependent—subjectively, that is, in the sense of subjects united for the purpose of organized science. No matter how instrumentally the moments of the mode of procedure are defined, their adequacy for the object is still always demanded, even if this is concealed. Procedures are unproductive when they are lacking in such adequacy. In the method, the object [*Sache*] must be treated in accord with its significance and importance, otherwise even the most polished method is bad. This involves no less than that, in the very form of the theory, that of the object must appear. The content of the theorem which is to be criticized, decides when the critique of sociological categories is only that of the method, and when the discrepancy between concept and object is to the latter's detriment since it claims to be that which it is not. The critical path is not merely formal but also material. If its concepts are to be true, critical sociology is, according to its own idea, necessarily also a critique of society, as Horkheimer developed it in his work on traditional and critical theory. Kant's critical philosophy also contained something of this. The arguments he advanced against scientific judgments on God, freedom and immortality were in opposition to a situation in which, long after these ideas had lost their theological binding force, people endeavoured to preserve them for rationality by surreptitious means. The Kantian term, 'subreption' confronts the apologists' lie in its intellectual error. Critical philosophy [*Kritizismus*] was militant enlightenment. The critical impulse, however, which halts before reality and is satisfied with work in itself, would, in comparison, hardly be an advanced form of enlightenment. By curtailing the motives of enlightenment, it would itself also be retarded, as is so convincingly demonstrated by the comparison of administrative research with critical theories of societies. It is time that sociology resisted such atrophy which is entrenched behind the intangible method. For, knowledge lives in relation to that which it is not, in relation to its other. This relation will not of itself suffice as long as it prevails merely indirectly in critical self-reflection; it must become a critique of the sociological object. If social science—and, for the moment, I do not prejudge the content of such statements—on the one hand, takes the concept of a liberal society as implying freedom and equality and, on the other hand, disputes, in principle, the truth-content of these categories under liberalism—in view of the inequality of the social power which determines the relations between people—then these are not logical contradictions which could be eliminated by means of more sophisticated definitions, nor are they subsequently emergent empirical restrictions or differentiations of a provisional definition, but rather, they are the structural constitution of society itself. Thus criticism does not merely mean the reformulation of contradictory statements for the sake of consistency in the scientific realm. Such logicity, by shifting the real substance, can become false. I should like to add that this change in approach likewise affects the conceptual means of sociological knowledge. A critical theory of society guides the permanent self-criticism of sociological knowledge into another dimension. I would simply recall what I implied about naïve trust in organized social science as a guarantor of truth.

But all this presupposes the distinction between truth and false-hood to which Popper so strictly adheres. As a critic of sceptical relativism, he argues polemically against the sociology of knowl-edge and, in particular, against that of Pareto and Mannheim just as sharply as I have always done. But the so-called total concept of ideology, and the elimination of the distinction between true and untrue, does not correspond to the classical doctrine of ideologies, if one might call it that. It represents a degenerate form of the latter. It allies itself with the attempt to blunt the critical edge of that doctrine and to neutralize it to a branch in the domain of science. Once ideology was called socially necessary illusion. Then the critique of ideology was under obligation to provide concrete proof of the falsehood of a theorem or of a doctrine; the mere mistrust of ideology, as Mannheim called it, was not sufficient. Marx, in keeping with Hegel, would have ridiculed it as abstract negation. The deduction of ideologies from societal necessity has not weakened judgment upon their falseness. It sought to submit their derivation from structural laws such as that of the fetish character of commodities, which denotes the πρῶτον ψεῦδος, to

the very standard of scientific objectivity which even Popper
applies. Even the now customary reference to superstructure and
base renders this trite. Whilst the sociology of knowledge, which
dissolves the distinction between true and false consciousness,
believes that it is advancing the cause of scientific objectivity, it
has, through such dissolution, reverted to a pre-Marxian conception of science—a conception which Marx understood in a fully
objective sense. Only through embellishment and neologisms
such as perspectivism, and not through material determinations
[*sachhaltige Bestimmungen*], can the total concept of ideology
distance itself from the empty rhetorical world-view of vulgar
relativism. For this reason, one has the open or concealed subjectivism of the sociology of knowledge which Popper rightly
denounces, and in criticizing which the great philosophical
tradition is at one with concrete scientific work. The latter has
never seriously allowed itself to be misled by the general stipulation of the relativity of all human knowledge. When Popper
criticizes the fact that the objectivity of science is confused with
the objectivity of the scientist, he seizes upon the concept of
ideology which has been degraded to a total one, but does not
apprehend its authentic conception. The latter implied the
objective determination of false consciousness, a determination
largely independent of the individual subjects, and of their much-
quoted standpoints, and verifiable in the analysis of the social
structure; a notion, incidentally, which dates back to Helvétius, if
not to Bacon. The zealous concern for the standpoint-boundedness
[*Standortgebundenheit*] of individual thinkers emanates from the
powerlessness to hold fast the insight gained into the objective
distortion of truth. It has little to do with the thinkers and nothing
at all with their psychology. In short, I am in agreement with
Popper's critique of the sociology of knowledge; but it also is the
undiluted doctrine of ideology.

Popper, like Max Weber before him in his famous essay, con-
nects the question of social-scientific objectivity with that of value
freedom. It has not escaped him that this category, which has been
dogmatized in the meantime and which comes to terms all too
well with pragmatistic scientific activity, must be thought out
anew. The disjunction between objectivity and value is not so
secure as it seems in Max Weber's writings. In his texts, it is, however, more qualified than his slogan might lead one to expect.
When Popper calls the demand for unconditional value freedom

paradoxical, since scientific objectivity and value freedom are themselves values, this insight is hardly as unimportant as Popper regards it. One might draw philosophical-scientific consequences from it. Popper underlines the fact that the scientist's evaluations could not be prohibited or destroyed without destroying him as a human being and also as a scientist. This, however, is to say more than merely something about the practice of knowledge; 'destroying him . . . as a scientist' involves the objective concept of science as such. The separation of evaluative and value-free behaviour is false in so far as value, and thus value freedom, are reifications; correct, in so far as the behaviour of the mind cannot extricate itself at will from the state of reification. What is referred to as the problem of value can only be constituted in a phase in which means and ends are split asunder for the sake of a frictionless domination of nature in which the rationality of means advances with a constant or, if possible, increasing irrationality of ends. Kant and Hegel did not use the concept of value already current in political economy. Presumably it first entered philosophical terminology with Lotze; Kant's distinction between dignity and price in practical reason would be incompatible with it. The concept of value is formed in the exchange relationship, a being for the other. In a society in which every relationship has become an exchange relationship, has become fungible—and the denial of truth which Popper observes reveals the same state of affairs—this 'for the other' has been magically transformed [*verhext*] into an 'in itself', into something substantial. As such, it then became false and was suited to fill the sensitive vacuum by following the caprice of dominant interests. What was subsequently sanctioned as a value does not operate externally to the object, does not oppose it χωρίς, but rather is immanent to it. Reality, the object of societal knowledge, can no more be imperative-free [*Sollensfreies*] or merely existent [*Daseiendes*]—it only becomes the latter through the disections of abstraction—than can the values be nailed into a firmament of ideas. The judgment upon an entity [*Sache*], which certainly requires subjective spontaneity, is always simultaneously prescribed by the entity and is not exhausted in subjectively ir-rational decision, as it is in Weber's conception. Every judgment is, in the language of philosophy, a judgment of the entity upon itself; the judgment recalls the fragmentariness of the entity. It is constituted, however, in each relation to that whole which is contained in it, without being immediately given, without being facticity; this is the intention of the statement that the entity must be measured against its concept. The whole problem of value, which sociology and other disciplines haul about with them like a ballast, is accordingly falsely posed. Scientific awareness of society, which sets itself up as value-free, fails to apprehend reality just as much as one which appeals to more or less preordained and arbitrarily established values. If one assents to the alternative, then one becomes involved in antinomies. Even positivism was not able to extricate itself from them. Durkheim, whose *chosisme* outstripped Weber in positivist sentiments—the latter himself had his *thema probandum* in the sociology of religion—did not recognize value freedom. Popper pays his tribute to the antinomy in so far as, on the one hand, he rejects the separation of value and knowledge but, on the other hand, desires that the self-reflection of knowledge become aware of its implicit values; that is, he desires that self-reflection does not falsify its truth content in order to prove something. Both desiderata are legitimate. But the awareness of this antimony should be incorporated into sociology itself. The dichotomy of what is [*Sein*] and what should be [*Sollen*] is as false as it is historically compelling and, for this reason, it cannot be ignored. It only achieves an insight into its own inevitability through societal critique. In actual fact, value-free behaviour is prohibited not merely psychologically but also substantively. Society, the knowledge of which is ultimately the aim of sociology if it is to be more than a mere technique, can only crystallize at all around a conception of the just society. The latter, however, is not to be contrasted with existing society in an abstract manner, simply as an ostensible value, but rather it arises from criticism, that is, from society's awareness of its contradictions and its necessity. When Popper says, 'For although we cannot justify our theories rationally and cannot even prove that they are probable, we can criticize them rationally', then this is no less true for society than for theories about society. The result would be a form of behaviour which neither doggedly entrenches itself in a value freedom that blinds one to the essential interest of sociology, nor permits itself to be guided by abstract and static value dogmatism.

Popper sees through the latent subjectivism of a value-free sociology of knowledge, which is especially proud of its scientistic lack of prejudice, and consequently he attacks sociological psychologism. Here too, I share his view and may perhaps draw attention to my essay in the Horkheimer Festschrift in which the discontinuity of the two disciplines is developed, both of which are subsumed under the vague encompassing concept of the science of man. But the motives which lead Popper and myself to the same result differ. The division between man and social environment seems to me to be somewhat external, much too orientated towards the existing map of the sciences, whose hypostatization Popper basically rejects. The human subjects, whom psychology pledges itself to examine, are not merely, as it were, influenced by society but are in their innermost core formed by it. The substratum of a human being in himself who might resist the environment—and this has been resuscitated in existentialism—would remain an empty abstraction. On the contrary, the socially active environment, no matter how indirectly and imperceptibly, is produced by human beings, by organized society. Despite this, psychology may not be regarded as the basic science of the social sciences. I would simply point out that the form of socialization [*Vergesellschaftung*], in English termed 'institutions', has, on account of its immanent dynamics, made itself independent of real people and their psychology. It has confronted them as something so alien, and yet so overpowering, that reduction to primary modes of human behaviour, in the manner in which psychology studies them, cannot even be equated either with typical behaviour patterns which can be plausibly generalized or with societal processes which take place over people's heads. Nevertheless, I would not conclude from the priority of society over psychology that there is such a radical independence of the two sciences as Popper seems to believe. Society is a total process in which human beings surrounded, guided and formed by objectivity do, in turn, act back upon society; psychology, for its part, can no more be absorbed into sociology than can the individual being be absorbed into its biological species and its natural history. Certainly, fascism cannot be explained in social-psychological terms, but the 'Authoritarian Personality' has occasionally been misunderstood as just such an attempt. But if the authoritarian character type had not been so widespread for reasons which, in their turn, are sociologically intelligible, then fascism, at any rate, would not have found its mass basis, without which it would not have achieved power in a society like that of the Weimar democracy. The autonomy of social processes is itself not an 'in itself' but rather it is grounded in reification; even the processes estranged from human beings remain human. For this reason, the boundary between the two sciences is no more absolute that that between sociology and economics, or sociology and history. Insight into society as a totality also implies that all the moments which are active in this totality, and in no way perfectly reducible one to another, must be incorporated in knowledge; it cannot permit itself to be terrorized by the academic division of labour. The priority of what is societal over what is individual is explained in reality itself, that is, that powerlessness of the individual in the face of society which for Durkheim was precisely the criterion for the *faits sociaux*. The self-reflection of sociology, however, must be on guard against its historical-scientific inheritance which induces one to overstrain the autarchy of the recent science, still not accepted in Europe as an equal by the *universitas literarum*.

In our correspondence which preceded the formulation of my reply, Popper characterized the difference in our positions by saying that he believed that we live in the best world which ever existed and that I did not believe it. As far as he is concerned, he presumably exaggerated a little for the sake of sharpening the discussion. Comparisons between the degree of badness in societies of various epochs are precarious. I find it hard to assume that no society is claimed to have been better than that which gave birth to Auschwitz and, to this extent, Popper has unquestionably given a correct characterization of my view. But I do not regard the difference as one of mere standpoint but rather as determinable. Both of us surely adopt an equally negative attitude towards a philosophy based on standpoints and, consequently, to a sociology based on standpoints. The experience of the contradictory character of societal reality is not an arbitrary starting point but rather the motive which first constitutes the possibility of sociology as such. In Popper's language, only the person who can conceptualize a different society from the existing one can experience it as a problem. Only through that which it is not, will it reveal itself as that which it is and this would presumably be fundamental in a sociology which, unlike the majority of its projects, would not be satisfied with ends laid down by public and private administration. Perhaps we find here precisely the reason why, in sociology, as the finding of an individual science, society has no place. If in Comte, the outline of a new discipline was born out of the desire to protect the productive tendencies of his age, the unleashing of productive forces, that is, from the destructive potential which was emerging in them at that time, then subsequently nothing has altered in this original situation unless it has become more extreme, in which case sociology should take this into account. The arch-positivist Comte was aware of the antagonistic character of society as the decisive aspect which the development of later positivism desired to conjure away as metaphysical speculation. Hence the follies of his late phase which, in turn, demonstrated how much societal reality scorns the aspirations of those whose profession it is to apprehend it. In the meantime, the crisis, to which sociology must prove itself equal, is no longer that of bourgeois order alone but rather it literally threatens the physical continuance of society as a whole. In view of the nakedly emergent coercive force of relations, Comte's hope that sociology might guide social force reveals itself as naïve except when it provides plans for totalitarian rulers. Sociology's abandonment of a critical theory of society is resignatory: one no longer dares to conceive of the whole since one must despair of changing it. But if sociology then desired to commit itself to the apprehension of facts and figures in the service of that which exists, then such progress under conditions of unfreedom would increasingly detract from the detailed insights through which sociology thinks it triumphs over theory and condemn them completely to irrelevance. Popper concluded his paper with a quotation from Xenophanes which is symptomatic of the fact that neither of us is satisfied with the separation of philosophy and sociology, a separation which nowadays ensures the sociology's peace of mind. But Xenophanes too, despite his Eleatic ontology, represents the enlightenment. It is not without good reason that, even in him, one can find an idea which recurs in Anatole France, namely, that if an animal species could conceive of a deity it would be in its own image. Criticism of this type has been handed down by the entire European enlightenment from antiquity onwards. Today its inheritance has fallen to a great extent to social science. Criticism implies demythologization. This, however, is no mere theoretical concept nor one of indiscriminate iconoclasm which, with the distinction between true and untrue, would also destroy the distinction between justice and injustice. Whatever enlightenment achieves in the form of disenchantment it must necessarily desire to liberate human beings from such spells—formerly from that of the demons, nowadays from the spell which human relations exert

over them. An enlightenment which forgets this, which disinterestedly takes the spell as given and exhausts itself in the
production of utilizable conceptual apparatuses sabotages itself,
along with the very concept of truth with which Popper confronts
the sociology of knowledge. The just organization of society is
incorporated in the emphatic concept of truth without being filled
out as an image of the future. The *reductio ad hominem* which
inspires all critical enlightenment is substantiated in the human
being who would first have to be produced in a society which
was master of itself. In contemporary society, however, its sole
indicator is the socially untrue.

RALF DAHRENDORF

REMARKS ON THE DISCUSSION OF THE PAPERS BY KARL R. POPPER AND THEODOR W. ADORNO

1

The topic of the two main papers—the Logic of the Social Sciences—was selected by the planners of the Tübingen working session of the German Sociological Association with a definite intention. It is no secret that manifold differences not only in research orientation but also in theoretical position and, beyond this, differences in basic moral and political attitudes, divide the present generation of university teachers of sociology in Germany. After several discussions in recent years, it seemed as if a discussion of the logical-scientific foundations of sociology could be an appropriate way in which to make the existing differences emerge more clearly and thereby render them fruitful for research. The Tübingen working session did not however confirm this assumption. Although both symposiasts did not hesitate, in their expositions, to adopt unequivocally a definite position, the discussion generally lacked the intensity that would have been appropriate to the actual differences in views. In addition, most of the contributions to the discussion adhered so strictly to the narrow confines of the topic that the underlying moral and political positions were not expressed very clearly. Principally, then, one can record a certain increase in precision in the views of the two speakers as a result of the discussion. Consequently, this must also remain central to this report on the discussion.

2

Several contributors to the discussion regretted the lack of tension between the symposiasts' papers. At times, it could indeed have appeared, astonishingly enough, as if Popper and Adorno were in agreement. But the irony of such points of agreement could hardly escape the attentive listener. The discussion provided a series of amusing instances of similarities in the formulations of the symposiasts behind which profound differences in the matters discussed were hidden.

Thus, Popper and Adorno were in complete agreement that the attempt at a sharp demarcation between sociology and philosophy would have detrimental effects for both. Adorno formulated this forcefully, 'If one draws the dividing line in the way which has constantly been suggested *ad nauseam* then this dividing line is transformed—you will forgive me the false image —into a trench in which the fundamental interest of both disciplines disappears.' Nevertheless, the symposiasts were wise in not talking about what can or should be thought or said at the boundary of the disciplines (if such a boundary is even conceivable). But Georg Heinrich Weippert was surely correct in drawing attention to the 'extraordinary difference in the concept of philosophy' held by the two symposiasts.

Certainly, the shared preference of the two symposiasts for the category of criticism, which Peter Ludz commented upon in the discussion, was just as superficial. Criticism (or more precisely, 'a critical theory of society') means for Adorno the unfolding of the contradictions of reality through their apprehension [*Erkenntnis*]. One is tempted to examine this concept of a critical theory—which, in the Kantian sense, is, at least potentially, thoroughly dogmatic—in its derivation from the critique of the Left Hegelians. For Popper, on the other hand, the category of criticism is completely lacking in definite content; it is a pure mechanism of the provisional confirmation of general scientific statements: 'We cannot ground our assertions', we can only 'expose them to criticism'.

Points of agreement and dissension in the views of the two symposiasts on the logic of science emerged with particular force in the question of the distinction between the natural and human sciences. Neither Popper nor Adorno were inclined to adhere unreservedly to this distinction. In their respective lines of argument, they emphasized, however, very diverse aspects. Popper advocated the view that the traditional distinction largely rested upon a misunderstood conception of the natural sciences. If one corrected this misunderstanding, the result would be that all sciences were 'theoretical', namely, that they all exposed general statements to criticism. Distinctions between domains of science could therefore only be those of degree, and of historical development; that is, these distinctions are in principle transcendable. Adorno, on the other hand, drew attention to a methodic distinction of quite a different kind which he does not in fact regard as 'fundamental' but, nevertheless—since it is determined by the object—as untranscendable: 'In natural science we are mainly concerned with unmediated materials, that is, with materials which have not already been humanly performed and, to this extent, we are dealing with materials which are, to a large extent, unqualified. The result is that natural science gives us— if you like—a freer choice of our categorial system than is the case in sociology whose object is determined in itself to such an extent that the object forces us to take up the categorial apparatus'.

In such formulations, the fundamental difference in the cognitive hopes and aspirations of Popper and Adorno becomes clear —a difference which permeated the entire discussion and which will be taken up again in its basic aspects below. Whilst Adorno regards it as possible to reproduce reality itself in the cognitive process and, consequently, even to apprehend and utilize a categorial apparatus inherent in the object, for Popper, knowledge is always a problematic attempt to capture reality by forcing upon it categories and, above all, theories. It is hardly necessary to mention the names of Kant and Hegel here.

3

In terms of time and subject matter, however, the discussion was dominated neither by Popper nor Adorno, but instead by a 'third man', conjured up by almost all participants in the discussion, but yet against whom the two symposiasts unreservedly adopted a common stance. This 'third man' was given several names by his friends and enemies alike—'positive method', 'unmetaphysical positivism', 'empiricism', 'empirical research', and so on. Even before the discussion, Eduard Baumgarten noted certain shortcomings. These were then commented upon by Emerich Francis, and emphasized by Leopold Rosenmayr, Weippert and others, namely, that in both papers there had actually been very little mention of the methodical problems of a sociology which, in its daily business at least, principally engages in empirical research. Weippert's formulation, directed towards Popper, can be applied to both symposiasts. Weippert claims that, contrary to the representatives of empirical research, both symposiasts possessed 'an extraordinarily narrow conception of the empirical and an extraordinarily broad conception of theory'. For both, science largely exhausts itself in general statements, in theories, whilst systematic experience is accorded only a limited place as a corrective or as a testing-instrument. Individual contributors to the discussion indicated that both symposiasts thus failed to apprehend precisely what constitutes modern sociology and what distinguishes it from the speculative early stages of the discipline.

Faced with such objections, Popper and Adorno adopted a rigorous methodological position. Both characterized themselves (using Popper's term) as 'negativists' in so far as they saw the task of the empirical as being that of critical correction. Beyond this, both repeatedly emphasized the primacy of theory in science. For Popper, this primacy results from the unambiguous connection of the theoretical and the empirical in the 'hypothetico-deductive method' of science which he has developed in his works and presupposed in his paper: 'There is no observation without hypothesis . . . Induction is the false thesis that one can take observation as the starting point. There simply is no induction.' For Adorno, the relationship of theory and empirical research is more complicated: 'I do not believe that one can simply bridge the divergency between the concept of a critical theory of society and empirical social research through the application of the former to the latter.' 'From what I have characterized as the critical theory of society, there constantly arises an indescribable number of problematic questions for empirical research which the latter, if it is simply confined to itself, could not crystallize.' Here too, the primacy of theory is unambiguously asserted.

Although the rigour of such a view is logically plausible, one must object that not all questions of scientific activity can be answered with its help. Thus both Weippert's question about the 'concrete research process' and Rosenmayr's questions concerning an intelligible definition of the concept of theory, and of the notion of theoretical cumulation, remained unanswered. In a liberal definition of scientific procedure, one should not fail to recognize that empirical research also has tasks other than that of testing theories; for example, that of stimulating but also of systematically ascertaining and mediating information. But rightly, both symposiasts repeatedly emphasized that such tasks of empirical research are in no way capable of establishing a concept of sociology as a science. According to them, science remains theoretical even when the actual research activity is primarily empirical.

4

In individual contributions to the discussion, a series of subsidiary motifs were introduced which were partly taken up later and partly only mentioned once. These included the problem of the encyclopaedia of the sciences (Hans L. Stoltenberg), the classification of individual methods of social-scientific knowledge, in particular that of the interpretative method (Weippert) and the question of the justification of Popper's comments on the changes in the relationship of sociology to ethnology (Wilhelm E. Mühlmann). Amongst these subsidiary motifs, there was one, however, which emerged so frequently and created such apparent interest that one can assume that it represents a necessary topic of discussion within German sociology: this was the problem of value judgments. A series of speakers, including Hofmann, Mühlmann, Rosenmayr and Weippert, demanded a reappraisal of the concept of value freedom, that is, the reopening of the controversy over value judgments [*Werturteilsstreit*] dating from the period before the First World War. In their final remarks, the symposiasts hardly referred to this demand. One formed the impression that the problem of value judgment did not seem as urgent to either Popper or Adorno as it did to some of the participants in the discussion. In so far as this was the case, both symposiasts failed to take into account the question which, for the other participants at the conference, was clearly an urgent one. Possibly even a discussion of the ethics of social-scientific research and doctrine is more suited to provide expression for the opposing basic views within German sociology than the discussion of the logic of research. Even if the fronts have perhaps been reversed, the controversy over value judgments has forfeited little of its explosiveness in German sociology after fifty years.

5

Even in his first comment on the discussion, Adorno characterized the relation of his expositions to those of Popper with the remark that it was not simply a question of difference in standpoint but rather that the differences were determinable. In the course of the discussion, the listener, on the other hand, was increasingly confronted with the question of whether the first statement was correct but the latter false. One would have certainly characterized the positions of the speakers quite inadequately if one were to declare them to be mere standpoints which thus exclude discussion and argument. On the other hand, the differences are obviously profound, not only as far as content is concerned but also in the type of argumentation itself, so that one must doubt whether Popper and Adorno could even agree upon a procedure with the aid of which their differences could be decided. Particularly at the close of the discussion, these differences were again very clearly expressed. Here the relationship between the two symposiasts was virtually reversed when Adorno, in answer to a question by Ludz, very openly and clearly identified the political principles of his interpretation of sociological theory and thus occasioned Popper to formulate, for his part, polemically and in political categories, the bases of his logical-scientific conception. This closing dispute between the two speakers is sufficiently important to justify a somewhat more detailed reference.

Adorno first countered Ludz's accusation that in his critical theory of society he had 'retreated to a pre-Marxian position' with the following: 'Societal reality has changed in a manner such that one is forced back almost inevitably to the standpoint of Left Hegelianism, so scornfully criticized by Marx and Engels, and this simply because, in the first place, the theory developed by Marx and Engels has itself, in the meantime, taken on a completely dogmatic form. Secondly, because in this dogmatized and fossilized form of the theory, the notion of the transformation of the world has itself become an atrocious ideology which serves to justify the most wretched practice of the suppression of mankind. Thirdly, however—and this is perhaps the most serious—because the notion that through the theory, and through the enunciation of the theory, one can immediately stir people and arouse them to action has become doubly impossible. This results from the disposition of men who, as is well known, can no longer be aroused by theory in any way, and results from the form of reality which excludes the possibility of such actions which for Marx seemed to be just around the corner. If today one behaved as if one could change the world tomorrow, then one would be a liar.'

Popper described this sceptical attitude as a 'pessimism' which must necessarily spring from the disappointment arising from the foundering of over-extended utopian or revolutionary hopes. On the other hand, anyone who desired less, who was satisfied with small steps forward, with a piecemeal procedure [*Fussgänger-Vorgehen*] could, like himself, be an 'optimist'. 'I am an old representative of the Enlightenment and a liberal—and even a pre-Hegelian one.' Accordingly, Popper demanded that we must take up a pre-Hegelian position for 'Hegel destroyed liberalism in Germany'. The dualism of what is and what ought to be, necessary for the improvement of the world, has disappeared in the 'post-Hegelian enlightenment' and yet in it there lay a basic precondition for meaningful action. 'The conceit that we know such an overwhelming amount about the world is what is false . . . We know nothing and therefore we must be modest; and since we are modest, we can be optimists.'

It was only at this late point in the discussion that one was struck by the connection which had been predominant in the selection of the topic, namely, that there is an inner connection between certain conceptions of the task of sociology, between certain epistemological and logical-scientific positions and between certain moral principles which also possess political relevance. However, by no means all the syndromes of the interpretation of science and of political position which are represented in German sociology were mentioned.

6

It is almost too trivial to point out that the discussion of the papers by Popper and Adorno left many questions open. But there is some sense in such an assertion. For many participants, the Tübingen discussion left a keen feeling of disappointment. Consequently, the question arises as to what the discussion lacked in order to evoke this feeling—a question which is made more acute by the fact that the fruitfulness of the papers is beyond doubt. An answer to this question has already been hinted at several times. Contrary to the expectations of the organizers, the topic proved unsuitable for producing such controversies which perceptibly play an implicit role in many discussions amongst German sociologists. A further reason for the disappointment of many people might be sought in the following; namely, that the discussion did not lead to a precise clarification of general logical-scientific positions, for instance, to the detailed paradigmatic analysis of individual theories or to a sharp definition of the relationship between the theoretical and the empirical, between construction and analysis and research into facts. In general, references to specifically sociological problems, and perhaps also to the burning questions of the practitioners of social research who were present, remained loose. This did not make intensive participation in the discussion any easier. Along with such arguments, one should not overlook the fact that the willingness to discuss was restricted to a few participants and that consequently by no means all the opportunities for fruitful confrontation were taken up which the symposiasts had created in their papers.

JÜRGEN HABERMAS

THE ANALYTICAL THEORY OF SCIENCE AND DIALECTICS

A Postscript to the Controversy Between
Popper and Adorno

1

'Societal totality does not lead a life of its own over and above that which it unites and of which it, in its turn, is composed. It produces and reproduces itself through its individual moments ... This totality can no more be detached from life, from the co-operation and the antagonism of its elements than can an element be understood merely as it functions without insight into the whole which has its source [*Wesen*] in the motion of the individual entity itself. System and individual entity are reciprocal and can only be apprehended in their reciprocity.'[1] Adorno conceives of society in categories which do not deny their origins in Hegel's logic. He conceptualizes society as totality in the strictly dialectical sense, which prohibits one from approaching the whole organically in accordance with the statement that it is more than the sum of its parts. Nor is totality a class which might be determined in its logical extension by a collection of all the elements which it comprises. To this extent, the dialectical concept of the whole is not subsumed under the justified critique of the logical bases of those Gestalt theories,[2] which in their sphere recoil altogether from investigations following the formal rules of analytical techniques and thereby it oversteps the boundaries of formal logic in whose shadowy realm dialectics itself cannot appear as anything other than a chimera.

The logicians may react in any way they choose; sociologists

---

[1] T. W. Adorno, 'On the Logic of the Social Sciences', p. 107 above.
[2] Cf. E. Nagel, *The Structure of Science* (London, 1961), pp. 380ff.

have an excellent word for such chimeras which are not merely chimeras: expressions which relate to the totality of the social life-context are nowadays considered to be ideology. In as far as the self-understanding of the social sciences is determined by the analytical theory of science, the supposedly radical enlightenment senses in every dialectical move a piece of mythology. Perhaps this is not completely incorrect, for the dialectical enlightenment,[3] from whose stringency a superficial enlightenment tries to extricate itself, indeed retains from myth an insight forfeited by positivism, namely, that the research process instigated by human subjects belongs, through the act of cognition itself, to the objective context which should be apprehended. This insight, of course, pre-supposes society as totality and sociologists who reflect upon themselves from within this context. Certainly, the social sciences which proceed analytically and empirically are familiar with a concept of the whole. Their theories are theories of systems and a general theory would have to refer to the societal system as a whole. By means of this anticipatory concept, social phenomena are grasped as a functional connection of empirical regularities. In social-scientific models, the derived relations between the sum of covariant quantities are regarded as elements of an inter-dependent context. Nevertheless, this relationship of a system to its elements, which is hypothetically represented in the deductive connections of mathematical functions, has to be strictly dis-tinguished from the relationship of the totality and its moments which can be revealed only in a dialectical manner. The distinction between system and totality, in the sense mentioned, cannot be signified directly, for in the language of formal logic it would have to be dissolved, whilst in the language of dialectics it would have to be transcended. Instead of this we intend to approach— as it were, from outside—the two typical forms of social science, one of which restricts itself to the use of the functionalist concept of system whilst the other insists on a dialectical concept of totality. We shall elucidate both types, first of all, by means of four characteristic distinctions.

1. Within the framework of a strictly empirical scientific theory, the concept of system can only signify formally the inter-

---

[3] *See* Horkheimer and Adorno, *Dialektik der Aufklärung* (Amsterdam, 1947), pp. 13ff.; English trans. J. Cumming, *Dialectic of Enlightenment* (New York, 1972/ London, 1973).

dependent connection of functions which, for their part, are broadly interpreted as relations between variables of social behaviour. The concept of system itself remains as external to the realm of experience analysed as the theoretical statements which explicate it. The rules for analytical-empirical modes of procedure contain—alongside the formal logical rules for the construction of a deductive connection of hypothetical statements, that is, a calculus utilizable in an empirical scientific manner—merely the demand that the simplified basic assumptions be chosen in such a way that they permit the derivation of empirically meaningful law-like hypotheses. At times, it is claimed that the theory must be 'isomorphic' to its area of application, but even this manner of expression is misleading. For we know hardly anything about an ontological correspondence between scientific categories and the structures of reality. Theories are ordering schemata which we construct at will within a syntactically binding framework. They prove to be utilizable for a specific object domain if the real manifoldness of the object accommodates them. For this reason, the analytical theory of science, too, can adhere to the programme of unified science. A factual agreement between the derived law-like hypotheses and empirical uniformities is, in principle, fortuitous and as such remains external to theory. Any reflection which is not satisfied with this state of affairs is inadmissible.

A dialectical theory is guilty of this lack of satisfaction. It doubts whether science, with regard to the world produced by men, may proceed just as indifferently as it does with such success in the exact natural sciences. The social sciences must, in advance, ensure the appropriateness of their categories for the object because ordering schemata, which co-variant quantities only accommodate by chance, fail to meet our interest in society. Certainly, the institutionally reified relations are included in the catalogue of social science models as so many empirical regularities; and certainly analytical experiental knowledge of this kind may enable us, in the knowledge of isolated dependencies, to exert a technical control over social quantities just as we do over nature. But as soon as cognitive interest is directed beyond the domination of nature—and here this means beyond the manipulation of natural domains—the indifference of the system in the face of its area of application suddenly changes into a distortion of the object. The structure of the object, which has been neglected in favour of a general methodology, condemns to irrelevance the theory which it cannot penetrate. In the domain of nature, the triviality of true cognitions has no serious import; in the social sciences, however, the object takes its revenge if the human subject, who is still caught up in the act of cognition, remains bound to the constraints of the very sphere that he wishes to analyse. He only frees himself to the extent to which he grasps the societal life-context as a totality which determines even research itself. At the same time, however, social science forfeits its alleged freedom in the choice of categories and models. It knows now that it 'does not have unqualified data at its disposal but only such data as are structured through the context of societal totality'.[4]

For all that, the demand that theory in its construction and in the structure of its concept has to measure up to the object [*Sache*], and the demand that in the method the object has to be treated in accord with its significance can—beyond all representational theory [*Abbildtheorie*]—only be fulfilled dialectically. It is only the scientific apparatus which reveals an object whose structure must nevertheless previously be understood to some degree, if the categories chosen are not to remain external to it. This circle cannot be broken by any a priori or empiricist immediacy of approach, but is rather only to be explored dialectically in conjunction with the natural hermeneutics of the social life-world. The hypothetico-deductive system of statements is replaced by the hermeneutic explication of meaning. In place of a reversibly unambiguous co-ordination of symbols and meanings vaguely pre-understood, categories gain their determinacy gradually through their relative position in the context developed. Concepts of a relational form give way to concepts which are capable of expressing substance and function in one. Theories of this more flexible type even in the subjective organization of the scientific apparatus incorporate reflexively the fact that they themselves remain a moment of the objective context which, in their turn, they subject to analysis.

---

[4] T. W. Adorno, loc. cit., p. 106 above.

2. At the same time as the relationship of theory to its object is transformed, that of theory and experience is also transformed. The analytical-empirical modes of procedure tolerate only one type of experience which they themselves define. Only the controlled observation of physical behaviour, which is set up in an isolated field under reproducible conditions by subjects interchangeable at will, seems to permit intersubjectively valid judgments of perception. These represent the experiental basis upon which theories must rest if the deductively acquired hypotheses are to be not only logically correct but also empirically convincing. Empirical sciences in the strict sense insist that all discussable statements should be checked, at least indirectly, by means of this very narrowly channelled experience.

A dialectical theory of society opposes this. If the formal construction of theory, of the structure of concepts, of the choice of categories and models are not able to follow blindly the abstract rules of a general methodology, but rather, as we have seen, must, in advance, measure up to a pre-formed object, then theory cannot merely be united at a later stage with an experience which is then, of course, restricted. The required coherence of the theoretical approach with the total societal process, to which sociological research itself belongs, similarly points towards experience. But insights of this sort stem, in the last instance, from the fund of pre-scientifically accumulated experience which has not yet excluded, as merely subjective elements, the basic resonance of a life-historically centred social environment, that is, the education acquired by the total human subject.[5] This prior experience of society as totality shapes the outline of the theory in which it articulates itself and through whose constructions it is checked anew against experiences. For ultimately, even on that level at which empiricism as organized observation has completely separated itself from thought, and confronts from outside, as an alien instance, thought which has reduced itself to hypothetically necessary statements—even at that level, it must be possible to create consistency. Even a dialectical theory cannot clash with an experience, however restricted it may be. On the other

---

[5] In connection with Dilthey's and Husserl's concept of 'life-world' (*Lebenswelt*), Alfred Schutz rescues a concept of experience, which has not yet been positivistically circumscribed, for the methodology of the social sciences. *See Collected Papers* (The Hague, 1962), part 1, pp. 4ff.

hand, it is not bound to forego all those thoughts which cannot be checked in this manner. Not all its theorems can be translated into the formal language of a hypothetico-deductive connection; they cannot all be wholly resolved by empirical findings—least of all the central theorems: 'Probably no experiment could convincingly demonstrate the dependence of each social phenomenon on the totality, for the whole which preforms the tangible phenomena can never itself be reduced to particular experimental arrangements. Nevertheless, the dependence of that which can be socially observed upon the total structure is, in reality, more valid than any findings which can be irrefutably verified in the particular and this dependence is anything but a mere figment of the imagination.'[6]

The functionalist concept of system which analytical social science presupposes cannot, in accordance with its operational sense, be empirically confirmed or refuted as such; law-like hypotheses, no matter how tested or how great in number, could not provide proof that the structure of society itself fulfils the functional connection which necessarily is presupposed analytically as the framework of possible co-variants. On the other hand, the dialectical concept of society as totality demands that analytical tools and social structures act upon one another like cog-wheels. The hermeneutic anticipation of totality must prove itself in more than a merely instrumental manner. In the course of the explication, it must establish itself as correct—precisely as a concept appropriate to the object itself, whereas the manifoldness of appearances at best complies with a presupposed catalogue of hypotheses. Only against the background of this claim does the shift of emphasis in the relation of the theoretical and the empirical become clear. On the one hand, within the framework of dialectical theory, even the categorial means which otherwise merely lay claim to analytical validity must themselves be legitimated in experience. On the other hand, however, this experience is not to be so identified with controlled observation that a thought, even without being at least indirectly capable of strict falsification, can retain scientific legitimation.

3. The relationship of theory to experience also determines that

---

[6] T. W. Adorno, loc. cit., pp. 113f above.

of theory to history. The analytical-empirical modes of procedure repeatedly attempt to test law-like hypotheses in the same manner, regardless of whether they are dealing with historical material or with natural phenomena. In both cases, a science which lays claim to this title in the strict sense must proceed in a generalizing manner, and the law-like dependencies which it establishes are, in their logical form, basically the same. Out of the very procedure with which the validity of law-like hypotheses is checked against experience, there arises the specific achievement of empirical scientific theories: they permit limited predictions of objective or objectified processes. Since we test a theory by comparing the events predicted with those actually observed, a theory which has been sufficiently tested empirically allows us—on the basis of its general statements, that is the laws, and, with the aid of limiting conditions which determine a case under consideration —to subsume this case under the law and to set up a prognosis for the given situation. One usually calls the situation defined by the limiting condition the cause, and the predicted event the effect. If we use a theory in this way to forecast an event, then it is said that we can 'explain' this event. Limited prognosis and causal explanation are different expressions for the same achievement of the theoretical sciences.

According to the analytical theory of science, even the historical sciences are assessed by the same criteria. Of course, they combine the logical means for a different cognitive interest. Their aim is not the derivation and corroboration of universal laws but the explanation of individual events. Historians assume a number of trivial laws, mainly psychological or sociological rules derived from experience, in order to infer a hypothetical cause from a given event. The logical form of the causal explanation is the same in each case but the hypotheses, which are to be empirically tested, refer, in the generalizing sciences, to deductively acquired laws under limiting conditions given at random. Yet in the historical sciences, they refer to these limiting conditions themselves which, under the pragmatically presupposed rules of everyday experience, are of interest as the cause of a testified individual event.[7] In the analysis of certain causes of individual events,

---

[7] *See* K. Popper, *The Open Society and its Enemies*, vol. 2 (London, 1966), pp. 193ff.

the laws, upon which one tacitly relies, may become problematical. As soon as interest in the investigation swings away from the hypothetical singular statements which are to explain specific events, and directs itself towards hypothetical-general statements—for instance, the laws of social behaviour till then assumed to be trivial—then the historian becomes a sociologist; the analysis then belongs to the realm of theoretical science. From this, Popper infers that the testing of law-like hypotheses is not the concern of the historical sciences. Empirical regularities which are expressed in the form of general statements on the functional dependence of covariant quantities, belong to a different dimension than the concrete limiting conditions which can be understood as the cause of certain historical events. Accordingly, there can be no such thing as historical laws. The laws utilizable in the historical sciences have the same status as all other natural laws.

A dialectical theory of society, on the other hand, asserts the dependence of individual phenomena upon the totality; it must reject the restrictive use of the concept of law. Its analysis aims beyond the particular dependent relations of historically neutral quantities, towards an objective context which also plays a part in determining the direction of historical development. Of course, this does not imply those so-called dynamic law-like regularities which strict empirical sciences develop in the form of continuous flow models. The historical laws of movement claim a validity which is, at the same time, more comprehensive and more restricted. Since they do not abstract from the specific context of an epoch, they are in no way generally valid. They do not refer to anthropologically enduring structures, to historical constants, but rather to a particular concrete area of application, defined in terms of a process of development both unique *in toto* and irreversible in its stages. This means that it is defined not merely analytically but through the knowledge of the object itself. On the other hand, the realm of validity for dialectical laws is also more comprehensive, precisely because they do not take in the ubiquitous relations of individual functions and isolated connections, but rather such fundamental dependent relations from which a social life-world, an epochal situation as a whole, is determined as totality and is permeated in all its moments: 'The generality of social scientific laws is not at all that of a conceptual sphere into which the individual parts can be wholly incorporated, but rather always and essentially relates to the relationship of the general to the particular in its historical concretion.'[8]

Historical regularities of this type signify developments which mediated through the consciousness of the acting subjects, gradually prevail. At the same time, they claim to articulate the objective meaning of a historical life-context. To this extent, a dialectical theory of society proceeds hermeneutically. For such a theory, the comprehension of meaning, to which the analytical-empirical theories attach a merely heuristic value,[9] is constitutive. For it gains its categories primarily from the situational consciousness of acting individuals themselves; in the objective spirit of a social life-world, that meaning is articulated which sociological interpretation takes up through identification and critique. Dialectical thought does not simply eliminate the dogmatics of the lived situation through formalization, in fact it retains the subjectively intended meaning in its examination of the prevailing traditions and breaks this meaning up. For the dependence of these ideas and interpretations upon the interests of an objective configuration of societal reproduction makes it impossible to remain at the level of subjective meaning-comprehending hermeneutics; an objective meaning-comprehending theory must also account for that moment of reification which the objectifying procedures exclusively have in mind.

Just as dialectics eludes the objectivism under which societal relations of historically acting people are analysed as the law-like relations between things, so too it resists the danger of ideologizing which exists as long as hermeneutics naïvely measures the relationships solely in terms of that which they subjectively regard themselves to be. The theory will adhere to this meaning, but only in order to measure it—behind the back of subjects and institutions—against what they really are. In this way, it reveals for itself the historical totality of a social context whose concept even deciphers the subjectively meaningless constraint of the relationships which naturally rebound upon individuals as the fragments of an objective

---

[8] T. W. Adorno, 'Sociology and Empirical Research', p. 77 above.

[9] *See* W. Stegmüller, *Main Currents in Contemporary German, British and American Philosophy*, trans. A. Blumberg (Dordrecht, 1969), p. 342; T. Gomperz, *Über Sinn und Sinngebilde, Erklären und Verstehen* (Tübingen, 1929).

context of meaning—and thereby criticizes it: the theory, 'must transform the concepts which it brings, as it were, from outside into those which the object has of itself, into what the object, left to itself, seeks to be, and confront it with what it is. It must dissolve the rigidity of the temporally and spatially fixed object into a field of tension of the possible and the real . . . But, for this reason, hypotheses derived from it—forecasts of what can be regularly expected—are not completely sufficient for it.'[10] By linking the method of *Verstehen* in this manner with the objectivating procedures of causal-analytical science and by permitting the realization of both through a mutually transcending critique, the dialectical approach overcomes the separation of theory and history. According to one of these approaches, the study of history would remain devoid of theory in the explanation of specific events, whilst, according to an approach which recognizes the role of hermeneutics, it would remain devoid of theory in a contemplative realization of past horizons of meaning. In order that history itself can be penetrated theoretically in terms of an objective comprehension of meaning, the study of history must, if the historical-philosophical hypostatization of such meaning is to be avoided, keep itself open to the future. Society reveals itself in the tendencies of its historical development, that is, it reveals itself in the laws of its historical development primarily from that which it is not: 'Every concept of structure of the contemporary social order presupposes that a definite will to reshape in future this social structure, to give it this or that direction of development, shall be posited or recognized as historically valid, that is, as effective. Naturally, it remains another matter whether this future is practically intended, is actually formed in its direction, for instance, through politics— or whether it is applied as a constitutive element of theory, as hypothesis.'[11] Only in this way, with practical intent, can the social sciences proceed both historically and systematically, whereby, of course, this intention must also, in its turn, be reflected from within the same objective context whose analysis it facilitates. Precisely this legitimation distinguishes it from Max Weber's subjectively arbitrary 'value relations' (*Wertbeziehungen*).

---

[10] Adorno, 'Sociology and Empirical Research', loc. cit., p. 69 above.
[11] H. Freyer, *Soziologie als Wirklichkeitswissenschaft* (Leipzig/Berlin, 1930), p. 304.

4. The relationship of theory to history also transforms that of science to practice. A study of history which restricts itself in a rigorously empirical-scientific manner to the causal explanation of individual events has immediately only retrospective value; knowledge of this type is not suited to application in practical life. Relevant in this context is rather the knowledge of empirically proven law-like hypotheses; they permit limited prognoses and can, for this reason, be translated into technical recommendations for a purposive-rational choice of means only if the ends are pre-given practically. The technical realization of natural science prognoses rests upon this logical relationship. Correspondingly, techniques in the realm of societal practice can also be developed from social scientific laws, that is, precisely those social techniques with whose aid we can make social processes utilizable, as is the case with natural processes. A sociology which proceeds analytically and empirically can, for this reason, be called upon as an auxilliary science for rational administration. Of course, limited and, consequently, technically utilizable predictions can only be won from theories which refer to isolable fields and stationary connections with recurring and repeatable sequences. Social systems, however, stand in historical life-contexts, they do not belong to those repetitive systems for which empirical-scientifically cogent statements are possible. Correspondingly, the radius of social techniques restricts itself to partial relations between isolable quantities; more complex connections of a higher level of interdependence elude scientifically controllable operations—and this is even more true of social systems as a whole.

If, nevertheless, we look to the diverse and isolated techniques for assistance in planned political practice—roughly in the sense in which Mannheim intended to employ them for a reorganization of society, or Popper even for a realization of a meaning in history—then, even by positivistic standards, a total analysis is indispensable.[12] This analysis would have to develop out of historical contexts the perspective of an action imputable to a total society as subject, only within which can we become conscious of practically significant ends-means relations and possible social techniques. According to Popper,

---

[12] *See* Popper, loc. cit., vol. 2, pp. 259ff.

general interpretations of major historical developments are also permissible for the purpose of securing this heuristic goal. They do not lead to theories which would be empirically testable in the strict sense, since the same point of view, which guides the interpretation with regard to relevant contemporary problems, largely determines the selection of facts drawn upon for corroboration. Yet we permit such interpretations to glide over our past like searchlights in the expectation of illuminating the relevant sections of the past by the reflected light in such a way that partial relations can be recognized under practical viewpoints. The social techniques themselves are based on general law-like regularities which are neutral to historical development. Yet these techniques are formed within the framework of a heuristically fruitful historical total view which, in the last instance, is chosen arbitrarily. The social context, in which we intervene in a social-technical manner, remains strictly within the dimension of an existence [*Sein*] set apart from what ought to be [Sollen]. Conversely, the viewpoint of our interpretation and the projection of praxis remain within the dimension of what ought to be, which is split off from existence. The relationship of science to praxis rests, like that of theory to history, upon the strict distinction between facts and decisions: history has no more meaning than nature but we can posit a meaning by virtue of arbitrary decision [*Dezision*] and energetically strive to enforce it gradually in history with the aid of scientific social techniques.

In contrast, a dialectical theory of society must indicate the gaping discrepancy between practical questions and the accomplishment of technical tasks—not to mention the realization of a meaning which, far beyond the domination of nature achieved by manipulation of a reified relation, no matter how skillful that may be—would relate to the structure of a social life-context as a whole and would, in fact, demand its emancipation. The real contradictions are produced by this totality and its historical movement, and those interpretations are reactively evoked which guide the employment of social techniques for apparently freely chosen goals. Only in so far as the practical intentions of our total historical analysis, or the guiding viewpoints of that 'general interpretation' generously conceded by Popper, can be released from pure arbitrariness and can be legitimated, for their part, dialectically from the objective context—only to this extent may we expect scientific orientation in practical action. We can only make history in as much as it appears to us as capable of being made. Thus it is one of the advantages, but also one of the obligations of a critical social science, that it allows its problems to be posed by its object: 'one would fetishize science if one radically separated its immanent problems from the real ones, which are weakly reflected in its formalisms'.[13] Adorno's statement is the dialectical answer to the postulate of the analytical theory of science that knowledge-guiding interests should be relentlessly examined to ascertain whether they are motivated immanently to the science or whether they are motivated merely from the practice of life.[14]

Thus, the discussion of the relationship between science and practice necessarily leads to the fifth and last question which distinguishes the self-understanding of the two types of social science, namely, the problem of the so-called value freedom of historical and theoretical research.

I do not wish, however, to treat this question, as I did the previous ones, in a purely descriptive manner. A systematic investigation cannot be satisfied with a topological determination of philosophy of science standpoints. Since both parties basically raise the same rationalistic claim to a critical and self-critical mode of cognition, it must be possible to decide whether dialectics, as positivism asserts, oversteps the boundaries of verifiable reflection and merely usurps the name of reason for an obscurantism which is all the more dangerous;[15] or whether, on the contrary, the codex of strict empirical sciences arbitrarily silences a more comprehensive rationalization, and converts the strength of reflection, in the name of precise distinction and sturdy empiricism, into sanctions against thought itself. Dialectics bears the burden of proof for this assertion, for it does not, like positivism, remain confined to simple negation but rather it initially takes up, in an affirmative manner, intellectual thought institutionalized in the scientific sphere. It has to criticize the analytical-empirical modes of procedure immanently in the light of their own claim. Of course, the

---

[13] T. W. Adorno, 'On the Logic of the Social Sciences', loc. cit., p. 109 above.
[14] See K. Popper, 'The Logic of the Social Sciences', pp. 96f. above.
[15] See K. Popper, 'What is Dialectic?', Mind, 49, 1940, pp. 403ff.

reduction to methodological observation, that is, the methodical elimination of relevant contents, through which a logical absolutism justifies its validity, creates difficulties. Dialectics cannot legitimate its own validity within a dimension which it has *a limine* transcended—it can in no way be proven by means of principles, but rather its proof would simply be the expounded theory itself. Nevertheless, dialectical thought, if it is to take itself seriously, obliges one to take up the confrontation within the framework laid down by the opposing party. Nonetheless, commencing from its own standpoint, it must force empirical-scientific rationalism, in accordance with the recognized standards of partial reason, to realize that the binding reflection is impelled beyond such rationalism, since the latter is a form of incomplete rationalization.

2

The postulate of so-called value freedom rests upon a thesis which, following Popper, one can formulate as the dualism of facts [*Tatsachen*] and decisions [*Entscheidungen*]. The thesis can be elucidated by means of a distinction between various types of law. On the one hand, there are the empirical regularities in the sphere of natural and historical phenomena, that is, natural laws; on the other hand, there are rules of human behaviour, that is, social norms. Whilst the invariances of phenomena which are fixed by natural laws endure, in principle, without exception and independent of the influence of acting subjects, social norms are posited and implemented under the threat of sanctions: they are valid only mediately, through the consciousness of human subjects who accept them and alter their actions accordingly. But positivists assume that the sphere of each of the two types of law are autonomous. Correspondingly, even the judgments in which we accept laws of one type or the other lay claim to a basis independent of one another. Hypotheses which refer to natural laws are assertions which either hold good empirically or do not. Statements, on the other hand, with which we accept or repudiate, approve or reject social norms are assertions which can be neither empirically true nor false. The former judgments rest on knowledge, the latter on decision. The meaning of social norms no more depends—as has been presupposed—on factual natural laws or even the latter on the former, than can the normative content of value judgments be derived from the descriptive content of factual assertions or, even conversely, the descriptive be derived from the normative. The spheres of is [*Sein*] and ought [*Sollen*] are strictly differentiated in this model; statements of a descriptive language cannot be translated into a prescriptive language.[16] The dualism of facts and decisions corresponds, in the logic of science, to the separation of cognition and evaluation and, in methodology, to the demand for a restriction of the realm of empirical-scientific analyses to the empirical uniformities in natural and social processes. Practical questions which relate to the meaning of norms are distinguishable scientifically; value judgments can never legitimately take on the form of theoretical statements or be brought into a logically compelling connection with them. Empirical-scientific prognoses concerning a probable co-variance of certain empirical quantities permit, through given ends, a rationalization of the choice of means. The positing of ends itself, however, rests upon an acceptance of norms and lacks any means of being scientifically checked. Such practical questions should not be merged with theoretical-technical questions—that is, with scientific questions which refer to real entities, to the conclusiveness of causal hypotheses and to given ends-means relations. The postulate of value freedom gave rise to Wittgenstein's classic statement that 'We feel that even when all possible scientific questions have been answered, the problems of life remain completely untouched.'[17]

The dualism of facts and decisions necessitates a reduction of permissible knowledge to strict empirical sciences and thereby a complete elimination of questions of life-practice from the horizon of the sciences. The positivistically purified boundary between cognition and evaluation naturally signifies less a result than a problem. For philosophical interpretations now take possession anew of the eliminated realm of values, norms and decisions precisely on the basis of labour divided between philosophy and a restricted science.

Objective value ethics immediately makes of this a realm of ideal being which transcends sensory experience (Scheler, Hartmann). The value qualities ascribed independence as things of a peculiar ontological dignity, are considered to be comprehensible in a kind

---

[16] *See* R. M. Hare, *The Language of Morals* (Oxford, 1952).
[17] Ludwig Wittgenstein, *Tractatus logico-philosophicus*, loc. cit., 6.52.

of intuitive knowledge. *Subjective value philosophy* is no longer so certain of the references to meaning which are split off from the real life context and thus hypostatized. It too reclaims the existence of orders of value (Max Weber) and powers of belief (Jaspers) in a sphere removed from history. But scientifically controlled knowledge is not simply enlarged by intuitive knowledge. Philosophical belief, which takes a middle course between pure decision and rational comprehension, has to commit itself to one of the competing orders, without being able to transcend their pluralism and completely dissolve the dogmatic core on which philosophical belief itself lives. The responsible, although in principle undecidable, polemic between philosophers, the intellectually honest and existentially committed representatives of mental powers, is undoubtedly the most rational form of confrontation in this realm of practical questions. Ultimately, *decisionism* [*Dezisionismus*] is no longer afraid of reducing norms wholly to decisions [*Entscheidungen*]. In the language-analytical form of a non-cognitive ethics, the decisionistic enlargement into positivistically restricted science is itself positivistically conceived (R. M. Hare). As soon as one posits certain fundamental value judgments as axioms, a deductive connection of statements can be cogently analysed in each case. Here, of course, those principles are no more accessible to any kind of rational comprehension than are the norms in opposition to natural laws: their acceptance rests solely upon rational decision. No matter whether such arbitrary decisions are interpreted in an existential-personal sense (Sartre), in a public political sense (Carl Schmitt) or institutionally on the basis of anthropological presuppositions (Gehlen) the thesis remains the same—that decisions relevent in practical life, whether they consist in the acceptance of principles, in the choice of a life-historical outline or in the choice of an enemy, can never be replaced or even rationalized through scientific calculation. If, however, the practical questions which have been eliminated from empirical-scientifically restricted knowledge must be utterly dismissed in this manner from the scope of rational discussions; if decisions in questions of practical life must be absolved from every instance in some way committed to rationality, then the last attempt, a desperate one, is not surprising: to secure institutionally, through a return to the closed world of mythical images and powers, a socially binding precedent for practical questions (Walter Bröcker). This complementing of positivism by *mythology* does not lack, as Horkheimer and Adorno have shown,[18] a logical compulsion whose treacherous irony only dialectics could set free in laughter.

Honest positivists, whose laughter is dispelled by such perspectives, make do with the programme of an 'open society'. They too, of course, must insist on the boundary strictly drawn by the logic of science between cognition and evaluation. They too identify empirical scientific knowledge, gained in accordance with the rules of a generally binding methodology, with science as such. They too accept, for this reason, the residual determination of thought which extends beyond this, and do not ask whether perhaps it is not the monopolization of all possible knowledge, through a specific form of knowledge, which creates the norm that relegates everything which it cannot accommodate to the fetish form of evaluation, decision or belief. But if they shrink from the unarticulated metaphysics of objective value ethics and subjective value philosophy in the same manner as they shrink from the declared irrationalism of decisionism and even re-mythologization, then there only remains the alternative which Popper in fact has chosen, namely, of saving rationalism at least as a confession of faith.

Since positivism may admit reason only in its particularized form (as a faculty of the correct handling of formal logical and methodological rules), it can proclaim the relevance of cognition for a rational practice only through a 'faith in reason'. Here the problem 'cannot be the choice between knowledge and faith, but only between two kinds of faith'.[19] If scientific cognition lacks every meaning reference to practice and, conversely, every normative content is independent of insight into the real life-context—as is presupposed undialectically—then the dilemma must be admitted, namely, that I can compel no one to base his assumptions constantly on arguments and experiences; and, with the aid of such arguments and experiences, I can prove to no one that I myself must behave in this way; 'That is to say, a rationalist attitude must first be adopted [by means of an arbitrary decision—J.H.] if any argument or experience is to be effective, and it cannot

[18] Horkheimer and Adorno, *Dialectic of Enlightenment*, pp. 11f.; on Bröcker *see* my review, 'Der befremdliche Mythos—Reduktion oder Evokation', in *Philosophische Rundschau*, 6, 1958, pp. 215ff.
[19] Popper, loc. cit., vol. 2, p. 246.

therefore be based upon argument or experience.'[20] This rationalistic attitude is effective in practice to the extent to which it
determines the moral and political actions of individuals and, in
the last instance, of society as a whole. Above all, it commits us to
a social-technical appropriate behaviour. In social life, as in nature,
we discover empirical regularities which can be formulated in
scientific laws. We act rationally in so far as we establish social
norms and institutions in the knowledge of these natural laws and
select our measures according to the technical recommendations
which result from them. It is, therefore, precisely the problematical
separation of natural laws and norms, the dualism of facts and
decisions, which we make when assuming that history can have as
little meaning as nature, that appears as the precondition for the
practical effectiveness of a commitment to rationalism. It is a
precondition of our social-technical realization of a meaning,
naturally alien to history, in the dimension of historical facts. This
realization is achieved by means of an arbitrary decision and by
virtue of our theoretical knowledge of factual natural laws.

   Popper's attempt to preserve the rationalism of the logic of
science from the irrationalistic consequences of its necessarily
decisionistic basis—his rationalistic confession of faith in a
scientifically-guided political practice—develops naturally from
the questionable presupposition, which he shares with Dewey's
Quest for Certainty and with pragmatism as a whole, namely that
human beings can rationally direct their own fate to the extent to
which they utilize social techniques. We shall examine whether
this presupposition holds good: does a continuum of rationality
exist between the capacity for technical mastery over objectified
processes. on the one hand, and a practical domination of historical
processes, on the other—the history which we 'make' without up
till now being able to make it consciously ? The question at issue is
whether rational administration of the world coincides with the
solution of historically posed practical questions. Prior to this
however, another precondition, the fundamental one, upon which
the problem as a whole rests, is to be examined; namely, the strict
separation of natural laws and norms to which the dualism of facts
and decisions refers. Certainly the critique of natural law has
demonstrated that social norms are not directly founded in nature,
in that which is, nor can they be so grounded.[21] But does not this

[20] loc. cit., p. 230.
[21] Cf. E. Topitsch, *Vom Ursprung und Ende der Metaphysik* (Vienna, 1958).

withdraw the normative meaning from a rational discussion of the concrete life-context from which it emerged and upon which it either falls back ideologically or reacts critically? And conversely, the question poses itself more pointedly: is knowledge then—and not only that which, in the emphatic sense, aims at the concept of an object instead of merely at its existence, but also the knowledge which has been reduced positivistically to empirical science—in fact released from every normative bond?

3

We shall examine this question in connection with Popper's suggestions for the solution of the so-called basis-problem.[22] This problem is posed in the philosophy of sciences' analysis of the possible empirical testing of theories. Logically correct hypotheses prove their empirical validity only when they are confronted with experience. Strictly speaking, however, theoretical statements cannot be directly tested by means of experience, however objectified it may be, but rather only by other statements. Experiences or perceptions however, are not statements, they can at most be expressed in observation statements. For this reason, such protocol statements were regarded as the basis upon which the decision as to the conclusiveness of hypotheses could be taken. It was Popper himself who objected to this view of Carnap and Neurath, claiming that the vagueness in the relationship of theory and experience is merely set aside, only to return in the equally problematic relationship of protocol statements to protocolled experiences. For if we do not rely upon the historically superseded presupposition of earlier sensualism that elementary sensory data are intuitively and immediately manifest, then to us even protocolled sense-certainty provides no logically satisfying basis for the plausibility of empirical scientific theories.

Popper offers an alternative solution in connection with his general theory of falsification.[23] As is well known, he provides proof that law-like hypotheses cannot be verified at all. These hypotheses possess the form of unrestricted universal statements with an unlimited number of—in principle—possible instances of application whilst the series of observations, however, with whose

---

[22] Cf. K. R. Popper, *The Logic of Scientific Discovery* (London, 1959), pp. 93ff.
[23] Cf. loc. cit., pp. 78ff.

aid we examine the hypothesis in *one* particular case, is, in principle, finite. An inductive proof is therefore impossible. Law-like hypotheses can at most be confirmed indirectly by withstanding as many attempts at falsification as possible. A theory can founder on singular existential assertions which contradict the law-like hypothesis which has been reformulated as a negative prediction. But intersubjective recognition cannot be exacted from such basic statements, which express a result of observation. For analogous reasons, they themselves are no more accessible to a verification than are law-like hypotheses, whose empirical testing they are intended to serve. Inevitably, in every basic statement, universal terms are used which, with regard to verification, have the same status as hypothetical assumptions. The simple assertion that 'here is a glass of water' could not be proved by a finite series of observations, because the meaning of such general terms as 'glass' or 'water' consists of assumptions about the law-like behaviour of bodies. Even basic statements transcend all possible experience because their terms inexplicitly imply law-like hypotheses which, for their part, cannot be verified on account of the, in principle, unlimited number of instances of application. Popper clarifies this thesis with the comment that all universals are either 'dispositional words', or can be reduced to these. Even in the elementary terms of the simplest protocol statements, we discover the implied assumptions concerning law-like behaviour of observable objects as soon as we consider possible verification procedures, that is test situations, which, in doubtful cases, would be sufficient to clarify the significance of the universals used.[24]

It is no accident that Popper advances the logical objections to the naïve view that basic statements can be resolved directly through intuitive sense certainty, up to the point from which the pragmatic objections of Charles Sanders Peirce had once developed.[25] In his own way, Peirce repeats Hegel's critique of sense certainty. Of course, he does not dialectically transcend the illusion of naked facts and bare sensations in the experiential process of a phenomenology of the mind, nor does he remain content, as did a later phenomenology, with pushing perceptual judgments back into the associated realm of pre-predicative

---

[24] Cf. loc. cit., pp. 420ff.

[25] Cf. C. S. Peirce, *Collected Papers*, ed. Hartshorne and Weiss (Cambridge, 1960), Vol. V; above all, the essays, 'Questions Concerning Certain Faculties Claimed for Man'; 'Fixation of Belief'; and 'How to Make Our Ideas Clear'.

experiences.[26] That pre-systematic experiential knowledge, already sedimented in forms of aperception, into which each immediate perception is merged from the outset—that is, the network of the hypothetically pre-understood and the anticipatorily co-intended, in which even the simplest sensations are always encapsulated— Peirce links with feedback-regulated behaviour. The hypothetical surplus-beyond each specific content of an immediately perceived entity, which logically comes into its own in the universal terms of experiential protocols—implicitly refers to an anticipated behavioural regularity. Indeed, such meaning as is possessed by what is perceived can only be regarded as the sum of behavioural habits which are corroborated in it: 'for what a thing means is simply what habits it involves'. Hypothetically, the degree of generality of descriptive content in perceptual judgments far exceeds the particularity of what is perceived in each case because, under the selective pressure towards the stabilization of the results of actions, we always form experiences and articulated meanings.

Popper, in opposing a positivist solution to the basis problem, adheres to the view that the observational statements which lend themselves to the falsification of law-like hypotheses cannot be justified in an empirically compelling manner; instead, it must be decided in each case whether the acceptance of a basic statement is sufficiently motivated by experience. In the process of research, all the observers who are involved in attempts at falsifying certain theories must, by means of relevant observational statements, arrive at a provisional consensus which can be refuted at any time. This agreement rests, in the last instance, upon a decision; it can be neither enforced logically nor empirically. Even the limiting case is taken into account: should it be impossible one day for those involved to arrive at such an agreement at all, then this would be tantamount to the breakdown of language as a means of general communication.

Popper's 'solution' leads to consequences that are certainly unintended. For it involuntarily confirms that the empirical validity of basic statements, and thus the plausibility of theories, is by no means decided in a scientifically elucidated context, for instance, in a context of action which, for its part, could be theoretically elucidated or even capable of theoretical explication. But, rather, scientists discuss whether to accept a basic statement,

[26] Cf. E. Husserl, *Erfahrung und Urteil* (Hamburg, 1948).

and this means, whether or not they wish to apply a law-like
hypothesis, correctly derived, to a given, experimentally established state of affairs. Popper compares this process to the legal
process, and here the Anglo-Saxon organization of the trial well
exemplifies this. Through some kind of decision, the jurors agree
which representation of a factual occurence they intend to approve.
This corresponds to accepting a basic statement. It permits,
together with the system of norms of criminal law (empirical
scientific hypotheses), certain stringent deductions and the
verdict. We, of course, are only interested in the parallel with
regard to a circle which, when scientific law-like hypotheses are
applied to observed states of affairs, can apparently be no more
avoided than when juridical legal norms are applied to the events
investigated. In both cases, it would be impossible to apply the
system of laws if one had not previously agreed upon the establishment of the facts; this establishment, however, must, in its turn,
be reached in a procedure which corresponds to the system of
laws and, consequently, already applies them.[27] One cannot apply
general rules if a prior decision has not been taken concerning the
facts which can be subsumed under the rules; on the other hand,
these facts cannot be established as relevant cases prior to an
application of those rules. The inevitable circle[28] in the application of rules is evidence of the embedding of the research process
in a context which itself can no longer be explicated in an analytical-
empirical manner but only hermeneutically. The postulates of
strict cognition naturally conceal a non-explicated pre-understanding which, in fact, they presuppose; here the detachment of
methodology from the real research process and its social
functions takes its revenge.

Research is an institution composed of people who act together
and communicate with one another; as such it determines,
through the communication of the researchers, that which can
theoretically lay claim to validity. The demand for controlled
observation as the basis for decisions concerning the empirical
plausibility of law-like hypotheses, already presupposes a pre-
understanding of certain social norms. It is certainly not sufficient
to know the specific aim of an investigation and the relevance of
an observation for certain assumptions. Instead, the meaning of
the research process as a whole must be understood before I can

---

[27] Cf. Popper, loc. cit., p. 110.
[28] Cf. H. G. Gadamer, *Wahrheit und Methode* (Tübingen, 1960), pp. 292ff.

know to what the empirical validity of basic statements is related, just as the judge must always have grasped the meaning of judicature as such. The *quaestio facti* must be determined with reference to a given *quaestio juris*, that is, one understood in its immanent claims. In legal proceedings, this question is prominent in everyone's mind. The whole affair here revolves around the question of an offence against general prohibitive norms, positively set down and sanctioned by the state. Correspondingly, the empirical validity of basic statements is measured against a behavioural expectation governed by social norms. But, what does the *quaestio juris* look like in the research process, and how is the empirical validity of basic statements measured in this case? One indication is given by the pragmatist interpretation of the research process.

How can we explain the fact which Popper persistently ignores, namely, that we are normally in no doubt at all about the validity of a basic statement; that we are in no doubt that the assumptions implied in its universal terms, which refer to the law-like behaviour of bodies would also be corroborated in all future test situations? The regress of an—in principle—infinite series of basic statements, of which each succeeding one would have to corroborate the assumptions implied in the previous statement, is, to be sure, a logically grounded possibility. In the research process, however, it would only become acute if these assumptions were actually rendered problematic along the whole series. For, thus far, they in no way possess the uncertainty of hypotheses but represent the certainty of unproblematic convictions and pragmatically proven ideas. The theoretical floor of an undiscussed behavioural certainty is carpentered from the planks of such latent convictions (of 'beliefs' which the pragmatists take as their starting point). On this universal ground of belief, *single* pre-scientifically established convictions become problematic and are only recognizable in their hypothetical validity when, in a specific instance, the associated habit no longer guarantees the expected result.

The disturbed stability of pragmatically adopted behaviour necessitates a modification of the guiding 'conviction', which can now be formulated as a hypothesis and subjected to a test. In principle, the preconditions for the latter mirror the preconditions for the credibility of non-problematicized convictions: preconditions for the achievements of acting human beings who sustain and ease their life through societal labour. In the last instance, therefore, the empirical validity of basic statements, and thereby the plausibility of law-like hypotheses and empirical scientific theories as a whole, is related to the criteria for assessing the results of action which have been socially adopted in the necessarily intersubjective context of working groups. It is here that the hermeneutic pre-understanding, concealed by the analytical theory of science, is formed, a pre-understanding which first makes possible the application of rules for the acceptance of basic statements. The so-called basis-problem simply does not appear if we regard the research process as part of a comprehensive process of socially institutionalized actions, through which social groups sustain their naturally precarious life. For the basic statement no longer draws empirical validity solely from the motives of an individual observation, but also from the previous integration of individual perceptions into the realm of convictions which are unproblematic, and have proved themselves on a broad basis. This occurs under experimental conditions which, as such, imitate the control of the results of action which is naturally built into systems of societal labour. If, however, the empirical validity of experimentally tested law-like hypotheses is derived in this manner from the context of the work process, then strictly empirical scientific knowledge must tolerate being interpreted through the same life-reference to labour as a type of action and as the concrete domination of nature.

The technical recommendations for a rationalized choice of means under given ends cannot be derived from scientific theories merely at a later stage, and as if by chance. Instead, the latter provide, from the outset, information for rules of technical domination similar to the domination of matter as it is developed in the work process. Popper's 'decision' [*Entscheidung*] concerning the acceptance or rejection of basic statements is reached from the same hermeneutic pre-understanding that guides the self-regulation of the social labour process: even those involved in the work process must be in agreement about the criteria governing success or lack of success of a technical rule. The latter can prove itself or founder in specific tasks; but the tasks in which its validity is decided empirically possess, for their part, at most a social binding force. The regulated feedback of technical rules is measured against the tasks set down with the social labour process, and this means that they have been made socially binding;

this feedback is measured against norms which must be consensual with regard to their meaning if judgments as to success or failure are to be intersubjectively valid. Such a research process bound to analytical-empirical rules cannot probe behind this life-reference; it is always presupposed hermeneutically.

In the court case, the empirical validity of basic statements is measured antecedently against the meaning of socially defined behavioural expectations; in the research process, it is measured against the meaning of the socially defined (scientific) achievement. In both cases, it is a question of systems of socially posited norms, but with the crucial distinction that the meaning of work seems to be relatively constant within a large historical span of variation, whilst not only the legal systems but also the modes of production and the meaning of law as such changes with epochs and social structures. The situation is exactly the same in the case of other social norms. The practical interest in the domination of objective processes apparently stands out from all the other interests of practical life. The interest in the sustenance of life through societal labour under the constraint of natural circumstances seems to have been virtually constant throughout the previous stages in the development of the human race. For this reason, a consensus concerning the meaning of technical domination can be achieved without any difficulty, in principle, within historical and cultural boundaries; the intersubjective validity of empirical-scientific statements which follows the criteria of this pre-understanding is therefore secured. Indeed, the high level of intersubjectivity of this type of statement retroactively causes the very interest upon which it is based—and to whose historically and environmentally neutral constancy it is indebted—to fall, as it were, into oblivion. The interest which has now become self-evident and is no longer thematized, recedes into the background, so that, having become invested methodically in the grounds of cognition, it subjectively disappears from the consciousness of those involved in the research process.

Thus, the illusion of pure theory can preserve itself even in the self-understanding of modern empirical sciences. In classical philosophy from Plato to Hegel, the theoretical attitude has been conceptualized as contemplation which rests upon the need for a lack of need. In a continuation of this tradition, the analytical theory of science still adheres to the same attitude: regardless of the life-contexts from which the research process historically proceeds, as far as the validity of empirical scientific statements is concerned, the research process is to be emancipated from all life references and no less removed from praxis than the Greeks had claimed for all true theory. It is upon their classical pre-suppositions that a postulate is founded which, however, would have been alien to the classical philosophers—the demand for value freedom. It would indeed be endangered if, for the modern sciences, through an immanent critique, a connection were demonstrated with the social labour process, a connection which penetrates the innermost structures of the theory itself and determines what shall empirically possess validity.

The historical situation in which during the seventeenth century empirical science in the strict sense emerges with the new physics, is by no means external to the structure of empirical science. If it demands that the theoretical outline and the meaning of empirical validity be obtained from a technical attitude, then it would be true that henceforth research and knowledge would be practised from the perspective and the horizon of interests of the labouring human subject. Up to that point, the roles of theory and of the reproduction of material life had been strictly divided socially; the monopolization of the acquisition of knowledge by the leisure classes had remained unchallenged. It is only within the framework of modern bourgeois society, which legitimizes the acquisition of property through labour, that science can receive impulses from the experiential realm of manual crafts and research can gradually be integrated into the labour process.

The mechanics of Galileo and his contemporaries dissects nature with reference to a form of technical domination which had just been developed within the framework of the new modes of manufacture. It was, for its part, dependent upon the rational dissection of the manual labour process into elementary functions. To regard natural events mechanistically by analogy with labour processes in manufacturing concerns, meant focusing knowledge upon the need for technical rules.[29] That the life-practical refer-ence of cognition to work within the framework of a mechanistic world picture emerged at this moment, at the time of the so-called period of manufacture; that since then it has created universal—and in the prevailing positivistic self-understanding of the sciences—exclusive recognition for one specific form of knowledge, all

[29] Franz Borkenau, *Der Übergang vom Feudalen zum bürgerlichen Weltbild* (Paris, 1934), esp. pp. 1–15.

this is indeed connected historically with another developmental tendency within bourgeois society.

In so far as exchange relations also affect the work process and make the mode of production dependent upon the market, the life references—constitutive in the world of a social group—which are the concrete relations of human beings to things and of human beings with one another, are torn asunder. In a process of reification, that which things are for us in a concrete situation and that which human beings signify for us in a given situation, are hypostatized into entities in themselves, which can then be attributed to apparently neutralized objects in the form, so to speak, of the appended quality of a 'value'. The value freedom objectivated in the empirical sciences is just as much a product of this reification as are the values themselves which are abstracted from the life-context. On the one hand, just as in the exchange values the actually invested labour and the possible enjoyment of the consumer disappears so, on the other hand, the manifoldness of the social life-references and of the knowledge-guiding interests is obfuscated in the objects which remain when the veneer of subjectivized value qualities is stripped from them. It is all the more easy for the excluding domination of that particular interest to prevail unconsciously which, complimenting the process of utilization, incorporates the natural and the social world into the labour process and transforms them into productive forces.

This practical cognitive interest in the mastery of objective processes can be formalized to such an extent that it disappears *qua* practical cognitive interest in the grounds of cognition of the empirical sciences. The relationship between abstract measures and the anticipated rule-governed behaviour of isolated quantities is liberated from the context of action of social labour and becomes relevant in itself. Even the relevance of a need for technical rules ultimately becomes indiscernible within a canon of instructions which robs this instrumental relationship between intervention and reaction of the technical sense of applicability for practical ends in general. Eventually, left to itself, the research process is only concerned with the functional connections of co-variant quantities, with natural laws. In the face of this, our spontaneous achievements have to be restricted to our 'recognizing' them disinterestedly and in a manner quite removed from practical life; in short, in a theoretical attitude. The claim to exclusiveness raised by strict knowledge sublates all the other knowledge-

guiding interests in favour of a single interest of which it is not
even conscious.

The postulate of value freedom testifies that the analytical-
empirical procedures cannot ensure for themselves the life-
reference within which they themselves objectively stand. Within
a life-reference fixed by everyday language and stamped out in
social norms, we experience and judge things as human beings
with regard to a specific meaning, in which the unseparated
descriptive and normative content states just as much about the
human subjects who live in it as it does about the objects experienced themselves. 'Values' are constituted dialectically in the
relation between the two. As soon as they are subtracted, however,
as an independent quality from the apparently neutralized entities,
and are either objectified into ideal objects or subjectified into
forms of reactions, then the categories of the life-world are not
so much burst open as deceived. The latter only gain power over
a theory which devolves on practice because, in the illusion of
autonomy, it ridicules a connection which in reality cannot be
dissolved. No theory which is aware of this will be able to comprehend its object without simultaneously reflecting upon the
viewpoint under which, according to its own immanent claim,
the object has some validity: 'what was subsequently sanctioned
as a value does not operate externally to the object . . . but rather is
immanent to it'.[30]

4

Value neutrality has nothing to do with the theoretical attitude
in the classical sense. On the contrary, it corresponds to an
objectivity of the validity of statements, which is made possible
—and is purchased—through restriction to a technical cognitive
interest. This restriction does not, however, transcend the
normative commitment of the research process to the motives of
practical life; instead, without any discussion, it makes one
particular motive dominant over the others. No matter how
greatly repressed this may be in the scientific-theoretical self-
understanding, one may be quite sure that, in the practical
realization of social-scientific results, difficulties emerge which

---

[30] T. W. Adorno, 'On the Logic of the Social Sciences', loc. cit., p. 117.

arise solely from this. Gunnar Myrdal has drawn attention to this problem.[31]

Since Max Weber, what had long been pragmatically clarified in the relationship between natural sciences and technology seems to have been clarified for the realm of social sciences too; namely, that scientific prognoses can be realized in technical recommendations. These recommendations distinguish between a given initial situation, alternative means and hypothetical ends; all so-called value judgments are simply attached to the third member of this chain, whilst the if-then relations can themselves be investigated in a value-free manner. This translation presupposes, of course, that in societal practice, as in the technical domination of nature, it is always possible to isolate ends-means relations in which the value neutrality of the means and the value indifference of the subsidiary consequences are guaranteed; in which, then, a 'value' is only linked with ends so that these ends may not, for their part, be regarded as neutralized means for other ends. In those realms of practical life for which social-scientific analyses are required, none of the three conditions is, however, normally fulfilled. If practical decisions are to be grounded in a concrete situation, then technical recommendations must first be interpreted with regard to complex life-references. This interpretation must take into account what those recommendations ignore, namely, that initially isolated ends and subsidiary consequences must be regarded—if possible in relation to other ends—just as much as means as the initially neutralized means, in another respect, can gain a relative end in themselves.

Certainly, every social-technical measure, every technical recommendation to which it adheres, every strictly scientific prognosis upon which it is based, must *assume* means for isolated ends with isolable subsidiary consequences to be value-neutral. Isolation and neutralization are inevitable for analytical purposes. But the structure of the object, the social life-world itself, also imposes the reservation that practical questions cannot be sufficiently solved by the statement of a technical rule, but instead they require an interpretation which cancels that abstraction with respect to the life-practical consequences. Such interpretations demonstrate that the ends-means relations, which are unprob-

---

[31] Cf. Gunnar Myrdal, 'Ends and Means in Political Economy', in *Value in Social Theory* (London, 1958); on the whole problem, cf. Max Horkheimer, *Eclipse of Reason* (New York, 1947), esp. ch. 1.

lematic in the technical domination of nature, immediately become problematic with regard to society. Conditions which define the situations of action behave like the moments of a totality which cannot be dichotomously divided into dead and living, into facts and values, into value-free means and value-laden ends without failing to grasp them as such. Rather, it is here that Hegel's dialectic of ends and means comes into its own, since the societal context is literally a *life*-context, in which the smallest trifling part is as alive—and that means equally as vulnerable—as the whole. The means possess just as much expediency for certain ends as the ends themselves possess a correspondence to *certain* means. Consequently, practical questions cannot be sufficiently answered with a purposive-rational choice of value-neutral means. Practical questions demand theoretical guidance as to how one situation can be carried over into another. They demand (following a suggestion made by Paul Streeten) programmes and not prognoses. Programmes recommend strategies to bring about unproblematical situations, namely, the specific connection of a particular constellation of means, ends and subsidiary consequences, a connection which can certainly be dissected for analytical purposes but cannot be dissolved practically.

Myrdal's critique of Weber's ends-means scheme demonstrates that with the strict modes of procedure of value-free social sciences a technical cognitive interest comes into play which remains inappropriate to practical life and, in addition, requires a programmatic interpretation of the individual prognoses. Beyond this, it is shown how, under the exclusive validity of this type of science, the competing, apparently mediatized cognitive interests succeed *on the back* of that interest (in the domination of objectified processes) which is alone permitted. It becomes apparent that the practical realization of technical recommendations, in fact, has no need of the controlled, additional interpretation which had been demanded. But this is not because there is, after all, no discrepancy between technical recommendations and practical solutions, but simply because the social-scientific theories from which the prognoses are derived, do not, despite their own self-understanding, satisfy the strict demands of value neutrality. From the very beginning, they are guided by a pre-understanding relevant to a specific set of practical questions. This guiding understanding of meaning is decisive in the choice both of the theoretical foundations and of the hypotheses basic to the models.

On a high level of abstraction, the great majority of possible functional connections and of correspondingly manifold programmes is systematically excluded—in fact, rightly excluded as irrelevant—under the particular guiding programmatic viewpoints which are not reflected upon as such. The analysis itself develops in a formally universal manner and leads to value-neutral prognoses; but these prognoses result from analyses within a frame of reference which, as such, already proceeds from a programmatic pre-understanding, and consequently relates to the strategies sought after. The pre-understanding may certainly prove to be incomplete or useless. The exact knowledge of functional connections can lead both to a transformation of the techniques and to a correction of the goals, to an adaptation of the strategy as a whole, even to the demonstration that the tacit anticipation of the state of affairs into which the problematic situation is to be carried over is inappropriate. On the other hand, however, the analysis itself is directed by tacitly assumed programmatic viewpoints. Only for this reason can the analytically won ends-means relation be wholly merged into practical solutions at all.

Since not only the ends but *all* the components of a particular constellation of means, ends and subsidiary consequences are elements of a life-context, and since, in a choice of practical measures, these would have to be compared and weighed against other constellations *in their entireties*, it is necessary that the great mass of all conceivable constellations be eliminated before the value-neutral investigation can commence in formal agreement with the ends-means scheme. Thus it was the case that for Max Weber's ideal-typical series a particular historical-philosophical pre-understanding of the entire European development was decisive, and this means a programmatic viewpoint, namely the rationalization of all areas of culture.[32] And the case is, in principle,

---

[32] Cf. H. Freyer, *Soziologie als Wirklichkeitswissenschaft*, loc. cit., pp. 155f., 'It is extremely characteristic that in a typology of the forms of domination one deliberately starts from the specifically modern form of administration, "in order afterwards to be able to contrast the others with it" (*Wirtschaft und Gesellschaft*, p. 124). It is just as characteristic that the chapter on the sociology of the city . . . is designed to understand the specific nature of the western city, because in it lie the roots of the modern capitalist social system, and that here once again the other types of city are treated as contrasts. In these examples . . . the basic intention of Max Weber's sociology is revealed. It consists of the question: which is the autonomous form of the formation of modern European society, and through which

no different as far as more strictly formalized theories are concerned. It is precisely the domination of a technical cognitive interest, hidden to itself, which conceals the veiled investments of the relatively dogmatic total understanding of a situation, with which even the strictly empirical sociologist has implicitly identified himself before it slips through his hands in the initial stages of a formalized theory under the claim of hypothetical universality. If, however, even in the initial stages of mathematical social sciences, situationally-bound experiences are of necessity incorporated, if the knowledge-guiding interests can be merely formalized but not suspended, then the latter must be brought under control and criticized or legitimated as objective interests derived from the total societal context, unless one wishes to silence rationalization on the threshold of analytical-empirical procedures.

The reflection upon such interests impels recourse to dialectical thought, if dialectics simply means, in this context, the attempt to comprehend the analysis at every moment both as a part of the societal process analysed and as its possible critical self-awareness. But this means that we forego the assumption of that external, and merely fortuitous, relationship between the analytical instruments and the data analysed, a relationship which can, of course, be assumed in the relation of technical domination over objective and objectified processes. Only in this way, can the social sciences throw off the illusion—valuable in practical terms—that the scientific control of societal domains which results in an emancipation from natural constraint—secured by recourse to a scientifically produced technical force of domination—is possible in history in the same manner and with the same means as is already realized in the face of nature.

---

unique combination of circumstances is it made possible or enforced?... Sociology, as the systematic science of other types of societal reality, becomes the path along which contemporary reality learns to recognize itself in its historical reality.'

HANS ALBERT

THE MYTH OF TOTAL REASON

Dialectical Claims in the Light of
Undialectical Criticism

1 DIALECTICS VERSUS POSITIVISM

The problem of the connection between theory and practice has
repeatedly aroused the attention of philosophers and social
scientists. It has led to the debate which persists even today,
concerning the significance and possibility of *value freedom*, a
debate with whose commencement and first critical phase the
name of *Max Weber* is particularly linked. On the other hand, it
has given rise to the discussion on the meaning of *experiment*
for the social sciences whereby the methodological claim to
autonomy of a cultural-scientific [*geisteswissenschaftlich*] character
was questioned, a claim which is still made for these disciplines.
It is not surprising that such questions represent a point of
departure for philosophical reflections into the problems of the
sciences.

In recent times, the social sciences have developed to a considerable extent, under the influence—direct and indirect—of
positivistic trends. The social sciences have favoured positivistically determined solutions to these problems, and have worked
out new forms of corresponding methodological conceptions.
However, one can in no way claim that today these views prevail
everywhere. This is not even the case in the English-speaking
world where one would most readily expect it. In the German-
speaking world, it is difficult to clarify the situation in view of the
influence of various philosophical currents upon the social
sciences. In any case, more recent forms of positivism seem to
have had only a minor effect here, possibly no stronger than
historicism and neo-Kantianism, or than phenomenology and

hermeneutics. Finally, one should not underrate here the *influence of the Hegelian inheritance*, either direct, or mediated through Marxism, an inheritance which has, moreover, asserted itself in other ways too. Recently, an attack directed against positivistic trends has been made from this side and analysing it might be fruitful since it led to the heart of the above-mentioned problems.[1]

One recognizes in this attack the view that certain difficulties which emerge in the course of the realization of the scientific programme advanced by these positivistic trends, can be overcome if one is prepared to revert to ideas which stem from the Hegelian tradition. We might, first of all, confront this attempt at a dialectical overcoming of so-called positivistic weaknesses of the social sciences, with the question of the *problem situation* from which the author sets out. More specifically, we should consider the question of the difficulties inherent in this problem situation; namely, in what respect and to what extent, in the opinion of Habermas, a science of the 'positivistic' type must fall down. A further question would then be that of the *alternative* which he develops, of its usefulness for the solution of these difficulties and its tenability; and finally, perhaps, one could go beyond this and raise the question of *other possible solutions*.

The problem situation from which Habermas sets out can be characterized in roughly the following manner: in so far as the social sciences develop in a manner that brings them closer to the positivistic scientific ideal—and today this is already to a large extent the case—they grow more like the natural sciences. This is particularly true in the sense that in both types of science a purely technically rooted cognitive interest dominates,[2] and theory is carried out 'with the attitude of the technician'. Social sciences which are orientated in this way are no longer in a

---

[1] In connection with the controversy between Karl Popper and Theodor W. Adorno at the internal working session of the German Sociological Association in Tübingen in 1961 (*see* Karl R. Popper, 'The Logic of the Social Sciences', and Theodor W. Adorno, 'On the Logic of the Social Sciences'), Jürgen Habermas published under the title 'The Analytical Theory of Science and Dialectics. A Postscript to the Controversy Between Popper and Adorno') a critical contribution to Adorno's *Festschrift*. Soon afterwards his collection of essays *Theorie und Praxis: Sozial philosophische Studien* (Neuwied/Berlin, 1963) appeared, which merits interest in the same connection. English trans. J. Viertel, *Theory and Practice* (London/Boston, 1974). What was hinted at in Adorno appears to be clearer in Habermas.

[2] This idea has central significance for the understanding of Habermas' thought. It is constantly reformulated in his work, *see*: *Theory and Practice*, loc. cit., pp. 6of., 75, 114, 254f., 263f., 267f. and *passim*; *Theorie und Praxis*, pp. 224ff.; further 'The Analytical Theory of Science and Dialectics', pp. 137f., 141ff., 156ff. and *passim*.

position to offer normative viewpoints and conceptions for practical orientation. They are only able to give technical recommendations for the realization of pre-given ends: that is, they are only able to influence the selection of means. The rationalization of practice which they make possible only refers then to its technical aspect. Thus we are dealing with a restricted rationality, in contrast to that produced by earlier doctrines—namely, by those which continued to unite normative orientation and technical directions.

The usefulness of a social science orientated in this way is thus in no way in itself denied by Habermas. But he sees the danger of its limitations not being recognized when a simple identification of technical and practical use takes place, and where thereby an attempt is made to reduce the more comprehensive practical to the narrower technical problems, as would seem to be the case given the tendency inherent in the 'positivistic' theory of science. The restriction of rationality to the use of means which is legitimized by this view, entails that the other aspect of the practical problematic, the realm of ends, falls prey to pure decisionism, the whim of mere decisions not reflected upon by reason. The *decisionism* of unreflected, arbitrary decisions in the realm of practice corresponds to the *positivism* implied by the restriction to pure value-free theories in the realm of cognition, where technological problems are not at issue. 'The price paid for economy in the selection of means is an unconstrained decisionism in the selection of the highest goals.'[3]

Through rational reflection, the images of mythological interpretations of the world can penetrate unhindered into the realm which is left vacant through the reduction of rationality. As a result, positivism provides, de facto, not only for the rationalization of the technical aspect but, over and above this—even if unintentionally—it provides for the remythologizing of the ungrasped aspect of the practical problematic. This is a consequence from which, of course, the representatives of such views recoil. They respond with a critique of ideology which does not serve the shaping of reality, but instead the elucidation of

---

[3] Habermas, *Theory and Practice*, loc. cit., p. 265 [amended translation]; *see also* pp. 46f. Similarly, expressed metaphorically: 'A disinfected reason is purged of all moments of enlightened volition; external to itself, it has externalized—alienated—its own life. And life deprived of spirit leads an existence of arbitrariness that is a ghostly spirit indeed—all under the name of "decision" ', p. 263.

consciousness and, for that reason, does not really seem intelligible in terms of the conception of science upon which it is based, and which is only directed towards technical rationality. Here it becomes apparent, in Habermas' view, that positivism tends to overcome its own accepted restriction upon rationality in favour of a more comprehensive conception, one which involves the convergence of reason and decision.[4] But this tendency can only achieve a breakthrough if the limitations of positivism themselves are broken down, if its restricted reason is overcome dialectically by a reason which brings about the unity of theory and practice, and thereby the transcendence of the dualism of cognition and evaluation, of facts and decisions and the abolition of the positivistic division of consciousness. Apparently, only this dialectical reason is in a position to transcend both the decisionism of mere decision and the positivism of pure theory in order 'to comprehend society as a historically constituted totality for the purposes of a critical maieutics of political praxis'.[5] Basically, Habermas is concerned with regaining the lost realm by recourse to the Hegelian inheritance preserved in Marxism: that is, with regaining practice-orientated dialectical reason for rational reflection.

The basic lines of his critique of the 'positivistic' conception of science in the social sciences have now been presented, as have the claims which he associates with his dialectical supersession of this conception. We must now examine his objections and proposals in detail, in order to see to what extent they appear tenable.[6]

---

[4] The term 'positivism' is used very widely here—even, for example, for Karl Popper's view which differs from orthodox positivistic views in basic points. Popper himself has therefore constantly protested against his inclusion in this group. It also becomes clear that such imputation can lead to misunderstanding precisely in view of the problems dealt with by Habermas.

[5] The passage is taken from the chapter 'Between Philosophy and Science: Marxism as Critique' in the above-quoted book by Habermas, p. 205 [amended trans.]. It stands, therefore, in the context of an analysis of Marx, but in my view it represents very clearly what Habermas himself expects of dialectics, namely, a 'philosophy of history with practical intent', as he writes elsewhere. This also explains his uneasiness concerning the analyses of Marxism which fail to take into account the unity of the object: society as *totality*, its *dialectical* interpretation as a *historical* process and the *relationship* of theory *to practice*. On this reference to practice see also Habermas, loc. cit., pp. 78f.

[6] Here it is useful to refer to the above-mentioned postscript to the Popper-Adorno controversy in which he formulates his objections to Popper's critical rationalism in a precise form. Even with reference to this view, he regards his arguments against 'positivism' as sound.

2 ON THE PROBLEM OF THEORY FORMATION

In his confrontation with the analytical theory of science, Habermas takes as his starting point the distinction between the *functionalist concept of system* and the *dialectical concept of totality* which he regards as basic, but difficult to explicate. He assigns to each concept one of the two typical forms of social science with which he is concerned—analytical and dialectical social science—in order to take up the difference between them, on the basis of four problem areas. These problem areas comprise: the relationship between theory and object, between theory and experience, between theory and history and between science and practice. The relation between science and practice is subsequently analysed in more detail in the three following sections of his essay and here the problem of value freedom, and the so-called basis-problem, come to the fore.

It is well known that the dialectical concept of totality, which forms the starting-point of Habermas' discussion, constantly recurs in theoreticians who follow in Hegel's footsteps. Apparently they look upon this concept as being in some way fundamental. It is therefore all the more regrettable that Habermas makes no attempt to provide a more precise clarification of this concept, which he strongly emphasizes and frequently uses. He merely says of it that it is to be understood 'in the strictly dialectical sense, which prohibits one from approaching the whole organically according with the statement that it is more than the sum of its parts'. Nor, he claims, is totality 'a class which might be determined in its logical extension by a collection of all the elements which it comprises'. From this he believes he can conclude that the dialectical concept of the whole is not affected by the critical investigations of the concepts of wholeness such as for example, were carried out by Ernest Nagel.[7]

Nagel's studies, however, are in no way restricted to a concept of the whole which one could simply dismiss in this context as

---

[7] *See* Ernest Nagel, *The Structure of Science* (London, 1961), pp. 380ff., an analysis to which Habermas refers explicitly. One could also consult Karl Popper, *The Poverty of Historicism* (London, 1957), pp. 76ff. and *passim*, a study which he surprisingly did not take into account, although it refers precisely to the historical-philosophical holism which he himself represents; further, Jürgen v. Kempski, *Zur Logik der Ordnungsbegriffe, besonders in den Sozialwissenschaften*, 1952, reprinted in *Theorie und Realität*, edited by H. Albert (Tübingen, 1964).

irrelevant. Rather, he analyses various concepts which, one would imagine, might be worthy of consideration by a theoretician concerning himself with totalities of a social character.[8] Habermas, however, observes that the dialectical concept of the whole exceeds the limits of formal logic, 'in whose shadowy realm dialectics itself cannot appear as anything other than a chimera'.[9] From the context in which this statement appears one may conclude that Habermas wants to challenge the possibility of logically analysing his concept of totality. Without close elucidation, one will no longer be able to see in such a thesis how to protect both the expression from an 'arbitrary decision' [*Dezision*] (to use this term again which has proved its worth against the positivists)—in other words a decision [*Entscheidung*]—and the concept from the analysis. Anyone possessing sufficient mistrust will detect in this an immunization strategy which is based on the expectation that whatever recoils from analysis will escape criticism. Be that as it may; for Habermas the non-explicability of this concept seems particularly important since from it apparently stems the non-explicability of the distinction between 'totality' in the dialectical and 'system' in the functional sense—a distinction which he seems to regard as basic.[10] This distinction is particularly

---

[8] Nagel asserts that the vocabulary of wholeness is rather ambiguous, metaphorical and vague and therefore can hardly be judged without clarification. This would also apply to Habermas' 'totality'. Even if Adorno's somewhat vague remarks about totality, with which Habermas begins his article, in no way permit a firm classification of his concept, I would still assume that if Habermas had read Nagel's presentation more carefully he would have come across at least related concepts which could have further assisted him. (For example, pp. 391ff.) In any case, his short reference, which creates the impression that Nagel's analyses are irrelevant for his own concept of 'totality' is completely inadequate, especially since he himself has no equivalent at his disposal. It is unintelligible that the rejection of the alternatives 'organic whole' and 'class' can be sufficient to exclude the question of a possible logical analysis.

[9] Habermas, 'The Analytical Theory of Science and Dialectics', p. 131 above.

[10] He says of it that it cannot be directly 'signified', 'for in the language of formal logic it would have to be dissolved, whilst in the language of dialectics it would have to be transcended'. But it may be possible to find a language which would not be overtaxed. What grounds are there for this idea which so quickly establishes itself, namely, that it is not possible at any cost? And incidentally, to what extent is the language of formal logic supposed to 'dissolve' something? Habermas seems to imagine here that, with its help, one can make a distinction disappear which is present in the actual usage of two concepts. That is certainly possible—in an inadequate analysis. But where does the idea originate that there cannot be an adequate analysis? Here one may assume a certain connection with the unfortunate relationship which Hegelians in general are wont to have with logic which, on the one hand, they underestimate in importance and, on the other hand, they overestimate in its ('falsifying') effect.

concerned with his comparison of two types of social science, since he fosters the problematic notion that a *general* theory must 'refer to the social system as a whole'.

With respect to the relationship between theory and object, he explicates the distinction between the two types of social science in the following manner. Within the framework of empirical-scientific theory, the concept of system and the theoretical statements which explicate it remain '*external*' to the realm of experience analysed. Theories, he says, are here mere ordering schemata *randomly constructed* in a syntactically binding framework, utilizable if the real manifoldness of an object-domain *accomodates* them—but this is, in principle, fortuitous. Here then the impression of randomness, whim and chance is evoked through the mode of expression selected. The possibility of applying strict testing procedures, whose result is largely independent of subjective will, is made ridiculous, and this is presumably connected with the fact that it is later ruled out for dialectical theory. The reader is made to think that the latter theory, on the other hand, is *necessarily and internally*[11] in accord with reality and thus does not require factual testing.[12]

But for dialectical theory, on the contrary, the claim is made that it does *not* proceed so 'indifferently' in the face of its object domain as is the case in the exact natural sciences—where, it is admitted, this is successful. It 'must, in advance, ensure' the appropriateness of [its] categories for the object because ordering schemata, which co-variant quantities only accommodate by chance, fail to meet our interest in society'—which, in this case, is apparently *not* a purely technical one, an interest in the domination of nature. For, as soon as the cognitive interest is directed beyond this, says Habermas, 'the indifference of the system in the

---

[11] At this point, agreement with the typical arguments of social-scientific essentialism is blatant; *see*, for example, Werner Sombart, *Die drei Nationalökonomien* (Munich and Leipzig, 1930), pp. 193ff. and *passim*; also my critique 'Der moderne Methodenstreit und die Grenzen des Methodenpluralismus', in *Jahrbuch für Sozialwissenschaft*, Band 13, 1962; reprinted as chapter 6 of my essay collection, *Marktsoziologie und Entscheidungslogik* (Neuwied/Berlin, 1967).

[12] The section closes with the sentence, 'Reflection which is not satisfied with this state of affairs is inadmissible'. In the next section this 'lack of satisfaction' is claimed for dialectical theory. The word 'satisfy' suggests a restriction. It will not be so easy to produce evidence that Karl Popper—who is presumably the addressee of these objections—wishes to exclude the possibility of speculation. On the contrary, however, it is precisely the dialecticians who frequently seem to desire to 'satisfy' themselves with theories whose untestability they believe they can take for granted.

face of its area of application suddenly changes into a distortion of the object. The structure of the object, which has been neglected in favour of a general methodology, condemns to irrelevance the theory which it cannot penetrate'.[13] The diagnosis is 'distortion of the object'; the suggested cure: one must grasp the social life-context as a *totality* which, moreover, determines research itself. In this way, however, social science forfeits its alleged freedom in the choice of categories and models. Theory 'in its construction and in the structure of its concept has to measure up to the object (*Sache*), and 'in the method the object has to be treated in accord with its significance', a demand which by its very nature can 'only be fulfilled dialectically'. The *circle*—produced when one claims that it is only the scientific apparatus reveals an object whose structure must, nevertheless, *previously* have been understood to some degree—is 'only to be explored dialectically in conjunction with the natural hermeneutics of the social life-world', so that here 'the hermeneutic explication of meaning' will replace the hypothetico-deductive system.[14]

The problem which Habermas here takes as his starting point is apparently connected with the fact that in analytical social science a *one-sided technical cognitive interest* leads to distortion of the object. At this point we come to the thesis, already mentioned, which provides him with one of his most basic objections to current procedures in the social sciences. In so doing, he adopts an *instrumentalist* interpretation of the empirical sciences and ignores the fact that the philosopher of science, to whom presumably his objections are basically addressed, has explicitly dealt with this interpretation and has attempted to demonstrate its dubious nature.[15] The fact that informative theories of a nomological character have proved themselves to be technically utilizable in

---

[13] Habermas, loc. cit., p. 134 above.

[14] Habermas, loc. cit., p. 134 above.

[15] In Popper's view, it is as dubious as the earlier essentialism which above all remains active in cultural-scientific thought; *see* Karl Popper, 'Three Views Concerning Human Knowledge' (1956), reprinted in his essay collection, *Conjectures and Refutations* (London, 1963), and also other essays in this volume; further his article 'Die Zielsetzung der Erfahrungswissenschaft', *Ratio*, I, 1957, revised English version, 'The Aim of Science' in K. R. Popper, *Objective Knowledge* (Oxford, 1972); further, Paul K. Feyerabend, 'Realism and Instrumentalism', in: *The Critical Approach to Science and Philosophy* (Glencoe, 1964). In fact, Habermas' instrumentalism seems to be more restrictive than the views of this sort that have been criticized in the above-mentioned essays.

many spheres is in no way a sufficient indication of the cognitive interest upon which they are based.[16]

An unbiased interpretation of this state of affairs can be geared to the fact that, from a deeper penetration into the structure of reality, one can expect insights which are also of importance for the orientation of action, for the orientation of a form of intercourse with real factors (*Gegebenheiten*). The methodology of the theoretical empirical sciences seeks, above all, to grasp law-like connections, and to suggest informative hypotheses concerning the structure of reality, and thereby the structure of actual events. Empirical checks and, connected with these, prognoses are made in order to ascertain whether the connections are as we presume them to be. Thus our 'prior knowledge' can, of course, be placed in question without any difficulty. Here a fundamental role is played by the idea that we can learn from our mistakes by exposing the theories in question to the risk of destruction at the hands of the facts.[17] Interventions into real events can thereby serve to create situations which make the risk relatively high. Technical successes, produced in connection with research, can be attributed to the fact that one has in part drawn closer to the real connections. To a certain extent, then, this is rephrased by Habermas 'dualectically' in the idea that a one-sided cognitive interest is present here. The most conspicuous consequences of scientific development, which, moreover, can easily be interpreted realistically, are made the occasion for reinterpreting the cognitive efforts accordingly, and 'denouncing' them—as one would presumably have to express it in neo-Hegelian terms—as purely technical.[18]

---

[16] It seems superfluous to point out that the personal interests of the researchers are largely not directed towards technical success as such. Habermas presumably does not wish to dispute anything of the sort. Apparently he is thinking more of an institutionally anchored or methodically channelled interest from which the researcher, despite other personal motives, can in no way withdraw. But he does not provide sufficient evidence for this. I shall return to this point.

[17] *See* the works of Karl Popper.

[18] The instrumentalist interpretation of the natural sciences seems to be endemic amongst Hegelians, as is the notoriously poor acquaintance with logic. One finds both, for instance, well developed in Benedetto Croce's *Logik als Wissenschaft vom reinen Begriff* (Tübingen, 1930), where the natural sciences are in principle accredited only with 'pseudo-concepts' without cognitive significance (pp. 216ff.), formal logic is devalued as being rather meaningless (pp. 86ff.), and philosophy and history are identified with one another in a curious manner as genuine knowledge (pp. 204ff.). *See* Jürgen v. Kempski, *Brechungen* (Hamburg, 1964), pp. 85f. In Habermas one finds the tendency to link both the technical rationality of science with the 'logic of subsumption' and the universal rationality of philosophy with dialectics.

For the present, let us take the alleged dominance of technical cognitive interests for granted. As long as it is present, says Habermas, theory remains indifferent towards its object-domain. But if interest is directed beyond this, then this indifference changes suddenly into the distortion of the object. How can a change of interest achieve this? Does the type of proposition perhaps, or the structure of the theory, change? How may we conceive of this? Habermas gives us no indications. In any case, he robs the social scientist who proceeds analytically of any hope of altering his desperate situation in any way through an appropriate alteration of his interest, unless he goes over to dialectics and, in so doing, relinquishes his freedom to choose categories and models.[19] The naïve advocate of analytical modes of procedure will be inclined to adopt the view that he can most readily guarantee the appropriateness of his categories by subjecting the theories in which they play a role to strict test procedures.[20] Habermas considers this to be insufficient. He thinks that he can guarantee the appropriateness of his categories in advance. This seems to be prescribed for him by his cognitive interest, which is of a different nature. What he has written in this connection indicates that he would like to start out from everyday language and from the stock of everyday knowledge, in order to gain access to correct theory formation.[21]

I am not aware of any objection which one could make against recourse to everyday knowledge unless it is linked with any false claims. Even the natural sciences have distanced themselves from experiential knowledge of everyday life, but this was only possible with the help of methods which rendered this knowledge problematic and subjected it to criticism—partially under the influence of ideas which radically contradicted this 'knowledge'

---

[19] If this freedom is greater in the type of social science which he criticizes, then one must still presume that the theories favoured by the dialectician are included in his margin of freedom, so that, at least by chance, he can stumble across the essential. Against this, only the thesis concerning the distortion of the object seems to help.

[20] See, for example, my article 'Die Problematik der ökonomischen Perspektive', in Zeitschrift für die gesamte Staatswissenschaft, vol. 117, 1961, also my introduction ('Probleme der Theoriebildung') to Theorie und Realität, loc. cit.

[21] It is interesting to see here how Habermas approaches not merely the hermeneutic-phenomenological trends in philosophy but, at the same time, those of the linguistic bent, whose methods lend themselves to a dogmatization of knowledge incorporated in everyday language. For both, see the relevant critical analyses in Jürgen v. Kempski's interesting collection of essays, Brechungen. Kritische Versuche zur Philosophie der Gegenwart, loc. cit.

and were corroborated in the face of 'common sense'.[22] Why should things be any different in the social sciences? Why should one not here too be able to draw upon ideas which contradict everyday knowledge? Does Habermas wish to exclude this? Does he wish to declare common sense—or somewhat more sublimely expressed, 'the natural hermeneutics of the social life-world'—to be sacrosanct? If not, then wherein does the specificity of his method lie? To what extent is 'the object' (*Sache*) treated more in accord with its own significance' than in the usual methods of the empirical sciences? Rather, it seems to me that certain prejudices are being expressed here. Does Habermas perhaps wish to deny a priori his assent, to theories which do not owe their emergence to a 'dialectical exploration' in conjunction with this 'natural hermeneutics'? Or does he wish to present them as being inessential? What can be done if, after empirical tests, other theories are better corroborated than are those with a higher pedigree? Or should these theories be so constructed that they cannot in principle be destroyed? Many of Habermas' statements suggest that he wishes to give preference to pedigree over performance. In general, the method of dialectical social science at times creates a more conservative than critical impression, just as this dialectic looks, in many respects, more conservative than it pretends to be.

3 THEORY, EXPERIENCE AND HISTORY

Habermas accuses the analytical conception of tolerating 'only one type of experience', namely 'the controlled observation of physical behaviour, which is set up in an isolated field under reproducible conditions by subjects interchangeable at will.'[23] Dialectical social theory opposes such a restriction. 'If the formal construction of theory, of the structure of concepts, of the choice of a general methodology, but rather . . . must, in advance, measure up to a preformed object, then theory cannot merely be united at a later stage with an experience which is then, of course, restricted.' The insights, to which dialectical social science has recourse, stem from 'the fund of pre-scientifically accumulated experience', apparently the same experience as that to which reference was

---

[22] *See* the essays of Karl Popper in *Conjectures and Refutations*, loc. cit.
[23] Habermas, 'The Analytical Theory of Science and Dialectics', p. 135 above.

made in connection with natural hermeneutics. This prior experience, which relates to society as a totality, 'shapes the outline of the theory' which 'cannot clash with an experience, however restricted it may be'; but, on the other hand, it need not forego thought which cannot be checked empirically either. Precisely its central statements are not to be 'wholly resolved by empirical findings'. This means, however, to be compensated for by the fact that, on the one hand, even the 'functionalist concept of the system' cannot be checked whilst, on the other hand, 'the hermeneutic anticipation of totality must . . . in the course of the explication . . . establish itself as correct'. The concepts, which are otherwise 'merely' analytically valid, must 'be legitimated in experience', whereby, of course, the latter is not to be identified with controlled observation. Here, the impression of a more appropriate, if not even a stricter, testing procedure is created than is otherwise normal in the empirical sciences.

In order to judge these objections and proposals, one has to be quite clear which problems are under discussion here. That the conception which Habermas criticizes tolerates 'only one type of experience' is, as it stands, simply false, no matter how familiar to its critics who are orientated to the cultural sciences, the reference to a too narrow concept of experience may be. Rather, for theory formation, this conception needs to make no restrictions in this respect—as opposed to the conception upheld by Habermas which commits one to a recourse to natural hermeneutics. The 'channelled' experience to which he alludes[24] becomes relevant for a definite task—namely, that of checking a theory on the basis of facts in order to ascertain its factual corroboration. For such a check it is essential to find situations which discriminate as much as possible.[25] The result of this is merely that one has occasion to favour such situations if a serious test is intended. Stated differently, the less a situation discriminates with regard to a certain theory, the less it is useful for testing the theory. If no relevant consequences for the situation in question result from the

---

[24] I do not intend to discuss at this point whether he has characterized it adequately in detail, but instead I wish to indicate the possibility of utilizing statistical methods in order to perform non-experimental checks and further draw attention to the fact that the whole realm of symbolic and, consequently, verbal behaviour is to be classified along with 'physical' behaviour.

[25] See Karl Popper, *The Logic of Scientific Discovery* (London, 1959), *passim*, as well as his essay 'Science: Conjectures and Refutations' in his above mentioned essay collection, where the risk of destruction at the hands of facts is stressed.

theory, then this situation is useless in this respect. Can the dialectical view raise any objection to this? We should bear in mind that, according to Habermas, even a dialectical theory cannot clash with experience, however restricted it may be. So far, his polemic against the narrow type of experience seems to me to rest largely on points of misunderstanding.

The further question of whether one must forego 'thoughts' which are not testable in this way can, without further ado, be answered negatively. No one expects such a sacrifice of the dialectician; not even, for example, in the name of the modern theory of science. One can simply expect that theories which claim to make statements about social reality are not so constructed as to admit random possibilities, with the result that they make no allowance for actual social events. Why should the thoughts of the dialecticians not be convertible into theories which, in principle, are testable?[26]

As far as the origin of dialectical insights in 'pre-scientifically accumulated experience' is concerned, we have just had the opportunity of discussing the question of emphasis upon this connection. The advocate of the view which Habermas criticizes has, as we have said, no occasion to overrate such problems of origin. In principle, he has no objection to 'prior experience' guiding theory formation, even if he would point out that this experience, as it is sketched out by Habermas, contains, amongst other things, the inherited mistakes which can, to a certain extent, help to 'shape' theory formation. There would be every reason, then, to invent strict tests for theories with this origin, in order to escape from these and other mistakes. Why should it be merely this origin which guarantees the quality of the categories? Why should not new ideas similarly receive a chance to prove themselves? It seems to me that, at this point, Habermas' methodology

---

[26] Habermas cites in this context Adorno's reference to the untestability of the dependence of each social phenomenon 'upon the totality'. The quotation stems from a context in which Adorno, with reference to Hegel, asserts that refutation is only fruitful as immanent critique; see Adorno, 'On the Logic of the Social Sciences', pp. 112f. Here the meaning of Popper's comments on the problem of the critical test is roughly reversed through 'further reflection'. It seems to me that the untestability of Adorno's assertion is basically linked with the fact that neither the concept of totality used, nor the nature of the dependence asserted, is clarified to any degree. Presumably, there is nothing more behind it than the idea that somehow everything is linked with everything else. To what extent some view could gain a methodical advantage from such an idea would really have to be demonstrated. In this matter, verbal exhortations of totality ought not to suffice.

becomes unnecessarily restrictive—in fact, as already mentioned, in a conservative direction—whilst the conception which he accuses of demanding that theory and concept formation be 'blindly' subjected to its abstract rules, makes no substantive prohibitions, because it does not believe it can presuppose any uncorrectable 'prior' knowledge. The extended concept of experience which Habermas invokes appears, at best, to have the methodical function of making respectable mistakes—which belong to so-called accumulated experience—difficult to correct.[27]

Habermas does not explain how the 'hermeneutic anticipation of totality' establishes itself as correct 'in the course of the explication' as a 'concept appropriate to the object itself'. It is clear, however, that he is not thinking here at any rate of a testing procedure along the lines of the methodology which he criticizes. After such methods of testing have been rejected as inadequate, there remains a claim, supported by metaphors, which is linked to the supposed existence of a method—not described in more detail but, nonetheless, better. Previously, Habermas had drawn attention to the untestability of the 'functionalist concept of system' whose appropriateness for the structure of society apparently seems problematical to him. I do not know whether he would accept the answer that this concept too could establish itself to be correct in the course of explication. Rather than such a boomerang argument, I prefer to question all the overstressing of concepts which one finds in Habermas, as in almost all the cultural scientific methodologists, as being the Hegelian inheritance of which they are apparently unable to rid themselves.[28] Here, that essentialism finds its expression which Popper has criticized and which has long been overcome in the natural sciences. The view which Habermas is attacking is not concerned with concepts but statements and systems of statements. In con-

---

[27] In contrast, the methodology which he criticizes also includes the possibility of theoretical corrections to previous experiences. In this respect, it is apparently less 'positivistic' than that of the dialecticians.

[28] Recently Jürgen v. Kempski has drawn attention to this point; *see* his essay 'Vorausetzungslosigkeit. Eine Studie zur Geschichte eines Wortes' in his *Brechungen*, p. 158. He points out that the shift of emphasis from the statement to the concept, which took place in post-Kantian German idealism, is closely connected with the transition to *raisonnements* whose logical structure is difficult to penetrate. German philosophers, as another critic has rightly stressed, have learned from Hegel above all darkness, apparent precision and the art of apparent proof; *see* Walter Kaufmann, 'Hegel: Contribution and Calamity', in *From Shakespeare to Existentialism* (Garden City, 1960).

junction with these, the concepts used in them can be corroborated or not corroborated. The demand that they should be
judged in isolation, independently of their theoretical context,
lacks any basis.[29] The overtaxing of concepts practised by
Hegelians, which reveals itself above all in words like 'totality',
'dialectical' and 'history', does not amount, in my opinion, to
anything other than their 'fetishization'—that, as far as I can see,
is their specialist term for such. It merely amounts to a word-
magic in the face of which their opponents lay down their
weapons—unfortunately too early in most cases.[30]

In his discussion of the relationship between theory and history,
Habermas contrasts prediction on the basis of *general laws*, which
is the specific achievement of empirical-scientific theories, with
the *interpretation* of a historical life-context, with the aid of a
definite type of *historical law-like regularities*. The latter is the
specific achievement of a dialectical theory of society. He rejects
the 'restrictive' use of the concept of law in favour of a type of
law which claims 'a validity which is, at the same time, more
comprehensive and more restricted', since the dialectical analysis,
which makes use of such historical laws of movement, apparently
aims to illuminate the concrete totality of a society undergoing
historical development. Such laws are not then generally valid,
they relate rather 'to a particular concrete area of application,
defined in terms of a process of development both unique *in toto*
and irreversible in its stages. This means that it is defined not
merely analytically but through the knowledge of the object
itself'. Habermas accounts for the fact that its realm of validity

---

[29] Otherwise too, Habermas' comments on concepts are quite problematical. He
concludes the section on theory and object (loc. cit., p. 134), for example, with the
statement that in dialectical social science 'concepts of a relational form give way
to concepts which are capable of expressing substance and function in one'. From
this stem theories of a more 'flexible type' which have the advantage of self-
reflexivity. I cannot imagine in what way logic is enriched here. One should really
expect a detailed explanation. At least one would like to see examples for such
concepts—preferably, of course, a logical analysis, and a more precise discussion
of where its special achievement lies.

[30] Analysis instead of accentuation ought to be recommended here. It is certainly
very refreshing when, for example, Theodor W. Adorno reveals the word-magic
of Heideggerism with well-formulated ironical turns of phrase; *see* his *The Jargon
of Authenticity*, trans. K. Tarnowski and F. Will, (Evanston/London, 1973). But
does not the language of dialectical obscuration which goes back to Hegel sometimes
appear to the unbiased very similar? Are the efforts which bear the characteristic of
strained intellectual, activity and which attempt to 'reduce the object to its concept'
always so far removed from the exhortation of being?

is at the same time more comprehensive, with the usual reference to the dependence of individual manifestations upon the totality, for such laws apparently express their fundamental dependent relations.[31] At the same time, however, they seek to 'articulate the objective meaning of a historical life-context'. Dialectical analysis then proceeds hermeneutically. It gains its categories 'from the situational consciousness of acting individuals' and takes up, 'through identification and critique', the 'objective spirit of a social life-world' in order to reveal, from this standpoint, 'the historical totality of a social context', which is to be understood as an objective context of meaning. Through the combination of the method of *Verstehen* with that of causal analysis in the dialectical approach, the 'separation of theory and history' is overcome.

Once again then, the methodological view of the analysts apparently proves to be too narrow. In its place, the outlines of a more grandiose conception are indicated; one that aims at grasping the historical process as a whole and disclosing its objective meaning. The impressive claims of this conception are clearly recognizable, but so far there has been no trace of a reasonably sober analysis of the procedure sketched out of its components. What does the logical structure of these historical laws look like, which have been acredited with such an interesting achievement, and how can one test them?[32] In what sense can a law which relates to a concrete, historical totality, to a unique and irreversible process as such, be anything other than a singular statement? Where does the law-like character of such a statement lie? How can one identify the fundamental relations of dependency of a concrete totality? What procedure is available in order to proceed from the subjective hermeneutics, which has to be overcome, to the objective meaning? Amongst dialecticians these might all be questions of lesser importance. One is acquainted with this in theology. The interested outsider, however, feels his credulity over-taxed. He sees the claims which are produced with superior reference to the restrictedness of other views, but he

---

[31] *See* Habermas, loc. cit., pp. 138ff.

[32] What differentiates them, for example, from the law-like regularities of a historicist character which Karl Popper in *The Poverty of Historicism*, loc. cit., has, to some extent, effectively criticized? May one presume that Habermas assumes this criticism is irrelevant, just as earlier he characterized Nagel's investigations as being irrelevant to his problems?

would really like to know to what extent such claims are well-founded.[33]

4 THEORY AND PRACTICE: THE PROBLEM OF VALUE FREEDOM

Habermas' next topic is the relationship between theory and practice, a problem which is of basic importance for him, since what he strives for is apparently nothing less than a scientifically organized philosophy of history with practical intent. Even his transcendence of the division between theory and history, by means of a dialectical combination of historical and systematic analysis, goes back, as he stresses earlier, to just such a practical orientation. This is certainly to be distinguished from a merely technical interest—the alleged source of undialectical empirical science. This opposition, to which reference has already been made, becomes central to his investigation in this context. Apparently we have now reached the core of his argument.[34]

His basic concern here is to overcome the already criticized restriction of positivistic social science to the solution of technical problems, in favour of a normative orientation. This is to be accomplished, in fact, with the help of that total historical analysis whose practical intentions 'can be released from pure arbitrariness and can be legitimated, for their part, dialectically from the objective context'.[35] In other words, he is looking for an *objective justification of practical action derived from the meaning of history*, a justification which a sociology with an empirical-scientific character cannot, by its nature, produce. But in all this, he cannot ignore the fact that Popper too concedes a certain place

---

[33] It is well known that even the so-called method of subjective understanding has met with strong criticism for some time within the social sciences, and this cannot be simply brushed aside. A hermeneutics, which alleges to break through to an objective meaning, may be far more problematic even if it does not become immediately conspicuous, of course, in the current milieu of German philosophy. On this, see Jürgen v. Kempski, 'Aspekte der Wahrheit', in *Brechungen*, especially 2: 'Die Welt als Text', where he tracks down the background to the exegetic model of knowledge referred to here.

[34] To this problematic he devotes not only a considerable section of his contribution to Adorno's *Festschrift* but also the systematic parts of his book *Theory and Practice*.

[35] Habermas, 'The Analytical Theory of Science and Dialectics', p. 138 above; *see* also *Theory and Practice*, loc. cit., pp. 114ff.

in his conception for histroical interpretations.[36] Popper, however, sharply attacks historical-philosophical theories which, in some mysterious manner, seek to unveil a hidden objective meaning in history that is to serve practical orientation and justification. He upholds the view that such projections usually rest on self-deception, and that we must decide to give history itself the meaning which we believe we can uphold. Such a 'meaning' can then also provide viewpoints for historical interpretation, which in each case involves a selection that is dependent upon our interest, yet without the objectivity of the connections chosen for the analysis having to be excluded.[37]

Habermas, who wishes to legitimate practical intentions from an objective total historical context—a desire usually relegated by his opponents to the realm of ideological thought—can, by its very nature, make little use of the type of historical analysis which Popper concedes, for various historical interpretations are possible according to the selective viewpoints chosen in each case. But Habermas, for his purposes, requires the *single* superior interpretation which can be drawn upon for legitimation. For this reason, he plays off against the Popper 'pure arbitrariness' of the particular viewpoints selected, and apparently claims for his interpretation—which relates to totality, and which reveals the real meaning of events (the aim *of society* as it is called elsewhere[38]) —an objectivity which can only be achieved dialectically. But the supposed arbitrariness of Popper's interpretation is not particularly damaging, for such an interpretation does not make any of the claims which are to be found in Habermas. In view of his criticism, however, one must ask how he, for his part, avoids such arbitrariness. Given the fact that one finds no solution in his

---

[36] *See* the last chapter of his book *The Open Society and its Enemies* (1944): 'Has History any Meaning?', or perhaps his essay 'Selbstbefreiung durch das Wissen' in *Der Sinn der Geschichte*, edited by Leonhard Reinisch (Munich, 1961). English trans. 'Emancipation Through Knowledge' in *The Humanist Outlook*, A. J. Ayer ed., (London, 1968).

[37] Popper has repeatedly drawn attention to the selective character of each statement and set of statements and also to that of the theoretical conceptions in the empirical sciences. With reference to historical interpretations, he says expressly 'Since all history depends upon our interests, *there can be only histories, and never a "history"*, a story of the development of mankind "as it happened"'. *See The Open Society and its Enemies*, loc. cit., p. 364, note 9. Similarly Otto Brunner in 'Abendländisches Geschichtsdenken' in his essay collection: *Neue Wege der Sozialgeschichte* (Göttingen, 1956), pp. 171f.

[38] Habermas, *Theory and Practice*, loc. cit., p. 321, in connection with an analysis of a discussion of Marxism which is, in other aspects too, extremely interesting.

writings to the legitimation problem which he himself raises, one has every reason to assume that arbitrariness is no less problematical in his case—the only difference being that it appears under the mask of an objective interpretation. It is difficult to gauge to what extent he can reject the Popperian critique of such supposedly objective interpretations, and the critique of ideology of the 'superficial' enlightenment in general. To some extent, totality proved to be a 'fetish' which serves to allow 'arbitrary' decisions to appear as objective knowledge.

As Habermas rightly asserts, this brings us to the problem of the so-called *value freedom* of historical and theoretical research. The postulate of value freedom rests, as he says, on 'a thesis which, following Popper, one can formulate as the dualism of facts and decisions',[39] and which can be explained on the basis of the distinction between natural laws and norms. He regards the 'strict separation' of these 'two types of law' as problematical. With reference to this, he formulates two questions, the answers to which allow us to clarify the issues involved; namely, on the one hand, whether the normative meaning is excluded from a rational discussion of the concrete life-context from which it emerged and upon which it still reacts and, on the other hand, the question of whether knowledge reduced positivistically to empirical science is, in fact, released from every normative bond.[40] The manner of posing the questions in itself shows that he appears to interpret the dualism mentioned in a way that rests upon misunderstanding, for that which he questions here has little to do with the meaning of this distinction.

The second of the two questions leads him to the investigation of Popper's suggestions concerning the basis-problem.[41] He discovers in them unintended consequences which allegedly involve a circle, and he sees in this evidence for the embedding of the research process in a context which is only explicable hermeneutically. The problem revolves around the following: Popper, in opposition to the advocates of a protocol language, insists that even basic statements can, in principle, be revised, since they themselves contain a theoretically determined element

---

[39] Habermas, 'The Analytical Theory of Science and Dialectics', p. 144 above.

[40] Habermas, p. 148 above.

[41] We are concerned here with the problem of the character of basic statements—statements which describe observable states of affairs—and of their significance for the testability of theories; see Karl Popper, *The Logic of Scientific Discovery*, loc. cit., ch. 5.

of interpretation.[42] One has to apply the conceptual apparatus of the theory in question in order to obtain basic statements. Habermas detects a circularity in the fact that, in order to apply laws, one needs to have previously established the facts; but this can only be achieved in a process in which these laws are already applied. There is a misunderstanding here. The application of laws—and that means here the application of theoretical statements—demands the use of the relevant *conceptual apparatus* to formulate the conditions of application which come into question, and to which the application of *the laws themselves* can attach itself. I do not see what circularity is involved here nor, in particular, how in this case Habermas' *deus ex machina*, hermeneutic explication, would be of more help. Nor do I see to what extent 'the detachment of methodology from the real research process and its social functions' takes its revenge, here—whatever he means by this.

The reference made by Habermas in this context to the institutional character of research and the role of normative regulations in the research process, is in no way suited to solving previously unsolved problems.[43] As far as the 'fact' is concerned which Popper is supposed to 'persistently ignore' namely 'that we are normally in no doubt at all about the validity of a basic statement', and that, as a result, the logical possibility of an infinite regress *de facto* does not come into question, one can only make the following reply: namely, that, in itself, the factual certainty of a statement can only with difficulty be considered as a criterion of the statement's validity, and that, this apart, Popper himself solves the problem of regress without resorting to problematical states of affairs of this sort. His concern is not an analysis of factual behaviour but rather a solution of methodological problems. Reference to unformulated criteria, which are applied *de facto* in the institutionally channelled research process, is no solution to such a problem. The assertion that the problem really does not arise in this process, in no way serves to eliminate it as a methodological problem. One has only to recall that, for many

---

[42] This point of view is even more strongly expressed in Popper's later works; *see*, for example, the essays in his above-mentioned collection.

[43] In any case, Popper himself has already analysed such connections. In his book *The Logic of Scientific Discovery*, he critized naturalism with regard to methodological questions and, in his major social philosophical work *The Open Society and its Enemies*, he deals explicitly with the institutional aspects of scientific method. His *distinction* between natural laws and norms in no way led him to overlook the role of normative regulation in research.

scientists, the problem of information content—incidentally a related problem—does not present itself, and this frequently has the result that, under certain conditions, they tautologize their systems and render them devoid of content. Problems must present themselves to the methodologists which other people often do not think of.

The norms and criteria, upon which Habermas reflects in a very general manner in this section of his essay, are characteristically treated from the perspective of the sociologist as social states of affairs, as factors in a research process based on the division of labour, a process embedded in the context of societal labour. This is a perspective which can certainly be of great interest. For methodology, however, it is not a question of the acceptance of social data, but rather of the critical elucidation and rational reconstruction of the relevant rules and criteria with reference to possible aims; for example, the aim of more closely approximating to the truth. It is interesting that the dialectician becomes, at this point, the real 'positivist' by imagining he can eliminate problems of the logic of research by reference to factual social data. This is not a transcendence of Popperian methodology but rather an attempt to 'circumvent' its problems by drawing upon what one is wont to disavow in other contexts as 'mere facticity'.

As far as the sociological aspects are concerned, one must likewise doubt whether they can be adequately treated in the way in which Habermas suggests. It is in this respect—with respect to the so-called life-references of research—that one must take into account the fact that there are institutions which stabilize an independent interest in the knowledge of objective contexts, so that there exists in these spheres the possibility of largely emancipating oneself from the direct pressure of everyday practice. The freedom to engage in scientific work, made possible in this way, has made no small contribution to the advance of knowledge. In this respect, the inference of technical utilization from technical rootedness proves to be a 'short-circuit'.*

Habermas, in treating the basis-problem, introduces the question of the normative regulation of the cognitive process and from this can return to the *problem of value freedom* which formed his starting point. He can now say that this problem testifies 'that the analytical-empirical procedures cannot ensure for themselves

---

* Albert here makes a pun on *Rück*schluss (inference) and *Kurz*schluss (short-circuit). Unfortunately this cannot be rendered into English.

the life-reference within which they themselves objectively stand.[44] His succeeding comments suffer, however, from the fact that at no point does he formulate the postulate of value freedom, whose questionability he wishes to emphasize, in such a way that one can be sure with which assertion he is actually concerned. One can understand the value freedom of science in a variety of ways. I do not suppose that Habermas thinks that anyone upholding such a principle in *any* sense of the word could any longer form a clear picture of the social context in which research stands.[45]

Modern advocates of a methodical value freedom principle are in no way wont to overlook the normative references of research and the knowledge-guiding interests.[46] Generally they propose more detailed solutions in which various aspects of the problem are distinguished.

Similarly, Adorno's remarks on the problem of value, referred to by Habermas, will scarcely take us further. When he points out that the separation of evaluative and value free behaviour is false in so far as value, and thus value freedom, are themselves reifications, then similarly we may ask to whom such remarks are addressed. Who would relate the above-mentioned dichotomy so simply to 'behaviour'? Who would take up the concept of value in such a simple manner as is implied here?[47] Adorno's judgment that the whole value problem is falsely posed,[48] bears no relation

---

[44] *Habermas*, p. 158.

[45] As far as the reference which he makes at the start of his essay (p. 132 above), is concerned, that positivism has abandoned the insight 'that the research process instigated by human subjects belongs, through the act of cognition itself, to the objective context which should be apprehended', one only needs to refer to the relevant works, above all, Ernst Topitsch, 'Sozialtheorie und Gesellschaftsgestaltung' (1956) reprinted in his volume of essays *Sozialphilosophie zwischen Ideologie und Wissenschaft* (Neuwied, 1961). There one also finds critical material on the dialectical processing of this insight.

[46] Such an objection could also hardly be made against Max Weber. Similarly, such objections could not be applied to Karl Popper who has explicitly distanced himself from the demand for an *unconditional* value freedom (*see* his paper 'The Logic of the Social Sciences', pp. 87ff.) nor to Ernst Topitsch. I have frequently expressed myself on these problems, most recently in 'Wertfreiheit als methodisches Prinzip', in *Schriften des Vereins für Sozialpolitik*, Neue Folge, vol. 29 (Berlin, 1963).

[47] *See*, for example, the study of Viktor Kraft in his book *Grundlagen einer wissenschaftlichen Werttheorie*, 2nd ed. (Vienna, 1951), which can serve as a starting point for a more differentiated treatment of the value freedom problem. There can be no talk of 'reification' or of a value concept which can be criticized in this way. If one speaks of value freedom and similar terms as if they were Platonic essences which everyone can see then the ambiguity of such terms is inadequately represented.

[48] *Adorno*, 'On the Logic of the Social Sciences', p. 118 above.

to a definite formulation of this problem, and can therefore hardly be judged; it is an assertion which sounds comprehensive but carries no risk. He alludes to antinomies from which positivism cannot extricate itself, without even giving an indication of where they might lie. Neither the views criticized, nor the objections raised against them can be identified in such a way that an unbiased person could judge them.[49] In a very interesting manner, Habermas too talks of value freedom as the problem of reification, of categories of the life-world which gain power over a theory which devolves on practice, and similar things which presumably have escaped the 'superficial' enlightenment, but he does not condescend to analyse concrete solutions of the value problem.

In connection with the problem of the practical application of social-scientific theories, he then discusses Myrdal's *critique of ends-means thought*.[50] The difficulties to which Myrdal draws attention in connection with the question of value-neutrality lead him to attempt to demonstrate that one is forced into dialectical thought in order to overcome them. His thesis concerning the purely technical orientation of empirical-scientific knowledge plays a role here; *de facto* this makes necessary the guidance of 'programmatic viewpoints which are not reflected upon as such'.[51] Thus, technically utilizable social-scientific theories could not 'despite their own self-understanding, satisfy the strict demands of value-neutrality'. 'It is precisely the domination of a technical cognitive interest, hidden to itself,' he says, 'which conceals the veiled investments of the relatively dogmatic total understanding of a situation, with which even the strictly empirical sociologist has implicitly identified himself before it slips through his hands in the initial stages of a formalized theory under the claim of hypothetical universality.' He then concludes that if these interests, which *de facto* guide knowledge, *cannot be suspended* then they must 'be brought under control and criticized or legitimated as objective

---

[49] The passage to which Habermas refers ('What was subsequently sanctioned as a value does not operate externally to the object . . . but rather is immanent to it') suggests an interpretation of Adorno's position which one presumes would hardly please him, that is, an interpretation along the lines of a naïve value-realism which is still to be found in the Scholastics.

[50] These are thoughts which Myrdal published in 1933 in his essay, 'Das Zweck-Mittel-Denken in der Nationalökonomie' in *Zeitschrift für Nationalökonomie*, vol. IV; English translation in his essay collection *Value in Social Theory* (London, 1958). I am pleased that this essay, to which I have been constantly drawing attention over the last ten years, is gradually receiving general attention.

[51] Habermas, 'The Analytical Theory of Science and Dialectics', p. 161 above.

interests derived from the total societal context'; this, however, forces one into dialectical thought.

Here the fact that dialecticians persistently refuse to dissect the complex value-problematic and to treat its particular problems separately apparently takes its revenge in the fear that 'the whole' —which they, as if spellbound, seek never to let out of their sight —could slip through their fingers. In order to reach solutions at all, one has, now and again, to avert one's gaze from the whole and, temporarily at least, to bracket off totality. As a consequence of this thought which is directed to the whole, we find constant reference to the connection of all details in the totality, which compels one to dialectical thinking, but which results in not a single actual solution to a problem. Studies which show that here one can make progress without dialectical thought are, on the other hand, ignored.[52]

5 CRITIQUE OF IDEOLOGY AND DIALECTICAL JUSTIFICATION

It can hardly be doubted that Habermas sees the problem of the relation between theory and practice mainly from the perspective of the justification of practical action, and that he understands it as a *problem of legitimation*. This perspective also explains his attitude towards a critique of ideology which provides no substitute for that which it disavows. In addition, there is his *instrumentalist interpretation* of pure science which makes more difficult his own access to the understanding of such a critique of ideology. He links both with modern *irrationalism* which makes plausible his demand for a dialectical transcendence of 'positivistic' limitations.

He believes that the restriction of the social sciences to 'pure'

---

[52] In my view, Habermas does not sufficiently distinguish between the possible aspects of the value problem. I will not bother going into details here in order not to repeat myself; *see*, for instance, my essay 'Wissenschaft und Politik' in *Probleme der Wissenschaftstheorie. Festschrift für Viktor Kraft*, edited by Ernst Topitsch (Vienna, 1960), as well as the above-mentioned essay 'Wertfreiheit als methodisches Prinzip'. I have written on the problem of ends-means thought discussed by Myrdal in *Ökonomische Ideologie und politische Theorie* (Göttingen, 1954); 'Die Problematik der ökonomischen Perspektive', in *Zeitschrift für die gesamte Staatswissenschaft*, vol. 117 1961, reprinted as the first chapter in my *Marktsoziologie und Entscheidungslogik* and the section 'Allgemeine Wertproblematik' of the article 'Wert' in *Handwörterbuch der Sozialwissenschaften*. For a critique of the Myrdal book mentioned in note 50 *see* 'Das Wertproblem in den Sozialwissenschaften' in *Schweizer Zeitschrift für Volkswirtschaft und Statistik*, vol. 94, 1958. In my view, my suggested solutions for the problems in question render the leap into dialectics unnecessary.

knowledge—whose purity seems to him, in any case, problematical—eliminates from the horizon of the sciences the
questions of life-practice in such a way that they are henceforth
exposed to irrational and dogmatic attempts at interpretation.[53]
These attempts at interpretation are then subjected to a 'positivistically circumscribed critique of ideology', which is basically
indebted to the same purely technically rooted cognitive interest
as is technologically utilizable social science; and consequently,
like the latter, it accepts the dualism of facts and decisions. Since
such a social science, similar to the natural sciences, can only
guarantee the economy of the choice of means whilst action over
and above this demands normative orientation; and since
ultimately, the 'positivistic' type of critique of ideology is in a
position to reduce the interpretations which it criticizes merely
to the decisions upon which they rest, then the result is 'an
unconstrained decisionism in the selection of the highest goals'.
Positivism in the domain of knowledge is matched by decisionism
in the domain of practice; a too narrowly conceived rationalism
in the one realm matches irrationalism in the other. 'Thus on this
level the critique of ideology involuntarily furnishes the proof
that progress of a rationalization limited in terms of empirical
science to technical control is paid for with the corresponding
growth of a mass of irrationality in the domain of praxis itself'.[54]
In this context, Habermas is not afraid to relate quite closely the
diverse forms of decisionism represented, amongst others, by Jean
Paul Sartre, Carl Schmitt and Arnold Gehlen as in some degree
complementary views to a very broadly conceived positivism.[55]
In view of the irrationality of decisions accepted by positivists
and decisionists alike, the return to *mythology* is understandable,
Habermas believes, as a last desperate attempt 'to secure institutionally . . . a socially binding precedent for practical questions'.[56]

---

[53] *See* the section 'The positivistic isolation of reason and decision', in his essay
'Dogmatism, Reason, and Decision' in *Theory and Practice*, loc. cit., pp. 263f.; further
'The Analytical Theory of Science and Dialectics', pp. 146f.

[54] Habermas, *Theory and Practice*, loc. cit., p. 265.

[55] One finds a certain analogy to Habermas' complementary thesis in Wolfgang
de Boer's essay, 'Positivismus und Existenzphilosophie' in *Merkur*, vol. 6, 1952,
47, pp. 12ff., where the two intellectual currents are interpreted as two answers to
the 'same tremendous event of the constitution of existence'. As a remedy, the
author recommends a 'fundamental anthropological interpretation', 'a science of
man which we do not, as yet, possess'.

[56] Habermas, *Theory and Practice*, loc. cit., p. 267 [amended trans.]. In this connection, he refers to a very interesting book by Max Horkheimer and Theodor W.

Given his understanding of positive science, Habermas' thesis
is at least plausible, even if it does not do justice to the fact that
the relapse into mythology, where it has actually occurred, can
in no way be attributed to the specific rationality of the scientific
attitude.[57] Usually the positivism which Habermas criticizes
makes itself quite unpopular in totalitarian societies, in which such
a remythologization is on the agenda, whilst dialectical attempts
at the interpretation of reality are frequently able to gain recognition there.[58] Of course, it can always be said later that this was
not true dialectics. But how can true dialectics actually be
recognized? Habermas' treatment of Polish revisionism is interesting in this connection.[59] This revisionism developed in
reaction to Stalinist orthodoxy in an intellectual milieu which was
greatly determined by the influence of the Warsaw school of
philosophy. Amongst other things, its critique was directed
against the characteristics of a holistic philosophy of history with
practical intent—characteristics which determine the ideological
character of Marxism. Habermas wishes to take up positively
those characteristics of Marxist thought which fell prey to
revisionism's critique. This development is not accidental. It is
connected with the fact that in Poland, after the opportunities
for a certain amount of free discussion had been created, the

---

Adorno, *Dialectic of Enlightenment*, loc. cit., where, within the framework of an
analysis of the 'dialectics of myth and enlightenment', positivism is 'denounced' and
Hegel's poor acquaintance with logic, mathematics and positive science is renewed.

[57] It is interesting that in the Third Reich Carl Schmitt's 'decisionism' which
yielded to a 'concrete thought devoted to the upholding of order (*Ordnungsdenken*)'
readily recalls Hegel, as attested to by the Hegelian Karl Larenz at that time; *see*
Karl Larenz's review of Carl Schmitt's book, *Über die drei Arten des rechtswissen-
schaftlichen Denkens* (Hamburg, 1934), in *Zeitschrift für Deutsche Kulturphilosophie*,
vol. I, 1935, pp. 112ff. This periodical also contains testimonies to a mode of
thought which draws considerably upon Hegel and is right-wing in orientation. It
is not difficult to incorporate it into the realm of fascist ideology.

[58] *See* Ernst Topitsch's paper 'Max Weber and sociology today' in O. Stammer
(ed.), *Max Weber and Sociology Today* (Oxford, 1971). Also very interesting in this
respect is the book by Z. A. Jordan, *Philosophy and Ideology. The Development of
Philosophy and Marxism–Leninism in Poland since the Second World War* (Dordrecht,
1963), in which the confrontation between the Warsaw school of philosophy,
which ought to fall under Habermas' broad concept of 'positivism', and the dialectically orientated Polish Marxism, is analysed in detail.

[59] *See Theorie und Praxis*, loc. cit., pp. 324ff. This is the final section—'Immanente
Kritik am Marxismus'—of a very interesting essay, 'Zur philosophischen Diskussion
um Marx und den Marxismus' which also includes a discussion of Sartre and Marcuse. In this essay, Habermas' intentions concerning a philosophy of history with
practical intent, one which reworks the insights of the empirical social sciences, are
well expressed.

arguments of the dialecticians collapsed—one could say, all along the line—under the impact of the counter-arguments from the Warsaw school.[60] It is a bit too simple to attribute an epistemological naïvety, as Habermas does, to the theoreticians who were compelled to relinquish untenable positions in the face of the critical arguments of philosophers who belonged to a dominant tradition in the theory of knowledge. Leszek Kolakowski's retreat to a 'methodological rationalism' and a more 'positivistic revisionism', which Habermas so sharply criticizes, was motivated by a challenge to which our own inheritors of Hegelian thought must first prove equal, before they have cause to dismiss lightly the results of the Polish discussion.[61]

It seems to me that a close connection exists between the particular features of dialectical thought and the fact that dialectical attempts to interpret reality, in contrast to the 'positivism' which Habermas criticizes, are frequently quite popular in totalitarian societies. One can recognize a basic achievement of such forms of thought precisely in the fact that they are appropriate for disguising random decisions as knowledge, and thereby legitimating them in such a way as to remove them from the possibility of discussion.[62] A 'decision' veiled in this manner, will look no better even in the light of reason—however comprehensive it may be—than that 'mere' decision which one imagines one can overcome in this way. Unmasking through critical analysis can then, only with difficulty, be criticized in the name of reason.[63]

Habermas cannot, it is true, completely incorporate this

---

[60] *See* the above mentioned book by Jordan, *Philosophy and Ideology*, parts 4–6. The relevant argument for Habermas' conception is to be found in part 6: 'Marxist–Leninist Historicism and the Concept of Ideology.'

[61] This is especially true since one can hardly claim that the Polish Marxists did not have access to the arguments which our representatives of dialectical thought believe they have at their disposal.

[62] *See*, for example, the critical examination by Ernst Topitsch in his book *Sozialphilosophie zwischen Ideologie und Wissenschaft*, loc. cit., and also his essay 'Entfremdung und Ideologie. Zur Entmythologisierung des Marxismus' in *Hamburger Jahrbuch für Wirtschafts- und Gesellschaftspolitik*, 9, 1964.

[63] The 'superficial' enlightenment, which has to be overcome dialectically seems to me largely identical with the 'flat' and 'shallow' enlightenment which, for a long time in Germany, has been met with suspicion as a dubious metaphysics of the state, or as the name of concrete life-references; on this subject *see* Karl Popper, 'Emancipation Through Knowledge', loc. cit., Ernst Topitsch, *Sozialphilosophie zwischen Ideologie und Wissenschaft,* loc. cit., and my contribution to the *Jahrbuch für Kritische Aufklärung 'Club Voltaire'*, 1 (Munich, 1963), 'Die Idee der kritischen Vernunft'.

critique of ideology into his scheme of a technically rooted, and therefore randomly utilizable, knowledge. He is compelled to recognize a 'reified critique of ideology' which apparently has, to a certain extent, severed itself from this root,[64] and in which 'honest positivists, whose laughter is dispelled by such perspectives' namely those who shrink back from irrationalism and remythologization 'seek their foothold'. He regards the motivation of such a critique of ideology as unclarified but, this is only true because here he can hardly impute the only motive which he finds plausible, namely that of the provision of new techniques. He sees that this critique 'is making an attempt to enlighten consciousness' but fails to see from whence it draws its strength 'if reason divorced from decision must be wholly devoid of any interest in an emancipation of consciousness from dogmatic bias'.[65] Here he encounters the *dilemma* that scientific knowledge of this sort is, in his opinion, only possible as 'a kind of committed reason, the *justified* possibility of which is precisely what the critique of ideology denies' but with a renunciation of justification however 'the dispute of reason with dogmatism itself remains a matter of dogmatic opinion'.[65a] He sees behind this dilemma the fact that 'the critique of ideology must tacitly presuppose as its own motivation just what it attacks as dogmatic, namely, the convergence of reason and decision—thus precisely a comprehensive concept of rationality'.[65b] In other words, this form of critique of ideology is not in a position to see through itself. Habermas, however, sees through it; it is, for him, a veiled form of decided reason, a thwarted dialectics. One sees where his restrictive interpretation of non-dialectical social science has led him.

The critique of ideology analysed in this manner can, on the other hand, readily admit an underlying interest in an 'emancipation of consciousness from dogmatic bias'. It is even capable of reflecting on its foundations without running into difficulties. But as far as Habermas' *alternative of dogmatism and rational*

---

[64] *See* Habermas, *Theory and Practice*, loc. cit., pp. 267ff. He refers initially to the studies of Ernst Topitsch which are printed in *Sozialphilosophie zwischen Ideologie und Wissenschaft*, loc. cit. The book seems to provide him with certain difficulties of categorization.

[65] Habermas, loc. cit., p. 267 (amended translation).

[65a] ibid., p. 268.

[65b] ibid., p. 268 (amended translation).

justification is concerned it has every cause to expect information as to how dialectics is capable of solving the problem of rational justification which arises here. Above all *dialectics* is dependent upon such a solution since it sets out from the standpoint of the legimation of practical intentions. Whether positivism is in a position to offer a solution, indeed whether it is interested at all in a solution of such problems, is a question whose answer will depend, amongst other things, upon what one understands by 'positivism'. We shall return to this point.

According to Habermas, one can distinguish between one type of critique of ideology and, corresponding to it, a rationality which is only orientated to the value of scientific techniques, and another which, over and above this, also develops from 'the significance of a scientific emancipation for adult autonomy'.[66] He is prepared to admit that possibly 'even in its positivistic form the critique of ideology can pursue an interest in adult autonomy'. The Popperian conception, to which he makes this concession, apparently, in his opinion,[67] comes closest to the comprehensive rationality of the dialectical sort. For it cannot be denied that Popper's critical rationalism, which was developed precisely as a reaction to the logical positivism of the thirties, recognizes in principle no boundaries to rational discussion, and consequently can take up problems which a more narrowly understood positivism is not wont to discuss.[68] But he has no cause however to attribute all such problems to positive science. Critical reason in Popper's sense does not stop at the boundaries of science. Habermas concedes to him the motive of enlightenment but draws attention to the 'resigned reservation' which, it is claimed,

[66] *Theory and Practice*, loc. cit., pp. 268ff. and p. 276.

[67] Habermas, loc. cit., p. 276. Ernst Topitsch, on the other hand, if I understand correctly, must it seems be classified under the first type. I am unable to recognize the basis for this classification. Nor do I see how one can carry out a cataloguing in accordance with this scheme at all. What criteria are applied here? Does not the first form of the critique of ideology perhaps owe its fictive existence to its restrictive interpretation of scientific knowledge?

[68] Incidentally, it is thoroughly questionable to discuss such problems against the background of the positivism of the thirties, which has long been abandoned by its early representatives. Even at that time, there was also, for example, the Warsaw school, which never indulged in some of the restrictions. Wittgenstein's statement quoted by Habermas in connection with the question of value freedom—'We feel that even when all possible scientific questions have been answered, the problems of life remain completely untouched' (p. 171)—seems to me to be rather uncharacteristic for most positivists. It has nothing to do with Popper's view which makes its appearance in connection with a critique of Popper unintelligible.

lies in the fact that here rationalism only appears 'as his professed faith'.[69] One can assume that his critique at this point is linked with the above-mentioned expectation of justification.

Undoubtedly this expectation remains unfulfilled. Popper develops his view in a confrontation with a 'comprehensive rationalism' which is uncritical in so far as it—analogous to the paradox of the liar—implies its own transcendence.[70] Since, for logical reasons, a self-grounding of rationalism is impossible, Popper calls the assumption of a rationalist attitude a decision which, because it logically lies *prior* to the application of rational arguments, can be termed irrational.[71] However, he then makes a sharp distinction between a blind decision and one taken with open eyes, that is, with a clear knowledge of its consequences. What is Habermas' position on this problem? He passes over it, presumably on the assumption that a dialectician is not confronted with it.[72] He does not take up Popper's arguments against comprehensive rationalism. He admits that 'if scientific insight purged of the interest of reason is devoid of all immanent reference to praxis and if, inversely, every normative content is detached nominalistically from insights into its real relation to life—as Popper presupposes undialectically—then indeed the dilemma must be conceded: that I cannot rationally compel anyone to support his assumptions with arguments and evidence from experiences'.[73] He does not show, however, how far the assump-

---

[69] Habermas, *Theory and Practice*, loc. cit., p. 276.

[70] Karl Popper, *The Open Society and its Enemies*, loc. cit., p. 230.

[71] One can argue here as to whether the expressions used are problematica in so far as they can possibly evoke misleading associations. One could, for example, restrict the use of the dichotomy 'rational-irrational' to cases in which both possibilities exist. The word 'faith' which appears in this context in Popper is similarly loaded in many respects, above all on account of the widespread idea that there hardly exists a connection between faith and knowledge. But, despite this, it is not here primarily a matter of the mode of expression.

[72] It is not without interest in this connection that the founder of dialectics, in the form in which it is played off against 'positivism' by Habermas, failed to get by without a 'resolution' 'which one can also regard as an arbitrary action'; *see* G. F. W. Hegel, *Wissenschaft der Logik*, edited by Georg Lasson, Erster Teil, vol. 56 of the Meiner Library, p. 54. Jürgen von Kempski has specifically drawn attention to this point in the essay already mentioned, 'Voraussetzungslosigkeit' in *Brechungen*, loc. cit., p. 142, p. 146 and *passim*. Besides this von Kempski points out that 'the so-called German idealists have made the Kantian position on the primacy of practical reason and the doctrine of postulates into a focal point for a reinterpretation of the critique of reason—a reinterpretation subservient, in the last analysis, to theological motives', loc. cit., p. 146.

[73] Habermas, *Theory and Practice*, loc. cit., p. 276.

tion of an 'immanent reference to praxis' in knowledge, or a combination of normative content and insight into things can be relevant here. His remarks, in the last analysis, amount to the fact that the problems of a comprehensive 'decided' reason can be adequately resolved. One does not learn, however, what this solution looks like. His idea that 'in rational discussion as such a tendency is inherent, irrevocably, which is precisely a decisive commitment entailed by rationality itself, and which therefore does not require arbitrary decision, or pure faith',[74] presupposes rational discussion as a fact, and consequently overlooks the problem raised by Popper. The thesis that even 'in the simplest discussion of methodological question . . . a prior understanding of a rationality is presupposed that is not yet divested of its normative elements,'[75] is scarcely appropriate as an objection to Popper, who has not denied the normative background of such discussions but rather has analysed it. Once again, Habermas' tendency to point to 'naked' facts instead of discussing problems and solutions to problems is revealed.

In the meantime, Popper has further developed his views in a way that should be relevant to the problems which Habermas treats.[76] He aims at the transcendence of views which are directed towards the *idea of positive justification*,[77] and he opposes to this the idea of *the critical test*, detached from justificatory thought, which only has the choice between an infinite regress that cannot be fulfilled, and a dogmatic solution. Habermas, too, is still in the grip of this justificatory thought when he has recourse to factual certainties of some kind, when he wishes to legitimate practical intentions from an objective context, and when he expects that meta-ethical criteria be derived and justified from underlying

---

[74] Habermas, loc. cit., p. 279 (amended translation).

[75] Habermas refers here to David Pole's interesting book, *Conditions of Rational Inquiry* (London, 1961), a book which, despite partial critique of Popper, adopts a great number of his views. Pole discusses his work *The Open Society and its Enemies* but not, however, later publications in which Popper has further developed his critical rationalism.

[76] *See* in particular his essay 'On the Sources of Knowledge and Ignorance' in *Proceedings of the British Academy*, vol. XLVI, 1960, reprinted in *Conjectures and Refutations*; *see* also William Warren Bartley, *The Retreat to Commitment* (New York, 1962); Paul K. Feyerabend, *Knowledge without Foundations* (Oberlin/Ohio, 1961), and my above-mentioned contribution, 'Die Idee der kritischen Vernunft'.

[77] Even in his *Logik der Forschung* (Vienna, 1935), one can find the basis for this development; *see* his treatment of the Friesian trilemma of dogmatism, infinite regress and psychologism in the chapter on the problem of an empirical basis.

interests.[78] The alternative of dogmatism and rational justification,
which he considers important is affected, no matter how obvious
it sounds, by the argument that recourse to positive reasons is
itself a dogmatic procedure. The demand for legitimation which
Habermas' philosophy of history with practical intent inspires,
makes respectable the recourse to dogmas which can only be
obscured by dialectics. The critique of ideology aims at making
such obscurations transparent, at laying bare the dogmatic core
of such arguments, and relating them to the social context of
consequences in which they fulfil their legitimating function. In
this respect, it counteracts precisely such edifices of statement as
Habermas demands for the normative orientation of practice—
it must provide not legitimating but critical achievements. Anyone
undertaking to solve the problem of the relationships between
theory and practice, between social science and politics from the
perspective of justification is left—if he wishes to avoid open
recourse to a normative dogmatics—only with retreat to a form
of obscurantism such as can be achieved by means of dialectical
or hermeneutic thought. In this, language plays no small part;
namely, one which stands in the way of a clear and precise
formulation of ideas. That such a language dominates even
methodological reflections which precede the actual undertaking,
and also the confrontation with other conceptions on this level,
can presumably only be understood from the angle of aesthetic
motives if one disregards the obvious idea of a strategy of relative
immunization.[79]

---

[78] See *Theory and Practice*, loc. cit., p. 280, where he discusses my essay 'Ethik und
Meta-Ethik' which appears in *Archiv für Philosophie*, vol. 11, 1961. In my treatment
of the problem of corroboration for ethical systems, he objects to the fact that here
the positivistic limitations would involuntarily become evident, since substantive
questions would be prejudiced in the form of methodological decisions, and the
practical consequences of the application of the relevant criteria would be excluded
from reflection. Instead of this, he suggests a hermeneutic clarification of historically
appropriate concepts and, in addition, the justification from interests mentioned.
Just before this, however, he quotes a passage of mine from which it becomes clear
that a rational discussion of such criteria is quite possible. Here nothing is excluded
from reflection nor is anything prejudiced in the sense of decisions which cannot
be revised. It would be difficult to determine whether something is 'in itself' a
'substantive question' and, for this reason, has to be discussed on a quite specific
level.

[79] However, one has the impression that wherever this language makes an
appearance in works by members of the Frankfurt School, even when their ideas
seem quite interesting, they are themselves 'setting up a hedgehog defence' (*einigeln*)
in advance against possible critics.

6 CRITICAL PHILOSOPHY VERSUS DIALECTICS

The problem of the relations between theory and practice, central to Habermas' thought, is interesting from many standpoints. The representatives of other views also have to come to grips with this.[80] It is a problem in whose treatment philosophical views inevitably play a role. This may lead to useful solutions, but may also in certain circumstances render a solution more difficult. Habermas' manner of tackling the problem suffers from the fact that he exaggerates the difficulties of the views he criticizes by means of restrictive interpretations and, at best, indicates his own solutions vaguely and in metaphorical turns of phrase.[81] He behaves hypocritically towards his opponents but more than generously towards dialecticians. He is unsparing with advice to his opponents that they should overcome their restrictedness by creating the unity of reason and decision, the transition to a comprehensive rationality, and whatever other formulations he might suggest. But what he positively opposes to their 'specific' rationality are more metaphors than methods. He makes thorough use of the advantage that lies in the fact that Popper, for instance, formulates his views clearly, but he exposes his readers to the disadvantage that they must painstakingly find their way through his own exposition.

Substantively, the fundamental weakness of his presentation lies in the manner in which he outlines the problem situation. His instrumentalist interpretation of the theoretical empirical sciences forces him towards an interpretation of the 'positivistic' critique of ideology for which there are surely no indications in social reality. Where he cannot help but concede the motive of enlightenment, the emancipation of consciousness from dogmatic bias, he

---

[80] Over a long period, for example, Gerhard Weisser, schooled in the Fries-Nelson version of Kantianism, has concerned himself with this problem. In economics we find the so-called welfare-economics, which primarily has utilitarian roots. Particularly in this discipline it has become evident what difficulties the undertaking of the justification of political measures through theoretical considerations faces. It frequently seems here that the greatest difficulties lie in the details.

[81] I do not in any way wish to dispute that his book *Theory and Practice* contains interesting, partly historical analyses and confrontations which I cannot discuss within the framework of the problems at hand. I have only been able here to deal with systematic ideas which are important for his critique of 'positivism'. The relevant sections may not necessarily be decisive for an appreciation of the book as a whole.

indicates restrictions which are difficult to identify merely on the basis of his formulations. The thesis of the complimentarity of positivism and decisionism which he upholds does not lack a certain plausibility, if one relates it to the unreflected 'positivism' of everyday life. It may even have something in its favour if one presupposes his instrumentalist interpretation of science, but it can hardly be applied in a meaningful manner to the philosophical views which he wishes to attack with his thesis. In his attempts to demonstrate the questionability of the distinction between facts and decisions, between natural laws and norms, distinctions which he regards as mistaken oppositions, he has to constantly presuppose such distinction. It is precisely because of the obliteration of the distinction that a clarification of the relations between these things is made more difficult. That there *are* relations between them is in no way denied in the views he criticizes. Instead, such relations are analysed.

The crude 'positivism' of common sense may tend not only to distinguish *pure* theories, *bare* facts, and *mere* decisions but also to *isolate* them from one another if it seeks to free itself from the original *fusion* of these elements in the language and thought of everyday life. But this is in no way true of the philosophical views which Habermas criticizes. Instead, they reveal manifold *relations* between these moments which can be relevant for knowledge and action. The facts then appear as theoretically interpreted aspects of reality,[82] the thories as selective interpretations in whose judgment facts once again play a part and whose acceptance involves decisions. These decisions are made according to stand-points which, on a meta-theoretical level, are accessible to objective discussion.[83] As far as the decisions of practical life are concerned, they can be made in the light of a situational analysis which makes use of theoretical results and takes into consideration consequences which are actually expected. The distinction between facts and decisions, nomological and normative statements,

---

[82] *See*, for example, Karl R. Popper 'Why are the Calculi of Logic and Arithmetic Applicable to Reality?' in *Conjectures and Refutations*, loc. cit., esp. pp. 213f.

[83] Habermas admits (*Theory and Practice*, loc. cit., pp. 280–1) that 'as soon as argument with rational warrants is carried on at the methodological—the so-called meta-theoretical and meta-ethical—level, the threshold to the dimension of comprehensive rationality has already been breached', as if the discussion of such problems with critical arguments had not always been characteristic precisely for the types of rationalistic view which he covers with the collective name of positivism. One only has to glance at certain periodicals to determine this.

theories and states of affairs, in no way involves a lack of connection. It would hardly be meaningful to 'dialectically transcend' all such distinctions in a unity of reason and decision postulated *ad hoc*, and thus to allow the various aspects of problems and the levels of argumentation to perish in a totality which may certainly encompass all simultaneously, but which then makes it necessary to solve all the problems simultaneously. Such a procedure can only lead to problems being hinted at but no longer analysed, to a pretence at solutions but not their implementation. The dialectical cult of total reason is too fastidious to content itself with 'specific' solutions. Since there are no solutions which meet its demands, it is forced to rest content with insinuation, allusion and metaphor.

Habermas is not in agreement with the solutions to problems offered by his partners in discussion. That is his right. They themselves are now particularly satisfied with them. They are prepared to discuss alternatives if these are offered, and to respond to critical reflections in so far as arguments can be recognized in them. They do not suffer from that restriction of rationality to problems of positive science which Habermas frequently believes he has to impute to them, nor do they suffer under the restrictive interpretation of scientific knowledge which he makes the foundation of his critique. They do not see, in the positive sciences, simply the means of technical rationalization, but instead, in particular, a paradigm of critical rationality, a social realm in which the solution of problems using critical arguments was developed in a way which can be of great significance for other realms.[84] They believe, however, that they must meet the dialectics which Habermas favours with scepticism, among other reasons because, with its assistance, pure decisions can so easily be masked and dogmatized as knowledge. If he sets store by the elucidation of the connections between theory and practice, and not merely by their metaphorical paraphrase, then Habermas has sought out the false opponents, and a false ally; for dialectics will offer him not solutions, but simply masks under which lurk unsolved problems.

---

[84] That even science is not immune from dogmatization is quite familiar to them, since science too is a human undertaking; *see*, for example, Paul K. Feyerabend, 'Über konservative Züge in den Wissenschaften und insbesondere in der Quantentheorie und ihre Beseitigung' in *Club Voltaire, Jahrbuch für kritische Aufklärung* 1, edited by Gerhard Szczesny (Munich, 1963).

JÜRGEN HABERMAS

A POSITIVISTICALLY BISECTED RATIONALISM

A Reply to a Pamphlet[1]

Hans Albert has criticized an essay on the analytical theory of science and dialectics in which I took up a controversy which developed between Karl R. Popper and Theodor W. Adorno at the Tübingen working session of the German Sociological Association.[2] The strategy of mutually shrugging one's shoulders, which has been practised up until now, is not exactly productive. For this reason, then, I welcome the existence of this polemic no matter how problematical its form. I shall restrict myself to its substance.

Before entering into the discussion, I must make certain comments in order to establish agreement concerning the basis of our dispute. My criticism is not aimed at research practices in the exact empirical sciences, nor against those in behavioural-scientific sociology, in so far as the latter exists. It is another question whether this can exist beyond the confines of small-group research with a social-psychological orientation. My critique is exclusively directed at the positivistic interpretation of such research processes. For the false consciousness of a correct practice affect the latter. I do not dispute that the analytical theory of science has stimulated actual research and has helped to elucidate methodological judgments. At the same time, however, the positivistic self-understanding has restrictive effects; it silences

---

[1] Cf. Hans Albert, 'The Myth of Total Reason'. Page references in the text refer to this essay.

[2] *The Positivist Dispute*, pp. 131ff.; in addition, Albert refers to several passages in my essay 'Dogmatism, Reason, and Decision' in Jürgen Habermas, *Theory and Practice* (London/Boston, 1974), pp. 253ff. He does not take the book as a whole into account.

any binding reflection beyond the boundaries of the empirical-
analytical (and formal) sciences. I reject this masked normative
function of a false consciousness. According to positivistic
prohibitive norms, whole problem areas would have to be
excluded from discussion and relinquished to irrational attitudes,
although, in my opinion, they are perfectly open to critical
elucidation. Moreover, if those problems connected with the
selection of standards and the influence of arguments on attitudes
were inaccessible to critical discussion and had to be abandoned
to arbitrary decisions, then the methodology of the empirical
sciences themselves would be no less irrational. Since our chances
of reaching agreement on contentious problems in a rational
manner, are in fact, quite limited, I consider reservations of
principle, which prevent us from exhausting these chances, to be
dangerous. In order to guarantee the dimension of comprehensive
rationality and to penetrate the illusion of positivistic barriers, I
shall adopt what is really an old-fashioned course. I shall trust
in the power of self-reflection. When we reflect on what happens
in research processes, we realize that we move the whole time
within a spectrum of rational discussion, which is broader than
positivism regards as permissible.

Albert isolates my arguments from the context of an immanent
critique of Popper's view. Consequently, they become confused—
I myself scarcely recognize them. What is more, Albert creates the
impression that, with their help, I intend to introduce something
approaching a new 'method' alongside the already well-established
methods of social-scientific research. I have nothing of the sort in
mind. I selected Popper's theory for discussion because he himself
had already confirmed, in some measure, my doubts about
positivism. Influenced by Russell and the early Wittgenstein, it
was above all the Vienna Circle around Moritz Schlick who had
sketched out the now classic features of a theory of science.
Within this tradition, Popper occupies a peculiar position. He is,
on the one hand, a leading representative of the analytical theory
of science and, as far back as the twenties, he criticized, in a convincing manner, the empiricist presuppositions of this new
positivism. Popper's critique concentrates on the first level of self-
reflection of a positivism to which he remains bound in so far as he
does not see through the objectivistic illusion which suggests that
scientific theories represent facts. Popper does not reflect upon
the technical cognitive interest of empirical sciences; what is more,

he deliberately repulses pragmatic viewpoints. I am left with no alternative but to reconstruct the context of my arguments utilizing Popper's problems—a context which Albert distorts beyond recognition. In reformulating my previous critique in the light of Albert's strictures, I hope that, in its new form, it will give rise to fewer misunderstandings.

The charge of misunderstanding, however, has already been levelled at me by Albert. In his opinion, I am mistaken on the following points:

on the *methodological role of experience*,
on the so-called *basis-problem*,
on the *relationship between methodological and empirical statements*,
on the *dualism of facts and standards*.

Furthermore, Albert asserts that the pragmatist interpretation of the empirical-analytical sciences is erroneous. In the last analysis, he considers that the opposition between dogmatically fixed and rationally substantiated positions is a falsely posed alternative which has been made redundant by Popper's critical rationalism itself. I shall discuss these two objections in the context of those four 'misunderstandings', which I wish to resolve in that order. The reader may then decide on whose side they lay.

I do not like encumbering a sociological journal with details of the theory of science, but we cannot carry on a discussion as long as we stand above matters instead of in their midst.

1   CRITIQUE OF EMPIRICISM

The first misunderstanding relates to the methodological role of experience in the empirical-analytical sciences. Albert rightly points out that experiences of diverse origin can intervene in theories regardless of whether they spring from the potential of everyday experience, from historically transmitted myths, or from spontaneous impressions. They merely have to fulfil the condition that they can be translated into testable hypotheses. For the test itself, on the other hand, only a specific mode of experience is permitted, namely, sense experience, which is organized by experimental or analogous procedures. We also speak of systematic observation. I, for my part, have in no way questioned this influx of unordered experiences into the stream of imaginative leaps out of which hypotheses are created, nor would I fail to recognize the merits of test situations which organize sense experiences through replicable tests. But if one does not wish to enthrone philosophical innocence at any price, the question must be permitted whether, through such a definition of the preconditions for testing, the possible meaning of the empirical validity of statements has not been established in advance. And if this is the case, one might ask what meaning of validity is thereby prejudiced. The experiential basis of the exact sciences is not independent of the standards which these sciences themselves attribute to experience. Apparently, the test procedure, which Albert suggests is the only legitimate one, is merely one amongst several. Moral feelings, privations and frustrations, crises in the individual's life history, changes in attitude in the course of reflection—all these mediate different experiences. Through corresponding standards they can be raised to the level of a validating instance. The transference situation existing between doctor and patient, which is utilized by the psychoanalyst, provides an example of this. I do not wish to compare the advantages and disadvantages of the various test procedures; instead, I simply wish to elucidate my questions. Albert is unable to discuss them because he calmly identifies tests with the possible testing of theories against experience in general. What I regard as a problem he continues to accept without discussion.

This question interests me in connection with Popper's objections to the empiricist presuppositions of more recent positivism. Popper challenges the thesis of the manifest self-givenness of the existent in sense experience. The idea of an immediately attested reality, and of a manifest truth, has not withstood critical epistemological reflection. Since Kant's proof of the categorial elements of our perception, the claim of sense experience to be the final court of evidence has been dismissed. Hegel's critique of sense certainty, Peirce's analysis of perception incorporated in systems of action, Husserl's explication of pre-predicative experience, and Adorno's attack on First Philosophy have all, from their various points of departure, proved that there is no such thing as immediate knowledge. The search for the primary experience of a manifest immediacy is in vain. Even the simplest perception is not only performed categorially by physiological apparatus—it is just as determined by previous experience, through what has been handed down, and what has been learned as by what is anticipated, through the horizon of expectations, and even of dreams and fears. Popper formulates this insight in the statement that observations always imply interpretations in the light of experiences made and knowledge acquired. More simply, empirical data are interpretations within the framework of previous theories; as a result, they themselves share the latter's hypothetical character.[3]

Popper draws radical conclusions from this state of affairs. He reduces all knowledge to the level of assertions, of conjectures, with whose help we hypothetically complete an insufficient experience and interpret our uncertainties concerning a concealed reality. Such assertions and conjectures are differentiated merely in the extent to which they may be tested. Even tested conjectures which are constantly subjected to rigorous tests do not attain the status of proven statements; they remain suppositions, admittedly of a kind that hitherto have withstood all attempts to eliminate them—in short, they are well-tried hypotheses.

Empiricism, like the traditional critique of knowledge in general, attempts to justify the validity of exact knowledge by recourse to the sources of knowledge. Yet the sources of knowledge—pure thought, established tradition and sense experience— all lack authority. None of them can lay claim to immediate evidence and primary validity and consequently to the power of legitimation. The sources of knowledge are always contaminated; the way to their origins is barred to us. Hence the question of the source of knowledge must be replaced by the question of its validity. The demand for the verification of scientific statements is authoritarian because it makes the validity of statements dependent upon the false authority of the senses. Instead of inquiring after the legitimating origin of knowledge, we have to inquire after the method by means of which definitively false assertions can be discovered and apprehended amidst the mass of assertions which are, in principle, uncertain.[4]

Popper carries this critique so far that it unintentionally makes even his own suggested solution problematical. Popper strips the origins of knowledge, enlisted in empiricist studies, of their false authority. He rightly discredits every form of primary knowledge. But even mistakes can only be falsified on the basis of criteria of validity. For their justification we must adduce argu-

---

[3] Karl R. Popper, *Conjectures and Refutations* (London, 1963), pp. 23 and 387.
[4] *Conjectures*, pp. 3ff., 24ff.

ments; but where, then, are we to look for these if not in the very dimension—not of the origin but of the formation of knowledge—which has been ruled out? Otherwise, the standards of falsification remain arbitrary. Popper wants to sublate the *origins* of theories, namely, observations, thought and tradition alike, in favour of the method of testing which is to be the only way of measuring empirical validity. Unfortunately, however, this method, in its turn, can only be grounded by recourse to at least one of the sources of knowledge, to tradition, in fact to the tradition which Popper calls the critical tradition. It becomes clear that tradition is the independent variable upon which, in the final instance, thought and observations are just as dependent as the testing procedures, which are composed of thought and observations. Popper is too unhesitating in his trust in the autonomy of the experience which is organized in the testing procedure. He thinks that he can dismiss the question of standards in this procedure because, for all his criticism, he shares, in the last analysis, a deep-seated positivistic prejudice. He assumes the epistemological independence of facts from the theories which should descriptively grasp these facts and the relations between them. Accordingly, tests examine theories against 'independent' facts. This thesis is the pivot of the residual positivistic problematic in Popper. Albert does not indicate that I might have succeeded in even making him aware of what is at issue here.

On the one hand, Popper rightly counters empiricism with the objection that we can only apprehend and determine facts in the light of theories.[5] Moreover, he occasionally describes even facts as the common product of language and reality.[6] On the other hand, he assumes for protocol statements, which are dependent on a methodically secured organization of our experiences, a simple relationship of correspondence to the 'facts'. Popper's adherence to the correspondence theory of truth does not seem to me to be consistent. This theory presupposes that 'facts' exist in themselves, without taking into account that the meaning of the empirical validity of factual statements (and, indirectly, the meaning of theories in the empirical sciences too) is determined in advance by the definition of the testing conditions. It would instead be more meaningful to attempt a basic analysis of the connection between the theories of the empirical sciences and the

---

[5] *Conjectures*, p. 41, note 8.
[6] *Conjectures*, p. 214.

so-called facts. For in this way, we would apprehend the framework of a prior interpretation of experience. At this level of reflection, it would seem obvious to apply the term 'facts' only to the class of what can be experienced, a class which has been antecedently organized to test scientific theories. Then one would conceive of the facts as that which they are: namely, produced. One would thus recognize the concept of 'facts' in positivism as a fetish which merely grants to the mediated the illusion of immediacy. Popper does not complete the retreat into the transcendental dimension but the consistency of his own critique leads in this direction. Popper's presentation of the basis-problem shows as much.

2 THE PRAGMATIC INTERPRETATION OF EMPIRICAL-ANALYTICAL RESEARCH

The second misunderstanding, of which Albert accuses me, refers to the so-called 'basis-problem'. Popper gives the name 'basic statements' to those singular existential statements which lend themselves to the refutation of a law-like hypothesis expressed in the form of negative existential statements. Normally, these formulate the result of systematic observations. They mark the point of contact at which theories strike the basis of experience. Basic statements cannot, of course, rest upon experience without contact with it, for none of the universal expressions which occur in them could be verified, not even with the aid of a large number of observations. The acceptance or rejection of basic statements rests, in the last instance, on a decision; but the decisions are not made in an arbitrary fashion. Rather, they are made in accordance with rules. Such rules are only laid down institutionally, not logically. They encourage us to direct decisions of this sort towards an implicitly pre-understood goal, but they do not define it. We behave in this way in the course of everyday communication and also in the interpretation of texts. We have no choice when we move in a circle and yet do not wish to forego explication. The basis problem reminds us that even applying formal theories to reality entangles us in a circle. I have learned of this circle from Popper; I did not invent it myself, as Albert seems to suppose. Even in Albert's own formulation (p. 181) it is not difficult to discover it.

Popper explains it in a comparison of the research process with the process of trial by jury.[7] A system of laws, regardless of whether we are dealing with a system of legal norms or empirical-scientific hypotheses, cannot be applied unless agreement has previously been attained concerning the facts of the case to which the system should be applied. Through some kind of decision, the jurors agree which representation of a factual occurrence they intend to approve. This corresponds to accepting a basic statement. The decision is more complicated, however, since the system of laws and the facts of the case are not given independently of one another. On the contrary, the facts of the case are even sought under categories of the system of laws. The comparison of the research process with the process of trial by jury is intended to make us aware of this circle which is inevitable when general rules are applied. 'The analogy between this procedure and that by which we decide basic statements is clear. It throws light, for example, upon their relativity, and the way in which they depend upon questions raised by the theory. In the case of the trial by jury, it would be clearly impossible to *apply* the "theory" unless there is first a verdict arrived at by decision; yet the verdict has to be found in a procedure that conforms to, and thus applies, part of the general legal code. The case is analogous to that of basic statements. Their acceptance is part of the application of a theoretical system; and it is only this application which makes any further applications of the theoretical system possible.'[8]

What does this circle, resulting when theories are applied to reality, signify? I think that the area of the empirical is established in advance by means of theoretical assumptions concerning a certain structure, in combination with a certain type of testing conditions. Such things as experimentally established facts, upon which empirical scientific theories could founder, are only constituted in a prior context of the interpretation of possible experience. This context is produced in an interplay of argumentative discourse and experimental action. The combination is organized with a view to controlling predictions. An implicit pre-understanding of the rules of the game guides the discussion of the investigators when they are deciding whether to accept basic statements. For the circle within which they inevitably move

---

[7] Karl R. Popper, *The Logic of Scientific Discovery* (London, 1960), pp. 109ff. (hereafter cited as *Logic*).

[8] *Logic*, pp. 110ff.

when they apply theories to what has been observed refers them to a dimension in which rational discussion is only possible with the assistance of hermeneutics.

The demand for controlled observation as the basis for decisions concerning the empirical plausibility of law-like hypotheses presupposes a pre-understanding of definite rules. It is certainly not sufficient to know the specific aim of an investigation and the relevance of an observation for certain assumptions. Instead, the meaning of the research process as a whole must be understood before I can know to what the empirical validity of basic statements is related, just as the judge must always have grasped the meaning of judicature as such. The *quaestio facti* must be determined with reference to a *quaestio juris* understood in its immanent claims. In legal proceedings, this question is prominent in everyone's mind. The whole affair revolves around the question of an offence against general prohibitive norms, positively set down and sanctioned by the state. But, what does the *quaestio juris* look like in the research process, and how is the empirical validity of basic statements measured in this case? The form of propositional systems and the type of testing conditions which are used to measure their validity, suggest the pragmatist interpretation: namely, that empirical-scientific theories reveal reality under the guiding interest in the possible informative safeguarding and extension of feedback-regulated action.

Popper himself provides clues to this interpretation in his own work. Empirical-scientific theories are significant in that they permit the derivation of universal propositions concerning the covariance of empirical quantities. We develop such law-like hypotheses in anticipation of law-like regularity itself, without being able to justify empirically such anticipation. This methodical anticipation of possible empirical uniformity, however, corresponds to the elementary requirements of behavioural stability. Feedback-regulated actions can only be secured for a long period of time if they are guided by information as to empirical uniformities. In addition, this information must be capable of translation into expectations of behavioural regularity under given conditions. The pragmatist interpretation refers the logical general to general behavioural expectations. Viewed pragmatically, the disjunction between universal propositions, on the one hand, and the, in principle, finite set of observations and the corresponding singular existential statements, on the other hand, can be explained by the structure of feedback-regulated action, which always allows itself to be guided by anticipations of behavioural regularity.[9]

This interpretation, according to which the empirical-analytical sciences allow themselves to be guided by a technical cognitive interest, enjoys the advantage of taking account of Popper's critique of empiricism, without sharing a weakness of his falsification theory. For how is our uncertainty—in principle— about the truth of scientific information to accord with its generally varied and quite permanent technical utilization? Certainly, by the time that knowledge of empirical uniformities is incorporated into technical productive forces and becomes the basis of a scientific civilization, the evidence of everyday experience and of a permanent regulated feedback is overwhelming; logical misgivings are unable to assert themselves against the plebiscite of functioning technical systems, a plebiscite which is renewed daily. However great the weight of Popper's objections to verificationism, his own alternative thus seems less plausible, since it is only an alternative under the positivistic presupposition

---

[9] In this context, Popper's comment that all universal terms can be regarded as dispositional terms, is of interest. (*Logic*, pp. 94f.; appendix X, pp. 423ff.; and *Conjectures*, pp. 118f.). On the level of individual universal terms, the problem of universal statements is repeated. For the dispositional concepts implied in such terms can, in their turn, only be explicated by means of assumptions about a lawlike behaviour of objects. This is shown in doubtful cases when we imagine possible tests which would be sufficient to elucidate the significance of the universal terms used. In all this, recourse to the testing conditions is hardly fortuitous. For it is only the relation of the theoretical elements to the experiment which closes the functional circle of feedback-regulated action, within which such things as empirical regularities first exist. The hypothetical surplus beyond each specific content of an immediately perceived entity which, in the logical form of law-like statements and in the universal expression of observational terms, comes into its own, does not relate to a regular behaviour of things 'in themselves' but instead to a behaviour of things in so far as this forms a part of the horizon of expectations of actions requiring orientation. Thus, hypothetically, the degree of generality of descriptive content in perceptual judgments far exceeds the particularity of what is perceived in each case because, under the selective pressure towards the stabilization of the results of actions, we always gather experiences and articulate meanings—'for what a thing means is simply what habits it involves' (Peirce).

A further clue for a pragmatist interpretation is given by Popper in connection with a sociology of tradition ('Towards a Rational Theory of Tradition', in: *Conjectures*, pp. 120ff.). He compares the analogous roles which traditions and theories acquire in social systems. Both inform us about reactions which we can regularly expect, and in accordance with which we can confidently orientate our behaviour. Likewise, they bring order into a chaotic environment in which, without the capacity for prognosticating answers or events, we would not be able to form suitable behavioural habits.

of a correspondence between statements and actual states of affairs. The moment we abandon this supposition, and take technique in its widest sense seriously as a socially institutionalized regulatory system which, in accordance with its methodical meaning, is designed to be technically utilizable, one can conceive of another form of verification. The latter is exempt from Popper's objections and concurs, in fact, with our pre-scientific experiences. All the assumptions, then, are empirically true which can guide feedback-regulated action without having been previously rendered problematic through errors experimentally striven for.[10]

Albert imagines that by referring to Popper's criticism of instrumentalism he is released from any argument of his own against my interpretation, which he does not even reproduce. But I do not really need to answer his criticism since it is directed against theses which I do not expound. In the first instance, Popper concentrates on the thesis that theories are instruments.[11] Here he can easily counter that rules of technical application must be tried out, whilst scientific information must be tested. The logical relationships in the case of suitability tests for instruments and the testing of theories are not symmetrical—instruments cannot be refuted. The pragmatic interpretation which I wish to give to empirical-analytical sciences, does not include this form of instrumentalism. It is not the theories themselves which are instruments but rather that their information is technically utilizable. Even from a pragmatic viewpoint the failures, whereby law-like hypotheses founder under experimental conditions, possess the character of refutations. The hypotheses refer to empirical regularities; they determine the horizon of expectation of feedback-regulated action, and consequently can be falsified by disappointed expectations of success. Yet the law-like hypotheses,

---

[10] According to this view, Popper's reservation regarding incontestably valid knowledge can be quite compatible with the pragmatic corroboration of knowledge. Popper admits experimental tests exclusively as an instance of falsification, whilst in the pragmatic view, they are controlled experiments which refute assumptions but can also confirm them. However, corroboration through the results of an action can only be globally allocated, and not in a strictly correlative manner, since, with a given theory, neither in their scope nor in respect of their area of application can we definitely ascertain the factually working elements of knowledge. Definitively, we only know that parts of a theory which is controlled through the results of an action—and that means that it is a prognostically tested theory—are proved correct in the sphere of application of the test situation.

[11] 'Three Views Concerning Knowledge', in: *Conjectures*, pp. 111ff.

in their methodical sense, refer to experiences which are constituted exclusively in the functional sphere of such action. Technical recommendations for a rationalized choice of means under given ends cannot be derived from scientific theories merely at a later stage, and as if by chance. But these theories themselves are not therefore technical implements. This is possibly true in a figurative sense. Technical utilization of knowledge is, of course, in no way intended in the research process: actually, in many cases, it is even excluded. Nevertheless, with the structure of propositions (restricted prognoses concerning observable behaviour), and with the type of testing conditions (imitation of the control of the results of action which is built naturally into systems of societal labour), a methodical decision has been taken in advance concerning the technical utility of empirical scientific information. Similarly, the realm of possible experience is prejudiced, namely, that realm to which hypotheses refer and upon which they can founder.

The descriptive value of scientific information cannot be disputed, but it is not to be understood in such a way that theories represent facts and relations between facts. The descriptive content is only valid with reference to prognoses for feedback-regulated actions in predictable situations. All the answers which the empirical sciences can supply are relative to the methodical significance of the questions they raise and nothing more. No matter how trivial this restriction may be, it contradicts the illusion of pure theory which has been preserved in positivistic self understanding.[12]

---

[12] Another of Popper's objections is directed against operationalism, according to which basic concepts can be defined through modes of procedure (*Conjectures*, p. 62; *Logic*, pp. 440f.). Rightly, Popper asserts that the attempt to trace dispositional concepts back to measurement operations, in its turn presupposes a theory of measurement, for no operation could be described without universal terms. This circle, in which universal terms point to empirically regular behaviour, whilst the regularity of behaviour can only be established through measuring operations, which in turn presuppose general categories, seems to me, however, to require interpretation. The operationalist point of departure rightly insists that the semantic content of empirical scientific information is only valid within a frame of reference which has been transcendentally posited by the structure of feedback-regulated action, and furthermore the semantic content cannot be projected onto reality 'in itself'. It is incorrect to assume that such content could be simply reduced to criteria of observable behaviour. The circle in which this attempt is ensnared shows instead that the systems of action, of which the research process forms a part, are mediated through language, but, at the same time, language is not subsumed in categories of behaviour.

3 CRITICAL JUSTIFICATION AND DEDUCTIVE PROOF

The third misunderstanding to which, according to Albert, I have succumbed, refers to the relationship between methodological and empirical statements. He finds me guilty of a particularly crass positivism since I do not forego empirical arguments in methodological contexts and thereby confound in an unacceptable manner the logic of inquiry with the sociology of knowledge. After Moore and Husserl, from different standpoints, had effected the strict division between logical and psychological studies, and, in so doing, had reinstated the old Kantian insight, even the positivists broke with their naturalism. Influenced in the meantime by the advances which had been made in formal logic, Wittgenstein and the Vienna Circle made the dualism of statements and states of affairs the basis of their linguistic analyses. Since then, it has not been possible to lump together naïvely questions of genesis with those of validity. Presumably Albert wished to draw attention to this triviality. Once again, in so doing, he does not touch upon the questions I raised. For I am interested in the following peculiar state of affairs, namely, that, despite this clear distinction, non-deductive relationships between formal and empirical statements are produced precisely in the methodology of the empirical sciences and in the dimension of scientific criticism. The logic of science possesses an element of the empirical precisely in that sector in which the truth of empirical scientific theories should prove itself. For criticism, even in Popper's sense, cannot be fitted in an axiomatized form into the formal sciences. Criticism is the unreserved discussion of propositions. It employs all available techniques of refutation. Such a technique is a juxtaposition of hypotheses to the results of systematic observation. Though test results find a place in critical discussion, they do not constitute criticism. Criticism is not a method of testing, it is this test itself as discussion. On the other hand, the dimension in which critical discussion of the validity of theories is made is not that of the theories themselves. For not only do statements and their logical relations find a place in criticism but so also do empirical attitudes, which are influenced with the aid of arguments. Albert can of course rule out, by means of a postulate, that we consider in any way a connection which is neither completely logical nor completely empirical. In so doing, he would at most evade a discussion which I should like to develop in order to elucidate the question whether such a postulate can be justified for the realm of meta-theoretical discussion. Rather, it seems to me that there is reason to repeat Hegel's critique of Kant's division between the transcendental and empirical realms in the form of a contemporary critique of the division between the logical-methodological and the empirical realms. In both cases the critique is far removed from ignoring the distinctions mentioned; rather, it uses them as a starting point.

Reflection on what Popper himself does, makes us aware of the peculiar form of meta-theoretical discussions in so far as they advance beyond linguistic analysis. On the one hand, Popper pursues the immanent critique of given theories and, in so doing, employs the systematic comparison of logically compelling deductions. On the other hand, he develops alternative solutions; he makes suggestions of his own and attempts to support them with arguments. In this case, he cannot confine himself to the verification of deductive connections. Rather, his interpretation is aimed at critically altering old attitudes, of making new standards of judgment plausible and new normative points of view acceptable. This takes place in the hermeneutical form of argumentation which evades the rigid monologues of deductive systems of propositions. It sets standards for critical discussion as such. This is revealed in every choice between possible techniques of inquiry, between several theoretical starting points, between various definitions of basic predicates; it is revealed in decisions as to the linguistic framework within which I express a given problem and form its hypothetical solutions. A choice of standards is constantly repeated, as is the attempt to support this choice through suitable arguments. Morton White has shown that, even at the highest level, meta-theoretical discussions remain bound to this form of argumentation. Even the distinction between categorial and non-categorial being, between analytic and synthetic statements, between descriptive and emotive contents, between logical rules and law-like regularities, between controlled observation and moral experience—even these fundamental distinctions, upon which exact empirical science rests, are in no way exempt from discussion. They presuppose criteria which do not result from reality itself, that is, criticizable standards which, in their turn, cannot be strictly substantiated by arguments but can be supported or weakened by them.[13]

White makes the attempt which Popper neglects; the attempt to examine the logical relations of this non-deductive form of argumentation. He demonstrates that methodological decisions are quasi-moral decisions and, as a result, can only be justified in discussion of the kind familiar from the old topics and rhetorics. For neither the conventionalistic nor the naturalistic interpretation does justice to the choice of methodological rules.

Critical argumentation differs from deductive argumentation in progressing beyond the dimension of the logical connection of statements and includes a moment which transcends language—attitudes or outlooks. A logical relationship of implication between outlooks and statements is impossible: attitudes cannot be deduced from statements nor, vice versa, statements from attitudes. Nevertheless, agreement upon a mode of procedure and the acceptance of a rule can be supported or weakened by arguments; at any rate, it can be rationally considered and judged. This is the task of critique with reference to both practical and meta-theoretical decisions. Since the supporting or weakening arguments do not stand in a strictly logical relation to the statements which express the application of standards, but instead only in a relation of rational motivation, meta-theoretical discussions can also include empirical propositions. However, the relation between arguments and attitudes does not, in this way, itself become an empirical one. It can be taken as such, as for instance in a Festinger experiment on change of attitude, but then the argumentation would be reduced to the level of observable language behaviour, and the moment of rational validity, which forms part of every motivation, would be suppressed.

Popper does not consider that a rationalization of attitude is out of the question. This form of argumentation is the only possible one for tentatively justifying decisions. Yet since it is never conclusive, he considers it to be unscientific in comparison with logical deduction. He prefers the certainty of descriptive knowledge, a certainty guaranteed by the deductive combination of theories and the empirical constraint of facts. Yet even the interplay of statements and experiences of this particular type presupposes standards which require justification. Popper evades

---

[13] Morton White, *Toward Reunion in Philosophy* (Cambridge, Mass., 1956).

this objection by insisting on the irrationality of the decision which precedes the application of his critical method. According to him, the rationalistic attitude consists in the willingness to decide upon the acceptance of theories on the basis of experiences and arguments. It cannot, however, be grounded either through arguments or through experiences. Certainly it cannot be justified in the sense of a deductive proof but it can in the form of a supporting argumentation. Popper himself, in fact, makes use of it at some length. He explains every critical attitude in terms of certain philosophical traditions. He analyses the empirical presuppositions and consequences of scientific criticism. He examines its functions within the given structure of public political life. In fact, his methodology as a whole is a critical justification of criticism itself. It may be that this non-deductive justification is unsatisfactory for a logical absolutism. However, no other form of justification is known to scientific criticism which goes beyond an immanent critique and tests methodological decisions.

Popper terms the critical attitude a belief in reason. Therefore he claims, the problem of rationalism does not consist of the choice between knowledge and faith but rather in a choice between two sorts of faith. But, he adds paradoxically, the new problem is which faith is the right one and which the wrong one.[14] He does not totally reject non-deductive justification, but he believes that he can avoid its problematical combination of logical and empirical relations if he foregoes a justification of criticism—as if the 'Black Peter' were not already present in the criticism itself.

Albert saddles me with the onus of proof for the problem of foundation [*Begründungsproblem*]. He seems to assume that all problems are resolved for him with the abstention of rationalism from the problem of self-foundation [*Selbstbegründung*]. Apparently, he draws upon William W. Bartley, who attempted to demonstrate conclusively the possibility of such an abstention.[15] However, it seems to me that this attempt was not successful.

Bartley starts out from the assumption that, for logical reasons, a deductive self-foundation of rationalism is out of the question. Instead, he discusses the possibility of a critical philosophy

---

[14] Karl R. Popper, *The Open Society and its Enemies* (London, 1957), vol. II., p. 246.

[15] *The Retreat to Commitment* (New York, 1962), esp. chs. 3 and 4; also, 'Rationality Versus the Theory of Rationality' in: M. Bunge (ed.), *The Critical Approach to Science and Philosophy* (London, 1964), pp. 3ff.

(*Kritizismus*) which does in fact accept every proposition which can be rationally grounded, but not exclusively such propositions. He holds no views which cannot be accountable to criticism but neither does he demand that all views, including the critical attitude itself, be rationally grounded. Is this view still tenable, however, when logically the conditions of critical testing are themselves exposed to criticism? Bartley neither questions the standards according to which experience is organized in test situations, nor does he pose sufficiently radically the question of the sphere of validity of deductive justifications. For by means of a stipulation, he exempts from criticism all those standards which we must presuppose in order to criticize. He introduces a so-called revisibility criterion: 'namely, whatever is presupposed by the argument-revisibility situation is not itself revisable within that situation'.[16] We cannot accept this criterion. It is introduced in order to secure the argumentation, but it would stifle argumentation in the very dimension in which the latter's peculiar achievement is revealed; namely, in the subsequent revision of previously applied standards. Something approaching critical justification consists precisely in the fact that it produces a non-deductive connection between selected standards and empirically secured propositions. Consequently, it also supports or weakens attitudes by means of arguments which, for their part, are first found within the sphere of these attitudes. As soon as it progresses beyond the verification of deductive systems, argumentation takes a reflexive course. It employs standards which it can only reflect upon in their applications. Argumentation differs from mere deduction by always subjecting the principles, according to which it proceeds, to discussion. To this extent, criticism cannot be restricted in advance to conditions which form the framework of possible criticism. What can pass as criticism always has to be determined on the basis of criteria which are only found, elucidated and possibly revised again in the process of criticism. This is the dimension of comprehensive rationality which, although incapable of a final grounding [*Letztbegründung*], develops in a circle of reflexive self-justification.

Bartley's unconditional rationalism makes too many reservations. He does not recognize criticism as the sole and ultimate horizon within which the validity of theories about reality is

<hr/>

[16] ibid., p. 173.

science and ethics. For, on the one hand, theoretical knowledge determined. As a makeshift, we can conceive of criticism—which cannot be defined because the standards of rationality can only be explained within criticism itself—as a process which, in a domination-free discussion, includes a progressive resolution of disagreement. Such a discussion is guided by the idea of a general and unconstrained consensus amongst those who participate in it. Here, 'agreement' should not reduce the idea of truth to observable behaviour. Rather, the categories, with whose help agreement can be achieved in each case, are themselves dependent upon the process which we interpret as a process for achieving consensus. The idea of agreement does not therefore exclude the distinction between true and false consensus; but this truth cannot be so defined that future revision is ruled out.[17] Albert objects that I presuppose as a fact something resembling a rational discussion in methodological contexts (p. 193). I presuppose it as a fact since we always find ourselves in a communication which is intended to lead to agreement [*Verständigung*]. At the same time, however, this empirical fact possesses a distinctive feature: namely, a transcendental precondition. Only in discussion can agreement on the standards be reached on the basis of which we differentiate facts from mere spectres. The discarded link between formal and empirical statements attempts to do justice to a context in which methodological questions can no longer be meaningfully separated from questions of communication.

4   THE SEPARATION OF STANDARDS AND FACTS

The fourth misunderstanding with which Albert charges me relates to the dualism of facts and decisions. This can be elucidated on the basis of the difference between natural laws and cultural norms. Assumptions about empirical regularities can decisively founder on the facts, whilst the choice of standards can at most be supported critically by additional arguments. One can easily differentiate a realm of scientifically reliable information from that realm of practical knowledge which we only secure through a hermeneutic form of argument. I want to question this optimistic distinction, which is traditionally termed the separation between

---

[17] *See* D. Pole, *Conditions of Rational Inquiry* (London, 1961), p. 92.

which has been proven against facts is constituted within a normative framework which is capable of a critical but not of a deductive-empirical justification. On the other hand, the critical discussion of standards certainly involves empirical considerations —that is, recourse to so-called facts. A critique which creates a rational connection between attitudes and arguments forms the comprehensive dimension of science itself. Even theoretical knowledge can be no more certain than can critical knowledge. Yet again, the 'misunderstanding' appears to result from Albert having in no way apprehended my intention. I do not deny the distinction between facts and standards. I merely ask whether the positivistic distinction, which permits a dualism of facts and decisions, and correspondingly a dualism of propositions and proposals—that is, a dualism of descriptive and normative knowledge—is an appropriate one.

In the appendix to *The Open Society*,[18] Popper develops the asymmetrical relation between standards and facts: '. . . through the decision to accept a proposal (at least tentatively) we create the corresponding standard (at least tentatively); yet through the decision to accept a proposition we do *not* create the corresponding fact'.[19] I should like to examine this relation in more detail. We can discuss proposals and statements. Yet the discussion entailed no more produces the standards than it does the facts. Rather, in the first case, it draws upon arguments in order to justify or contest the act of accepting standards. Such arguments can include empirical considerations. But these, for their part, are not under discussion. In the second case, the reverse occurs. Here it is not the choice of standards which is under discussion, but their application to a state of affairs. The discussion draws upon arguments in order to justify or contest the act of incorporating a basic statement with reference to a given hypothesis. These arguments include methodological considerations. Their principles, however, are not under discussion in this case. The critique of an empirical-scientific hypothesis and the critical discussion of the choice of a standard is not symmetrical. Yet this is not because the logical structure of the discussion is different in the two cases—it is the same.

Popper terminates this reflection by reference to the correspondence theory of truth. Ultimately, the dualism of facts and

---

[18] 4th Edition, London, 1962, vol. 2, pp. 369ff.: 'Facts, Standards and Truth'.
[19] ibid., p. 384.

standards is based upon the assumption that, independent of our discussions, there exists something resembling facts and relations between facts to which propositions can correspond. Popper denies that the facts themselves are only constituted in combination with the standards of systematic observation or controlled experience. In so far as we intend true propositions, we always know that their truth is measured against a correspondence of propositions and facts. In the following manner, Popper meets the obvious objection that this concept of truth necessarily implies that the criterion or the standard or the definition has been introduced which itself must be exposed to critical discussion: 'It is decisive to realize that knowing what truth means, or under what conditions a statement is called true, is not the same as, and must be clearly distinguished from, possessing a means of deciding—a *criterion* for deciding—whether a given statement is true or false.'[20] We must forego a criterion, a definable standard of truth; we cannot define truth—but, nevertheless, we 'understand' in each individual case what we intend when we test the truth of a proposition: 'I believe that it is the demand for a criterion of truth which has made so many people feel that the question "what is truth" is unanswerable. But the absence of a criterion of truth does not render the notion of truth non-significant any more than the absence of a criterion of health renders the notion of health non-significant. A sick man may seek health even though he has no criterion for it.'[21]

In this passage, Popper makes use of the hermeneutic insight that we understand the meaning of statements from the context even before we can define individual terms and apply a general standard. Anyone familiar with the business of hermeneutics would certainly not conclude that we intend the meaning of such terms and statements without any standard at all. Rather, the pre-understanding which guides interpretation prior to any definition —even Popper's interpretation of truth—always includes standards implicitly. The justification of these prior standards is not really excluded; instead, it is the abstention from a definition which permits a continuous self-correction of the diffuse pre-understanding in the progress of the explication of the texts in hand. The interpretation throws the light of a growing understanding from the text back onto the standards through which it was initially

---

[20] *The Open Society*, vol. 2., op. cit., p. 371.
[21] ibid., p. 373.

made accessible. With the adaptation of the originally employed standards, the hermeneutic course of exigesis also provides their own justification. The standards and the descriptions which they permit when applied to the text still stand in a dialectical relationship. It is just the same with the standard of a truth based on correspondence. It is only the definition of standards and the establishment of criteria which tears apart the standards and the descriptions which make them possible. It is only they which create a deductive connection which excludes a retrospective correction of the standards through the object measured. Only at this point does the critical discussion of standards free itself from thier usage. Yet standards are also used implicitly before a critical justification on the meta-theoretical level is differentiated from the object level of applied standards.

For this reason, Popper does not manage to evade the dialectical connection between descriptive, postulatory and critical statements by reference to the correspondence concept of truth. Even this concept of truth, which allows such strict differentiation between standards and facts, is, no matter how implicitly we orientate ourselves by it, still in its turn a standard which requires critical justification. A critical discussion, regardless of whether it concerns the acceptance of proposals or propositions, includes a threefold usage of language: the descriptive, in order to describe states of affairs; the postulatory, in order to establish rules of procedure; and the critical, in order to justify such decisions. Logically, these forms of speech mutually presuppose each other. The descriptive usage is in no way limited to a certain class of 'facts'. The postulatory usage covers the establishment of norms, standards, criteria and definitions of all types, no matter whether practical, logical or methodological rules are involved. The critical usage employs arguments for considering, evaluating, judging and justifying the choice of standards; it includes, therefore, language-transcendent outlooks and attitudes in the discussion. No proposition concerning reality is capable of a rational test without the explication of a connection between arguments and attitudes. Descriptions are not independent of standards which are used, and standards rest upon attitudes which are in need of justification through supporting arguments, but which are, at the same time, incapable of deduction from assertions. If attitudes are altered under the influence of arguments, then such a motivation apparently combines a logically incomplete constraint with an empirical one. The only constraint of this sort originates in the power of reflection, which breaks the power of the unpenetrated by rendering it conscious. Emancipatory insight translates logical constraint into empirical constraint. This is achieved by critique; the latter overcomes the dualism of facts and standards, and in this way, first produces the continuum of a rational discussion which otherwise would degenerate immediately into arbitrary decisions and deductions.

As soon as we discuss a problem at all with the aim of reaching a consensus rationally and without constraint, we find ourselves in a dimension of comprehensive rationality which embraces as its moments langauge and action, statements and attitudes. Critique is always the transition from one moment to another. It is, if I may put it like this, an empirical fact in a transcendental role of which we become aware in the execution of criticism. It can also, of course, be repressed and disguised from that moment on in which, with the definition of the initially implicitly applied standards, a language-immanent realm of logical relations is freed from living reflection. This repression is expressed in Popper's critique of Hegel: 'To transcend this dualism of facts and standards is the decisive aim of Hegel's *philosophy of identity*—the identity of the ideal and the real, of right and might. All standards are historical: they are *historical facts*, stages in the development of reason, which is the same as the development of the ideal and of the real. There is nothing but fact; and some of the social or historical facts are, at the same time, standards.'[22] Nothing was further removed from Hegel's mind than this metaphysical positivism which Popper counters with the insight of logical positivism that statements and states of affairs belong to different spheres. Hegel in no way reduced the logical and empirical, the criteria of validation and factual relations, the normative and the descriptive to the level of historical facts. However, he did not negelct the experience of critical consciousness, namely, that reflection also holds together the well separated moments. The critique moves from the argument to the attitude, and from the attitude to the argument, and acquires, in this movement, the comprehensive rationality which, in the natural hermeneutics of everyday language, is still, as it were, naturally at work. In the sciences, however, this rationality must be re-established between

---

[22] *The Open Society*, vol. 2, op. cit., pp. 394–5.

the now-separated moments of formalized language and object-
ivized experience by means of critical discussion. Only because
this criticism relates chosen standards non-deductively to
empirical states of affairs, and can measure one moment against
another, is the statement correct—which according to Popper's
own presuppositions would be untenable, namely: '. . . that we
can learn; by our mistakes and by criticism; and that we can learn
in the realm of standards just as well as in the realm of facts.'[23]

5 TWO STRATEGIES AND A DISCUSSION

Albert seizes upon a series of questions, polemicizes and lets them
drop again. I cannot discover any principle behind this sequence.
I have attempted to clear up four fundamental misunderstandings
in order to create a basis of agreement upon which further
problems—for instance, the role of historical reflection, the
postulate of value freedom, or the position of the critique of
ideology—could be discussed without linguistic confusion. Now,
I believe, my intention will no longer be open to misunderstanding.
In opposition to positivism, I should like to justify the view that
the research process, which is carried out by human subjects,
belongs to the objective context which itself constitutes the
object of cognition, by virtue of cognitive acts.

The dimension in which this combination of the research process
with the social life-process is formed belongs neither to the sphere
of facts nor to that of theories. It stands apart from this dualism,
which only has meaning for empirical scientific theories. Rather,
in the comprehensive communicative context of scientific
criticism one moment links itself to another. I would say, in old-
fashioned language, that the transcendental preconditions of
possible knowledge are here created under empirical conditions.
As a result, neither the sociology of knowledge nor a pure
methodology are sufficiently appropriate at this level of reflection.
Their combination, which used to be called the critique of
ideology, is more appropriate. I do not like to use this expression,
for I do not wish the present discussion to cover all randomly
situated interests. I am concerned with knowledge-guiding
interests which, in each case, form the basis for a whole research

[23] ibid., p. 386.

system. In contrast to positivistic self-understanding, I should like to point out the connection of the empirical-analytical sciences with a technical cognitive interest. But this has nothing to do with 'denunciation', as Albert insinuates. It has quite escaped Albert's notice that it is far from my intention to criticize empirical-analytical research itself. He imagines that I wished to play off the methods of understanding against those of explanation. On the contrary, I regard as abortive, even reactionary, the attempts which characterized the old methodological dispute, namely, attempts to set up barriers from the outset in order to protect whole sectors from the clutches of a certain type of research. It would be a bad dialectician who immunized himself in this way.

Naturally, reflection upon cognitive interests is not without consequences. It makes us aware of attitudes upon which fundamental decisions concerning the methodological framework of whole research systems are dependent. Only in this way, do we learn to know what we are doing; only in this way, do we know what, when we do something, we can learn. We become aware, for instance, of the fact that empirical-analytical research produces technically utilizable knowledge, but not knowledge which makes possible a hermeneutical elucidation of the self-understanding of acting subjects. So far, sociology has primarily—and by no means in an unproblematic manner—assisted the self-reflection of social groups in given historical situations. It cannot escape this today, not even where it has professed its intention to provide mere information on empirical regularities of social behaviour. I agree with Albert that in our discipline we ought to devote all efforts to acquiring more and better information of this kind. I do not agree with him that we could, should or even must restrict ourselves to this. I shall not examine here the reason why in this country sociology has taken over the role of a historically orientated theory of society, whilst other social sciences were free from this burden and have therefore made faster progress within the limits of an exact empirical science. But what would it be like if a successful, positivistic, scientific strategy were able to reject this task completely and banish it to the vestibules of scientific discussion? For in the hands of the positivists, the critique of ideology serves this purpose. It concerns itself with cleansing the practical consciousness of social groups of those theories which cannot be reduced to technically utilizable knowledge, and yet defends their theoretical claims. How would it be then if this purge were feasible and were successfully carried out?

Under the conditions of reproduction of an industrial society, individuals who only possessed technically utilizable knowledge, and who were no longer in a position to expect a rational enlightenment of themselves nor of the aims behind their action, would lose their identity. Since the power of myth cannot be broken positivistically, their demythologized world would be full of demons. I fully accept the risk of this language. It belongs to a sphere of experience which is in no way reserved for a clairvoyant élite. However, I do have to admit that the power of imagination is only formed in contact with traditions which one initially acquires and does not immediately immerse oneself in. The possibility of rational agreement even in this dimension can be verified by reading a recently published book by Klaus Heinrich.[24]

A sociology which restricted itself in its critical intention to empirical-analytical research would only be in a position to examine the self-preservation and self-destruction of social systems in the sphere of pragmatically successful adjustment processes, and would have to deny other dimensions. Within sociology as a strict behavioural science, questions relating to the self-understanding of social groups cannot be formulated. Yet they are not meaningless on that count, nor are they beyond binding discussion. They arise objectively from the fact that the reproduction of social life not only poses technically soluble questions; instead, it includes more than the processes of adaptation along the lines of the purposive-rational use of means. Socialized individuals are only sustained through group identity, which contrasts with animal societies which must be constantly built up, destroyed and formed anew. They can only secure their existence through processes of adaptation to their natural environment, and through re-adaptation to the system of social labour in so far as they mediate their metabolism with nature by means of an extremely precarious equilibrium of individuals amongst themselves. The material conditions for survival are most closely bound up with the most sublime conditions; organic equilibrium is bound up with the distorted balance between separation and unification. Only in this balance, through communication with others, is the identity of each ego established.

---

[24] *Versuch über die Schwierigkeit, Nein zu sagen* (Frankfurt, 1964); cf. my review in *Merkur*, November, 1964.

A failing identity for people attempting to assert themselves, and an unsuccessful communication between those talking to one another, are both self-destructive—this ultimately has physical effects. In the individual sphere, these are familiar in the form of psychosomatic disturbances; the dismembered life-histories reflect the dismembered reality of institutions. We are acquainted with the painful processes of constantly renewing our identity from Hegel's *Phenomenology of Mind* as well as from Freud's psycho-analysis. The problem of an identity which can only be produced through identifications, and that means solely through external-izing identity, is at the same time the problem of communication, which makes possible the happy balance between silent, isolated existence and silent estrangement, between the sacrificing of individuality and the isolation of abstract individual persons. Everyone repeats such experiences of impending loss of identity and the silting up of verbal communication in the crises of his life-history. Yet they are no more real than the collective experiences in the history of the species, which the total societal subjects have made for themselves in their confrontation with nature. Questions concerning this realm of experience, because they cannot be answered by technically utilizable information, are not capable of explanation by empirical-analytical research. Never-theless, since its beginnings in the eighteenth century, sociology tried to discuss these very questions. In so doing, it cannot do without historically-orientated interpretations; nor, apparently, can it evade a form of communication under the spell of which alone these problems pose themselves. I refer to the dialectical network of a communicative context in which individuals develop their fragile identity between the dangers of reification and formlessness. This is the empirical core of the logical form of identity. In the evolution of consciousness, the problem of identity presents itself as a problem of survival and, at the same time, of reflection. From here dialectical philosophy once developed.

In the shirt-sleeved world picture of many a positivist, dialectics plays the part of a bogeyman. For others, who occasionally become aware of the fact that they lapse into dialectical trains of thought, dialectics only expresses the fact that we think and are able to think when, according to the traditional rules of logical inference, we really should not be able to do so. In dialectics, thought does not become entangled because it scorns the rules of formal logic but because it clings to them in a particularly stubborn manner—even on the level of self-reflection, rather than breaking off reflection at this point. The self-reflection of the strict empirical sciences, in my opinion, strikes a cautionary note as far as positivistic expectations are concerned. It includes the realization that our theories do not simply describe reality. On the other hand, it does not permit itself to be discouraged by definitions from explaining such connections which, according to the demarcations upon which—for good reason—empirical scientific analysis is based, should not exist.

Given these points of departure, a discussion between positivists and those who are not ashamed of dialectical trains of thought has its moments of treachery. Nevertheless, since both parties are convinced of the unity of human reason, as well as of the possibility of a consensus achieved in a rational manner and, in addition, do not intentionally deny the comprehensive rationality of an unreserved criticism, it is possible for them to carry on a discussion. In so doing, however, both parties pursue a different strategy.

Albert accuses me of a quite unscientific strategy. He calls it immunization and masking. If one considers that I subject to discussion the very conditions of validation themselves—upon whose exclusiveness Albert insists—then neither description seems particularly meaningful to me. I should prefer to talk of a flanking strategy. You have to make it clear to the positivist that you have already taken up a position behind his back. I have no idea whether this is a sympathetic manner in which to proceed but, at any rate, it was dictated to me by the course of the discussion. Albert's objections rest on presuppositions which, in their turn, I have questioned. Albert's strategy,[25] on the other hand, I could characterize, with a certain symmetry to his accusation of obscurantism, as one of pretending to be stupid. One refuses to understand what the other person is saying. This strategy, intended to force the opponent to accept one's own language, is several centuries old and has been extraordinarily successful since the days of Bacon. The advances of the exact sciences rest, to a large extent, upon translating traditional questions into a new language. They find no answer to questions which they themselves have not

[25] I do not wish to include here Albert's slip which creeps in on pp. 188f. I do not imagine that Albert makes a commonplace anti-communism a part of his strategy.

formulated. Yet, on the other hand, this very same strategy becomes a formidable hindrance if one wishes to discuss the status of such research as a whole. The systematic pretence of inability to understand dries up a discussion since any discussion must always move within the compass of a pre-understanding which is mutually taken for granted. In this way, one promotes an ethno-centricity of scientific subcultures which destroys the candour of scientific criticism.

The accusation of unintelligibility belongs to this context. In so far as this touches me as an empirical subject, I take it repentantly to heart. But in so far as it is aimed at a structure of thought and expression, it requires explanation. Understanding is a two-sided relationship. Whilst carrying out my required reading of ingenious positivistic studies, I have had the painful experience of not, or not immediately, understanding a great deal. I attributed the difficulty to my defective learning processes and not to the unintelligibility of the texts. I would not venture to exclude altogether the impression that the same thing could happen the other way round with someone who quotes Hegel at second hand.

I speak here of tradition with regard to learning processes which it makes possible and not in the anticipation of authorities to which a descent could be traced back. Perhaps it is precisely for this reason that Popper's works belong to the series of great philosophical theories, because he still maintains learned acquaintance with traditions which many a member of his retinue hardly knows even by name.

HANS ALBERT

BEHIND POSITIVISM'S BACK?

A Critical Illumination of Dialectical Digressions

'Honest positivists, whose laughter is dispelled by such perspectives . . .'
Jürgen Habermas, *Theory and Practice*

In his reply[1] to my critique,[2] Jürgen Habermas attempts to re-formulate his objections to Karl Popper's critical rationalism so as to avoid the misunderstandings produced by the essays which I criticized. His arguments in the present reply, however, could not convince me either that I had misunderstood him up till now, or that his objections hold good. I can hardly contest his impression that I have isolated his arguments from the context of an immanent critique of Popper's views and that, in this way, they have become so confused that he can scarcely recognize them. I took pains to reconstruct his arguments in such a manner that the reader could recognize what I was answering, and now I can only trust that anyone interested in this discussion will see for himself, by comparing the texts, whether this reproof is justified. For my part, however, I have gained the impression that, in his reply, Habermas has not only reformulated his existing critique but has altered its contents in quite important respects. Be that as it may, I too prefer open controversy to the 'strategy of mutually shrugging one's shoulders' and, like Habermas, I am prepared to forego discussion of questions of form. Despite our opposing views, interest in critical discussion seems to unite us.

In his preliminary remarks, Habermas attaches importance to the fact that his critique is not aimed at research practices in the

---

[1] Jürgen Habermas, 'A Positivistically Bisected Rationalism. A reply to a pamphlet'.

[2] Cf. my essay, 'The Myth of Total Reason. Dialectical Claims in the Light of Undialectical Criticisms'.

exact empirical sciences but rather at their positivistic interpretation. This is interesting because Karl Popper, whose views
Habermas criticizes, also puts forward arguments against such
an interpretation. But in order to implement his critique of
Popper, Habermas must insinuate that in basic respects Popper
must be incorporated into the positivist tradition. The solution
of such problems of incorporation depends on demarcations
which can be made in a variety of ways.[3] This means that an
unequivocal answer cannot be expected. The crucial point here,
however, would be proof that the specific objections which
Habermas raises against the representatives of this philosophical
tradition can also be made against Popper. Further, that the general
reproach concerning a restriction of critical thought seems to be
Habermas' central objection—and is expressed even in the title
of his reply—also applies to Popper. Habermas asserts that
positivistic self-understanding has restrictive effects, 'it silences
any binding reflection beyond the boundaries of the empirical-
analytical (and formal) sciences'.[4] He goes on to speak of
'positivistic prohibitive norms' according to which 'whole
problem-areas would have to be excluded from discussion and
relinquished to irrational attitudes'. In this context, he draws
attention to 'those problems connected with the selection of
standards and the influence of arguments on attitudes'. As far as
I am aware, such limitations, prohibitive norms and reservations
in principle are certainly not to be found in Popper, nor can such
assertions be maintained as far as the present-day representatives
of positivism in the narrow sense are concerned.[5]

Habermas refers to my representation of his view and claims
that I insinuated that, by his arguments, he intended 'to introduce
something approaching a new "method" alongside the already
well-established methods of social-scientific research' even
though he claims that de facto he had nothing of the sort in mind.[6]
I do not wish to decide in what sense Habermas' suggestion

---

[3] In our discussion of Popper's conception on 22.2.1965 at the Cologne Alpbach
seminar this became quickly evident, and we soon dropped the point for this reason.

[4] Habermas, 'A Positivistically Bisected Rationalism', p. 198–9 above.

[5] The neo-pragmatism of Morton G. White, to which Habermas draws attention
in his reply, and the views of the representatives of analytical philosophy following
the later *Wittgenstein*, may differ in many ways but hardly in that the latter would
prefer to exclude certain problems from discussion which the former is prepared to
deal with.

[6] Habermas, p. 199 above.

represents a counter-proposal to Popper's philosophy of science
and can be described as a 'new method'. In any case, my objections
are directed against the alleged superiority of Habermas' views
for solving problems which cannot be solved with Popper's
conception. Whether or not one is willing to call what Habermas
offers a new method, he does at least indicate the basic features
of a methodological conception for a dialectical social science,
which claims to overcome the limitations of a social science
fashioned after Popper's views. In my above-mentioned essay, I
undertook to subject this methodological conception to criticism
and to test its claims. I do not feel that this was sufficiently taken
into account in Habermas' reply. In this reply, one finds not so
much an attempt to support the claims of the *dialectical* conception with reference to the social sciences as an attempt to
utilize the results of *neo-pragmatism* for a critique of Popper's
rationalism. Certainly, Habermas' critique of Popper proves
considerably milder than does his critique of my view. Here he
seeks to locate basic misunderstandings not only with respect to
his own conception but, moreover, with regard to Popper's.
I shall now turn to the details of his attempt to clarify my misunderstandings.[7]

1 ON THE METHODOLOGICAL ROLE
OF EXPERIENCE

My first misunderstanding, according to Habermas, relates to
the methodological role of experience in the empirical sciences.
In this respect it seems to me that he represents the situation
under discussion in a peculiar manner. In fact, he represents it
in such a way that it seems as if he never doubted what I reproached
him with; namely, that the conception of theory formation which
he criticized need make no restrictions with regard to the type of
experience permitted, whilst his own view necessitates recourse
to natural hermeneutics.[8] In his objection, Habermas referred

---

[7] In the following pages, I shall basically discuss the problems in the same order
in which they appear in Habermas' article so that the reader might be in a position
to recognize a principle behind them.

[8] Cf. in this connection the relevant sections in 'The Analytical Theory of Science
and Dialectics', loc. cit., pp. 132ff., and my critique, loc. cit., pp. 173ff., as well as
his rejoinder, loc. cit., pp. 200f.

explicitly to the origin of insights which guide the outline of the dialectical theory which he has in mind, a theory which, in its construction must, *'in advance'* measure up to a pre-formed object and cannot *merely* be united *at a later stage* with a restricted experience. From these and other statements one might infer that he wishes to tie theory formation to prior experience. In fact, he refers to experience which has been accumulated pre-scientifically, that is, everyday experience, and he intends to tie theory formation to prior experience in a way no longer acceptable to Popper's conception. Here, I have already drawn attention to the remarkable conservatism which lies in this emphasis on the problem of origin and in a concept of experience which can, at best, serve the methodological function of making respectable mistakes difficult to correct. For it is not uncommon that successful theories contradict existing experience. [9]

In his reply, Habermas does not pursue this point any further; moreover, he rejects the suggestion that he might fail to recognize the merits of the test situations which I had emphasized in order to clarify critically the role of what he calls restricted experience. Instead, he turns to another question which is undoubtedly connected with it, namely, the question 'whether, through such a definition of the preconditions for testing, the possible meaning of the empirical validity of statements has not been established in advance. And if this is the case, one might ask what meaning of validity is thereby prejudiced'. [10] I do not know why, by rejecting such a question, I allegedly seek to 'enthrone philosophical innocence at any price'. The test conditions must be fashioned, in each case, in agreement with the meaning and the content of the respective theory; they are in no way imposed upon it 'from outside'. One can only ask that a theory should be subjected to as strict a test as possible and this means, of course, that full use should be made of test conditions which correspond to its hypotheses. One can also ask that its corroboration should be judged in connection with such attempts

---

[9] Cf. Here, for example, Paul K. Feyerabend, 'Problems of Empiricism' in R. G. Colodny (ed.), *Beyond the Edge of Certainty. Essays in Contemporary Science and Philosophy*, vol. 2, University of Pittsburgh Series in the Philosophy of Science (Englewood Cliffs, 1965), pp. 152ff. It is interesting that Feyerabend, who represents the Popperian conception, attempts here to counter precisely that radical empiricism to which Habermas, in this respect, is presumably attached.

[10] loc. cit., pp. 200f.

at validation. Theories which intend to make some statement about the world, and this means, amongst other things, about man and his socio-cultural world are confronted, whilst they are being tested, with 'facts' which appear to be relevant for them. The composition of such facts must depend upon the statements made by the particular theories. This is nothing more than a way of exposing theories to criticism, and this to the risk of destruction; by this, nothing is prejudiced which was not already established by these theories themselves.

In order to demonstrate the restrictive character of my methodological views, Habermas draws attention to the fact that moral feelings, privations and frustrations, crises in the individual's life-history, changes in attitude in the course of reflection, all mediate *different experiences* which 'through corresponding standards . . . can be raised to the level of a validating instance', apparently in opposition to the experiential basis of the exact sciences. Since this reference is apparently intended to function as an objection, it would be of some interest to have a more precise specification with regard to the question of *what kind of statements* are to be tested with the aid of such experiences, and *how* this is to take place. Certainly there exists no reason not to treat problems of this kind, but it is, to some extent, difficult to discuss references to possible solutions or even permit them as objections if these solutions themselves remain in the background.

Primarily, one could draw attention to the fact that the empirical sciences already deal with experiences of the kind quoted by Habermas, precisely in the way that they utilize them as 'facts' and connect them with theories which relate to facts of this kind. In this manner, such experiences are drawn upon to test theories without one being compelled to give up the methodological view criticized by Habermas. For this reason, one can assume that he does not intend such a utilization of these experiences. The very wording of his statement suggests, rather, that it is intended differently. It is not suggested that a frustration, for example, be utilized as a validating instance for a theory which makes same statement about frustration, but rather, that one raises such experiences *directly* to a validating instance, that is, that one tests a theory according to whether it frustrates someone, and possibly permits it to be so destroyed. In the present context, this would certainly be an interesting suggestion whose consequences would have to be considered. New ideas, critical arguments and reference to unpleasant facts quite often lead to frustrations in the case of advocates of particular views. One does not have to think here of the famous examples of Galileo, Darwin, Marx and Freud, where the dangerous consequences for the traditional world view were very clear, with the result that major defensive reactions were evoked. Even for scientific problems of less importance to world views, one can frequently reckon with the fact that the emotional investment in particular theories is large enough to lead to frustrations in similar cases. If one were to raise this seriously to a critical instance, then I do not know how methodologically one could see in it anything other than the attempt to place immunizing strategies at a premium. One might suppose that such irrationalism would hardly be acceptable even for Habermas.

Perhaps, therefore, another interpretation of his statement is to be preferred. One could start out from the assumption that a scientist is normally so trained that certain characteristics of theories frustrate him; for example, inner contradictions if he is not prepared to 'overcome' them dialectically, lack of informative content, or difficulties which arise in their empirical testing. Such an assumption can possibly be significant for the explanation of the research process, and thus for the sociology of science. It would, however, not permit any negative conclusions with regard to the methodological conception under scrutiny. Such an interpretation is hardly productive here. A further possibility would be that Habermas is not thinking at all of theories which claim to provide information about reality, to describe it and explain it, but rather he is thinking of approaches of a different kind. The reference to moral feelings as possibly validating instances suggests that he is concerned, for example, with normative conceptions. Even the above-mentioned statement concerning the prejudicing of the meaning of validity could point in this direction. Anyone who is not prepared to see in a view's claim to validity anything other than the claim to general recognition, and consequently does not appreciate the necessity for a differentiation in this respect, will nevertheless admit that the foundations of the validity of normative statements may be of a different nature from the foundations of the validity of empirical scientific theories. Even this would create no difficulties for the conception criticized by Habermas as restrictive but such a conception allows us to expose even normative views to critical arguments.[11] Presumably there is no need to discuss the fact that a connection can be established between the meaning of statements and their testing conditions, and that not all statements convey the meaning of empirical scientific hypotheses.[12] The real problems only arise when one has to analyse this connection for certain types of statements. Thus the relevance of Habermas' 'other experiences' could reveal itself in the case of the other test procedures which he indicates. For the present, I am not yet in a position to recognize that an argument for the restrictedness of the methodological conception which Habermas criticized, can be developed from this. I am most willing to discuss methodological innovations but they must be recognizable at some point.

The problem set out above interests Habermas as it relates to Popper's critique of positivism, which is allegedly carried so far 'that it unintentionally makes even his own suggested solution problematical'.[13] The point at issue here is as follows: Popper not only criticizes the positivistic conception in particular but also every epistemological view which intends to justify and thereby guarantee any knowledge by recourse to its certain final sources.[14] He replaces it with an epistemological fallibilism which excludes such guarantees of truth but is instead linked to a methodology of critical testing. Habermas, however, objects that mistakes are detected only on the basis of criteria for whose justification arguments must be adduced. Such arguments must be sought in order to avoid arbitrariness 'in the very dimension—not of the origin but of the formation of knowledge—which has been ruled out'.[15] Habermas claims that the Popper's 'sublation'

[11] Cf. on this point, my contributions, 'Die Idee der kritischen Vernunft. Zur Problematik der rationalen Begründung und des Dogmatismus', in *Club Voltaire I* (Munich, 1963); and 'Social Science and Moral Philosophy', in M. Bunge (ed.), *The Critical Approach to Science and Philosophy. In Honor of Karl R. Popper* (London, 1964).

[12] Perhaps this is the place to refer to the fact that there is scarcely any philosophical tendency which has contributed so much to the clarification of these problems as logical positivism and its related movements.

[13] Thus Habermas, p. 202, after a short presentation of Popper's critique. I can accept this presentation in its fundamentals, even if several formulations appear questionable, for example, the assertion (p. 202) that Popper *reduces* all knowledge to the level of assertions and the associated observations which, for readers lacking any knowledge of Popper's view, are liable to evoke completely misleading associations.

[14] Cf. Karl Popper, 'On the Sources of Knowledge and Ignorance' reprinted in, *Conjectures and Refutations* (London, 1963), pp. 3–30.

[15] Habermas, p. 203.

of the origins of theories is questionable, since this method itself can only be founded by recourse to the critical tradition, and thus by recourse to at least one of the sources of knowledge. The argument aims to show that even Popper is compelled to resort to such a justification invoking the sources, if not on the level of theory formation then at least on the methodological level. Popper himself has emphasized the significance of tradition as a source, in fact as one of the most important sources, of our knowledge as opposed to rationalistic anti-traditionalism. But he denies that there is a source which could lay claim to infallibility. Every source is thus subjected to criticism, even that of tradition, regardless of whether it provides theoretical or meta-theoretical views. Recourse to tradition can itself not be considered a foundation. One might counter Habermas' contention that Popper's method can only be so founded by asking how one can conceive of such a foundation if one wishes to avoid recourse to an instance which can no longer be criticized, that is, to a dogma.[16] But here it is not the case that Popper seeks a foundation in tradition—he believes rather that he can do without a foundation—but that Habermas presents it as inevitable because he believes that he must orientate his arguments towards justificatory thought. We shall return to this point.

Yet Habermas believes that he can diagnose the pivot of the residual positivistic problematic in Popper as the epistemological independence of facts—assumed by Popper—from the theories related to them, an independence which supports the idea of a test on the basis of the facts.[17] In my critique, I had pointed out that Popper explicitly criticizes the positivistic idea of pure givenness, of the naked fact not tainted by theory and does not require it for his methodological standpoint. Habermas is not

---

[16] In my critique I pointed out that the alternative of dogmatism and justification set up by Habermas is exposed to an objection formulated by Popper, namely, that recourse to positive grounds itself possesses the character of a dogmatic procedure or implies an infinite regress. Cf. pp. 189ff. The methodology of a critical test must, therefore, forego positive justification. On the possibility of a criticistic conception emancipated in this sense from justificatory thought, cf. for example, apart from the works of Popper, William Warren Bartley, *The Retreat to Commitment* (New York, 1962), a book which Habermas dismisses without sufficient analysis in his essay; cf. his answer, loc. cit., pp. 213ff. *See also* below.

[17] Habermas, p. 203; on this and on the observation of my discussion partner that he has apparently not succeeded in making me aware of what is at issue, here cf. The Analytical Theory of Science and Dialectics', pp 149ff. and *passim* and also my reply. I leave it to the reader to judge this attempt and its failure.

satisfied with this. Here he criticizes Popper's adherence to the correspondence theory of truth which presupposes that 'facts' are entities in themselves, without taking into account the prior decision made with the definition of the testing conditions upon the question of meaning. But I do not know how this characterization can be equated with Popper's view—quoted by Habermas himself—namely, that facts are the common product of language and reality.[18] The correspondence theory of truth is in no way confined to naked, theory-free and, in this sense, facts 'in themselves'. Nor must they be understood in terms of a picture-theory as is frequently insinuated by dialecticians,[19] for example, when, in connection with descriptive statements, the metaphor of the 'mere duplication of reality' occurs. Moreover, Popper's philosophy of science is not even dependent upon the correspondence theory of truth,[20] nor upon the realism associated with it in his work. Rather, it is sufficient that the possibility exists that, in the application of a theory to specific situations, the basic statements, adequate for these situations, contradict the theory in question, that is, the possibility of the emergence of counter instances which is already given, if this theory is to have any informative content at all.[21] I am unable to appreciate to what extent there is any justification—in view of the situation described

---

[18] I can however explain how this passage came about, since Habermas had originally assumed the indispensability of theory-free facts for falsification.

[19] Cf. Karl Popper, 'Truth, Rationality, and the Growth of Scientific Knowledge', in *Conjectures and Refutations*, loc. cit., pp. 223ff. where the correspondence theory is dealt with. Amongst other things, Popper draws attention here to Wittgenstein's 'surprisingly naïve picture theory', to Schlick's clear and devastating criticism of various versions of the correspondence theory (including the picture or projection theory) and finally to Tarski's version of the theory which does not repeat the old errors. Also on this problem see Günther Patzig, 'Satz und Tatsache', in *Argumentation. Festschrift für Josef König*, ed. Harold Delius and Günther Patzig (Göttingen, 1964), in which, amongst others, Wittgenstein's picture-theory is criticized, but above all it is shown in what sense one can readily adhere to the mode of reference to facts and their agreement with statements.

[20] Cf. the recent remarks on Tarski in Popper's *The Logic of Scientific Discovery* (London, 1959), p. 274.

[21] One sees here incidentally how Habermas comes to associate Popper with positivism, although explicitly represents a realist view. He sets out here from the treatment of the problem of 'Facts'. In order to throw the positivistic residue overboard, Popper would presumably have to agree to interpret concrete situations of application not only *in the light* of the theories which come into question but also, beyond this, *in the sense* of these theories, that is, in each case, conforming to the theory. Popper himself has drawn attention to the fact that one *can* carry out such a strategy of immunization; however, he has also drawn attention to the unpleasant consequences of such a procedure.

—in referring Popper to the 'fetish-character' of the positivistic concept of facts.

2 THE BASIS PROBLEM AND THE QUESTION OF INSTRUMENTALISM

In my critique of his analysis of Popper's philosophy of science, I reproached Habermas, amongst other things, for his inadequate treatment of the basis problem.[22] In particular, I contested the claim that a vicious circle would occur when empirical-scientific theories are applied—a point to which Habermas had drawn attention—and, in addition, I questioned to what extent hermeneutic explication can provide any further help in this connection. In his reply, Habermas has now attempted to clarify once again how this circle comes about[23]—he claims to have learned about this vicious circle from Popper himself. Habermas argues from an analogy between the process of trial by jury and the application of theories—an analogy which Popper draws upon in order to illustrate his views. In the passage in question, the distinction is made between the jury's verdict—a reply to a factual question arrived at after proceedings which are governed by certain rules—and the judge's sentence, which must be justified by means of the application of the relevant legal statutes to the facts of the case, which have been established in the verdict. Popper compares the acceptance of a basic statement with a verdict and the application of a theory with that of the relevant legal norms and points out that, in both cases, the establishment of the basis of application—both of the basic statement and of the verdict—itself belongs to the application of the propositional system—that is, of the theory or of the legal code—and, consequently, must take place according to the rules of procedure for the system in question. The passage which Habermas extracts from the context of Popper's argument can, however, lead the reader to project a circle into this whole procedure, but only if one does not draw upon the previous sections for interpretation. For in the latter, it is evident that the procedural rules, according to which the verdict is reached, are in no way identical with the

---

[22] Cf. Habermas, 'The Analytical Theory of Science and Dialectics', pp. 143ff. and my reply, pp. 181f.

[23] Habermas, 'A Positivistically Bisected Rationalism', pp. 204f.

legal norms which are to be applied to the facts of the case, although both of course belong to the legal system. Consequently, there can be no question of a circle in any relevant sense of the word. Nor can the acceptance of basic statements as part of the application of a theory be regarded as a circle. The modes of procedure, which determine their acceptance, rest upon rules which certainly belong to the theory but are in no way identical with the theoretical laws to be applied. In my critique, therefore, I distinguished between the use of theoretical language[24] for the formulation of the conditions of application, and the application of the laws themselves, If one could not make the distinction which Popper has clearly expressed, then an application of a theory would always result in its confirmation. Thus, the organization of attempts tests would be a futile venture. I do not wish to decide whether one could reasonably speak of a circle in this case. At any rate, this state of affairs would be somewhat fatal for the content and testability of theories—a situation which could not be altered even by means of hermeneutic explication.

After he has set out his circle thesis, Habermas attempts to substantiate his pragmatic interpretation of the empirical sciences, for which he believes he has found clues in Popper himself. I have no objection to his assertion that the demand for controlled observation as the basis for decision upon hypotheses presupposes that the meaning of the research process as a whole has been understood. For a long time, the philosophy of the empirical sciences has been involved in the clarification of such problems without recourse to any prompting from hermeneutic philosophical currents.[25] If one is so inclined one can, for instance,

---

[24] The language of an empirical scientific theory is normally not merely a formal system but rather it contains rules of application which are partially embodied even in certain techniques of measurement. These rules also underlie the decision concerning the acceptance or rejection of basic statements, as Habermas himself admits. Cf. his reply, p. 204. That these rules are only laid down institutionally and not logically, as he claims, is however a somewhat remarkable rider when one considers that to some extent, they belong to the grammar of the relevant theoretical language. Undoubtedly, even logical rules can be embedded in the same sense that grammatical rules can be embedded institutionally, with the result that the opposition does not appear to be very plausible.

[25] This also applies to logical positivism, which exposed itself to critical analysis precisely because its contributions to this problem-complex have the advantage of being lucid, definite and concrete, a feature which is generally lacking in contributions from hermeneutic and dialectical circles. This is not a remark which refers specifically to my present discussion partner, whose publications in this context undoubtedly reveal the desire to take up discussion of concrete problems and

regard Popper's *Logic of Scientific Discovery* quite simply as a 'hermeneutic' undertaking, all the more so since the philosophical currents which normally claim this designation for themselves have not provided anything like a method—as opposed to a vocabulary—in the use of which one might recognize them.[26] The pragmatistic result of Habermas' hermeneutic attempts, however, surely gets no closer to the meaning of the research process than that which is put forward by realist theoreticians. Undoubtedly it is true that the methodical anticipation of possible regularities corresponds to 'elementary needs of behavioural stability'. Nevertheless, the same can be said for all kinds of mythical, religious and metaphysical views, and even for every system of ordering the world. Science is only possible where there are social spheres in which cognitive interest emancipates itself from such elementary needs. Despite this, its results can of course still be connected to such needs, for it would surely be difficult to imagine knowledge of any kind which cannot be utilized in some way for the aim of orientating and stabilizing action. To this extent then, Habermas' thesis is stamped with a certain plausibility.[27] But it is here that the weakness lies. For the plausibility of this thesis stems, at least in part, from the fact that for successful action we are dependent on information concerning the nature of reality, so that a realist interpretation of knowledge is, to some extent, to be regarded as the natural prerequisite for the emphasis on its pragmatic utilizability. From a more profound

---

thereby achieve clarity and precision. One should, however, compare this with what Theodor W. Adorno writes in 'Skoteinos oder Wie zu lesen sei', *Drei Studien zu Hegel* (Frankfurt, 1963), pp. 115ff., in defence of obscurity, for which he would like to make the nature of the object responsible—as if a clear mode of expression could distort the object. Even in Habermas' contribution to the Popper–Adorno controversy, one finds a similar argument for distortion with regard to non-dialectical sociology. Cf. pp. 132ff.

[26] Ironically, one can discover such a method much more readily in the analytical currents in philosophy, above all in the pupils of the later Wittgenstein who, it would appear, is also being gradually taken up into the circle of the hermeneutic church elders and, interestingly enough, is drawing near to Martin Heidegger, whose exercises in language magic, rather than language criticism, continue to find support in this country.

[27] Earlier, I myself gave the action-reference of the sciences a prominent place, cf. e.g. my essay 'Theorie und Prognose in den Sozialwissenschaften', *Schweitzerische Zeitschrift für Volkswirtschaft und Statistik*, 93, 1957, pp. 60ff, reprinted in Ernst Topitsch (ed.), *Logik der Sozialwissenschaften* (Cologne, 1965). In the meantime, influenced by Popper's criticism, I have distanced myself from positivism and, from the overemphasis on those aspects of science which are dominant from prgamatic viewpoints—without thereby wishing to contest their significance.

penetration into the structure of the real world, one can expect insights which are also of significance for coping practically with real entities. The fact that information is practically utilizable, and that one can best test informative theories by means of practical interventions into real events, in no way compels one to conceal its cognitive significance in favour of its practical relevance.[28]

At this point, a further question arises which must be of significance for an appraisal of Habermas' perspective. Habermas develops his critique of the 'positivistic' type of social science in accordance with a view which states that dialectical social science has to overcome the restriction of the cognitive interest associated with the former type of social science. In his latest essay, this alternative to positivist social science is no longer mentioned. Nor is there any mention in his later essay of the thesis that a non-dialectical social science tends towards a distortion of the object. I, however, had explicitly questioned this alternative and its alleged advantages. I was not concerned with an adequate interpretation of a so-called analytical social science and, in this connection, with a critique of the instrumentalist thesis. Rather, I was concerned with a critique of the claims made for a dialectical social science; in particular, with the claim to realize, with the aid of historical regularities of a certain type, the fundamental relations of dependence of a concrete totality and also the objective meaning of a historical life-context[29] and, beyond this, with the claim to legitimate practical intentions from the objective context.[30] I had expressed my reservations with regard to the logical and methodological aspects of this undertaking which, in many respects seem to me problematical. One might well ask what are these regularities, what logical structure do the relevant statements and theories possess, and what methods of interpretation and legitimation are to be used here. Above all, it

---

[28] One should not object here that this argument does not cover the pragmatic significance of the anticipation of possible regularity at all. Such an anticipation can be interpreted quite easily as an attempt to penetrate ever deeper into the nature of reality, fully independent of whether positive consequences of successful action are the result, cf. Popper, 'Die Zielsetzung der Erfahrungswissenschaft', in *Ratio*, vol. 1, 1957 [Trans. note. A revised version appears as 'The Aim of Science' in K. R. Popper, *Objective Knowledge. An Evolutionary Approach* (Oxford, 1972)]. The pragmatic interpretation is neither prominent in the 'hermeneutic' sense, nor does it represent a 'retreat to the transcendental dimension' of a kind that the realist interpretation could not claim for itself.

[29] Cf. Habermas, 'The Analytical Theory of Science and Dialectics', pp. 137ff.

[30] Cf. pp. 140ff.

should also be asked whether it is not precisely here that a primary, practical orientation lies in the background; practical, in fact, in the normative sense of this word, that is, in a sense which renders the associated cognitive claim problematical, unless one agrees to eradicate the distinction between cognitive and normative statements. We shall return to these problems.

Indeed, the core of this procedure which becomes evident in the confrontation of a so-called positivistically restricted social science with a dialectical social science seems to me to lie in the fact that the attempt is made to render an instrumentalist interpretation of the empirical sciences plausible through hermeneutics, in order to make room for an undertaking which conceals those of its characteristics which *de facto* transcend knowledge under the mask of knowledge itself.[31] Without wishing to imply any kind of reproach, one can detect ideological traits here which, for a long time, have been both familiar and intelligible to the so-called positivistic critique of ideology.[32] When Habermas elsewhere emphasizes the fact that 'an analytic-empirical science . . . as long as it does not impair positivistic self-restriction, either deliberately or through negligence, is incapable of producing goals and ordering standpoints itself, of establishing priorities and developing programmes',[33] then he draws attention to a state of affairs which is valid for all empirical sciences and, beyond these, for all systems which, within their propositional connections, do not contain any prescriptive elements. Anyone who considers this to be a shortcoming can attempt to overcome it without associating the prescriptive statements—which require complimentation—with cognitive claims, as for example German neo-normativism does.[34] This path does not seem inviting to the

---

[31] This also holds for the authors of this undertaking, the Frankfurt School of sociology and its pupils—of which Habermas can still be counted a member. I emphasize this aspect of self-deception specifically in order not to earn such reproaches as Habermas expressed in his reply to my critique. In no way do I wish to transfer to the level of motivational research. It is not a question of the sincerity of intentions but rather of the characterization of a line of thought.

[32] Moreover, I no longer see how the previously contested thesis of object distortion—under the influence of a technical cognitive interest—can be reconciled with the present line of argument, even excluding the question as to how this thesis can be understood without a minimal realism.

[33] Habermas, 'Kritische und Konservative Aufgaben der Soziologie', *Theorie und Praxis* (Neuwied/Berlin, 1963), p. 226.

[34] I have criticized this in 'Wertfreiheit als methodisches Prinzip', *Schriften des Vereins für Sozialpolitik*, New Series, vol. 29 (Berlin, 1963), reprinted in *Logik der Sozialwissenschaften*, loc. cit., and in other writings.

advocates of a dialectical social science. They prefer to encumber
the social sciences with ideological statements and functions and
postulate a form of cognition whose exclusively practical achievement[35] strangely contrasts with the claim that, precisely in the
cognitive respect, it overcomes positivistic limitations.

Habermas claims for his pragmatist interpretation of the
empirical sciences that it takes Popper's criticism of empiricism
into account, without sharing the weakness of his falsification
theory,[36] which lies in the fact that the associated assertion,
concerning an uncertainty in principle about the truth of statements, appears to clash with the overwhelming evidence in their
technical utilization. There are two points here. Firstly, this
evidence has often proved to be deceptive, and this is quite
understandable when one considers that false theories can possibly
be very useful in a technological sense.[37] The progress of the
sciences normally overcomes such pieces of 'evidence'. We then
have no grounds for playing them off against such uncertainty
which we constantly experience in this matter. Secondly, the
problem of uncertainty in principle is not serious if we take as our
basis Popper's theory of approximation which is capable of
unifying fallibilism with the idea of truth and scientific progress.
Moreover, it seems to me that Habermas' counter-suggestion
only contains a verbal solution of the problems which in no way
alters the state of affairs which Popper has analysed. For Habermas
advocates that we permit as empirically true 'all the assumptions
. . . which can guide feedback-regulated action without having
been previously rendered problematic through errors experimentally striven for'.[38] Why should we so alter our concept of
truth that it coincides with the already existing concept of

---

[35] On this aspect of dialectical thought *see*, e.g., Ernst Topitsch, 'Sprachlogische
Probleme der sozialwissenschaftlichen Theoriebildung', *Logik der Sozialwissenschaften*, pp. 30ff; also his 'Das Verhältnis zwischen Sozial- und Naturwissenschaften',
loc. cit., pp. 62ff.

[36] For clues which Popper himself supposedly provides for this interpretation,
see Habermas, 'A Positivistically Bisected Rationalism', p. 206, also note 9, p. 207,
where Habermas discusses Popper's treatment of dispositional terms. A comparison
with Popper's *Logic of Scientific Discovery*, pp. 423ff., reveals that this analysis contains
nothing of special relevance for the problem of a pragmatic interpretation. The
same applies to his analysis of the role of traditions. It is not denied that there are
pragmatic aspects in the empirical sciences. What is problematical is their exclusive
accentuation.

[37] Popper has emphasized this point. As an example one might mention here the
ballistic utilization of the parabola.

[38] Habermas, p. 208.

corroboration, and thereby accept the consequence that, in Newton's age, the notion of truth differs from that held today? Apart from this verbal substitution, what alterations are made to Popper's theory of corroboration?[39]

As far as my reference to Popper's critique of instrumentalism is concerned—which Habermas thinks he does not need to answer, since it is allegedly directed against theses which he does not expound[40]—I must insist that it is clearly taken from views found in his writings, and particularly in those sections of his present reply which are supposed to prove the opposite. Habermas certainly claims that the pragmatic interpretation which he expounds does not encompass the type of instrumentalism criticized by Popper. According to this interpretation, theories themselves are not instruments but rather it is their information which is technically utilizable—a statement not challenged from any side. After a lengthy exposition intended to render intelligible my misunderstanding, Habermas states, however, that the descriptive value of scientific information is certainly not to be disputed, but it is not to be understood in such a way that theories represent facts and relations between facts. Rather, their descriptive content is only valid with reference to prognoses for feedback-regulated actions in predictable situations. Quite apart from the fact that the correspondence theory expounded by Popper is not a picture-theory, it is evident from this passage that here theories are interpreted as instruments of calculation in that sense which Popper criticizes; that is, contrary to his view, in which they can be understood as attempts to illuminate the structural characteristics of reality.[41] Habermas, as far as I can see, specifically rejects the realist alternative to the instrumentalist interpretation, as well as the correspondence theory of truth. It is

---

[39] Habermas in fact recognizes Popper's reservations with regard to incontestably valid knowledge, cf. his note 10, p. 208, where, however, he mistakenly asserts that Popper 'admits experimental tests exclusively as an instance of falsification' whilst he *de facto* develops a theory of corroboration.

[40] Cf. Habermas, pp. 208f., and my reference in 'The Myth of Total Reason', p. 170; the relevant arguments by Popper are to be found in his essay, 'Three Views Concerning Human Knowledge' in *Conjectures and Refutations*, loc. cit., pp. 97ff., which Habermas himself quotes, and in other works by Popper.

[41] Cf. Popper, 'Die Zielsetzung der Erfahrungswissenschaft', loc. cit., p. 76. Revised version as 'The Aims of Science' in K. R. Popper, *Objective Knowledge* (Oxford, 1972); further Paul K. Feyerabend, 'Realism and Instrumentalism: Comments on the Logic of Factual Support', in *The Critical Approach to Science and Philosophy*, loc. cit., pp. 280 ff.

quite compatible with the instrumental character of theories, in
the sense Popper criticizes, that the descriptive content is claimed
for singular statements produced with their aid—in particular,
prognoses—although of course, at this level, the question of
correspondence can arise again. I admit that not all Habermas'
statements have to be interpreted in this manner. But surely those
statements must be so interpreted where, in opposition to Popper,
he seeks to demonstrate the inadequacy of the views which Popper
has developed as a critique of the positivist conception of science.
The reduction of empirical scientific knowledge claimed by
Habermas, corresponds more readily to the positivist tradition.
Moreover, his statements in this connection surely do correspond
to the 'positivistic self-understanding' of many a physicist—but
this self-understanding is increasingly exposed to a critique from
the realist side, and partially, in fact, from within their own
camp.[42] One may therefore justly doubt whether Habermas has
positioned himself 'behind' the positivists' backs—especially
since the literature which he falls back upon to an ever-increasing
extent can easily be attributed to the realm of analytical philosophy.[43]

3   THE PROBLEM OF JUSTIFICATION

In my criticism of Habermas' contribution to the Adorno
Festschrift, I objected that the reference to the fact which—it is
alleged—'Popper persistently ignores, namely, that we are
normally in no doubt at all about the validity of a basic statement'
as well as further reference to unformulated criteria which play a
role in the institutionally regulated research process, cannot be
regarded as the solution to a methodological problem treated by
Popper. In this connection, I have pointed out that here the
dialectician becomes the real 'positivist' if he thinks that he can
eliminate problems of the logic of research by reference to actual
social phenomena. Habermas in no way takes up my criticism but

---

[42] Cf. Alfred Landé, 'Why Do Quantum Theorists Ignore the Quantum Theory?'
in *The British Journal for the Philosophy of Science*, vol. 15, no. 60, 1965, pp. 307ff., as
well as note 41 above.

[43] Naturally, I have no objection to this since I am more inclined to regard the
consultation of such literature as a step forward. I simply have the impression that
this is connected with a departure from dialectics which would create a headache
for 'typical' dialecticians—if such still exist. Far be it from me to want to protect
the Frankfurt School from such an analytical contamination.

rather asserts that I did not understand the question he raised and passes on to a new problem—namely, that of the relation between methodological and empirical statements.[44] Initially, his remarks on this problem are basically not contentious, because they correspond to those already made by his opponents. In the extension of his argument, he intends to express his critique of the division between logico-methodological and empirical domains, even though this distinction itself should not be overlooked. Primarily, he supports his argument with reference to the views of neo-pragmatism[45] which he attempts to confront with Popper's solution to the problem of rationalism. In so doing, he particularly emphasizes the fact that critical argumentation intends to influence attitudes, and that such argumentation goes beyond the sphere of the logical connection of statements. In this respect, he contrasts it with deductive argumentation so as to demonstrate, at a later point, that a justification of rationalism is possible with its help.

One might make the following comments here. Arguments usually exist as a given series of propositions which rest upon logical connections, regardless of whether they intend to influence attitudes, alter substantive convictions or attain a different result. The inclusion of the pragmatics of a communicative situation creates no new problems in this respect. Naturally there exists a distinction between a logical relation between statements of the same level and a relation such as exists between statements and their object-domain, whereby, in its turn, the object-domain can of course consist of statements.[46] But even this distinction does

---

[44] The objection I raised here was not that in methodological questions he did not draw upon empirical arguments, but rather that he sought to make methodological problems disappear by mere reference to facts. He claims that the problems do not arise if we see the research process in a way which corresponds to the sociologist's perspective. From the 'hermeneutic' standpoint, it would presumably be necessary to reconstruct the problem situation from which Popper's solution to the basis problem has sprung. Then it would have been shown that here it was not a question of factual certainties—such as must be constantly questioned in the research process —but rather of an independent problem of justification which can be raised even when 'in fact' it should not appear in many contexts. Empirical arguments which could be drawn upon today for these problems will generally have to rest upon modern theories of perception.

[45] Specifically Morton G. White's well-known book, *Toward Reunion in Philosophy* (Cambridge, Mass., 1956), in which Quine's holism is extended to ethics.

[46] Analytical philosophy has long been acquainted with the problem of language levels and similarly with that of the relationship between language and object-domain.

not oblige one to deny the fundamental role of the logical
relations in the formation of arguments, not even for those
arguments which aim at an alteration of attitudes. One can
examine and evaluate the logic of a line of argument quite independently of whether it can *de facto* influence attitudes or not. On
the other hand, one can carry out investigations of such factual
connections, as Habermas himself mentions. One can further
attempt to translate the relevant aspects of possible attitudes into
corresponding statements, for instance of a prescriptive character,
and then establish logical connections between the latter and the
arguments which they support. These are all things which can be
interesting in certain contexts, but which one can keep apart. A
rationalization of attitudes such as Popper considers possible,
would consist, above all, in attaining the readiness to participate
in critical arguments. This presupposes that one accepts the logic
up to this point. It does not presuppose that one prefers the
'certainty of descriptive knowledge'—which, as we know, does
not play an important role for Popper—to some form of
argumentation.[47]

In a sense, it may be true to say that even the interplay of
statements and experiences presupposes standards; but that
standards require justification is, firstly, a very problematical and,
secondly, an insufficiently specific thesis for one to be able to
adopt a definite view on it.[48] I am not able to discover here an
objection which Popper could evade. His problem is that of the
possibility of a foundation of rationalism through arguments.
Since the acceptance of arguments of any type presupposes a
rationalist attitude, the latter cannot be founded on arguments.[49]
Popper does not evade such consequences, but instead he tries to
show how a critical rationalism which relinquishes the claim to
positive foundation, without thereby sacrificing the possibility

---

[47] Cf. Habermas, p. 212.

[48] Standards of this type are seldom justified and, if they are, then in a given
context in which certain aims are presupposed, which themselves can appear
unproblematical. In my view, this has little to do with the problem of rationalism.

[49] One should note that *nothing* is changed in this state of affairs if one distinguishes
deductive proof from supporting argumentation, on the assumption that Popper is
only correct regarding the first form of argument. Quite apart from the extent to
which types of argument in which logic does not play a fundamental role can be
produced at all—so that the above-mentioned opposition could become in any way
relevant—one would also have to include the second type of argument in the
characterization of the rational attitude. Thus, the same state of affairs would be
observed as in Popper's solution to the problem.

of a critical test, is nevertheless possible. At this point, Habermas accuses him of an undialectical procedure, without having discussed the structure of Popper's arguments, and without having shown how this problem could be solved more adequately by dialectics.[50] In this context, I pointed out that the alternatives of dogmatism and rational foundation (*Begrundung*), which apparently underlie Habermas' arguments, are exposed to a serious objection, namely, that recourse to positive grounds itself implies a dogmatic procedure.

Instead of a detailed elaboration of the dialectical arguments which one could compare with Popper's arguments in order to ascertain what advantages they possess over the latter, one finds the surprising comment that Popper himself makes use of a 'supporting argumentation', which is sufficient as justification even if it might appear 'unsatisfactory for a logical absolutism'. In other words, Popper—who otherwise figures as a representative of a positivistically restricted rationalism—has solved Habermas' problem of rational foundation in a thoroughly adequate manner, without however sufficiently recognizing it himself. What does Popper's justification of rationalism consist of? It consists of the explication of the critical attitude in terms of philosophical traditions, the analysis of the presuppositions and consequences of criticism, and the examination of its function in public political life.[51] These are certainly achievements which apparently can also be produced with regard to other views, yet this is no justification for them. Popper carries out this analysis in order to clarify the possibilities between which one can decide; that is, in order to permit an open decision which—despite the impossibility already demonstrated by him, of a self-foundation of rationalism—can certainly be influenced, in his view, by such an analysis. As far as I can see, Habermas recognizes this way of proceeding, but adds three riders. On the one hand, he calls it a critical justification of criticism. On the other hand, he opposes Popper's assertion that the problem treated here consists in the choice between two sorts of faith. Finally, he asserts that Popper avoids the problematical combination of logical and empirical relations in non-deductive justifications when he foregoes a justification of criticism. As a result, the 'Black Peter' is already

[50] Cf. Habermas, 'Dogmatism, Reason, and Decision', in *Theory and Practice*, loc. cit., pp. 276ff., and my reply in 'The Myth of Total Reason', loc. cit., pp. 190ff.
[51] Cf. Habermas, 'A Positivistically Bisected Rationalism', p. 213.

present in the criticism itself. These three riders are basically verbal in character. They in no way alter the logic of the situation analysed by Popper, but rather relate to its linguistic paraphrase.[52] The logical grammar of 'justification' and 'faith' is certainly not sacrosanct, but I cannot detect what is has to do with a dialectical mastery of this problem as an alternative to that suggested by Popper. Popper essentially foregoes nothing which Habermas regards desirable—he merely refrains from calling his arguments a justification, and does so for very plausible reasons.[53]

In my analysis of Habermas' arguments, I pointed out that a consistent critical philosophy (*Kritizismus*) is in a position to overcome the dilemma of justificatory thought which only permits the choice between infinite regress and recourse to dogma.[54] In this connection, I took up Habermas' alternative of dogmatism and rational foundation, and his endeavour to replace Popper's solution of the problem with a better one. It is to this context that my reference to Bartley's analysis belongs. His analysis demonstrates that a consistent critical philosophy such as Popper's, in contrast to other views, does not succumb to the so-called *tu quoque* argument,[55] and consequently avoids the above-mentioned dilemma. Habermas declares that Bartley's attempt was not successful on the grounds that, by means of a premise, the latter exempts from criticism all the standards which we must presuppose for criticism. It is interesting that Habermas does not direct his critical objection at the core of Bartley's

[52] I too devoted a note to such questions—without regarding them as being serious, cf. 'The Myth of Total Reason', p. 192, note 71.

[53] Nor has the moral character of the problem escaped him, and this without him having recourse to neo-pragmatism, which found itself confronted by similar problems over ten years later, cf. Popper, *The Open Society and Its Enemies*, loc. cit., 1950, pp. 232ff.

[54] This view goes back to Popper. Cf. apart from the earlier writings, 'On the Sources of Knowledge and Ignorance' in *Conjectures and Refutations*; also William Warren Bartley, *The Retreat to Commitment* (New York, 1962), and other writings from the school of critical rationalism to which I have already, in part, referred.

[55] The argument has the character of a boomerang. Its intention is to demonstrate that precisely the same objection can be made to another view as to one's own; more specifically, that certain forms of rationalism are, in the last analysis, just as compelled to resort to a dogmatically fixed authority as is one's own irrationalism. This *tu-quoque* argument also applies—as Bartley has shown—to Morton G. White's form of rationalism from which Habermas in part draws support, cf. Bartley, loc. cit., pp. 124ff. It is interesting that this philosophy also contains recourse to a commitment not subjected to criticism, and is to be regarded in this sense as a 'restricted rationalism'.

arguments, but rather at certain of his 'technological' considerations which are appended to them. These considerations must appear wherever the claim is made to allow the validity of critical arguments. We are concerned here with the role of logic in argumentation. Bartley examines the notion of the revisability of logic introduced into the discussion by neo-pragmatism and demonstrates its limitations. For he shows that a revision in which certain essential characteristics are lost would mean a collapse of critical argumentation,[56] so that a task of logic would amount to a task of rationalism in general. Here, he makes a distinction between convictions revisable *within* a given argument-situation and those where this is not the case, and goes on to introduce the revisability criterion attacked by Habermas—'. . . whatever is presupposed by the argument-revisability situation is not itself revisable *within that situation.*'[57] This criterion apparently excludes nothing from criticism, so that all the objections made by Habermas are of no significance. Bartley makes no reservations or restrictions here which could conceivably be of consequence. In other respects he offers for discussion this whole train of thought which in no way possesses the relevance for his arguments which Habermas ascribes to it. Anyone who declares it unacceptable would, however, have to show how one can give up logic and yet use critical arguments.[58] Here lies the essential point of this train of thought. Bartley's criterion is a further point which can readily be discussed without affecting the position of critical philosophy. However, as we previously mentioned, it is not met by Habermas' objections, since Bartley excludes nothing from criticism—neither themes, nor standards, nor testing conditions.[59] It seems to me that the refutation of Bartley's argumentation is

---

[56] Bartley, loc. cit., pp. 161ff.; cf. *see also* Karl Popper, 'What is Dialectic?', *Conjectures and Refutations,* loc. cit.

[57] Bartley, loc. cit., p. 173; the italics, which emphasize the most important point of this criterion, stem from Bartley himself. Habermas omitted them. This is plausible if one looks at his arguments on this matter.

[58] For the evaluation of dialectical attempts at the 'overcoming' of logic, cf. Karl Popper, 'What is Dialectic?', note 56, as well as Z. A. Jordan, *Philosophy and Ideology* (Dordrecht, 1963), part 4, which contains the Polish discussion on formal logic.

[59] Even 'the subsequent revision of previously applied standards' is not excluded, as one might assume, not only from the context but also from the wording of the passage quoted by Habermas. In addition, Bartley even shows what form an argument might take which would refute this consistent critical philosophy itself; cf. loc. cit., pp. 148f.

not successful because its core was not even touched. Moreover, when I objected that Habermas presupposes free discussion as a fact,[60] then this was not because I am incapable of appreciating such a fact and would fail to recognize its significance, but rather because this pre-supposition, if it is made in the context he has explicated, is liable to obscure the problem with whose solution we are concerned here both in Popper's and Bartley's analysis.

4 THE DUALISM OF STANDARDS AND FACTS

In his contribution to Adorno's *Festschrift*, Habermas subjected Popper's thesis concerning the dualism of facts and decisions to criticism[61] which I, in turn, rejected as resting on misunderstandings.[62] I based my conjecture—namely, that a misinterpretation of Popper's position underlies his arguments—on the many considerations which he attached to this dualism thesis and which, in my view, have little to do with its meaning. This is particularly true of the two questions which he apparently regards as important: firstly, the question whether the normative meaning recoils from a rational discussion of the concrete life-context from which it proceeds and upon which it reacts; and secondly, the question whether knowledge, positivistically reduced to empirical science, is freed from every normative constraint. In my reply, I dealt with these questions. Here I would simply like to point out that even the assumption which apparently underlies this question illustrates this misunderstanding—the assumption that through the dualism thesis critical rationalism must provide a positive answer. But in his reply Habermas asserts that I have falsely apprehended his intention.[63] He seeks to question the optimistic distinction expressed in Popper's thesis for, on the one hand, theoretical knowledge is constituted within a normative framework which is only capable of critical justification, whilst on the other hand the critical discussion of standards includes empirical considerations and hence recourse to so-called facts. He

[60] Cf. 'The Myth of Total Reason', pp. 193f., and his reply, pp. 215f.
[61] Habermas, pp. 144ff.
[62] Cf. 'The Myth of Total Reason', pp. 181ff.
[63] Cf. 'A Positivistically Bisected Rationalism', p. 215.

does not deny the distinction between facts and standards but merely asks whether the distinction associated with the dualism thesis is an appropriate one. He goes on to discuss details on the basis of a new statement by Popper on this problem.[64]

As far as the problem of the normative framework of theoretical science is concerned, I pointed out, even in my first criticism, that there exist no grounds for the assumption that one could derive from it an objection to the views criticized by Habermas.[65] Even for the consideration of actual conditions in the discussion of standards there exist examples within the framework of these views[66] which show that the distinction criticized is readily compatible with them. It can hardly be asserted, then, that the advocates of dualism have not seen or taken into account connections of the type he quotes. I must confess that I am really no longer clear what Habermas is aiming at in his analysis. His earlier arguments on the problem of dualism and value freedom were directed at 'the problematic *separation*' of natural laws and norms, of cognition and evaluation. He has been unable to substantiate any objections to either the possibility of such a *differentiation*, or to the possibility of taking into account *connections* despite this differentiation, or even to the fact that the advocates of the dualism thesis have taken into consideration such connections and analysed them. His article which takes up Popper's recent work now brings into play arguments which basically displace the topic of the discussion, take up new problems and, on the whole, prevent one from correctly recognizing what is supposed to be at stake here—apart from the fact that in some way Popper's views are deficient.

Initially, Habermas takes up Popper's thesis concerning the asymmetry between standards and facts, but only in order to

---

[64] We refer here to the addendum, 'Facts, Standards and Truth. A Further Criticism of Relativism' which first appeared in the fourth edition of Popper's *The Open Society and its Enemies* (London ,1962) ,vol. 2, pp. 369–396, and consequently he did not alude to the book earlier.

[65] The problem was explicitly treated even within the framework of these views. Cf. for example, the relevant sections in Popper's *The Open Society* and other works, e.g. in *Conjectures and Refutations*; the following passage is characteristic of Popper's position, 'Ethics is not a science. But although there is no "rational scientific basis" of ethics, *there is an ethical basis of science*, and of rationalism', *The Open Society*, loc. cit., p. 238, my italics. I have also frequently taken up this problem, e.g. in 'Wertfreiheit als methodisches Prinzip', loc. cit.

[66] Consider the methodological utilization of scientific and other facts by Popper himself; but also by Feyerabend, Agassi, Bartley and others.

demonstrate that the logical structure of the discussion of both,[67] which Popper has not dealt with at all, is in no way differentiated. In this respect, without going into detail, Popper himself has drawn attention to the fundamental identity which lies in the fact that we can discuss and criticize both proposals and propositions, and that we can reach a decision. He has further pointed out that, in both cases, we can orientate ourselves by regulative ideas, in the former, by the truth, in the latter, by an idea which we can designate by means of the expressions 'the right' or 'the good'. Habermas now claims that Popper has 'terminated' the reflection already undertaken by reference to the correspondence theory of truth—what is meant here baffles me—and, as earlier, discusses this theory, but only in order to criticize the distinction made here by Popper between the definition of truth and the criterion of truth. He provides, however, no special arguments against the possibility—explicated by Popper—of utilizing the idea of truth as a *regulative idea*, without having at one's disposal a *criterion* of truth.[68] Instead, he makes the general objection that the 'pre-understanding' which guides the interpretation prior to any definition always implicitly includes standards, whose justification is provided in the hermeneutic course of exigesis. He then stresses the 'dialectical relationship' of standards and descriptions in this interpretative process, which apparently is then only disturbed by a 'definition of standards' and the 'establishment of criteria'. For it is only such determinations which 'create a deductive connection which excludes a retrospective correction of the standards through the object measured'.[69] One can easily see how, through determinations of this sort, the dialectical relationship corresponding to the object is solidified into an un-correctable deductive connection in which 'the critical discussion of standards frees itself from their usage'. Since the advocates of critical rationalism, despite their utilization of the usual logic, are just as much in a position to expose their standards to critical discussion as are those theoreticians whose vocabulary permits

---

[67] Incidentally, it is interesting that, in this connection, Habermas expresses himself in a way which hardly harmonizes with his critique of Bartley's revisability criterion; cf. pp. 214 and 217 above. What he says on p. 217 appears as if he himself wanted to exemplify at this point the criterion criticized two pages previously.

[68] Cf. his attempt analysed above to identify the concept of truth with that of corroboration, an attempt which does not solve the problem of truth but is merely liable to obfuscate it.

[69] Habermas, p. 218.

them to speak of dialectical relations where they do not wish to analyse complex connections in detail, I can recognize in this whole train of thought nothing which could count as an argument against the views which Habermas has in mind. Neither the correspondence theory of truth nor the dualism thesis in question is affected in any way here; nor are they affected by the subsequent thesis that the concept of truth, which permits so strict a distinction between standards and facts, is in turn a standard which requires critical justification. Popper himself has emphasized the regulative character of the idea of truth. The critical discussion of this idea can similarly be found in his work.[70] What Habermas has to say in this context on the 'threefold usage of language' and on the 'dialectical connection between descriptive, postulatory and critical statements', which Popper 'does not manage to evade' by reference to the correspondence concept of truth, is hardly an argument which endangers Popper's position.[71] The metaphorical conclusion of the whole section cannot cure this deficiency.

At any rate, the dualism of facts and standards is not overcome through Habermas' line of argument. What Habermas asserts are merely connections whose existence in themselves no one has contested. His initial question whether the differentiation itself was an adequate one has not been answered. Instead, this question has been lost in the discussion of connections in which this differentiation was already presupposed. The dimension of a comprehensive rationality, which Habermas concludes with, contains nothing which would have to be repressed or displaced by a 'positivistically restricted' rationalism—even if the words which he uses in his remarks indicate possible moves which seem to be denied to the critics of dialectics.[72]

---

[70] On the idea of justification see the earlier discussion.

[71] The relevant assertions, pp. 218f. are, in part, plausible and acceptable; in part, problematical as, for example, when he draws a parallel between, or even identifies, his threefold language usage with a threefold division of statements. For in critical arguments, statements of various types can appear. I shall not discuss this since I cannot recognize in these thoughts any point relevant to our problem.

[72] I do not wish to enter into the question whether Popper has incorrectly interpreted the Hegelian philosophy of identity. Presumably, questions of the interpretation of Hegel will always remain largely controversial for, as anyone who has attempted to wrest a meaning from Hegelian texts can confirm, Hegel is a philosopher—if not necessarily 'the only one'—'with whom at times one literally does not know, and cannot conclusively decide, what in fact is being talked about, and with whom even the possibility of such a decision is not guaranteed', thus Theodor W. Adorno in 'Skoteinos oder Wie zu lesen sei', loc. cit., p. 107. It is well known

5 DIALECTICS AND THE CRITIQUE OF IDEOLOGY

The attempt to demonstrate the positivistic restrictions of critical rationalism is, in my opinion, unsuccessful. I am unable to detect fundamental misunderstandings on my side. Nor are the advantages of a dialectical view shown in Habermas' reply. In certain places, he has adopted interpretations from the domain of neo-pragmatism, on the assumption that he could thus overcome Popper's critical philosophy. These newly-worked elements have proved in this respect just as problematical as those stressed earlier from the realm of hermeneutic thought. Much of what he represents in his reply seems to me to indicate a change, if not a very noticeable one, in his views which brings him closer to analytical views, and distances him somewhat further from those of the Frankfurt School than could already be detected. Dialectics is not so prominent as previously. What it should actually achieve, and what constitutes its basic characteristics has still not, however, become very clear. What is relatively certain is merely that it offers itself as a weapon against the restrictedness of positivism and other undialectical views, whose advocates are allegedly not in a position to reflect upon those things which the dialectician is capable of reflecting upon.

In many instances, Habermas relies upon investigations which can be attributed more readily to the wider realm of analytical philosophy than to dialectics. In several of his analyses, which can be simply reconstructed, one also recognizes that thoughts from this philosophical direction have been incorporated. On the level of detail, it appears that everything possible is acceptable to him. If, beyond this, he lays claim to hermeneutic modes of procedure then this partially amounts to a restriction of criticism,[73] partially to the solution of interpretative problems which, within the framework of other views, are easily soluble, but which, in the German-

---

that Hegel has his followers in this respect. Habermas counters Popper's interpretation with the assertion that it is incorrect. Besides this, however, he asserts that in this interpretation is 'reflected' the repression of criticism. I fail to recognize how he knows this. Even if Popper's interpretation of Hegel is problematical, it would be difficult to reach a negative conclusion regarding Popper's other views, for apparently Popper regards Hegel, *thus interpreted*, just as critically as does Habermas. Only by the indirect means of his remarkable repression thesis is Habermas able to evoke the impression that here an argument is provided against critical philosophy.
[73] Cf. my objections in 'The Myth of Total Reason'.

speaking world, seem to call forth a hermeneutic vocabulary.[74] It will not be possible, however, simply to establish the objective meaning of the historical process without recourse to modes of procedure which must appear dubious to critical rationalism, but which are more intimately linked with dogmatic, theological thought. Much would suggest that dialectical philosophy contains such a meaning—even if this is usually only intimated. In so far as an ideological undertaking of this type is renounced, an elucidation of practical consciousness, a 'critical maieutics of political practice' is possible with means and modes of procedure which fully lie within the range of critical rationalism.[75] Nor is an analysis of what Habermas calls 'knowledge-guiding interests' in any way excluded. Reflection upon what we do when we seek to extend our knowledge is a privilege of neither dialectical nor hermeneutical philosophy. I cannot appreciate what sense there is in the claim that representatives of other philosophical views suffer from the restrictions imposed upon their capacity for reflection, if the latter have *de facto* made contributions to the problems at issue, which the advocate of this thesis has himself partially utilized and if, on the other hand, the differences in these directions merely lie in the fact that their solutions to these problems look partially different and make possible criticism of certain dialectical theses.

---

[74] To what extent this hermeneutics can produce results inaccessible to language-analytical currents in philosophy is difficult to see. What it shares with several representatives of post-Wittgensteinian Oxford philosophy is the conservative tendency which does not criticize 'language games' but leaves them as they are. In the Oxford form of analysis, too, the original critical impulse of positivistic observance has ended in the analysis of the given, which is directed more at its conservation than its transformation. Hermeneutics shares this tendency and only transcends it in that one can assert, even with a certain justification, that in it one can see a 'continuation of the theology by other means' (Topitsch). The quasi-theological 'interrogatory reason' degenerates here into a liturgy of being. We must wait and see what emerges from a dialectical-hermeneutic amalgam. The conservative traits of Frankfurt philosophy are nonetheless clearly discernible. An analysis of the theological background of the dialectical critique of ideology can also be found in Ernst Topitsch, 'Entfremdung und Ideologie. Zur Entmythologisierung des Marxismus', *Hamburger Jahrbuch für Wirtschafts und Gesellschaftspolitik*, vol. 9, 1964, pp. 139ff.

[75] The elucidation of practical consciousness as a topic runs through Habermas' *Theory and Practice* as a continuous thread. I am fully able to understand such a problem, but I am of the opinion that one can still do justice to it within the framework of a rationalism of the Max Weber variety, quite apart from the fact that Popper's critical rationalism surely transcends Max Weber's, in so far as he does not claim the immunity of so-called final evaluations against critical argument.

The assertion which Habermas presents as the result of a reflection upon cognitive interests—that 'empirical-analytical research produces technically utilizable knowledge, but not knowledge which makes possible a hermeneutical elucidation of the self-understanding of acting subjects'[76]—suggests an opposition which does not reflect the actual restrictions of the empirical sciences, but merely a restrictive interpretation on the basis of an imputed restriction of cognitive interests. Neither theoretical nor historical investigations, of whatever form, are extinguished through the view attacked by Habermas. Even normative problems can be discussed and are discussed within the framework of such a view. That the solution of such problems does not consist here in the establishment of a normative dogmatics is one of the characteristics of critical rationalism which is connected to the rejection of dogmatic views in general. As far as a historically orientated theory of society is concerned—of the type which Habermas strives for—the traits of such an undertaking are still too vague for one to do more than press for a clarification, and raise the question as to how far this undertaking differs from others of a similar sort which have fallen prey to the critique of ideology.[77]

According to Habermas, the critique of ideology in the hands of the positivists seems to have the purpose of 'completely reject'[ing] the task, which he envisages, of a historically oriented theory of society 'and banish[ing] it to the vestibules of scientific discussion'; 'it concerns itself with cleansing the practical consciousness of social groups of those theories which cannot be reduced to technically utilizable knowledge, and yet defend their theoretical claims.'[78] He adheres then to his thesis of the 'positivistically circumscribed critique of ideology' which I had already analysed in my first criticism,[79] although he recognizes the interest

---

[76] Habermas, 'A Positivistically Bisected Rationalism' p. 221.

[77] Quasi-laws of spatio-temporally limited validity are also familiar to the view criticized by Habermas, even if it must emphatically point out the restriction which would lie in the attempt to raise the development of such hypotheses to a cognitive ideal. I have dealt with this point elsewhere. Law-like regularities of the type indicated by Habermas seem, however, to combine the restricted character of such quasi-laws with further properties which render such statements no less problematical: with a reference both to a totality which cannot be further characterized and to a normative claim. Amalgamations of this type, however, usually express what one might term, in a certain sense, 'a decided reason', namely ideological thought. It is difficult to see why one should burden social science with it.

[78] Habermas, p. 221.

[79] Cf. 'The Myth of Total Reason', pp. 186ff.

in enlightenment on the part of the theoreticians he apostroph-izes,[80] so that his emphasis upon the purely technically orientated cognitive interest appears forced, even in this respect. In reality, this critique of ideology does not need to neglect any knowledge which can serve enlightenment, nor that clarification of practical consciousness which Habermas envisages. Only where justifi-catory thought erects ideological façades in order to disguise decisions as knowledge, where strategies of dogmatization and immunization are applied in order to protect statements of all types against arguments, where connections are obscured, and knowledge distorted, is there cause to regard the critique of ideology of this type as dangerous.[81]

The thesis has often been advanced that problems of a certain type cannot be dealt with, clarified or solved within the realm of the views he criticizes. I have discussed this thesis often enough.[82] What he calls the 'self-reflection of the strict empirical sciences' is at least as accessible to critical rationalism as to dialectical

---

[80] Cf. See especially, Ernst Topitsch, *Socialphilosophie zwischen Ideologie und Wis-senschaft* (Neuwied/Berlin, 1961).

[81] In my reply to Habermas, I drew attention to the role of dialectics as an ideological weapon, and in particular to the Polish discussion between Marxism and the Warsaw School, pp 188f. Habermas refers to this as a 'slip' and goes on to remark that he does not assume that I make a commonplace anticommunism a part of my strategy. I must say that this disturbs me a little, since I neither see where the 'slip' can be found nor what could have induced him to associate me at all with a narrow sort of anticommunism which, up to a certain point, one can term 'common-place'. I do not know how far one can call Leszek Kolakowski, for instance, a com-munist. As far as I am acquainted with it, his philosophy possesses characteristics which bring it close to critical rationalism. Habermas, on the other hand, criticizes Kolakowski in the name of a view which is supposed to permit one 'to grasp and derive' decisions from history (*Theorie und Praxis*, loc. cit., p. 328), i.e. according to what he has said elsewhere on such problems, presumably to legitimate them historically. That he thinks he must protect this view against the 'restricted' critique of ideology of the so-called positivists is a state of affairs which gives cause for consideration. I would prefer here Kolakowski's philosophy, which does not claim a justification of this sort. Incidentally, it would be interesting to learn where the methodical distinction lies between the dialectics advocated by Habermas and that of right-wing thinkers like Karl Larenz to whom I have already referred (p. 188, note 57). Cf. Ernst Topitsch, 'Max Weber and Sociology Today' in O. Stammer (ed.), *Max Weber and Sociology Today*, loc. cit.

[82] The clarification of the identity problem (on pp. 222ff. of Habermas' reply) does not provide a new argument in this respect. The assertion that questions in this realm 'cannot be clarified through empirical-analytical investigations' simply does not correspond to the facts in my view. Psychology which, over a long period, has analysed such problems for the individual realm, has advanced into the realm of the analogous collective problem with the creation of modern social psychology. Only since the methods of experimental psychology have penetrated in this way into sociological thought have many problems of this type have become soluble.

philosophy.[83] It is merely that the former often reaches different results from the latter. But one can easily discuss this, as I have done. In such a discussion, it is always worthwhile to credit the other person with at least the will to understand what one has said oneself. That one's opponent expresses the understandable wish for clarification, does not necessarily have anything to do with commitment to a particular language. Who could object to another language if, with its aid, certain problems or states of affairs can be better expressed. What, on the other hand, is regrettable, since it promotes the 'ethnocentricity of scientific sub-cultures', is an esoteric language which does not achieve such expression, but rather whose essential function seems to lie in paraphrasing the central points of an argument metaphorically.[84] If, in connection with the critique of ideology, reference is made to the effects of masking and immunization then, with such references, one usually, but by no means necessarily, enters upon the level of motivational research. Strategies which lead to such results can stem from the most diverse motives. They belong to the traditional stock of broadly practised justificatory thought which is exposed to the illumination of the critique of ideology. It can hardly be denied that such modes of procedure are to be found under the name of dialectics.[85] There is, then, some reason

To expect explanations with the aid of less developed methods for the more complex area of macro-sociological thought is, in my view, an illusion. It is well known that, in the course of history, the attempt has constantly been made to set, in principle, the boundary for the application of so-called natural scientific methods at the point which the latter have just reached and to declare any further advance impossible.

[83] Incidentally, one might point out here that even positivism in the narrower sense of the word has made contributions in this connection which, as far as I can see, are more expert than the existing contributions on the part of dialectics. Habermas, too, constantly takes up works which more readily belong to the compass of this philosophy when he wishes to say something more concrete than simply that all connections must always be included in the analysis and that all separations must be overcome, and that all distinctions made by others are dubious.

[84] I firmly reject the wish to bind an opponent to my language, particularly as I was neither born a positivist nor have remained such. Given the present situation I cannot omit an autobiographical comment. I only became acquainted with the philosophy of the Vienna Circle after I had previously had 'acquaintance' with almost all philosophical traditions within my reach, in fact, also with the explicitly anti-positivistically orientated ones typical of German culture. I too have more recently had the experience of which Habermas speaks (p. 225) in my reading of positivist studies. With reference to the intelligibility of Hegel I concur, for good reasons, with Theodor W. Adorno's view quoted above (cf. above, note 72), and in fact on the basis of my own readings.

[85] Among others see Ernst Topitsch, 'Sprachlogische Probleme der sozialwissenschaftlichen Theoriebildung', also his 'Das Verhältnis zwischen Sozial- und

for mistrust when, within the framework of an analysis which aims at the legitimation of interests from the concrete totality of the historical process, the claims of a dialectics are raised, which uses similar language forms and at decisive points lacks clarity. It has in no way escaped me that Habermas, in his critique of so-called 'positivistically restricted rationalism', has attempted to question presuppositions which I took as the starting point of my reply. But this attempt seems to me to have failed. I would doubt that his dialectical detour via neo-pragmatism has led him behind positivism's back, particularly since, in so doing, he has burdened his dialectics with views which, in some respects, are subject to the very restrictions which he censures in his opponents. It seems to me even less true that he has advanced behind the back of critical rationalism. The question of what actually constitutes dialectics, of what advantages it possesses as opposed to other views and what methods it uses, has not been answered in his reply. At any rate, one may presume that there is contained in it an unrivalled instrument for the mastery of complex connections, even if the secret of how it functions has remained concealed up till now.

In reading Habermas' reply, the intentions of his polemic have become partially more distinct, even if they have not become less problematical. He opposes the restrictions of critical thought, even at the point where they are not to be found. He believes that, in the dialectical tradition, he has found a starting point for transcending such restrictions, even if it is not clear what constitutes the achievements which justify such a hope. One may unreservedly welcome the fact that he seeks discussion with other schools of thought. Misunderstandings are presumably inevitable in such an undertaking—this is true for both sides. But sometimes it is not so simple to identify them.

Naturwissenscnaften', loc. cit., pp. 30ff. and pp. 62ff. See also Ernst Topitsch, 'Über Leerformeln' in *Probleme der Wissenschaftstheorie. Festschrift für Viktor Kraft* (Vienna, 1960), pp. 245ff.

HARALD PILOT

JÜRGEN HABERMAS' EMPIRICALLY FALSIFIABLE PHILOSOPHY OF HISTORY

Every thorough critique of the objectivating procedures in the social sciences is liable to be suspected of intrigues involving the philosophy of history. Jürgen Habermas abruptly terminates mere suspicion: the declared goal of his writings is a 'philosophy of history with practical intent'.[1] He does not intend, however, that this philosophy of history should formulate necessary historical laws or even a metaphysical meaning, but instead that it should formulate programmes for social action.[2] Such goals for the future of a society must be possible, however, in real terms even in the present time. Consequently, the projections of a philosophy of history are dependent upon the results of empirical research and can, in fact, be refuted by the latter.

Habermas believes that the Marxist philosophy of history, if properly understood, is able to dispense with metaphysical transcendency, since it derives the guiding aims of future action from the 'factual contradictions' of contemporary society. The 'meaning of history' is simply its possible future which is realized through action. 'The experimental philosophy of history no longer searches for a hidden meaning; it rescues the latter by establishing it.'[3]

Since meaning refers to something which will be real in the

---

[1] Cf. especially Jürgen Habermas, *Theorie und Praxis* (Neuwied/Berlin, 1963), pp. 261ff. [Trans. note: The essay referred to here does not appear in the English translation of this volume], and his 'Zur Logik der Sozialwissenschaften', in *Philosophische Rundschau*, Beiheft 5, Feb. 1967, p. 180.

[2] Popper has convincingly criticized the possibility of laws which permit prognoses concerning the historical future. Cf. Karl R. Popper, *The Poverty of Historicism*, London 1961; and his *The Open Society and its Enemies*, 2 vols. (London, 1962).

[3] Habermas, *Theorie und Praxis*, loc. cit., p. 303

future, its preconditions can be empirically tested in the present. The philosophy of history with practical intent 'aims both at an historical-sociological analysis of the preconditions for the possibility of revolutionary praxis and at a historical-philosophical derivation out of the contradiction within existing society, of the concept of society itself, the concept which is the standard of its own critique and the idea of critical-practical activity'.[4]

In this way, the projections of a philosophy of history are subjected to a double check before their realization. Both the guiding aims themselves and the means for their realization must be gained from the empirical knowledge of the present. A given projection is impossible if it contradicts empirical analyses. It is, however, only possible in real terms if it is not only compatible with the latter but also expedient for resolving the existing contradictions of a society. It has to prove itself to be society's 'determinate negation'.

But even if a projection meets both conditions, its guiding aims are not theoretically but merely practically necessary. The philosophy of history does not formulate prognoses about the historical future but simply guidelines for action, 'which do not prevail "objectively", but through the will and consciousness of human beings; consequently, they can be calculated and forecast only in their objective preconditions of possibility but not however as such'.[5] '. . . its correctness, namely the correctness of all verifiable preconditions of a possible revolution is secured empirically, whilst its truth is only certain in the practical establishment of the very meaning which it expresses.'[6] In this way, the revolutionary philosophy of history eludes decisionistic and deterministic pitfalls.

But this programme can only be realized if the 'determinate negation' of existing contradictions can be gained from the results of empirical research. For it is only then that the hope of checking empirically the guiding aims of future action exists. But the self-interpretation of empirical research presents several obstacles to such an attempt. According to the methodological rules of the 'analytical theory of science'[7] it is, in fact, possible to

---

[4] ibid., p. 299.
[5] ibid., p. 289.
[6] ibid., p. 310
[7] Cf. for terminology, Habermas, 'The Analytical Theory of Science and Dialectics'.

'transform technologically'[8] nomological hypotheses, to utilize them as means for pre-given ends—but these rules in no way permit the derivation of the ends themselves from empirical analyses. For this reason, Habermas has 'to criticize the analytical-empirical modes of procedure immanently in the light of their own claim'.[9]

Nevertheless, a crucial limitation is imposed upon this criticism if the empirical control over the philosophy of history is not to dissolve into scepticism. It cannot destroy the criteria of empirical testability but rather its goal can simply be a margin of interpretation within which a hermeneutic procedure can be applied to a domain previously secured. Although Habermas' starting point does not in principle exclude such a 'determination of boundaries', his writings up to now have extended across this boundary in the direction of a 'dialectics of utopian reason'.[10] I wish to discuss this thesis in four steps:

1. Contingent dialectics and empirical analysis: the formal conditions of 'determinate negation'.
2. Value implications of social scientific theories—Habermas' critique of the 'analytical theory of science' and its meta-critique.
3. 'Domination-free communication' as the regulative principle of the philosophy of history.
4. Sceptical consequences of a 'dialectics of utopian reason'.

1

The 'determinate negation' of a contradiction-laden society is supposed to permit the 'dialectical derivation' of situationally related projections for future action out of a contradiction-laden

---

[8] Cf. Hans Albert, 'Wissenschaft als Politik', in Ernst Topitsch (ed.), *Probleme der Wissenschaftstheorie* (Vienna, 1960), p. 213: 'By means of tautological transformation, a theory is . . . converted into its technological form, from a set of nomological hypotheses emerges a set of propositions concerning the possibilities of human action with reference to certain goals. This transformation merely presupposes that certain desiderata are hypothetically imputed and does not therefore require the introduction of explicit value-premises'.

[9] Habermas, 'The Analytical Theory of Science and Dialectics', p. 143.

[10] The latter results when a dialectics of the present situation is extrapolated into the future, when the 'ideological distortion' also embraces the principles of critical practice. Then it is to be feared that the 'dialectical process of mediation' will become infinite.

society. This is disputed by the 'analytical theory of science' for the following reasons: (a) Dialectical thought is devoid of content since it operates through contradictions from which everything follows;[11] (b) facts cannot contradict one another; (c) empirical hypotheses are descriptive statements from which guidelines for action cannot follow.

Habermas seeks to evade these objections by means of a 'contingent dialectics'. This is not an a priori principle of thought, it does not take place 'prior to and underlying all history, at the stroke of metaphysical necessity . . .',[12] but rather it results from the structures of domination in a society which has not yet been able to liberate itself from natural constraints. 'As a whole it [contingent dialectics] is as contingent as the dominating conditions of labour whose inner contradiction and outer movement it expresses.'[13]

In an ideologically distorted society, thought becomes dialectical since it cannot realize itself as a free dialogue. 'If things can be grasped in a categorial manner whilst human beings can only be conceived adequately through dialogue in their relations with things and with one another, then dialectics may be understood from within the dialogue; certainly not itself as a dialogue but as a consequence of its repression.'[14] Since constraint is its necessary condition, the dissolution of constraint is also the dissolution of dialectics. By opposing constraint through 'critical praxis', dialectics simultaneously turns upon itself. 'Dialectics fulfilled in practice is simultaneously transcended dialectics . . .'[15] It changes into what it always was in terms of its own intention: a 'domination-free dialogue which could be universally practised'.[16] In the latter, dialectics realizes its second precondition: the interest in emancipation [Mündigkeit], in 'domination-free communication'. Only if both conditions can be fulfilled is a check on dialectical movement possible. Two things, then, are necessary: 1. To demonstrate empirically the constraint in 'actual contradictions' and, 2. to legitimate the 'interest in emancipation [Mündigkeit]'. Only with the aid of these two preconditions is it possible to

---

[11] Cf. Popper, 'What is Dialectic?', *Conjectures and Refutations* (London/New York, 1962), pp. 312f.
[12] Habermas, *Theorie und Praxis*, loc. cit., p. 321.
[13] ibid., p. 319.
[14] ibid., p. 318.
[15] ibid., p. 319.
[16] Cf. Habermas, *Knowledge and Human Interests*, p. 314 [amended translation].

'derive dialectically' projections into the future as the 'determinate negation' of a contradiction-laden society.

'Actual contradictions' are given in the antagonistic intentions of social groups which, in the form of 'interests', 'attitudes' and 'norms', belong to the object-domain of social scientific hypotheses. Intentions contradict one another if their illusorily real goals are mutually exclusive. From such contrary intentions, however, there does not result directly a further intention which resolves the 'contradiction'; but rather, in order to maintain the 'determinate negation', another 'objective intention' is required: the 'interest in emancipation'. The latter restricts contrary intentions and 'unifies' them in a new intention which negates the first two. Only in so far as the 'determinate negation' resolves the 'contradiction' of contrary intentions does it negate this contradiction. It implies the logical negation[17] of the latter, but distinguishes itself from it, however, through its determinate content. In it, the guiding aim is given whose realization would transcend the actual contradiction 'through critical praxis'.[18]

If this procedure could be carried out, the objections mentioned would no longer hold. For the 'determinate negation' is not deduced from a contradiction but instead it resolves the latter. It relates to intentions not to facts; ultimately it derives normative conclusions, not from descriptive but rather from normative premises.

But the empirical confirmation of 'actual contradictions' between intentions encounters considerable difficulties. For since

---

[17] This is, of course, a trivial implication, for the formal logical negation of a contradiction is always a tautology and follows from every conceivable statement. Formal logic in propositional calculus permits no difference between contrary and contradictory statements. Both are the negation of a tautology. Nevertheless, contrary and contradictory statements can be distinguished by means of formal logic. According to the statement concerning the excluded third (which is valid in a two-value logic), when there are two contradictory statements one is necessarily true, whilst in the case of two contrary statements *both* can be false (although they need not be false). Consequently, at least without contradiction, one can conceive of a resolution of contrary intention by means of a third, 'objective' intention. But if, on the other hand, the intentions (i.e. statements about them) were opposed to one another in a contradictory manner then one of the two would have to be selected.

[18] This interpretation of 'determinate negation' cannot rest upon statements by Habermas since the exact meaning of this principle has not so far been sufficiently explicated. Consequently, it is little more than a suggestion—but there is one reservation: I do not indeed consider the two given moments of 'dialectical mediation' to be its necessary conditions, so that my critical reflections are valid even independently of the 'dialectical theory' which has been expounded.

intentions are not contained directly in observable behaviour they can only be extracted from empirical hypotheses if their content. In it, the guiding aim is given whose realization would pretation can be tested in an 'empirical-analytic' manner. If the methodological rules of the analytic theory of science are valid for *all* empirical statements but, according to these rules, interpretations cannot be tested empirically, then an empirical control of statements concerning intentions and consequently a control of the 'determinate negation' is impossible. The philosophy of history with practical intent would have failed.

Yet could there not exist an intention in the hypotheses themselves, a certain 'value-reference' of the methodological rules which contradicted other 'value-references'? Then the 'universal objectivity' of empirical-analytic rules would open up only one of several domains of possible experience—and in other domains other methodological rules would be conceivable. If, moreover, the 'value-reference' of another domain could claim priority over that of the analytic-empirical rules, the latter could, with its aid, be restricted. This is precisely what Habermas attempts to demonstrate.

Underlying the empirical-analytic procedures is a 'technical cognitive interest' which is partially opposed to the 'interest in emancipation' yet, nevertheless, subordinated to it. It follows from this that the methodological rules of the 'analytical theory of science' can—and even must—be restricted to the conditions for the 'interest in emancipation', for the 'emancipatory cognitive interest'.

The 'technical cognitive interest' contradicts the 'emancipatory' in so far as it demands general theories of social action which impede progress towards emancipation—or even make it impossible, since they are not able to apprehend the specific character of 'social facts', the intentional component of action. For 'actions cannot be construed without reference to the guiding intentions, that is, they cannot be examined independently of something approximating to ideas'.[19] Intentions can, however, only be determined for a certain domain of culturally and historically specific norms. For this reason, every hypothesis concerning social action implies an understanding of the 'referential norms' (Bezugsnormen), which constitute the 'meaning' of the action.

---

[19] Habermas, *Zur Logik der Sozialwissenschaften*, loc. cit., p. 76.

For behaviour can 'express' very diverse forms of action, according to the norms which guide it. Since the rules of action are 'not guaranteed objectively through a natural law but rather inter-subjectively through the act of recognition of the interpreters involved . . .',[20] they can merely be understood but not explained in a hypothetico-deductive manner. Understanding, however, is realized in the normative context of a tradition and cannot be extended to random contexts. Consequently, hypotheses relating to social action are, of necessity, valid within the same limitations as the relevant norms—and are not generally valid.

Since the 'interest in emancipation . . . can be apprehended a priori'[21] whilst the norms are historically fortuitous, one can initially only postulate, with the aid of this interest, that the validity of social scientific hypotheses must be restricted, but that the norms do not lay down the given domain of the latter. Since it is claimed that statements about norms cannot be tested empirically and analytically yet nevertheless must be open to checks (for they contain assertions about 'historical states of affairs'), the rules for testing understanding, 'the methodological rules of hermeneutics', must be developed. Otherwise, social scientific hypotheses could arbitrarily be restricted in their validity. If, however, the rules of hermeneutics, in their turn, had to be limited by empirical-analytical prodecures, as would seem to follow from Habermas' critique of Gadamer's hermeneutics,[22] then Habermas would be caught in a circle. I shall attempt to demonstrate that Habermas' dual critique of empirical-analytical and hermeneutic procedures can only be compelling at the price of sceptical consequences. How, then, can a 'value-reference' of the empirical social sciences be demonstrated and does Habermas' critical programme follow from this?

2

Empirical theories in the social sciences possess value relevance in three respects:

(a) The selection of research areas (the 'relevance standpoints') depends upon value decisions.

[20] ibid., p. 75.
[21] loc. cit. *Knowledge and Human Interests*, p. 314 (amended translation).
[22] Cf. Hans Georg Gadamer, *Wahrheit und Methode*, 2nd ed. (Tübingen, 1965).

(b) 'Basic statements', by means of which theories refer to reality, are accepted through a 'resolution' on the part of the researchers involved in discussion.

(c) The operationalization of 'theoretical concepts' presupposes a pre-understanding which attributes observable behaviour to the intentional structures of such terms as 'role', 'institution' and 'expectation'.

This threefold reference to meaning postulates is combined in the 'technical cognitive interest' and it is this reference which, in turn, establishes the 'objectivity' and 'value freedom' of empirical research. Now for the social sciences, a value reference on the 'meta-level' is supposed to prove itself incapable of clear delineation from the intentional references of the object domain. 'In opposition to positivism', Habermas [would] 'like to justify the view that the research process, which is carried out by human subjects, belongs to the objective context, which itself has to be recognized by virtue of cognitive acts'.[23]

The 'analytical theory of science' does not dispute that the selection of research areas is dependent upon value decisions.[24] Since this value reference does not affect the validity of the hypotheses so formed, I shall restrict myself to a discussion of the other two points.

Using Popper's explication of the 'basis problem', Habermas demonstrates that empirical theses can only be related to reality by means of an interest. From empirical theories (together with the initial conditions) one can derive the most elementary statements which refer to observable facts. In this relationship, however, there also lies the decisive problem: how can observable facts and statements about such facts be unambiguously co-ordinated? According to Popper, this problem of co-ordination leads to the 'Friesian trilemma' of dogmatism, infinite regress and psychologism.[25] Popper solves this trilemma by applying his criterion of

---

[23] Habermas, 'A Positivistically Bisected Rationalism', p. 220.

[24] Cf. Hans Albert, 'The Myth of Total Reason', pp. 183f.; and his 'Wertfreiheit als methodisches Prinzip. Zur Frage der Notwendigkeit einer normativen Sozialwissenschaft', in Ernst Topitsch (ed.), *Logik der Sozialwissenschaften*, loc. cit., p. 190; 'Scientific activity demands . . . *standpoints* which make an evaluation of *relevance* possible. Every approach to a problem, every conceptual apparatus and every theory contains such selective standpoints, in which the direction of our interest finds expression.'

[25] Cf. K. R. Popper, *The Logic of Scientific Discovery* (London, 1959/New York, 1965), p. 94.

testability even to basic statements. This criterion is to replace the principle of induction.[26] It establishes the empirical content of theories and statements in 'degrees of testability'. The better a statement can be tested (without being falsified) the greater its empirical content. 'Potential falsifiers' are statements whose confirmation would refute a theory. The empirical content grows with the number of potential falsifiers: the best theory is the most prohibitive. For this reason, theories must be as improbable as possible—up to the borderline case of contradiction, which naturally remains excluded.

If the 'testability' of a theory determines its empirical content, then all its statements must permit the derivation of consequences. The statements of a theory can only be universal statements, from which—together with the marginal limiting conditions—basic statements can also be deduced. 'Every test of a theory . . . must stop at some basic statement or other which we *decide to accept*.'[27] Although we must break off the testing process at a given statement, this too can still be tested further.[28] 'This . . . makes the chain of deduction in principle infinite.'[29] Even basic statements are in no way 'immediate' empirical statements. 'Experiences can *motivate a decision*, and hence an acceptance or a rejection of a statement, but a basic statement cannot be *justified* by them—no more than by thumping the table.'[30]

Since even basic statements must be testable whilst theories can only be refuted by means of basic statements, even the refutation of theories is only possible 'for the time being',[31] and can be revised. The corroboration and refutation of theories is reached through a decision on the part of the community of researchers, who discuss whether a theory has been sufficiently tested according to the current knowledge of possible test procedures (or alternatively, a basic statement which refutes a theory). This

[26] Cf. ibid., ch. 1.
[27] ibid., p. 104.
[28] For possible testing procedures (as well as for the whole problem), cf. Albrecht Wellmer, *Methodologie als Erkenntnistheorie* (Frankfurt, 1967), esp., pp. 158ff.
[29] Popper, loc. cit., p. 105.
[30] ibid., p. 105.
[31] Cf. ibid., p. 111, and also the discussion in Wellmer, loc. cit., pp. 164ff. Wellmer concludes that 'Doubting the verifiability of empirical statements would mean doubting the possibility of experience; even if experience can err, it can be corrected by new experience' (p. 170). He disputes the possibility of an infinite testability of basic statements, since he considers that the decision in favour of a given statement would thus be a blind one.

decision, for its part, cannot be secured through observation since then the problem would again arise as to how these observations, in their turn, are to be tested. Consequently, this decision must be taken according to teleological standpoints (*Zweckgesichtspunkte*) which are determined by a given interest. This means, however, that although empirical theories do not contain any value judgments, they are, nevertheless, related to an interest with regard to their validity—even if it is only a 'suspended' validity. The 'objectivity' of empirical research therefore implies a normative component, which first makes inter-subjective validity and 'value freedom' possible; normative and descriptive structural determinations are inseparably linked with one another in their validity.[32]

But if even the empirical basis is affected by decisions, does not empirical science then have to become a function of social connections, so that, in an extreme case, every political system and every 'cultural circle' would have its own social science? This consequence only arises if the scientists' interest involved in discussion cannot be apprehended in rules which can be secured through institutions; even if the scientists' decisions are determined through the life-context. Nevertheless, even Popper writes: '. . . what is usually called "*scientific objectivity*" is based, to some extent, on social institutions'.[33]

But even if the motivations, through which the scientists' 'objective' decisions are reached, are dependent upon a given organization of the research institutions, they nonetheless *also* remain related to experience. The scientists are motivated through experiments, by their perceptions and by reports on the perceptions of others. As long as it is a question of objects and of their relations, the latitude for possible decisions is thus narrowly defined. It is not so easy to break through the manifest evidence of judgments of perception.

The object domain, to which hypotheses in the social sciences refer, is composed primarily of intentional structures. Social action is structured by means of the 'subjective meaning' of action, which is present in the intentions of those acting and is determined by norms. The 'immediate experience' of the social

---

[32] This in no way implies that 'value-judgments' must be incorporated into empirical theories; instead, it can only be asserted that methodological rules do not permit such a separation.

[33] Popper, *The Poverty of Historicism*, loc. cit., p. 155.

scientist itself already contains normative components, upon which there can be no judgments of perception. Consequently, one might think there can only be a culturally and historically special social science, in which the rules of socialization at the same time largely determine the rules of research. General theories of social action would be impossible, since the methodological rules would have to alter with the social system. Social science would then have to orientate itself in an essentially historical manner in order to explicate the meaning of the very traditions to which it belonged, even in its rules for testing.

This consequence is, however, only compelling if intentional structures cannot be adequately expressed by means of behavioural variables. But up till now it has not been possible to translate statements about intentions *synonymously* into statements about behaviour.[34] Certainly, too, in the social sciences, 'the law-like hypotheses (must) be formulated with regard to the covariance of intelligible quantities . . .'[35] But a restriction of the *generality* of

---

[34] Cf. Rudolf Carnap, *Meaning and Necessity*, 3rd ed. (Chicago 1960), paras. 13ff., and the Appendix. Carnap's explication of 'belief sentences' is convincing if the rules of an artificial language, in the form in which he introduces them, can be conceded. Nevertheless, even for such an artificial language one must presuppose the existence of an ordinary language, since the correspondence rules for translation into the artificial language must be established with the aid of ordinary language. The intentional structure of statements can only be expressed by means of dispositions. In this manner, of course, hypotheses can be formulated concerning the meaning content of statements *for* one person, but it is not evident how, in the absence of a homogeneous understanding of the question 'Do you believe that "p"?' the exact intentional content can be ascertained. The homogeneous understanding of the symbols must either be taken for granted or the translation can only achieve an approximate success. In my view, however, a 'behaviouristic' research strategy is still possible even if it were not possible to apprehend the intentiona structures completely. For prognoses concerning future behaviour merely presuppose an if-then relation between 'verbal behaviour' and the 'results of the action' prognosticated.

[35] Habermas, *Zur Logik der Sozialwissenschaften*, loc. cit., p. 65. In my opinion, Habermas' argumentation on the function of understanding in the research process contains an apparent contradiction. Against Theodor Abel's 'The Operation Called Verstehen' (in H. Feigl and M. Brodbeck (eds.), *Readings in the Philosophy of Science* (New York, 1953), Habermas rightly raises the objection that understanding should not refer to the relations between social facts but only to the latter themselves: 'Interpretive sociology . . . draws upon understanding for analytical purposes only in so far as the law-like hypotheses must be formulated with regard to the covariance of intelligible quantities—but the operation of Verstehen is immaterial for the logical form of the analysis of law-like regularities of social action' (ibid., p. 65). On the other hand, in his confrontation with functionalism, he advocates the strong thesis that even the relations between social facts must be understandable: 'The meaning intended in action, and objectivated both in language and in actions, is transferred from social facts to the relations between facts. In the domain of social

social scientific hypotheses only follows from this if 'a deception with language as such'[36] is possible, if symbolic understanding can be ideologically channelled. It is precisely then, however, that sceptical consequences are inevitable. But to what extent does the specific character of the object domain bind the social sciences to methodological rules, which make even the process of testing itself dependent upon social context?

Social action is rule-governed. Rules, however, can only be determined with the aid of behavioural expectations which are given in a reference group. These expectations refer to *future* behaviour which cannot yet be observed. For this reason, they cannot be apprehended through future behaviour. Instead, the members fo a reference group must be *questioned* about their expectations. Their replies are then, however, statements about *future* behaviour. They signify a state of affairs and are thus statements about facts but are not facts in themselves. Nevertheless, a theory of social action must link up the domain of the interview with the domain of manifest if it behaviour is to prognosticate actions. Now this linkage can either be realized by interpreting even the inquiry into behavioural expectations as a behavioural relation, or by projecting both the interview and the prognosticated 'behaviour' onto an intelligible level. In the first case, language is 'behaviouristically' reduced to verbal behaviour; in the second case, on the other hand, even the results of the action must be intelligible and 'hermeneutically' explicable. The logical type rule drives us to this alternative. According to this rule, propositions about future behaviour should not be combined hypothetically with this behaviour itself. For this relation would have to be formulated in hypotheses whose object domain would consist of staetments and facts.[37]

If social scientific hypotheses refer 'behaviouristically' to an

---

action, there is no empirical uniformity which, though not intended, would not be intelligible. But if the covariances asserted in law-like hypotheses are to be meaningful in this mode of understanding (Verstand) then they themselves must be conceptualised as part of an intentional context' (ibid., p. 81).

[36] ibid., p. 178.

[37] Cf. ibid., p. 67. It is certainly questionable whether the problems of reflexive statement structures (which would reveal themselves in logical antinomies) can simply be transferred to constitutive problems of the social scientific object domain. For reflexive phrases cannot always be avoided, for which reason, the necessity of a strict separation between object domain and meta-domain has to be specifically demonstrated (cf. Popper's essay 'Self-Reference and Meaning in Ordinary Language', in *Conjectures and Refutations*, loc. cit., pp. 304-311).

object domain of behaviour, then behavioural expectations appear as relations of 'verbal behaviour'. The communicative experience of the interview is apprehended through linguistic hypotheses, by means of which the norms of action are expressed in probabilities of verbal behaviour and can be linked through social-scientific hypotheses to the observed results of actions. Social-scientific hypotheses thus combine 'verbal behaviour' with the actual results of the action of a reference group. This leads to a unified object domain within which all hypothetical relations can be tested by means of observations. All that remains problematical is the co-ordination of behaviour with the intentional structures which are expressed in it. This is particularly valid for linguistic hypotheses. They require correspondence rules in order to translate meanings into probabilities of verbal behaviour. Such rules, however, remain tied to everyday language, since even the rules of an artificial language, in accordance with which expressions of everyday language could be apprehended through verbal behaviour, in their turn already presuppose translation from everyday language. An infinite regress of meta-languages can only be avoided if everyday language is the ultimate meta-language. But then the process of understanding in everyday language determine even the operationalization of behavioural dispositions, which are contained in the form of 'theoretical concepts' in linguistic hypotheses. In statements such as 'X believes (or: expects, thinks, hopes) that p', we must always understand 'believe' if we seek the verbal behaviour in which 'believe' is expressed with sufficient precision.[38]

On account of these translation difficulties, the operationalization of 'theoretical concepts' implies a 'pre-understanding' of the intentional structures which are to be apprehended in behaviour. But this 'pre-understanding' cannot restrict the validity of hypotheses concerning the *relations* between social facts without simultaneously expressing itself in their logical structure. If the 'pre-understanding' defines the *validity* of hypotheses than, even according to the methodological rules of the analytical theory of

---

[38] Cf. Carnap, loc. cit., 'On Belief Sentences', p. 230. 'It seems best to reconstruct the language of science in such a way that terms like . . . "belief" in psychology are introduced as theoretical constructs rather than as intervening variables of the observation language. This means that a sentence containing a term of this kind can neither be translated into a sentence of the language of observables nor deduced from such sentences, but at best inferred with high probability.' In the social sciences, this state of affairs compels one to make heuristic use of 'pre-understanding'.

science, a hypothesis can be rejected. For, either the 'pre-understanding' is identical for the antecedent and the consequent of the hypothesis, in which case the relationship of the two can be subjected to a test, or, the 'pre-understanding' of the two terms is inconsistent, in which case they can be rejected. Then, only the following evaluations of the relational members are possible:

(a) False-True; then the initial conditions can be unrealizable or the antecedent is itself a contradictory concept, both of which can be avoided with a certain amount of care.

(b) True-False; then the hypothesis can always be falsified. (The possibly complicated epistemological structure of this refutation need not be examined.)

(c) False-False; in this case, what has been said concerning (a) holds for the antecedent.

Consequently, the diversity of the 'pre-understanding' can never decide *unnoticed* upon the truth or falsity of hypotheses. Even if a 'pre-understanding' is necessary for operationalization, it follows that *general* social scientific theories are possible which do not contain any ideological fundament.

This only applies, however, so long as the relations between social facts do not need to be determined similarly by a 'pre-understanding'. If, on the other hand, it should emerge that even the relations must be *intelligible*, then the character of hypotheses would have to alter according to the 'pre-understanding'. In which case, an ideological distortion, even of the operationalization of hypotheses, could no longer be excluded with any certainty—unless it proves possible to examine the particular 'pre-understanding' for its ideological implications.

Now Habermas claims both 'that the meaningful structuring of the facts which concern interpretative sociology only permits a general theory of social action if the relations between facts are also intelligible'[39], and that this consequence necessarily results from the structure of the object domain in the social sciences. For the reciprocal interaction between language and praxis requires an intelligible, universal context within which each rule is laid down. Rules change their meaning if they are transferred to a different context and cannot, therefore, be sufficiently determined from mere behaviour as the latter is ambiguous when confronted with the meanings which it acquires through contextual variations.

---

[39] Habermas, loc. cit., p. 87.

If, however, rules are, in this sense, contextually determined, they remain dependent upon the various practical contexts in which they appear—and thus upon the ideological distortions too, which are imposed upon action by structures of domination. But how can such a thesis be grounded? Why should the rules of language be dependent 'upon praxis, *by virtue of their immanent meaning . . .*'.?[40]

Habermas assumes that the programme of an artificial language cannot be realized because the translation rules, for their part, would have to be formulated in terms of everyday language. Consequently, everyday language is the ultimate meta-language and only through itself can it be handed down, learned and understood. However, this means that 'since everyday language is the ultimate meta-language, it contains within itself the dimension in which it can be learned. For this reason, however, it is not "merely" language but, at the same time, praxis. This connection is logically necessary, otherwise everyday languages would be hermetically sealed-off; they could not be handed down.'[41]

Habermas argues from a *reductio ad absurdum*. If it is granted that language is not bound to praxis, then rules cannot be explicated at all, since language would remain caught up within the circle of its own rules. But language is explicable. It does not, however, necessarily follow from this that it is related to *praxis*, for the circle of linguistic rules resolves itself if the rules are 'present' in another 'external dimension' of language: in behaviour. Both possibilities are at least logically equivalent. The decision in favour of reference to praxis cannot be motivated logically even if it cannot be refuted logically either.[42]

For Habermas, at any rate, language is necessarily related to action and not merely to behaviour. This leads to considerable difficulties but it can explain why even the relations between social facts must be intelligible. Language and action form a unified system of rules whose individual elements must be determined by the total context. The meaning of the rules does not, then, depend solely upon the immediate context of action and communication but, at the same time, upon previous processes of the inter-

[40] ibid., p. 139.
[41] ibid., p. 142.
[42] For the resolution of a circle (or of an infinite regress of meta-languages) does not follow from the latter itself. Nevertheless, in our case, there remains the possibility of resolving the circle through reference to behaviour. This possibility cannot be excluded simply by referring to another possibility.

nalization of norms and upon previous socialization processes. Correspondingly, this is true for nomological hypotheses. Understanding itself is a fictive learning process which virtually carries out a process of socialization. But as the latter, in turn, is determined by the internalized norms, understanding can only be realized as the progressive integration of the system of norms to be understood into the system of norms which has been internalized through previous socialization. The internalized norms of previous socialization processes determine the understanding of new norms, and are determined anew by the latter. For this reason, all understanding remains committed to a 'prejudice', which results from earlier socialization processes. These, however, are dependent upon the specific traditions in which the interpreter (*der Verstehende*) has grown up—and are, of course, dependent upon their ideological distortions.

Since, however, understanding remains bound to earlier socialization processes, to a prejudice which is given by the tradition in question, 'prejudice' must be apprehended reflexively and rendered harmless. This takes place with the aid of hermeneutic procedures. Yet pure hermeneutics 'converts insight into the prejudice-structure of understanding into a rehabilitation of prejudice as such.'[43] In the rules of language, however, a constraint is also articulated whose ideological consequences cannot be penetrated by pure hermeneutics. 'Language as tradition is . . . in its turn dependent upon societal processes, which cannot be reduced to normative connections. Language is *also* a medium of domination and of social power.'[44] Hermeneutics is incapable of apprehending this ideological moment of language, because it can, at most, integrate one linguistic norm into another, but does not recognize their being bound to natural constraints.

A pure hermeneutics has, therefore, an ideological character. This only appears, of course, when the 'pre-understanding' (prejudice) is related to the objective constraints upon which it occasionally depends. These constraints themselves can, however, be taken up by the objectivating procedures of the analytical theory of science. In the hermeneutic approach, they would have to dissolve into phenomena of consciousness. If, then, the methodological rules of an ideology-free hermeneutics are also to take up natural constraints, then the rules of the analytic theory

[43] ibid., p. 174.
[44] ibid., p. 178.

of science must be added to these hermeneutic rules. The complete set of methodological rules of hermeneutics would have to be compatible with *all* the rules of the analytical theory of science. This is particularly valid for the generality postulate. A hermeneutics which could not accept the general theories of social action would be suspected of ideology. For only at the price of having to accept every 'pre-understanding'—even one determined by constraint—can the objections to the analytical-empirical procedures in the social sciences be maintained.

Habermas' critique of hermeneutics is compelling if he can demonstrate at least one pre-understanding which possesses an ideological structure. But this is only possible if the constraint can also be objectivated from which the pre-understanding is derived. For this reason, the critique of hermeneutics presupposes the rules of the analytical theory of science and, in particular, the postulate of generality. On the other hand, the critique of general theories of social action presupposes that a 'pre-understanding' must also be assumed for relations between facts, a pre-understanding that reveals ideological traits. Habermas' critique of the analytical theory of science presupposes the ideology-free structure of hermeneutics, whilst his critique of hermeneutics presupposes the ideology-free validity of *general* hypotheses (generality is the precondition for their testability) and, to this extent, the ideology-free validity of the analytical theory of science. Both critiques, therefore, are mutually exclusive.

This contradiction in the critiques rests upon an incomplete disjunction, for the presuppositions of both critiques could differ from both procedures criticized. It would then be necessary to demonstrate ideological structures, independently of both, with the help of the emancipatory cognitive interest. But this presupposes its independent legitimation. Since the complex of rules in a society determines every structure, each realization of this interest must also be subject to the distortions which are claimed to be true for the rules criticized. Thus, Habermas' critique presupposes an 'ideology-free' interest in emancipation, yet asserts, on the other hand, that this interest is in no way real so long as the ideological distortions of the society criticized are not removed or at least penetrated: '. . . on the one hand, it is only possible to see through the dogmatism of a congealed society to the degree to which knowledge has committed itself to being guided by the anticipation of an emancipated society and by the actualised emancipation of all people; but at the same time, this interest demands successful insight into the processes of societal development, since in them alone it constitutes itself as an objective interest.'[45]

Even if the emancipatory cognitive interest can legitimate itself, one must ask in what manner the analytical theory of science can be criticized with its aid. For here proof is still required that the emancipatory cognitive interest has priority over the technical interest. This priority must make it possible to restrict the generality postulate of the analytical theory of science. This strong demand can only be implemented, however, if the technical cognitive interest not only presupposes the emancipatory interest but also implies it. For only then does a logical constraint exist which restricts all the results achieved with the methodological rules of the technical cognitive interest to the conditions of the emancipatory interest. Only then could one infer from an ideological distortion of the necessary precondition (for the emancipatory interest) an ideological distortion of the sufficient precondition (for the technical interest) according to the *modus tollens*. If hypotheses were to contradict the emancipatory interest they could be rejected, since their validity would depend upon the 'possibility' of the latter.

(If, on the other hand, we wished to reverse the logical relation and treat the technical interest as the necessary condition for the emancipatory interest, then, together with the technical interest, the objectivity of the empirical social sciences would also become logically independent of the emancipatory interest. Then Habermas' critique would no longer be logically compelling.[46])

Habermas' critique of empirical-analytical procedures therefore presupposes that the emancipatory cognitive interest is at least a necessary condition for empirical objectivity and, consequently, that it must always be actually achieved in successful empirical knowledge. Now since the interest in emancipation requires that undistorted (ideology-free) knowledge be gained in a 'domination-

---

[45] Habermas, *Theory and Practice*, trans. J. Viertel (London/Boston, 1974), p. 262 (amended translation).

[46] Habermas has not specifically classified the logical relations between the cognitive interests. In my view, however, it follows from his comments in *Knowledge and Human Interests* (Appendix) that the emancipatory interest precedes the technical interest. In any case, a compelling critique must assert the given logical relations. Nevertheless, logical relations between interests would have to be examined in 'deontic logic'.

free dialogue',[47] it must be possible to conceive at least of such a dialogue and thus of an 'emancipatory objectivity' of empirical analyses, even for an ideologically deformed society. But then the methodological rules themselves cannot be distorted. Rather this can only be true of their *usage*.[48]

If the usage is to be criticized, then the 'domination-free dialogue' must be real in the critique—otherwise the critique, in its turn, would be subject reflexively to a suspicion of ideology. Its standards could express an ideological distortion. Since the critique, however, cannot relate to the methodological rules themselves, but only to their usage, then the condition for its realization is nothing less than the existence of the 'domination-free dialogue of *scientists*'. For only in this way could ideological research results be distinguished from other research results.

This is not only a condition for a possible critique of empirical theories but also one for the philosophy of history with practical intent. 'For the interest in emancipation only posits a standpoint and not a domain.'[49] The concrete guiding aims of action, the means for their realization, and the possible subsidiary consequences only result with the aid of this standpoint from the store of tested hypotheses. If the *validity* of these hypotheses (which depends upon the decision of the community of scientists) could, for its part, be ideologically distorted, and if the relations between social facts could be represented 'ideologically' in the theory, then either the means and the subsidiary consequences could no longer be examined for their ideological content, or the standpoint itself would become the condition for 'validity'. The 'interest in emancipation' would then, in fact, have to permit a distinction between 'ideologically' determined validity and 'emancipatory validity'. Then the utopian standpoint and not the empirical sciences would decide upon the structure of the facts and their relations.

If, on the other hand, the discussion amongst scientists is a *real* anticipation of the 'domination-free dialogue', then firstly, general theories of social action can be permitted and secondly, even their 'ideologically' deformed initial conditions can be

---

[47] Cf. Habermas, *Knowledge and Human Interests*, loc. cit., p. 314.
[48] Habermas is naturally correct in insisting that the free dialogue of scientists is only, in part, a reality in contemporary institutions. For a free usage of the methodological rules, democratically organized research institutions are also necessary and these are not generally to be found in contemporary universities.
[49] Habermas, *Theorie und Praxis*, loc. cit., p. 289.

isolated in critical reflection and possibly removed through praxis. Must Habermas not, therefore, forego a *universal* rehistorization of sociology? After all, he does not take his bearings from a 'domination-free dialogue' even in an ideologically deformed society. How then, can the 'interest in emancipation' be conceptualized?

3

'The interest in emancipation is not mere fancy for it can be apprehended a priori. What raises us out of nature is the only thing whose nature we can know: language. Through its structure, emancipation is posited for us. Our first sentence expresses unequivocally the intention of universal and unconstrained consensus. Emancipation constitutes the only idea that we possess in the sense of the philosophical tradition.'[50] The interest in emancipation can be apprehended as a mere intention. The idea of domination-free consensus justifies itself in the anticipation of this intention: in linguistic communication. The understanding of a statement cannot be enforced. Linguistic communication is only possible if domination is at least partially eliminated.

But since language is also determined by the context of action, it remains constantly exposed to ideological deformations in a society distorted by constraints. Despite its intention to secure freedom from constraint, linguistic communication is marked by traces of violence in an unemancipated society. Consequently, 'only in an emancipated society, whose members' emancipation had been realised, would communication have developed into the domination-free dialogue which could be universally practised, from which both our model of reciprocally constituted ego-identity and our idea of true consensus are always implicitly derived'.[51]

This formulation permits two different interpretations corresponding to two positions of a critique of ideology which threaten to destroy Habermas' starting point. First of all, it can mean that in an unemancipated society the 'domination-free dialogue' cannot, of course, be 'universally' practised but nevertheless is possible, within narowly defined conditions, and then

---

[50] Habermas, *Knowledge and Human Interests*, p. 314 (amended translation).
[51] ibid., p. 314 (amended translation).

does not reveal any ideological distortions. Secondly, it means that in an unemancipated society ideological distortion is universal and includes even the idea of emancipation itself. In the first case, the idea of emancipation can be the principle of the philosophy of history with practical intent. In the second case, on the other hand, sceptical consequences are inevitable.

Given the first interpretation, the following conditions result for the philosophy of history with practical intent:

1. In the 'domination-free' discussion of the community of scientists, hypotheses must be formed and empirically tested which both describe the social facts and determine their relations by means of explanations. But the *empirical* content of such hypotheses then contains facts and relations whose structure 'contradicts' the 'interest in emancipation'. For this reason, the contents of social scientific theories 'contradict' the necessary conditions for their validity. This class of 'contradictions' is, at the same time, actually given, whilst the tendencies within society 'contradict' this free dialogue. But since the institutions are also a condition for validity, the 'objectivity' of the theoretical approach (upon which validity depends) implies an interest in the changing of ideological structures in society. This interest on the part of the scientist is primarily aimed, however, at the preservation and maximization of an already existing 'domination-free' dialogue of the sciences and is not aimed, for instance, at its gradual abolition in favour of certain social-political goals. Consequently, a free science is able to attack reactionary tendencies in society—and in fact it must do so—without abandoning its 'value freedom' which guarantees its 'objectivity'.

2. The store of tested hypotheses existing at any particular time is to be examined with the aid of critical reflection, 'to determine when theoretical statements grasp invariant regularities of social action as such and when they express ideologically frozen relations of dependence that can in principle be transformed. . . . Of course, to this end a critically mediated knowledge of laws cannot through reflection alone render a law itself inoperative, but it can render it inapplicable.'[52] For occasionally 'false consciousness' belongs to the initial conditions of

---

[52] ibid., p. 110.

hypotheses. (Thus, election results can express an apparent consensus, which rests upon psychologically controlled manipulation. A consensus reached in this manner does not result from objective constellations of interests but from 'fortuitous' response to a stimulus. This apparent consensus is dissolved if the human subjects are enlightened concerning the mechanism which brought it about.) If interpretations of the acting human subjects belong to the initial conditions of a hypothesis—interpretations resting upon ideological distortion —then reflection can eliminate these interpretations, and then the actions, which according to the hypotheses are hypothetically necessary, must also disappear.

But since not every external constraint reflected in subjective interpretations of a situation can be transcended by means of reflection, the possibility of such a reflectively conditioned transcendence must be confirmed by means of a test. Since the influence of external constraints upon subjective interpretations will be secured, in many cases, through institutions, the identity of each particular institution perpetuating the constraint must also be ascertained. To this end, a test situation in which it is merely possible to establish the abstract possibility *that* a subjective interpretation rests upon constraint and not upon anthropological invariants, is in no way sufficient. Knowledge of the given institutions which stabilize ideologically distorted socialization processes is also necessary. For only when the institutions are recognized can they possibly be abolished by means of emancipatory praxis.

Such an investigation of the interpretations would permit both an investigation of law-like hypotheses in terms of a critique of ideology (without a restriction of the validity of such hypotheses), and a check on the 'pre-understanding' which is determined by tradition—that is, on the hermeneutic procedures as well. A procedure involving random samples is conceivable which, with the aid of psychoanalytic techniques, tests 'emancipatory' hypotheses, according to which certain initial conditions of sociological laws can disappear if a general educational process is introduced and implemented in society. In this way, the chances of a revolutionary praxis can be estimated, but, above all, the possibly dangerous subsidiary effects can be better calculated.

3. The 'structural freedom from constraint' of linguistic com-

munication must be shown to be the 'intention focused on an emancipated society'.

This last condition leads us to the second—in my view, untenable—interpretation of the 'intention focused on emancipation'. For it is, above all, this interpretation which may have compelled Habermas to corroborate the regulative principle of his philosophy of history in a dialectic 'that takes the historical traces of suppressed dialogue and reconstructs what has been suppressed'.[53] For the attempt to infer the idea of emancipation from the structural conditions of language, but, nevertheless, to relate it necessarily to praxis, leads to the dilemma of only being able to assume a necessary reference of linguistic communication to praxis when not only 'deceptions in a language, but rather . . . deception with language as such'[54] is possible—or of having to forego the necessary connection between the two. Only if language is simultaneously a life-form can the linguistic intention be focused on a future emancipated society.[55] But it is precisely at this point that language participates in the ideological distortion of the society in which it is spoken. Then, however, the idea of emancipation itself would be distorted. In an unemancipated society, the idea of emancipation itself would still contain ideological distortions which could only be eliminated through a critical praxis. Together with the ideological distortions of the unemancipated society, the distorted utopia of an emancipated society would also disappear. It would be the actual 'domination-free dialogue which could be practised universally' which would make it possible to conceive of the 'true' idea of emancipation. From this it follows, of course, that the idea of emancipation cannot directly initiate a critical praxis since it is itself exposed to

---

[53] ibid., p. 315.

[54] Habermas, *Zur Logik der Sozialwissenschaften*, loc. cit., p. 178.

[55] A connection between language and praxis can certainly also be asserted if language is not ideologically deformed in a *structural* manner. But then one presumably cannot avoid the consequence that, since the rules of language are inseparable from the rules of life-praxis, they stabilize the conditions of domination. This consideration underlies the criticism of Ludwig Wittgenstein whose statement 'Philosophy can in no way temper with the actual usage of language. . . . It leaves everything as it is'. (*Philosophical Investigations*, Oxford, 1958, p. 51), has become a matter of scandal for Marxist theory (cf. Herbert Marcuse, *One-Dimensional Man* (London/Boston, 1964), pp. 148ff.). Nevertheless, Wittgenstein is able to evade the aporia in which a 'dynamic' critique of ideology becomes entangled when it determines linguistic rules as life-forms, yet suspects them of being ideological distortions.

the suspicion of ideology. Not only would the interpretation of the present have to proceed 'dialectically', but also the anticipation of future emancipation. A philosophy of history whose regulative principle would have to be identified as dialectical in this manner would require a 'dialectic of utopian reason'. Is this possible?

4

If the regulative principle of the philosophy of history is, for its part, structured 'dialectically', then the following dilemma results:

1. Either, its dialectic is not contingent but rather the universal structure of thought—this would contradict Habermas' presupposition and would presumably lead to an a priori metaphysics of history;
2. Or, its dialectic is contingent and rests upon ideological distortion—then one can neither see how the standards of self-reflection can still be certain a priori, nor how knowledge is supposed to be possible at all.

The universal dialectic of thought is suggested since the 'interest in emancipation' can be apprehended a priori. But if this interest itself is structured dialectically, yet nevertheless can be apprehended a priori, then its dialectic too must be posited a priori. Accordingly, on the other hand, a contingent dialectics of the 'interest in emancipation' would also have to imply a contingent a priori. We shall let the matter rest at this point and merely ask what consequences result for the philosophy of history with practical intent from a contingent dialectic of this sort.

The contingent 'dialectic' corresponds to the ideological distortions through societal constraints. The 'accident' which evokes them lies in the organization of the labour process. Thought becomes 'dialectical' when it is ideologically distorted. If this is also true of the 'interest in emancipation', then 'critical theory' begins to oscillate between its principle and the societal conditions analysed with its aid. The suspicion of ideology becomes reflexive, turns back upon its presuppositions and from these back to the conditions in society. This oscillation leads to a sceptical regress which can never be assuaged in any knowledge. Such a sceptical theory is no longer capable of initiating an emancipatory praxis. It persists in its scruples and ought to be left to them.

In my view, the motion of sceptical regress can only be brought to a halt if the regulative principle of the philosophy of history is determined as both '*objective*' interest and interest in objectivity, as an actual anticipation of the domination-free dialogue in the discussion between scientists. This means, of course, in a double function: on the one hand, as an interest in the stabilization, reproduction and maximization of scientific objectivity, but, on the other hand, as an interest in the practical negation of all the rules of social action which contradict this 'objectivity'.

The 'scientific approach' of the scientists requires institutional securities. These imply a *practically* orientated interest, a political interest of science. Such a 'contradiction' between the domination-free dialogue of the scientists and societal conditions may, of course, no longer be 'dialectical'—but what then constitutes dialectics?

HANS ALBERT

A SHORT SURPRISED POSTSCRIPT TO A LONG INTRODUCTION

The impartial reader might be surprised that a book of this sort has taken on such remarkable proportions. Anyone who is acquainted with its genesis will know, however, what conditions are responsible for this disproportion. The discussion reprinted here began in 1961 between Karl Popper and Theodor W. Adorno; it was continued in 1963 with Jürgen Habermas' postscript, to which I responded in 1964; he replied in the same year and in the following year I published my rejoinder. If I understood the editor correctly, it was his original idea to make this discussion accessible to a wider circle of readers. I agreed to this suggestion and even tolerated later modifications although, in them, there gradually emerged early indications of that peculiar redistribution of proportions, together with an inflation of the volume, which eventually resulted. Apparently, permission for a simple reprinting of the original contributions to this discussion was not forthcoming from the other side. Consequently, the appearance of the volume was repeatedly delayed over a period of three years. At the suggestion of the editor, I eventually agreed to forego my postscript in order to speed up publication. I could not anticipate, however, how one of those involved would exploit his function—that of writing the introduction to the volume—nor what dimensions the above-mentioned redistribution of proportions would assume. Nevertheless, as some readers will understand, I cannot entirely suppress a certain satisfaction in view of the zeal that was at work here.

Be that as it may. I shall allow myself in conclusion some brief comments on the matter itself. Primarily, I should like to establish that I am not only struck by the other side's extravagance in terms

of printed pages—although I naturally find this understandable—
but also by the way in which the extensions to the previous discussions have been shaped with regard to their subject matter. But
above all—to express it more clearly—I am struck by the mode of
expression which, despite its usual degree of complexity, is basically relatively simple. Utilizing this mode of expression, Adorno
reproduces all the possible misunderstandings which have gained
a footing in the German-speaking world in the general controversy
over positivism, aroused since the start of our discussion and
partly under its influence. These are misunderstandings which
could have been avoided from the outset—if not through reading
the existing contributions to the discussion, then through reading
the other writings of Adorno's discussion partners. Adorno, like
Habermas earlier and, in his footsteps, a whole series of theoreticians, now falls prey to his own somewhat vague concept of
positivism and to the method, tendentious but quite typical in this
country, of subsuming under this category whatever in his view
seems to merit criticism. Adorno, too, has adopted in his introduction a procedure which is today very widespread. He suggests to the reader that the opposing view, which is primarily at
issue in this discussion is identical—or at least closely related in
relevant respects—to a crude positivism, such as may well be
established, in part, in social scientific research. Alternatively, he
suggests a connection with the logical positivism of the twenties
and thirties and then gives vent to his objections to these views,
without thereby making the position of critical rationalism
sufficiently clear and without even taking it into account.

A fundamental part of his line of argument proves to be unfounded, and, what is more, misleading if one simply consults the
relevant writings of his opponents in this controversy in order to
ascertain what *they* have to say on the points in question. This
applies, for instance, to his objections to the positivistic criteria
of meaning, the hostility towards philosophy on the part of several
thinkers, the prohibition of fantasy and other so-called prohibitive
norms, the rejection of speculation, the appeal to unproblematical
certainty and absolute reliability, or the appeal to the unquestioned
authority of the scientific realm and freedom from prejudice, the
separation of knowledge from the real life-process, and the like.[1]

---

[1] On such questions, see the articles printed in Karl Popper, *Conjectures and Refutations* (London, 1963), and, in addition, my *Traktat über Kritische Vernunft* (Tübingen,
1968).

In this connection, Adorno's charge of subjectivism and the reference to Berkeley's *esse est percipi* sounds downright grotesque in view of the fact that one can obtain information about Popper's criticism without great effort.[2] I would draw attention to the fact that Lenin, for example—although he was not a professor of philosophy—was quite capable of distinguishing between positivism and realism. The Frankfurt School, on the other hand, seem to have great difficulties in this respect. This could possibly be connected with their idealist tendencies, to which I shall return in another context.

Even with regard to the problem of testability, I need only recommend a somewhat more precise reading of the relevant writings, quite apart from the fact that the more or less implicit concessions contained in the articles of my discussion partners which have appeared recently, hardly leave me anything to say.[3] What Adorno allows himself in the form of comments on simplicity and clarity has little connection with what his opponents have to say on this problem. Quite frequently in this introduction, he establishes a connection more through free association than through confrontation with his opponents' arguments. Adorno has apparently failed to grasp my objection to the conservative association of knowledge with 'prior experience'— the inductivist moment in Habermas' thought. He interprets my reference to the significance of new ideas in a manner which surely reveals his complete misunderstanding to the unbiased reader.[4] With regard to the value problem, the representatives of the Frankfurt School would be well advised to discuss in detail the solutions suggested by their critics and, in so doing, show to what extent they are exposed to their objections. The reification

[2] Cf. apart from the relevant sections of Popper's *Logic of Scientific Discovery* and in his *Conjectures and Refutations*, the following article in which his criticism of subjectivism in epistemology, the theory of probability and modern physics becomes clear—'Epistemology Without a Knowing Subject' in Karl R. Popper, *Objective Knowledge* (Oxford, 1972), pp. 106–52; 'Probability, Magic or Knowledge out of Ignorance', *Dialectica*, 11, 1957; 'Quantum Mechanics Without the Observer', *Studies in the Foundations, Methodology, and Philosophy of Sciences*, vol. 2, ed. M. Bunge (Berlin/Heidelberg/New York, 1967).

[3] This even applies to Adorno's introduction. Cf. the instructive subordinate clause which appears on p. 47, 'unless one were to light upon particularly ingenious experiments'. No comment is necessary here.

[4] See above, p. 8. Here too, amplification is hardly necessary. Even more striking is his reaction to Helmut F. Spinner's ironic use of the expression 'great philosophical tradition' in a context which would hardly confront the normal reader with difficulties of interpretation. See p. 9 above.

thesis, for instance, may appear reasonable when confronted with the widely current formulations of people who have not indulged in a rigorous examination of this problem. But it surely meets neither the views of Max Weber nor of Karl Popper, nor even the suggestions which I myself have formulated for solving the problems concerned.[5]

A basic point must be very briefly mentioned here, namely, the allegedly absolute primacy of logic which Adorno thinks he can detect in his opponents and what for him is then connected with this primacy in the form of objections and theses. His discussion partners, however, have so clearly drawn attention to the role played by logic in critical rationalism that it hardly seems necessary to clarify it again here:[6] above all, its role as an organon of criticism. I venture to doubt whether Adorno can manage without it in this respect. In general, he too will not be prepared to suspend the principle of non-contradiction, although in his introduction he again frequently provides the relevant formulations. Apparently, it does not occur to him that a 'dialectical contradiction' expressing 'the real antagonisms' could possibly be completely compatible with this principle. In no way does he seem to be interested either in the results of previous discussions on logic and dialectics—for example, in the Polish discussion—or in the suggestions of his discussion partners on this problem. When I take into account its origins, I quite understand the aversion to logic which he displays. It is the fatal inheritance of Hegelian thought which even today plays such an important role in German philosophy. I am not quite sure to what extent the Frankfurt School still represents a unified view on this point. Possibly, some representatives of this school of thought will, if anything, gradually become embarrassed by the careless polemic against logic, non-contradiction, deductive and systematic thought—a polemic which has recently found adherents in wide circles.

What Adorno says on the political manipulability of positivism should presumably be regarded as a reply to Ernst Topitsch's corresponding line of argument against dialectics.[7] I do not wish

---

[5] Since I have expressed myself in great detail on such problems, I shall refrain from discussing them once again.

[6] Cf. Popper's *Conjectures and Refutations* and my *Traktat*.

[7] Cf. Ernst Topitsch, *Die Sozialphilosophie Hegels als Heilslehre und Herrschaftsideologie* (Neuwied/Berlin, 1967).

to present a balance of the opposing arguments here, although one hardly need fear such a balance. I should like to point out, though, that Adorno makes matters a little too easy for himself, for critical rationalism—also an intended target here—is by no means the apolitical philosophy which Adorno makes it out to be. His polemic against the neutrality of positivistic scepticism and its ideological abuse is wide of the mark as far as our discussion is concerned. Why should such associations be evoked? Why does he actively support those confusions in the German controversy over positivism created by obviously uninformed participants? What is to be gained from the obliteration of his opponents' arguments by a strategy of unspecific objections? I cannot help seeing in this a confirmation of the charges brought against the Frankfurt School by many of its critics. In my view, a dialectics which incorporates the belief that it can dispense with logic, supports— presumably contrary to its underlying intention—one of the most dangerous features of German thought: the tendency towards irrationalism.

KARL R. POPPER

REASON OR REVOLUTION?

The trouble with a total revolution [. . .]
Is that it brings the same class up on top:
Executives of skilful execution
Will therefore plan to go halfway and stop.

Robert Frost
(from 'A Semi-Revolution', in *A Witness Tree*)

The following critical considerations are reactions to the book, *Der Positivismusstreit in der deutschen Soziologie* [now translated into English as *The Positivist Dispute in German Sociology*], which was published last year[1] and for which I unwittingly provided the original incentive.

1

I will begin by telling some of the history of the book and of its misleading title. In 1960 I was invited to open a discussion on 'The Logic of the Social Sciences' at a congress of German sociologists in Tübingen. I accepted; and I was told that my opening address would be followed by a reply from Professor Theodor W. Adorno of Frankfurt. It was suggested to me by the organizers that, in order to make a fruitful discussion possible, I should formulate my views in a number of definite theses. This I did: my opening address to that discussion, delivered in 1961, consisted of twenty-seven sharply formulated theses, plus a programmatic formulation of the task of the theoretical social sciences. Of course, I formulated these theses so as to make it difficult for any Hegelian or Marxist (such as Adorno) to accept them; and I supported them

---

[1] This paper, which has been added to the English translation of this volume, was first published in *Archives européennes de sociologie* XI, 1970, pp. 252–62. It has been revised for the present publication.

as well as I could by arguments. Owing to the limited time available, I confined myself to fundamentals, and I tried to avoid repeating what I had said elsewhere.

Adorno's reply was read with great force, but he hardly took up my challenge—that is, my twenty-seven theses. In the ensuing debate Professor Ralf Dahrendorf expressed his grave disappointment. He said that it had been the intention of the organizers to bring into the open some of the glaring differences—apparently he included political and ideological differences—between my approach to the social sciences and Adorno's. But the impression created by my address and Adorno's reply was, he said, one of sweet agreement; a fact which left him flabbergasted ('*als seien Herr Popper und Herr Adorno sich in verblüffender Weise einig*'). I was and I still am very sorry about this. But having been invited to speak about 'The Logic of the Social Sciences' I did not go out of my way to attack Adorno and the 'dialectical' school of Frankfurt (Adorno, Horkheimer, Habermas, *et al.*) which I never regarded as important, unless perhaps from a political point of view; and in 1960 I was not even aware of the political influence of this school. Although today I should not hesitate to describe this influence by such terms as 'irrationalist' and 'intelligence-destroying', I could never take their methodology (whatever that may mean) seriously from either an intellectual or a scholarly point of view. Knowing now a little more, I think that Dahrendorf was right in being disappointed: I ought to have attacked them, using arguments I had previously published in my *Open Society*[2] and *The Poverty of Historicism*[3] and in 'What is Dialectic?',[4] even though I do not think that these arguments fall under the heading of 'The Logic of the Social Sciences'; for terms do not matter. My only comfort is that the responsibility for avoiding a fight rests squarely on the second speaker.

However this may be, Dahrendorf's criticism stimulated a paper (almost twice as long as my original address) by Professor Jürgen Habermas, another member of the Frankfurt school. It was in this paper, I think, that the term 'positivism' first turned up in this particular discussion: I was criticized as a 'positivist'.

---

[2] *The Open Society and Its Enemies* (London, 1945), 5th ed. (rev.) 1969, 10th impr. 1974.
[3] *The Poverty of Historicism* (London, 1957 and later editions).
[4] 'What is Dialectic?', *Mind*, XLIX (1940), pp. 403ff. Reprinted in *Conjectures and Refutations* (London, 1963), 5th ed., 1974.

This is an old misunderstanding created and perpetuated by people who know of my work only at second-hand: owing to the tolerant attitude adopted by some members of the Vienna Circle, my book, *Logik der Forschung*,[5] in which I criticized this positivist Circle from a realist and anti-positivist point of view, was published in a series of books edited by Moritz Schlick and Philipp Frank, two leading members of the Circle;[6] and those who judge books by their covers (or by their editors) created the myth that I had been a member of the Vienna Circle, and a positivist. Nobody who has read that book (or any other book of mine) would agree—unless indeed he believed in the myth to start with, in which case he may of course find evidence to support his belief.

In my defence Professor Hans Albert (not a positivist either) wrote a spirited reply to Habermas' attack. The latter answered, and was answered a second time by Albert. This exchange was mainly concerned with the general character and tenability of my views. Thus there was little mention—and no serious criticism—of my opening address of 1961, and of its twenty-seven theses.

It was, I think, in 1964 that a German publisher asked me whether I would agree to have my address published in book form together with Adorno's reply and the debate between Habermas and Albert. I agreed.

But, as now published [in 1969, in German], the book consists of two quite new introductions by Adorno (94 pages), followed by my address of 1961 (20 pages) with Adorno's original reply (18 pages), Dahrendorf's complaint (9 pages), the debate between Habermas and Albert (150 pages), a new contribution by Harold Pilot (28 pages), and a 'Short Surprised Postscript to a Long Introduction' by Albert (5 pages). In this, Albert mentions briefly that the affair started with a discussion between Adorno and myself in 1961, and he says quite rightly that a reader of the book would hardly realize what it was all about. This is the only allusion in the book to the story behind it. There is no answer

---

[5] *Logik der Forschung* (Wien, Julius Springer, 1934; 5th ed., Tübingen, J. C. B. Mohr, 1973). English translation: *The Logic of Scientific Discovery* (London, Hutchinson, 1959), 7th impr. 1974.

[6] The Vienna Circle consisted of men of originality and of the highest intellectual and moral standards. Not all of them were 'positivists', if we mean by this term a condemnation of speculative thought, although most of them were. I have always been in favour of criticizable speculative thought and, of course, of its criticism.

to the question of how the book got a title which quite wrongly indicates that the opinions of some 'positivists' are discussed in the book. Even Albert's postscript does not answer this question.

What is the result? My twenty-seven theses, intended to start a discussion (and so they did, after all), are nowhere seriously taken up in this longish book—not a single one of them, although one or other passage from my address is mentioned here or there, usually out of context, to illustrate my 'positivism'. Moreover, my address is buried in the middle of the book, unconnected with the beginning and the end. No reader can see, and no reviewer can understand, why my address (which I cannot but regard as quite unsatisfactory in its present setting) is included in the book —or that it is the unadmitted theme of the whole book. Thus no reader would suspect, and no reviewer did suspect, what I suspect as being the truth of the matter. It is that my opponents literally did not know how to criticize rationally my twenty-seven theses. All they could do was to label me 'positivist' (thereby unwittingly giving a highly misleading name to a debate in which not one single 'positivist' was involved); and having done so, they drowned my short paper, and the original issue of the debate, in an ocean of words—which I found only partially comprehensible.

As it now stands, the main issue of the book has become Adorno's and Habermas' accusation that a 'positivist' like Popper is bound by his methodology to defend the political *status quo*. It is an accusation which I myself raised in my *Open Society* against Hegel, whose identity philosophy (what is real is reasonable) I described as a kind of 'moral and legal positivism'. In my address I had said nothing about this issue; and I had no opportunity to reply. But I have often combatted this form of 'positivism' along with other forms. And it is a fact that my *social theory* (which favours gradual and piecemeal reform, reform controlled by a critical comparison between expected and achieved results) contrasts strongly with my *theory of method*, which happens to be a theory of scientific and intellectual revolutions.

2

This fact and my attitude towards revolution can be easily explained. We may start from Darwinian evolution. Organisms evolve by trial and error, and their erroneous trials—their erroneous mutations—are eliminated, as a rule, by the elimination of the organism which is the 'carrier' of the error. It is part of my epistemology that, in man, through the evolution of a descriptive and argumentative language, all this has changed radically. Man has achieved the possibility of being *critical of his own tenative trials, of his own theories*. These theories are no longer incorporated in his organism, or in his genetic system: they may be formulated in books, or in journals; and they can be critically discussed, and shown to be erroneous, without killing any authors or burning any books: without destroying the 'carriers'.

In this way we arrive at a fundamental new possibility: our trials, our tentative hypotheses, may be critically eliminated by rational discussion, without eliminating ourselves. This indeed is the purpose of rational critical discussion.

The 'carrier' of a hypothesis has an important function in these discussions: he has to defend the hypothesis against erroneous criticism, and he may perhaps try to modify it if in its original form it cannot be successfully defended.

If the method of rational critical discussion should establish itself, then this should make the use of violence obsolete: *critical reason is the only alternative to violence so far discovered*.

It seems to me clear that it is the obvious duty of all intellectuals to work for *this* revolution—for the replacement of the eliminative function of violence by the eliminative function of rational criticism. But in order to work for this end, one has to train oneself constantly to write and to speak in clear and simple language. Every thought should be formulated as clearly and simply as possible. This can only be achieved by hard work.

3

I have been for many years a critic of the so-called 'sociology of knowledge'. Not that I thought that everything that Mannheim (and Scheler) said was mistaken. On the contrary, much of it was only too trivially true. What I combated, mainly, was Mannheim's belief that there was an essential difference with respect to objectivity between the social scientist and the natural scientist, or between the study of society and the study of nature. The thesis I combated was that it was easy to be 'objective' in the natural sciences, while objectivity in the social sciences could be achieved, if at all, only by very select intellects: by the 'freely poised intelligence' which is only 'loosely anchored in social traditions'.[7]

As against this I stressed that the objectivity of natural and social science is not based on an impartial state of mind in the scientists, but merely on the fact of the public and competitive character of the scientific enterprise and thus on certain social aspects of it. This is why I wrote: '*What the* [so-called] "*sociology of knowledge*" *overlooks is just the sociology of knowledge*—the social or public character of science'.[8] Objectivity is based, in brief, upon *mutual rational criticism*, upon the critical approach, the critical tradition.[9]

Thus natural scientists are not more objectively minded than social scientists. Nor are they more critical. If there is more 'objectivity' in the natural sciences, then this is because there is a better tradition, and higher standards, of clarity and of rational criticism.

In Germany, many social scientists are brought up as Hegelians, and this is, in my opinion, a tradition destructive of intelligence and critical thought. It is one of the points where I agree with Karl Marx who wrote: 'In its mystifying form dialectic became the accepted German fashion'.[10] It is the German fashion still.

4

The sociological explanation of this fact is simple. We all get our values, or most of them, from our social environment; often merely by imitation, simply by taking them over from others; sometimes by a revolutionary reaction to accepted values; and at other times—though this may be rare—by a critical examination of these values and of possible alternatives. However this may be,

---

[7] The quotation is from Mannheim. It is discussed more fully in my *Open Society* vol. II, p. 225.

[8] *The Poverty of Historicism*, p. 155.

[9] Cf. *Conjectures and Refutations*, especially chapter IV.

[10] Karl Marx, *Das Kapital*, 2. Aufl., 1872, 'Nachwort'. (In some later editions this is described as 'Preface to second edition'. The usual translation is not 'mystifying' but 'mystified'. To me this sounds like a Germanism.)

the social and intellectual climate, the tradition in which one is brought up, is often decisive for the moral and other standards and values which one adopts. All this is rather obvious. A very special case, but one which is all-important for our purpose, is that of intellectual values.

Many years ago I used to warn my students against the widespread idea that one goes to university in order to learn how to talk, and to write, impressively and incomprehensibly. At the time many students came to university with this ridiculous aim in mind, especially in Germany. And most of those students who, during their university studies, enter into an intellectual climate which accepts this kind of valuation—coming, perhaps under the influence of teachers who in their turn had been reared in a similar climate—are lost. They unconsciously learn and accept that highly impressive and difficult language is the intellectual value *par excellence*. There is little hope that they will ever understand that they are mistaken; or that they will ever realize that there are other standards and values: values such as truth; the search for truth; the approximation to truth through the critical elimination of error; and clarity. Nor will they find out that the standard of impressive incomprehensibility actually clashes with the standards of truth and rational criticism. For these latter values depend on clarity. One cannot tell truth from falsity, one cannot tell an adequate answer to a problem from an irrelevant one, one cannot tell good ideas from trite ones, one cannot evaluate ideas critically, unless they are presented with sufficient clarity. But to those brought up in the implicit admiration of brilliance and impressive opaqueness, all this (and all I have said here) would be *at best*, impressive talk: they do not know any other values.

Thus arose the cult of un-understandability, the cult of impressive and high-sounding language. This was intensified by the (for laymen) impenetrable and impressive formalism of mathematics. I suggest that in some of the more ambitious social sciences and philosophies, and especially in Germany, the traditional game, which has largely become the unconscious and unquestioned standard, is to state the utmost trivialities in high-sounding language.

If those who had been brought up on this kind of nourishment are presented with a book that is written simply, and that contains something unexpected or controversial or new, then usually they find that it is difficult or impossible to understand it. For it does not conform to their idea of 'understanding', which for them entails agreement. That there may be important ideas worth understanding with which one cannot at once agree or disagree is to them un-understandable.

5

There is here, at first sight, a difference between the social sciences and the natural sciences: in the so-called social sciences and in philosophy, the degeneration into impressive but more or less empty verbalism has gone further than in the natural sciences. Yet the danger is getting acute everywhere. Even among mathematicians a tendency to impress people may sometimes be discerned, although the incitement to do so is least in mathematics; for it is partly the wish to ape the mathematicians and the mathematical physicists in technicality and in difficulty that inspires the use of verbiage in other sciences.

Yet lack of critical creativeness—that is, of inventiveness paired with critical acumen—can be found everywhere; and everywhere this leads to the phenomenon of young scientists eager to pick up the latest fashion and the latest jargon. These 'normal' scientists[11] want a framework, a routine, a common and an exclusive language of their trade. But it is the non-normal scientist, the daring scientist, the critical scientist, who breaks through the barrier of normality, who opens the windows and lets in fresh air; who does not think about the impression he makes, but tries to be well understood.

The growth of normal science, which is linked to the growth of Big Science, is likely to prevent, or even to destroy, the growth of knowledge, the growth of great science.

I regard the situation as tragic if not desperate; and the present trend in the so-called empirical investigations into the sociology of the natural sciences is likely to contribute to the decay of

---

[11] The phenomenon of normal science was discovered, but not criticized, by Thomas Kuhn in *The Structure of Scientific Revolutions*. Kuhn is, I believe, mistaken in thinking that 'normal' science is not only normal *today* but always was so. On the contrary, in the past—until 1939—science was almost always critical, or 'extraordinary'; there was no scientific '*routine*'.

science. Super-imposed upon this danger is another danger, created by Big Science: its urgent need for scientific technicians. More and more Ph.D candidates receive a merely technical training, a training in certain techniques of measurement; they are not initiated into the scientific tradition, the critical tradition of questioning, of being tempted and guided by great and apparently insoluble riddles rather than by the solubility of little puzzles. True, these technicians, these specialists, are usually aware of their limitations. They call themselves specialists and reject any claim to authority outside their specialities. Yet they do so proudly, and proclaim that specialization is a necessity. But this means flying in the face of the facts which show that great advances still come from those with a wide range of interests.

If the many, the specialists, gain the day, it will be the end of science as we know it—of great science. It will be a spiritual catastrophe comparable in its consequences to nuclear armament.

6

I now come to my main point. It is this. Some of the famous leaders of German sociology who do their intellectual best, and do it with the best conscience in the world, are nevertheless, I believe, simply talking trivialities in high-sounding language, as they were taught. They teach this to their students, who are dissatisfied, yet who do the same. In fact, the genuine and general feeling of dissatisfaction which is manifest in their hostility to the society in which they live is, I think, a reflection of their unconscious dissatisfaction with the sterility of their own activities.

I will give a brief example from the writings of Professor Adorno. The example is a select one—selected, indeed, by Professor Habermas, who begins his first contribution to *Der Positivismusstreit* by quoting it. On the left I give the original German text, in the centre the text as translated in the present volume, and on the right a paraphrase into simple English of what seems to have been asserted.[12]

---

[12] In the original publication of this article in *Archives européennes de sociologie* the three columns contained, respectively, the original German, a paraphrase into simple German of what seemed to have been asserted, and a translation of this paraphrase into English.

Die gesellschaftliche Totalität führt kein Eigenleben oberhalb des von ihr Zusammengefassten, aus dem sie selbst besteht.	Societal totality does not lead a life of its own over and above that which it unites and of which it, in its turn, is composed.	Society consists of social relationships.
Sie produziert und reproduziert sich durch ihre einzelnen Momente hindurch. . . .	It produces and reproduces itself through its individual moments. . . .	The various social relationships somehow produce society. . . .
So wenig aber jenes Ganze vom Leben, von der Kooperation und dem Antagonismus seiner Elemente abzusondern ist,	This totality can no more be detached from life, from the co-operation and the antagonism of its elements	Among these relations are co-operation and antagonism; and since (as mentioned) society consists of these relations, it is impossible to separate it from them.
so wenig kann irgendein Element auch bloss in seinem Funktionieren verstanden werden ohne Einsicht in des Ganze, das an der Bewegung des Einzelnen selbst sein Wesen hat.	than can an element be understood merely as it functions without insight into the whole which has its source [*Wesen*, essence] in the motion of the individual entity itself.	The opposite is also true: none of the relations can be understood without the totality of all the others.
System und Einzelheit sind reziprok und nur in ihre Reziprozität zu erkennen.	System and individual entity are reciprocal and can only be apprehended in their reciprocity.	(Repetition of the preceding thought.)

Comment: the theory of social wholes developed here has been presented and developed, sometimes better and sometimes worse, by countless philosophers and sociologists. I do not assert that it is mistaken. I only assert the complete triviality of its content. Of course Adorno's *presentation* is very far from trivial.

7

It is for reasons such as these that I find it so difficult to discuss any serious problem with Professor Habermas. I am sure he is perfectly sincere. But I think that he does not know how to put things simply, clearly and modestly, rather than impressively. Most of what he says seems to me trivial; the rest seems to me mistaken.

So far as I can understand him, the following is his central complaint about my alleged views. My way of theorizing, Habermas suggests, violates the *principle of the identity of theory and practice*; perhaps because I say that theory should *help* action, that is, should help us to modify our actions. For I say that it is the task of the theoretical social sciences to try to anticipate the unintended consequences of our actions; thus I differentiate between this theoretical task and the action. But Professor Habermas seems to think that only one who is a practical critic of existing society can produce serious theoretical arguments about society, since social knowledge cannot be divorced from fundamental social attitudes. The indebtedness of this view to the 'sociology of knowledge' is obvious, and need not be laboured.

My reply is very simple. I think that we should welcome any suggestion as to how our problems might be solved, regardless of the attitude towards society of the man who puts them forward; provided that he has learned to express himself clearly and simply —in a way that can be understood and evaluated—and that he is aware of our fundamental ignorance, and of our responsibilities towards others. But I certainly do not think that the debate about the reform of society should be reserved for those who first put in a claim for recognition as practical revolutionaries, and who see the sole function of the revolutionary intellectual in pointing out as much as possible that is repulsive in our social life (excepting their own social roles).

It may be that revolutionaries have a greater sensitivity to social ills than other people. But obviously, there can be better and worse revolutions (as we all know from history), and the problem is not to do too badly. Most, if not all, revolutions have produced societies very different from those desired by the revolutionaries. *Here is a problem*, and it deserves thought from every serious critic of society. And this should include an effort to put one's ideas into simple, modest language, rather than high-sounding jargon. This is an effort which those fortunate ones who are able to devote themselves to study owe to society.

8

A last word about the term 'positivism'. Words do not matter, and I do not really mind if even a thoroughly misleading and mistaken label is applied to me. But the fact is that throughout my life I have combated positivist epistemology, under the name 'positivism'. I do not deny, of course, the possibility of stretching the term 'positivist' until it covers anybody who takes any interest in natural science, so that it can be applied even to opponents of positivism, such as myself. I only contend that such a procedure is neither honest nor apt to clarify matters.

The fact that the label 'positivism' was originally applied to me by a sheer blunder can be checked by anybody who is prepared to read my early *Logik der Forschung*.

It is, however, worth mentioning that one of the victims of the two misnomers, 'positivism' and '*Der Positivismusstreit*' is Dr Alfred Schmidt, who describes himself as a 'collaborator of many years standing' (*Langjähriger Mitarbeiter*) of Professors Adorno and Horkheimer. In a letter to a newspaper *Die Zeit*,[13] written to defend Adorno against the suggestion that he misused the term 'positivism' in *Der Positivismusstreit* or on similar occasions, Schmidt characterizes 'positivism' as a tendency of thought in which 'the method of the various single sciences is taken absolutely as the only valid method of knowledge' (*die einzelwis-senschaftlichen Verfahren als einzig gültige Erkenntnis verabsolutierende Denken*), and he identifies it, correctly, with an over-emphasis on 'sensually ascertainable facts'. He is clearly unaware of the fact that my alleged 'positivism', which was used to give the book *Der Positivismusstreit* its name, consisted in a fight against all this which he describes (in my opinion fairly correctly) as 'positivism'. I have always fought for the right to operate freely with specula-tive theories, against the narrowness of the 'scientistic' theories of knowledge and, especially, against all forms of sensualistic empiricism.

I have fought against the aping of the natural sciences by the social sciences,[14] and I have fought for the doctrine that positivistic epistemology is inadequate even in its analysis of the natural sciences which, in fact, are not 'careful generalizations from observation', as it is usually believed, but are essentially speculative and daring; moreover, I have taught, for more than thirty-eight years,[15] that all observations are theory-impregnated, and that

---

[13] 12th June 1970, p. 45.

[14] I have even done so, although briefly, in the lecture printed in the present volume. (See especially my seventh thesis.)

[15] See my book, *The Logic of Scientific Discovery*, new appendix i.

their main function is to check and refute, rather than to prove, our theories. Finally I have not only stressed the meaningfulness of metaphysical assertions and the fact that I am myself a metaphysical realist, but I have also analysed the important historical role played by metaphysics in the formation of scientific theories. Nobody before Adorno and Habermas has described such views as positivistic, and I can only suppose that these two did not know, originally, that I held such views. (In fact, I suspect that they were no more interested in my views than I am in theirs.)

It may be worth stating here that the suggestion that anybody interested in natural science is to be condemned as a positivist would make positivists not only of Marx and Engels but also of Lenin—the man who introduced the equation of 'positivism' and 'reaction'.

Terminology does not matter, however. Only it should not be used as an *argument*; and the title of a book ought not to be dishonest; nor should it attempt to prejudge an issue.

On the substantial issue between the Frankfurt school and myself—revolution versus piecemeal reform—I shall not comment here, since I have treated it as well as I could in my *Open Society*. Hans Albert too has said many incisive things on this topic, both in his replies to Habermas in *Der Positivismusstreit* and in his important book *Traktat über kritische Vernunft*.[16]

---

[16] H. Albert, *Traktat über kritische Vernunft* (Tübingen, Mohr, 1969).

SELECTED BIBLIOGRAPHY

History of the Dispute

Albert, H. & Topitsch, E. (eds.), *Werturteilsstreit*, Darmstadt, 1971

Aron, R., *German Sociology* (Trans. M. & T. Bottomore), Glencoe, Ill., 1964

Boese, F., 'Geschichte des Vereins für Sozialpolitik, 1872–1932', *Verein für Sozialpolitik, Schriften*, vol. 188, Berlin, 1939

Böhm-Bawerk, E. v., 'The historical versus the deductive method in political economy', *Annals of the American Academy of Political and Social Science*, vol. 1, no. 2, 1890

Cahnman, W., 'Weber and the methodological controversy', in Cahnman, W. & Boskoff, A. (eds.), *Sociology and History*, New York, 1964

Dilthey, W., *Gesammelte Schriften*, 12 vols., 2nd Ed., Stuttgart/Göttingen, 1958. (See especially volumes 1, 5 and 7.)

Eisermann, G., 'Die deutsche Soziologie im Zeitraum von 1918 bis 1933', *Kölner Zeitschrift für Soziologie*, vol. 11, 1959

Engel-Reimers, C., 'Der Methodenstreit in der Soziologie', *Schmollers Jahrbuch*, vol. 56, 1932

Ferber, C. v., 'Der Werturteilsstreit 1909/59', *Kölner Zeitschrift für Soziologie*, vol. 11, 1959

Freyer, H., *Soziologie als Wirklichkeitswissenschaft*, Leipzig/Berlin, 1930

Habermas, J., 'Zur Logik der Sozialwissenschaften', *Philosophische Rundschau, Beiheft 5*, Tübingen, 1967. (Reprinted Frankfurt 1971, with additional material.)

Hansen, R., 'Der Methodenstreit in den Sozialwissenschaften zwischen Gustav Schmoller und Karl Menger', in Diemer, A. (ed.), *Beiträge zur Entwicklung der Wissenschaftstheorie in 19 Jahrhundert*, Meisenheim, 1968

Hodges, H. A., *The Philosophy of Wilhelm Dilthey*, London, 1952

Hodges, H. A., *Wilhelm Dilthey: an Introduction*, London 1944

Hofmann, W., *Gesellschaftslehre als Ordnungsmacht: Die Werturteilsfrage heute*, Berlin, 1961

Holborn, H., 'Wilhelm Dilthey and the critique of historical reason', *Journal of the History of Ideas*, 1950

Horkheimer, M., 'Traditionelle und kritische Theorie', *Zeitschrift für Soziologie*, vol. 6, 1937

Horkheimer, M., *Critical Theory* (trans. M. O'Connell *et al.*), New York, 1973/London, 1974. (Contains above article.)

Horkheimer, M., *The Eclipse of Reason*, New York, 1947, 1974

Huessi, K., *Die Krisis des Historismus*, Tübingen, 1932

Kaufmann, F., 'Logik und Wirtschaftswissenschaft. Eine Untersuchung über die Grundlagen der ökonomischen Theorie', *Archiv für Sozialwissenschaft*, vol. 54, 1925

Kaufmann, F., *Methodenlehre der Sozialwissenschaften*, Vienna, 1936

Kaufmann, F., *Methodology of the Social Sciences*, New York, 1944. (Not the same book as above.)

Kraft, V., *Der Wiener Kreis. Der Ursprung des Neopositivismus*, Vienna, 1950

Landshut, S., *Kritik der Soziologie-Freiheit und Gleichheit als Ursprungsproblem der Soziologie*, Munich/Leipzig, 1929

Lindenlaub, D., 'Richtungskämpfe im Verein für Sozialpolitik', *Vierteljahrsschrift für Sozial und Wirtschaftsgeschichte*, Beiheft 52, 1967

Lukacs, G., *Geschichte und Klassenbewusstsein*, Berlin, 1923. (English translation R. Livingstone.) *History and Class Consciousness*, London/Cambridge, Mass., 1971

Mannheim, K., 'Problems of sociology in Germany', in K. Wolff (ed.), *From Karl Mannheim*, New York, 1971

Marcuse, H., *Reason and Revolution*, New York, 1941

Menger, C., *Untersuchungen über die Methode der Sozialwissenschaften und der politischen ökonomie insbesondere*, Leipzig, 1883

Menger, C., 'Irrtümer des Historismus in der deutschen National-ökonomie', in *Kleinere Schriften zur Methode und Geschichte der Volkswirtschaftslehre*, London, 1935

Menger, C., *Problems of Economics and Sociology* (trans. F. J. Nock, ed. and introd. L. Schneider), Urbana, 1963

Mommsen, W., *Max Weber. Gesellschaft, Politik und Geschichte*, Frankfurt, 1974

Morf, O., *Geschichte und Dialektik in der politischen ökonomie*, Frankfurt, 1970

Pfister, B., *Die Entwicklung zum Idealtypus. Eine methodologische Untersuchung über das Verhältnis von Theorie und Geschichte bei Menger, Schmoller und Max Weber*, Tübingen, 1928

Rickert, H., *Die Grenzen der Naturwissenschaftlichen Begriffsbildung. Eine logische Einleitung in die historischen Wissenschaften*, Tübingen/Leipzig, 1902

Rickert, H., *Kulturwissenschaft und Naturwissenschaft*, 6th and 7th editions, Tübingen, 1926

Rickert, H., *Science and History* (trans. G. Reisman), Princeton, 1962

Ritzel, G., *Schmoller versus Menger. Eine Analyze des Methodenstreits im Hinblick auf den Historismus in der Nationalökonomie*, Frankfurt, 1950

Schelting, A. v., 'Die logische Theorie der historischen Kulturwissenschaft von Max Weber', *Archiv für Sozialwissenschaft*, vol. 49, 1922

Schelting, A. v., *Max Webers Wissenschaftslehre*, Tübingen, 1934

Schmoller, G., 'Zur Methodologie der Staats-und Sozialwissenschaften', *Jahrbuch für Gesetzgebung, Verwaltung and Volkswirtschaft im deutschen Reich*, vol. 7, 1883

Schmoller, G., 'Die Volkswirtschaft, die Volkswirtschaftslehre und ihre Methode', *Handwörterbuch der Staatswissenschaften*, 1893

Stammer, O. (ed.), *Max Weber and Sociology Today* (trans. K. Morris), Oxford, 1971

Sweezy, P. (ed.), *Karl Marx and the Close of his System and Böhm-Bawerk's Criticism of Marx*, New York, 1949

Tenbruck, F., 'Die Genesis der Methodologie Max Webers', *Kölner Zeitschrift für Soziologie*, vol. 11, 1959

Troeltsch, E., *Der Historismus und seine Probleme*, Tübingen, 1922

Troeltsch, E., 'Die Revolution in der Wissenschaft', *Schmollers Jahrbuch*, vol. 45, 1921. (Reprinted in Troeltsch, E., *Gesammelte Schriften*, vol. 4, Tübingen, 1925, and in Albert, H. & Topitsch, E., loc. cit.

Weber, M., 'Gutachten zur Werturteilsdiskussion im Ausschuss des Vereins für Sozialpolitik 1913', in E. Baumgarten, *Max Weber: Werk und Person*, Tübingen, 1964

Weber, M., *Gesammelte Aufsätze zur Wissenschaftslehre*, 2nd ed., Tübingen, 1951

Weber, M., *The Methodology of the Social Sciences* (trans. E. A. Shils & H. A. Finch), New York, 1949

Weber, W. & Topitsch, E., 'Das Werturteilsproblem seit Max Weber', *Zeitschrift für Nationalökonomie*, vol. 13, 1952

Windelband, W., 'Geschichte und Naturwissenschaft', in *Präludien*, vol. 2, Tübingen, 1924

Wittenberg, E., 'Die Wissenschaftskrisis in Deutschland im Jahre 1919. Ein Beitrag zur Wissenschaftsgeschichte', *Theoria*, vol. 3, 1937

Relevant Writings of Authors in the Dispute

Adorno, T. W., *Aufsätze zur Methodologie und Soziologie*, Frankfurt, 1971

Adorno, T. W., 'Contemporary German Sociology' (trans. N. Birnbaum), *Transactions of the Fourth World Congress of Sociology*, vol. 1, Washington, 1959

Adorno, T. W., 'Scientific experiences of a European scholar', in D. Fleming & B. Bailyn (eds.), *The Intellectual Migration—Europe and America, 1930-60*, Cambridge (Mass.), 1969

Adorno, T. W., *Soziologische Schriften 1*, Frankfurt, 1973

Adorno, T. W., *Vorlesungen zur Einleitung in die Soziologie* (summer semester 1968), Frankfurt, 1973

Albert, H., *Marktsoziologie und Entscheidungslogik*, Neuwied/Berlin, 1967

Albert, H., 'Social science and moral philosophy: A critical approach to the value problem in the social sciences', in M. Bunge (ed.), *The Critical Approach to Science and Philosophy, Essays in Honor of Karl R. Popper*, Glencoe, N.Y., 1964

Albert, H. (ed.), *Sozialtheorie und soziale Praxis—Eduard Baumgarten zum 70. Geburtstag*, Meisenheim am Glan, 1971

Albert, H. (ed.), *Theorie und Realität*, Tübingen, 1964

Albert, H., *Traktat über kritische Vernunft*, 2nd ed., Tübingen, 1969

Albert, H., 'Zur Logik der Sozialwissenschaften: Die These der Seinsgebundenheit und die Methode der kritischen Prüfung', *European Journal of Sociology*, vol. 5, 1964

Habermas, J., A postscript to *Knowledge and Human Interests* (trans. C. Leinhardt), *Philosophy of the Social Sciences*, vol. 3, 1973

Habermas, J., *Knowledge and Human Interests* (trans. J. Shapiro), Boston/London, 1971

Habermas, J., *Kultur und Kritik*, Frankfurt, 1973

Habermas, J., *Legitimationsprobleme im Spätkapitalismus*, Frankfurt, 1973 (English trans. T. McCarthy, *Legitimation Crisis*, Boston/London, 1975)

Habermas, J., *Philosophisch-politische Profile*, Frankfurt, 1971

Habermas, J., *Theory and Practice* (trans. J. Viertel), Boston/London, 1974

Habermas, J., *Toward a Rational Society* (trans. J. Shapiro), Boston/London, 1970

Habermas, J., 'Wahrheitstheorien', in Fahrenbach, H. (ed.), *Wirklichkeit und Reflexion: Festschrift für Walter Schulz*, Pfullingen, 1973

Habermas, J., *Zur Logik der Sozialwissenschaften*, loc. cit.

Popper, K. R., *Conjectures and Refutations*, London, 1963

Popper, K. R., *Objective Knowledge. An Evolutionary Approach*, Oxford, 1972

Popper, K. R., *The Logic of Scientific Discovery*, 2nd ed., London, 1968

Popper, K. R., *The Open Society and its Enemies*, 5th ed., London, 1966

Popper, K. R., *The Poverty of Historicism*, 2nd ed., London, 1960

The Succeeding Controversy

Adorno, T. W. (ed.), *Spätkapitalismus oder Industriegesellschaft? Verhandlungen des 16. Deutschen Soziologentages 1968*, Stuttgart, 1969

Albert, H., *Konstruktion und Kritik. Aufsätze zur Philosophie des kritischen Rationalismus*, Hamburg, 1972

Albert, H. & Keuth, H. (eds.), *Kritik der kritischen Psychologie*, Hamburg, 1973

Albert, H., *Plädoyer für kritischen Rationalismus*, Munich, 1971

Albert, H., *Transzendentale Träumereien. Karl-Otto Apels Sprachspiele und sein hermeneutischer Gott*, Hamburg, 1975

Apel, K.-O., *et al.*, *Hermeneutik und Ideologiekritik*, Frankfurt, 1971
Apel, K.-O., 'Das Problem der philosophischen Letztbegründung im Lichte einer transzendentalen Sprachpragmatik (Versuch einer Metakritik des "kritischen Rationalismus")', in Kanitscheider, B. (ed.), *Festschrift für Gerhard Frey*, 1974
Habermas, J./Luhmann, N., *Theorie der Gesellschaft oder Sozialtechnologie —Was leistet die Systemforschung?*, Frankfurt, 1971
Hochkeppel, W. (ed.), *T. W. Adorno, H. Albert, et al., Soziologie zwischen Theorie und Empirie*, Munich, 1970
Kambartel, F. (ed.), *Praktische Philosophie und konstruktive Wissenschaftstheorie*, Frankfurt, 1974
Maciejewski, F. (ed.), *Theorie-Diskussion Supplement 1. Theorie der Gesellschaft oder Sozialtechnologie*, Frankfurt, 1973
Maciejewski, F. (ed.), *Neue Beiträge zur Habermas-Luhmann-Diskussion*, Frankfurt, 1974
Stark, F. (ed.), *Reform oder Revolution? Herbert Marcuse und Karl Popper. Eine Konfrontation*, Munich, 1971

Commentary on the Controversy

Baier, H., 'Soziale Technologie oder soziale Emanzipation? Zum Streit zwischen Positivisten und Dialektikern über die Aufgabe der Soziologie', in B. Schäfers (ed.), *Thesen zur Kritik der Soziologie*, Frankfurt, 1969
Baier, H., 'Soziologie und Geschichte. Überlegungen zur Kontroverse zwischen dialektischer und neopositivistischer Soziologie', *Archiv für Rechts-und Sozialphilosophie*, vol. 52, 1966
Ballestrem, K. & McCarthy, A., 'Thesen zur Begründung einer kritischen Theorie der Gesellschaft', *Zeitschrift für allgemeine Wissenschaftstheorie*, vol. 3, 1972
Bubner, R., *Dialektik und Wissenschaft*, Frankfurt, 1973
Bühl, W., 'Dialektische Soziologie und soziologische Dialektik', *Kölner Zeitschrift für Soziologie*, vol. 21, 1969
Frisby, D., 'The Popper-Adorno controversy: the methodological dispute in German sociology', *Philosophy of the Social Sciences*, vol. 2, 1972
Ley, H. & Müller, T., *Kritische Vernunft und Revolution. Zur Kontroverse zwischen Hans Albert und Jürgen Habermas*, Cologne, 1971
Lichtheim, G., 'Marx or Weber: dialectical methodology', in *From Marx to Hegel*, New York/London, 1971
Lorenzen, P., 'Szientismus vs. Dialektik', in Bubner, R./Cramer, K./Wiehl, R. (eds.), *Hermeneutik und Dialektik I*, Tübingen, 1970
Munch, R., 'Realismus und transcendentale Erkenntniskritik', *Zeitschrift für allgemeine Wissenschaftstheorie*, vol. 4, 1973
Schnädelbach, H., 'Über den Realismus, Ein Nachtrag zum Posi-

tivismusstreit in der deutschen Soziologie', *Zeitschrift für allgemeine Wissenschaftstheorie*, vol. 3, 1972

Wellmer, A., *Critical Theory of Society* (trans. J. Cumming), New York, 1971

Willms, B., 'Theorie, Kritik und Dialektik', *Soziale Welt*, vol. 17, 1966; reprinted in *Über Theodor W. Adorno*, Frankfurt, 1968

General Works

Apel, K-O., 'Communication and the foundation of the humanities', *Man and World*, vol. 5, 1972

Apel, K-O., *Transformation der Philosophie*, 2 vols., Frankfurt, 1973

Bartley, W., *The Retreat to Commitment*, New York, 1962

Böhler, D., 'Paradigmawechsel in analytischer Wissenschaftstheorie?', *Zeitschrift für allgemeine Wissenschaftstheorie*, vol. 3, 1972

Bubner, R./Cramer, K./Wiehl, R. (eds.), *Hermeneutik und Dialektik*, 2 vols., Tübingen, 1970

Dahrendorf, R., 'Sociology and the sociologist. On the problem of theory and practice', in *Essays in the Theory of Society*, London, 1968

Dahrendorf, R., 'Values and social science. The value dispute in perspective', in *Essays in the Theory of Society*, loc. cit.

Feyerabend, P. K., *Against Method*, London, 1974

Fijalkowski, J., 'Über einige Theorie-Begriffe in der deutschen Soziologie der Gegenwart', *Kölner Zeitschrift für Soziologie*, vol. 13, 1961

Gadamer, H., *Wahrheit und Methode*, 2nd ed., Tübingen, 1965, (English trans, *Truth and Method*, New York, 1975)

Giddens, A. (ed.), *Positivism and Sociology*, London, 1974

Horkheimer, M., *Kritische Theorie*, 2 vols., Frankfurt, 1968

Hülsmann, H. (ed.), *Strategie und Hypothese*, Düsseldorf, 1972

Kolakowski, L., *The Alienation of Reason. A History of Positivist Thought*, New York, 1968

Kreckel, R., *Soziologische Erkenntnis und Geschichte*, Opladen, 1972

Lakatos, I. & Musgrave, A. (eds.), *Criticism and the Growth of Knowledge*, Cambridge, 1970

Lenk, H. (ed.), *Neue Aspekte der Wissenschaftstheorie*, Braunschweig, 1971

Lorenzen, P., *Normative Logic and Ethics*, Mannheim, 1969

Ludz, P., 'Zur Frage nach den Bedingungen der Möglichkeit einer kritischen Gesellschaftslehre', *Archiv für Rechts-und Sozialphilosophie*, vol. 49, 1963

Malewski, A., 'Two models of sociology', in H. Albert (ed.), *Theorie und Realität*, loc. cit.

Mittelstrass, J., *Die Möglichkeit von Wissenschaft*, Frankfurt, 1974

Munch, R., 'Zur Kritik der empirischen Forschungspraxis', *Zeitschrift für Soziologie*, vol. 1, 1972

O'Neill, J. (ed.), *Modes of Individualism and Collectivism*, London, 1973
Radnitsky, G., *Contemporary Schools of Metascience*, Göteborg, 1968/ Chicago 1973
Riedel, M. (ed.), *Rehabilitierung der praktischen Philosophie*, Freiburg, vol. 1, 1972; vol. 2, 1974
Ritsert, J., *Erkenntnistheorie, Soziologie und Empirie*, Frankfurt, 1971
Schäfers, B. (ed.), *Thesen zur Kritik der Soziologie*, loc. cit.
Schilpp, P. A. (ed.), *The Philosophy of Karl Popper*, La Salle, Ill., 1974 (contains complete bibliography of Poppers' works to 1974)
Schnädelbach, H., *Erfahrung, Begründung und Reflexion. Versuch über den Positivismus*, Frankfurt, 1971
Spinner, H., *Pluralismus als Erkenntnismodell*, Frankfurt, 1974
Stegmüller, W., *Main Currents in Contemporary German, British, and American Philosophy* (trans. A. Blumberg), Dordrecht, 1969
Stegmüller, W., *Metaphysik, Wissenschaft und Skepsis*, 2nd ed., Berlin/ Heidelberg/New York, 1969
Topitsch, E., *Sozialphilosophie zwischen Ideologie und Wissenschaft*, Neuwied/Berlin, 1961
Wellmer, A., *Kausalität und Erklärung* (unpublished Habilitationschrift), Frankfurt, 1970
Wellmer, A., *Methodologie als Erkenntnistheorie. Zur Wissenschaftslehre Karl R. Poppers*, Frankfurt, 1967
Wright, G. H. von, *Explanation and Understanding*, London, 1971